SPSS Trends™ 6.1

SPSS Inc.

SPSS Inc.
444 N. Michigan Avenue
Chicago, Illinois 60611
Tel: (312) 329-2400
Fax: (312) 329-3668

SPSS Federal Systems (U.S.)
SPSS Argentina srl
SPSS Asia Pacific Pte. Ltd.
SPSS Australasia Pty. Ltd.
SPSS Belgium
SPSS Benelux BV
SPSS Central and Eastern Europe
SPSS E. Mediterranea and Africa
SPSS France SARL
SPSS Finland Oy
SPSS Germany
SPSS Hellas SA
SPSS Hispanoportuguesa S.L.
SPSS Ireland
SPSS Israel Ltd.
SPSS Italia srl
SPSS Japan Inc.
SPSS Korea
SPSS Latin America
SPSS Malaysia Sdn Bhd
SPSS Mexico SA de CV
SPSS Middle East and Africa
SPSS Scandinavia AB
SPSS Schweiz AG
SPSS Singapore Pte. Ltd.
SPSS South Africa
SPSS Taiwan Corp.
SPSS UK Ltd.

For more information about SPSS® software products, please write or call

Marketing Department
SPSS Inc.
444 North Michigan Avenue
Chicago, IL 60611
Tel: (312) 329-2400
Fax: (312) 329-3668

ISBN 0-13-201055-0

Library of Congress Catalog Card Number: 94-068306

Preface

SPSS® 6.1 is a powerful software package for microcomputer data management and analysis. The Trends option is an add-on enhancement that provides a comprehensive set of procedures for analyzing and forecasting time series. These procedures include

- State-of-the-art ARIMA ("Box-Jenkins") modeling.
- Exponential smoothing.
- Regression with first-order autocorrelated errors.
- Seasonal decomposition.
- Spectral analysis.
- X11 ARIMA modeling.

The procedures in Trends must be used with the SPSS 6.1 Base system and are completely integrated into that system. The Base system itself contains facilities for plotting time series and autocorrelation functions, for curve fitting, and for many time-series-related data management tasks. The algorithms are identical to those used in SPSS software on mainframe computers, and the statistical results will be as precise as those computed on a mainframe.

SPSS with the Trends option will enable you to perform many analyses on your PC that were once possible only on much larger machines. We hope that this statistical power will make SPSS an even more useful tool in your work.

What's New in SPSS 6.1. The information in this manual is essentially the same as the information in *SPSS for Windows Trends Release 6.0.* Improvements to the Trends option of SPSS 6.1 do not affect the information on dialog boxes, the functionality of the statistics procedures, or the syntax. The new operational features of SPSS 6.1 are all available for use with the Trends option, including the following:

- Toolbar
- Case identification and labeling in scatterplots (discriminant analysis, factor analysis, multidimensional scaling)
- Exporting charts in various formats
- Variable information pop-up window
- Compatibility with Win32s

These features are described in the SPSS Base system documentation.

Installation

To install Trends, follow the instructions for adding and removing features in the Installation Instructions supplied with the SPSS Base system. (Hint: Double-click on the SPSS Setup icon in the SPSS program group.)

Compatibility

The SPSS system is designed to operate on many computer systems. See the installation instructions that came with your system for specific information on minimum and recommended requirements.

Serial Numbers

Your serial number is your identification number with SPSS Inc. You will need this serial number when you call SPSS Inc. for information regarding support, payment, or an upgraded system. The serial number can be found on Disk 2, which came with your Base system. Before using the system, please copy this number to the registration card.

Registration Card

STOP! Before continuing on, *fill out and send us your registration card*. Until we receive your registration card, you have an unregistered system. Even if you have previously sent a card to us, please fill out and return the card enclosed in your Trends package. Registering your system entitles you to:

- Technical support on our customer hotline
- Favored customer status
- New product announcements

Don't put it off—send your registration card now!

Customer Service

Contact Customer Service at 1-800-521-1337 if you have any questions concerning your shipment or account. Please have your serial number ready for identification when calling.

Training Seminars

SPSS Inc. provides both public and onsite training seminars for SPSS. All seminars feature hands-on workshops. SPSS seminars will be offered in major U.S. and European cities on a regular basis. For more information on these seminars, call the SPSS Inc. Training Department toll-free at 1-800-543-6607.

Technical Support

The services of SPSS Technical Support are available to registered customers. Customers may call Technical Support for assistance in using SPSS products or for installation help for one of the supported hardware environments.

To reach Technical Support, call 1-312-329-3410. Be prepared to identify yourself, your organization, and the serial number of your system.

If you are a Value Plus or Customer EXPress customer, use the priority 800 number you received with your materials. For information on subscribing to the Value Plus or Customer EXPress plan, call SPSS Software Sales at 1-800-543-2185.

Additional Publications

Additional copies of SPSS product manuals may be purchased from Prentice Hall, the exclusive distributor of SPSS publications. To order, fill out and mail the Publications order form included with your system or call toll-free. If you represent a bookstore or have an account with Prentice Hall, call 1-800-223-1360. If you are not an account customer, call 1-800-374-1200. In Canada, call 1-800-567-3800. Outside of North America, contact your local Prentice Hall office.

Lend Us Your Thoughts

Your comments are important. So send us a letter and let us know about your experiences with SPSS products. We especially like to hear about new and interesting applications using the SPSS system. Write to SPSS Inc. Marketing Department, Attn: Micro Software Products Manager, 444 N. Michigan Avenue, Chicago IL, 60611.

About This Manual

This manual is divided into two sections. The first section provides a guide to the various statistical techniques available with the Trends option and how to obtain the appropriate statistical analyses with the dialog box interface. Illustrations of dialog boxes are taken from SPSS for Windows. Dialog boxes in other operating systems are similar. The second section of this manual is a Syntax Reference section that provides complete command syntax for all the commands included in the Trends option. Most features of the system can be accessed through the dialog box interface, but some functionality can be accessed only through command syntax.

SPSS Inc.
Chicago, Illinois, U.S.A.
Tel: 1.312.329.2400
Fax: 1.312.329.3668
Customer Service:
1.800.521.1337
Sales:
1.800.543.2185
sales@spss.com
Training:
1.800.543.6607
Technical Support:
1.312.329.3410
support@spss.com

SPSS Federal Systems
Arlington, Virginia, U.S.A.
Tel: 1.703.527.6777
Fax: 1.703.527.6866

SPSS Argentina srl
Buenos Aires, Argentina
Tel: +541.816.4086
Fax: +541.814.5030

SPSS Asia Pacific Pte. Ltd.
Singapore, Singapore
Tel: +65.3922.738
Fax: +65.3922.739

SPSS Australasia Pty. Ltd.
Sydney, Australia
Tel: +61.2.9954.5660
Fax: +61.2.9954.5616

SPSS Belgium
Heverlee, Belgium
Tel: +32.162.389.82
Fax: +32.1620.0888

SPSS Benelux BV
Gorinchem, The Netherlands
Tel: +31.183.636711
Fax: +31.183.635839

**SPSS Central and
Eastern Europe**
Woking, Surrey, U.K.
Tel: +44.(0)1483.719200
Fax: +44.(0)1483.719290

SPSS East Mediterranea and Africa
Herzlia, Israel
Tel: +972.9.526700
Fax: +972.9.526715

SPSS Finland Oy
Sinikalliontie, Finland
Tel: +358.9.524.801
Fax: +358.9.524.854

SPSS France SARL
Boulogne, France
Tel: +33.1.4699.9670
Fax: +33.1.4684.0180

SPSS Germany
Munich, Germany
Tel: +49.89.4890740
Fax: +49.89.4483115

SPSS Hellas SA
Athens, Greece
Tel: +30.1.7251925
Fax: +30.1.7249124

SPSS Hispanoportuguesa S.L.
Madrid, Spain
Tel: +34.91.447.3700
Fax: +34.91.448.6692

SPSS Ireland
Dublin, Ireland
Tel: +353.1.66.13788
Fax: +353.1.661.5200

SPSS Israel Ltd.
Herzlia, Israel
Tel: +972.9.526700
Fax: +972.9.526715

SPSS Italia srl
Bologna, Italy
Tel: +39.51.252573
Fax: +39.51.253285

SPSS Japan Inc.
Tokyo, Japan
Tel: +81.3.5466.5511
Fax: +81.3.5466.5621

SPSS Korea
Seoul, Korea
Tel: +82.2.552.9415
Fax: +82.2.539.0136

SPSS Latin America
Chicago, Illinois, U.S.A.
Tel: 1.312.494.3226
Fax: 1.312. 494.3227

SPSS Malaysia Sdn Bhd
Selangor, Malaysia
Tel: +603.704.5877
Fax: +603.704.5790

SPSS Mexico SA de CV
Mexico DF, Mexico
Tel: +52.5.575.3091
Fax: +52.5.575.2527

**SPSS Middle East and
South Asia**
Dubai, UAE
Tel: +971.4.525536
Fax: +971.4.524669

SPSS Scandinavia AB
Stockholm, Sweden
Tel: +46.8.102610
Fax: +46.8.102550

SPSS Schweiz AG
Zurich, Switzerland
Tel: +41.1.201.0930
Fax: +41.1.201.0921

SPSS Singapore Pte. Ltd.
Singapore, Singapore
Tel: +65.2991238
Fax: +65.2990849

SPSS South Africa
Johannesburg, South Africa
Tel: +27.11.7067015
Fax: +27.11.7067091

SPSS Taiwan Corp.
Taipei, Republic of China
Tel: +886.2.5771100
Fax: +886.2.5701717

SPSS UK Ltd.
Woking, Surrey, U.K.
Tel: +44.1483.719200
Fax: +44.1483.719290

Contents

1

Overview

SPSS Trends provides the power and flexibility required by experienced time series analysts, while at the same time being easy enough for those not familiar with time series techniques to use and master quickly. Its power and flexibility can be seen in the wide variety of identification, estimation, forecasting, and diagnostic methods available, the opportunity for continuous interaction during the model-building process, and the ability to quickly create new series as functions, transformations, or components of the observed series for further analysis. Its graphical user interface, comprehensive manual, and online Help system ensure that you will find Trends easy to use.

The range of analytical techniques available in Trends extends from simple, basic tools to more sophisticated types of analysis. These include:

- *Plots.* With facilities in the SPSS Base system you can easily produce a variety of series and autocorrelation plots, including high-resolution plots that you can enhance with all of the facilities of the SPSS Chart Editor.

- *Smoothing.* You can use simple but efficient smoothing techniques that can yield high-quality forecasts with a minimum of effort.

- *Decomposition.* You can break down a series into its components, saving the seasonal factors and trend, cycle, and error components automatically—ready to use in further analysis.

- *Regression.* You can build regression models using a variety of techniques, including those in the SPSS Base system, such as ordinary least-squares regression and curve fitting. Trends adds a special facility for regression with autocorrelated errors.

- *ARIMA Modeling.* You can apply the powerful techniques of ARIMA modeling in a fully interactive environment where identification, estimation, and diagnosis lead you quickly to the best model.

- *Spectral Analysis.* You can examine a time series as a combination of periodic cycles of various lengths.

- *X11ARIMA.* You can estimate seasonal factors for monthly or quarterly series.

This chapter presents a brief introduction to time series analysis and an overview of the capabilities of Trends.

Time Series Analysis

A **time series** is a set of observations obtained by measuring a single variable regularly over a period of time. In a series of inventory data, for example, the observations might represent daily inventory levels for several months. A series showing the market share of a product might consist of weekly market share taken over a few years. A series of total sales figures might consist of one observation per month for many years. What each of these examples has in common is that some variable was observed at regular, known intervals over a certain length of time. Thus, the form of the data for a typical time series is a single sequence or list of observations representing measurements taken at regular intervals. Table 1.1 shows a portion of a series of daily inventory levels observed for 12 weeks.

Table 1.1   A daily inventory time series

Time	Week	Day	Inventory level
t_1	1	Monday	160
t_2	1	Tuesday	135
t_3	1	Wednesday	129
t_4	1	Thursday	122
t_5	1	Friday	108
t_6	2	Monday	150
		. . .	
t_{60}	12	Friday	120

Reasons for Analyzing Time Series

Why might someone collect such data? What kinds of questions could someone be trying to answer? One reason to collect time series data is to try to discover systematic patterns in the series so a mathematical model can be built to explain the past behavior of the series. The discovery of a strong seasonal pattern, for instance, might help explain large fluctuations in the data.

Explaining a variable's past behavior can be interesting and useful, but often one wants to do more than just evaluate the past. One of the most important reasons for doing time series analysis is to forecast future values of the series. The parameters of the model that explained the past values may also predict whether and how much the next few values will increase or decrease. The ability to make such predictions successfully is obviously important to any business or scientific field.

Another reason for analyzing time series data is to evaluate the effect of some event that intervenes and changes the normal behavior of a series. Intervention analysis examines the pattern of a time series before and after the occurrence of such an event. The goal is to see if the outside event had a significant impact on the series pattern. If it did, there is a significant upward or downward shift in the values of the series after the occurrence of the event. For this reason, such series are called *interrupted time series.* Weekly numbers of automobile fatalities before and after a new seat belt law, monthly totals of armed robberies before and after a new gun law, and daily measurements of productivity before and after initiation of an incentive plan are examples of interrupted time series. What they have in common is a hypothetical interruption in their usual pattern after the specific time when some outside event occurred. Since the time of the outside event is known and the pattern before and after the event is observable, you can evaluate the impact of the interruption.

A Model-Building Strategy

No matter what the primary goal of the time series analysis, the approach basically starts with building a model that will explain the series. The most popular strategy for building a model is the one developed by Box and Jenkins (1976), who defined three major stages of model building: identification, estimation, and diagnostic checking. Although Box and Jenkins originally demonstrated the usefulness of this strategy specifically for ARIMA model building, the general principles can be extended to all model building.

Identification involves selecting a tentative model type with which to work. This tentative model type includes initial judgements about the number and kind of parameters involved and how they are combined. In making these judgements, you should be parsimonious. The methods usually employed at this stage include plotting the series and its autocorrelation function to find out whether the series shows any upward or downward trend, whether some sort of data transformation might simplify analysis, and whether any kind of seasonal pattern is apparent.

Estimation is the process of fitting the tentative model to the data and estimating its parameters. This stage usually involves using a computerized model-fitting routine to estimate the parameters and test them for significance. The estimated parameters can then be used to see how well they would have predicted the observed values. If the parameter estimates are unsatisfactory on statistical grounds, you return to the identification stage, since the tentative model could not satisfactorily explain the behavior of the series.

Diagnosis is the stage in which you examine how well the tentative model fits the data. Methods used at this stage include plots and statistics describing the residual, or error, series. This information tells you whether the model can be used with confidence, or whether you should return to the first stage and try to identify a better model.

How Trends Can Help

SPSS Trends is designed to help you accomplish the goals of these model-building stages. The following sections describe some of the ways it simplifies your work.

Model Identification

The most useful tools for identifying a model are plots of the series itself or of various correlation functions. The SPSS Base system provides many plots that are helpful for analyzing time series, such as sequence charts and autocorrelation plots.

Plotting the Series. With the Sequence Charts procedure in the SPSS Base system you can plot the values of your series horizontally or vertically. You have the option of plotting the series itself, a log transformation of the series, or the differences between adjacent (or seasonally adjacent) points in the series.

Plotting Correlation Functions. The Base system provides facilities for plotting correlation functions. As with the series plots, you can show the function itself, a log transformation of the function, or the differences between adjacent (or seasonally adjacent) points. Confidence limits are included on the plots, and the values and standard errors of the correlation function are displayed in the output window. The following facilities are available:

- The Autocorrelations procedure displays and plots the autocorrelation function and the partial autocorrelation function among the values of a series at different lags. It also displays the Box-Ljung statistic and its probability level at each lag in the output window.

- The Cross-correlations procedure displays and plots the cross-correlation functions of two or more time series at different lags.

Parameter Estimation

SPSS Trends includes state-of-the-art techniques for estimating the coefficients of your model. These techniques can loosely be grouped under the general areas of smoothing, regression methods, Box-Jenkins or ARIMA analysis, and decomposition of cyclic data into their component frequencies.

Smoothing. The Exponential Smoothing procedure uses exponential smoothing methods to estimate up to three parameters for a wide variety of common models. Forecasts and forecast error values for one or more time series are produced using the most recent data in the series, previous forecasts and their errors, and estimates of trend and seasonality. You can specify your own estimates for any of the parameters or let Trends find them for you. The output includes statistics arranged to help you evaluate the estimates.

Trends also includes the Seasonal Decomposition procedure, which lets you estimate multiplicative or additive seasonal factors for periodic time series. New series containing seasonally adjusted values, seasonal factors, trend and cycle components, and error components can be automatically added to your working data file so you can perform further analyses.

Regression Methods. The Regression procedure in the SPSS Base system is useful when you want to analyze time series using ordinary least-squares regression. Additional procedures for regression methods include:

- The Curve Estimation procedure, which is part of the Base system, fits selected curves to time series and produces forecasts, forecast error values, and confidence interval values. The curve is chosen from a variety of trend-regression models that assume that the observed series is some function of the passage of time.

- The Autoregression procedure, which is part of Trends, allows you to estimate regression models reliably when the error from the regression is correlated between one time point and the next—a common situation in time series analysis. Autoregression offers two traditional methods (Prais-Winsten and Cochrane-Orcutt) as well as an innovative maximum-likelihood method that is able to handle missing data imbedded in the series.

Box-Jenkins Analysis. The ARIMA procedure lets you estimate nonseasonal and seasonal univariate ARIMA models. You can include predictor variables in the model to evaluate the effect of some outside event or influence while estimating the coefficients of the ARIMA process. ARIMA produces maximum-likelihood estimates and can process time series with missing observations. It uses the traditional ARIMA model syntax, so you can describe your model just as it would be described in a book on ARIMA analysis. Summary statistics for the parameter estimates help you evaluate the model. New series containing forecasts as well as their errors and confidence limits are automatically created.

Seasonal-Adjustment Methods. The Seasonal Decomposition procedure lets you estimate multiplicative or additive seasonal factors for periodic time series using the ratio-to-moving-average (Census I) method of seasonal decomposition. The X11 ARIMA procedure is a modified version of the Census II-X-11 program for seasonal adjustment. It lets you estimate ARIMA forecasts and/or backcasts, which can be added to the series before seasonal decomposition. Both Seasonal Decomposition and X11 ARIMA automatically create new series in your working data file containing seasonally adjusted values, seasonal factors, trend and cycle components, and error components so you can perform further analyses.

Frequency-Component Analysis. The Spectral Plots procedure lets you decompose a time series into its harmonic components, a set of regular periodic functions at different wavelengths or periods. By noting the prominent frequencies in this model-free analysis you can detect features of a periodic or cyclic series that would be obscured by other methods. Spectral Plots provides statistics, plots, and methods of tailoring them for univariate and bivariate spectral analysis, including periodograms, spectral density estimates, gain and phase spectra, popular spectral windows for smoothing the periododogram, and optional user-defined filters. Plots can be produced by period, frequency, or both.

Diagnosis

The ability to diagnose how well the model fits the data is a vital part of time series analysis. Several facilities are available to assist you in evaluating models:

- The automatic residual and confidence-interval series generated along with the forecasts aid you in assessing the accuracy of your models.
- Standard errors and other statistics help you to judge the significance of the coefficients estimated for your model.
- In regression analysis and elsewhere, you frequently need to determine whether the residuals from a model are normally distributed. The SPSS Base system offers Normal P-P and Normal Q-Q plots, which compare the observed values of a series against the values that would be observed if the series were normally distributed. They give you quick and effective visual checks for normality.

Other Facilities

In addition to the analytical commands surveyed above, Trends includes many facilities to simplify the process of analyzing time series data:

- *Forecasting.* Since most of the analytical commands in Trends automatically create predicted values and error terms, generating forecasts is virtually effortless and evaluating them is nearly as easy. You can easily tell Trends which period to use in estimating its models and which period you want to forecast—whether you are forecasting in a *validation period,* for which you have data, or forecasting into the future.
- *Easy interaction.* Trends shows you the results of your analysis immediately, so you can revise it on the spot if you like. The dialog boxes remember your specifications throughout the session, so it is easy to modify your analysis on the basis of previous results.
- *Utilities.* Trends includes all the utilities you need to analyze time series data flexibly and efficiently.
- *Alternate command-driven interface.* Like the rest of the SPSS system, Trends lets you dispense with the dialog boxes and execute command syntax, either directly from a window or in batch mode.
- *Online assistance.* The SPSS Help system provides immediate information about any aspect of Trends facilities and about the command syntax if you prefer to use it.

For information on how to use these facilities efficiently, refer to Chapter 2.

An Example

This simple example illustrates some of the procedures you can use to analyze a time series. The example uses only a few Trends procedures, but if you try entering the commands yourself you'll see how easy it is to work with Trends.

Let's say you're interested in predicting the monthly sales of a certain product for the next three months. Since you know how many have been sold each month for the last three years, you have a time series with which you can predict future sales of your product.

① After starting SPSS, you will see an empty Data Editor window entitled Newdata. Double-click on the column heading of the first column. This opens the Define Variable dialog box, as shown in Figure 1.1.

Figure 1.1   Define Variable dialog box

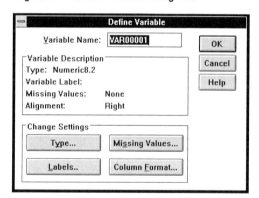

② Type sales into the Variable Name text box, and click on OK. This defines one series, or variable, which is named *sales*.

③ The first column in the Data Editor now has the heading *sales*, the variable name you assigned. The first cell in that column is highlighted. Type in some numbers to represent the sales records of your product. After each number, press ⏎Enter to move down to the next row in the Data Editor. Enter as many numbers as you like, preferably a dozen or more so that the results of your analysis will look plausible.

④ The next step is to attach real dates to these values and define the range of months to be predicted. You can do this by selecting Define Dates on the Data menu. This opens the Define Dates dialog box. Scroll up to the top of the list of date specifications in the Cases Are list and click on Years, months. The dialog box now looks like Figure 1.2.

Figure 1.2   Define Dates dialog box

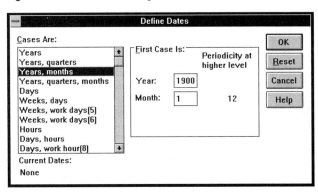

⑤ With the mouse, highlight the number 1900 that has appeared in the Year text box. Type 1985 to replace it with the first year of your data (Figure 1.3). If you like, you can change the starting month also. Click on OK and Trends will add three new time series to the Data Editor, containing date information for the *sales* series.

Figure 1.3   Define Dates dialog box filled in for starting date

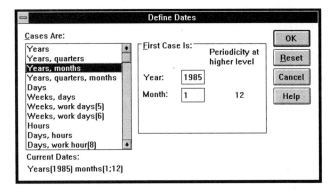

The Define Dates command assigns a date (a year, a month, and a labeling variable *date_* that shows both year and month) to each value in the series.

Click somewhere in the Data Editor window to bring it to the front, if necessary. Scroll to the bottom and notice the date assigned to the last data value you entered for *sales*. For example, if you entered 24 values and your starting date was year 1985, month 1, then the last data value will be for year 1986, month 12.

⑥ Now plot the series. From the menus choose:

Graphs
　Sequence...

This opens the Sequence Charts dialog box, as shown in Figure 1.4. Make sure the variable *sales* is highlighted in the source variable list (on the left). Click on the upper ▶ button to move *sales* into the Variables list. Then click on OK to produce a sequence chart of the data you entered.

Figure 1.4　Sequence Charts dialog box

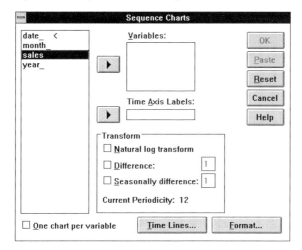

⑦ The sequence chart appears in the Chart Carousel, a holding area for high-resolution charts. At this point you could print it, save it on disk, or edit it to enhance its appearance. Instead, let's continue the analysis. From the menus choose:

Window
　Newdata

This brings the Data Editor window back, restoring the regular SPSS menu bar.

⑧ One model type you might try to fit to the data is a linear exponential smoothing model. From the menus choose:

Statistics
　Time Series ▶
　　Exponential Smoothing...

This opens the Exponential Smoothing dialog box, as shown in Figure 1.5.

Figure 1.5   Exponential Smoothing dialog box

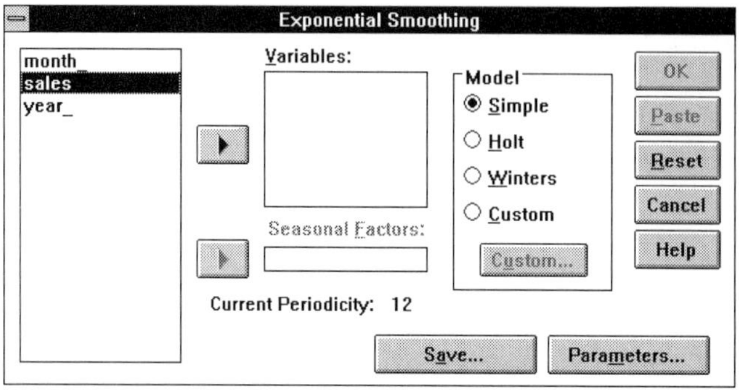

As before, click on the ▶ button to move sales into the Variables list and click on OK to carry out the analysis. This command fits a linear nonseasonal model to the series *sales*. By default, the general smoothing parameter, alpha, is set to 0.1. For this series, 0.1 may or may not be a good value for alpha; it depends on what values you typed into the Data Editor. Chapter 4 explains the ideas behind exponential smoothing and shows how Trends can determine the best values for the parameters.

⑨ When you run the Exponential Smoothing command, Trends smooths the *sales* series and adds two new series to the working data file: *fit_1*, which contains predicted values, and *err_1*, which contains residual values. To get an idea of how well the model fits the data, you can generate a plot of *sales* and *fit_1*. From the menus choose:

Graphs
  Sequence...

This opens the Sequence Charts dialog box, as shown above. The Variables list still contains sales from the last time you used this dialog box. The new variables *err_1* and *fit_1* are in the source variable list.

⑩ Click on *fit_1* in the source variable list and then click on the upper ▶ button to move it into the Variables list. Click on OK to generate a sequence chart showing both sales and the values predicted by the Exponential Smoothing model.

The predicted values probably don't follow your made-up data very closely. This is to be expected, since random numbers are hard to model. For a real time series you probably could have chosen a better value for the parameter alpha than the default 0.1. You'll see how in Chapter 4.

What Else?

This brief overview has only hinted at the facilities that SPSS Trends provides to make your sessions more productive. Chapter 2 shows you how to use these facilities.

2 Working with SPSS Trends

In addition to the commands for plotting and analyzing time series, SPSS Trends also provides the "nuts and bolts" commands that you need to deal with the special problems of time series analysis.

- Time series observations form a regularly spaced sequence, often a *dated* sequence. You need flexible ways of referring by date to portions of your series.
- Fitting, modeling, and forecasting time series are central goals. Often these activities require the creation of new series containing forecasts or residuals (errors), which you then subject to further analysis.
- Time series analysis is interactive. You usually examine or plot the results of one analysis before deciding what to do next. Frequently you repeat an analysis on a different series or a different portion of the same series, or you repeat an analysis with just a slight change in the specifications.

In this chapter you will learn how SPSS Trends lets you manipulate dates, modify your series, and generate new series for further analysis. At the end of this chapter you can find some tips for using Trends with the rest of SPSS for Windows, and for maximizing the efficiency of Trends.

Defining Time Series Data

A time series corresponds to a variable in ordinary data analysis. If you are accustomed to analyzing data that are not time series, or if you need to use the facilities from other parts of the SPSS system, you may find it helpful to remember that a series plays the role of a variable. Each observation in a time series corresponds to a case or observation. The main difference is that in time series analysis, the observations are taken at equally spaced time intervals.

When you define time series data for use with SPSS Trends, give each series a name exactly as if it were a variable. For example, to define a time series in the Data Editor, click in an unused column and from the menus select:

Data
  Define Variable...

11

Or you can simply double-click on the column heading of an unused column.

If you open a spreadsheet containing time series data, each series should be arranged in a column in the spreadsheet. If you already have a spreadsheet with time series arranged in rows, you can open it anyway and use the Transpose command (in the Data menu) to flip the rows into columns.

Missing Data

A time series by definition consists of equally spaced observations. Sometimes the value for a particular observation is simply not known and will be missing. In addition, missing data can result from any of the following:

- Each degree of differencing reduces the length of a series by 1.

- Each degree of seasonal differencing reduces the length of a series by one season.

- If you create new series that contain forecasts beyond the end of the existing series (by clicking on a Save... button and making suitable choices), the original series and the generated residual series will have missing data for the new observations.

- Some transformations (for example, the log transformation) produce missing data for certain values of the original series.

Missing data at the beginning or end of a series pose no particular problem; they simply shorten the useful length of the series. Gaps in the middle of a series (*imbedded* missing data) can be a much more serious problem. The extent of the problem depends on the analytical procedure you are using.

- Some commands require all observations to be *present* and *in order* but can accept imbedded missing data. For example, if you don't know last October's sales figures, you need to supply an empty observation for October to preserve the spacing between September and November. The commands that can handle imbedded missing data are Autoregression (with the exact maximum-likelihood method) and ARIMA. (See "Performance Considerations" on p. 20 for issues regarding imbedded missing data in these commands.)

- Some commands depend heavily on the unbroken sequence of observations. These commands are Autoregression, Exponential Smoothing, Seasonal Decomposition, Spectral Plots (on the Graphs menu), and X11 ARIMA. Before you can use these commands, you must fill in data for imbedded missing values using the Data Editor or the Remove Missing Values command (see "Handling Missing Data" on p. 19).

Facilities

Most of the facilities available in the SPSS Base system can be used with time series data.

- You can run any command or procedure on time series data, since the series names are SPSS variable names.
- You can use any transformation commands in the SPSS Base system to modify the data in a time series or to create new time series from existing ones.
- You can use file-manipulation facilities on the File and Data menus in exactly the same way as with any other file.
- You can use the SPSS Data Editor to enter or modify time series data.

In addition, there are a number of facilities specifically designed for manipulating time series data.

Data Transformation

The Create Time Series command in the SPSS Base system was designed expressly for time series data. In addition, you can take advantage of options on some of the Trends dialog boxes to temporarily transform your data before analyzing it. Remember also that many Trends commands create new series as transformations of your existing series.

Transformation Commands

A Base system command intended specifically for transforming time series data is:

Create Time Series. Produces new series as functions of existing series. This facility works somewhat like the Compute command in the SPSS Base system. It includes functions that use neighboring observations for smoothing, averaging, and differencing. If you use the name of an existing series as the "target" series, Create Time Series (unlike Compute) moves that series to the end of the file.

Create Time Series always causes the data to be read, regardless of the option you have chosen in the Preferences dialog box. Consult the *SPSS Base System User's Guide* for more information on Create Time Series.

Transformation Options

Many Trends procedures include options that transform data within the procedure, leaving the data in your working data file unchanged. These options are shortcuts to simplify your work. They include the following:

❏ **Difference.** This option tells Trends to analyze the differences between the values of adjacent observations, rather than the values themselves.

❏ **Seasonally difference.** Seasonal differencing takes differences at a lag equal to the seasonality of your series.

❑ **Log transformations.** These are available using both base 10 and base *e* (natural) logarithms.

Historical and Validation Periods

It is often useful to divide your time series into a *historical* or *estimation period* and a *validation period*. You develop a model on the basis of the observations in the historical period and then test it to see how well it works in the validation period. When you are not sure which model to choose, this technique is sometimes more efficient than comparing models based on the entire sample.

The facilities in the Select Cases dialog box (available through the Data menu) and the Save dialog box (available through the main dialog box for many procedures) make it easy to set aside part of your data for validation purposes.

Select Cases. Specifies a range of observations for analysis. The selection Based on time or case range allows you to specify a range of observations using date variables, if you have attached them to your time series, or using observation numbers if you have not. You normally define a historical period in this way.

Save. Specifies a range of observations for forecasts or validation. Trends commands that save new series containing such things as fit values and residuals allow you to predict values for observations past the end of the series being analyzed. To define a validation period, select the default Predict from estimation period through last case. Trends then uses the model developed from the historical period to "forecast" values through the validation period so that you can compare these forecasts to the actual data. Forecasts created in this way are *n*-step-ahead forecasts. For information on generating one-step-ahead forecasts, refer to "Forecasts" below.

Forecasts

Forecasts are ubiquitous in time series analysis—both real forecasts and the validation "forecasts" discussed above. It is often useful to distinguish between "one-step-ahead" forecasts and "*n*-step-ahead" forecasts. One-step-ahead forecasts use—and require—information in the time period immediately preceding the period being forecast, while *n*-step-ahead forecasts are based on older information. You can produce either type of forecast in Trends.

Real forecasts, i.e., forecasts for observations beyond the end of existing series, are always *n*-step-ahead forecasts. To generate these forecasts, specify the forecast range in a Save dialog box, using the Predict through alternative. Trends will automatically extend the series to allow room for the forecast observations. (This type of forecast can be generated by ARIMA and Exponential Smoothing, and by Curve Estimation in the Base system.)

Validation forecasts can be either one- or *n*-step-ahead. To generate *n*-step-ahead validation forecasts, simply specify the historical period in the Select Cases dialog box and the validation period in the Save dialog box, as discussed above. If you need one-step-ahead validation forecasts, you must use a certain amount of SPSS command syntax:

1. Specify the historical period in the Select Cases dialog box.

2. Estimate the model in which you are interested. Instead of executing it directly, click on the Paste button to paste its command syntax into a syntax window.

3. Execute the command from the syntax window by clicking on the Run button on the icon bar.

4. Go back to the Select Cases dialog box and specify both the historical and validation periods. Generally this means to select All cases.

5. Activate the syntax window and edit the command that you executed in step 3. Leave the command name (EXSMOOTH, ARIMA, SEASON, or whatever), but replace all of its specifications with the single specification /APPLY FIT. Then execute the command by clicking on Run. Trends generates a *fit* variable through both the historical and validation periods, based on the coefficients estimated in step 3 for the historical period.

Date Variables

The observations in a time series occur at equally spaced intervals. The actual date of each observation does not matter in the analysis but is useful for labeling output. It is also convenient when you want to specify a portion of the series. For example, it's easier to indicate that you want observations from 1965 through 1985 than to construct a logical condition such as

```
year >= 1965 & year <= 1985.
```

in the Select Cases If dialog box. For these reasons SPSS Trends is designed to work with *date variables*. Date variables are variables that indicate the time of an observation. Year, quarter, month, week, day, hour, minute, and second are possible date variables.

• Date variables are generally not defined or read like ordinary time series. They are created by SPSS when you use the Define Dates command (on the Data menu).

• The Define Dates dialog box lists about twenty time intervals, and combinations of time intervals, that you can use to indicate the spacing of your observations. When you click on OK, Trends creates a numeric date variable with the name of the time interval followed by an underscore: *year_*, *quarter_*, and so on. If you choose a combination of time intervals, Trends creates more than one such variable.

• When you use Define Dates, Trends always creates a string variable named *date_* in addition to the numeric date variables you specifically request in the Define Dates dialog box.

- The Define Dates facility assigns values to the numeric date variables in sequence for each observation in the series. You specify initial values for these variables in the dialog box.

- Define Dates also assigns values that correspond to the values of the numeric date variables to the string variable *date_*.

- Define Dates often establishes a default seasonal cycle. For example, for monthly data, Trends assumes a seasonal periodicity of 12 months.

- Date variables have meaning only as labels, as indicators of periodicity, and as a means of specifying part of a series in the Select Cases Range or Save dialog boxes.

- You should not modify the values of date variables in the Data Editor or with transformation commands. There is no reason to do so, and Trends expects these variables to have certain values.

Other Date Combinations

The Define Dates dialog box cannot anticipate every combination of date variables and periodicity. For example, there are two options for daily data collected on work days only, one for a 5-day work week and one for a 6-day work week. For hourly data collected on work days, however, only the 5-day work week is provided. To define date variables for hourly data collected 6 days a week, you would need to consult the *SPSS Base System Syntax Reference Guide* and execute a relatively simple command like this:

```
date week 1 day 1 6 hour 8.
```

If you open the Define Dates dialog box after using command syntax to define date variables in a manner not supported by the dialog box, SPSS highlights Custom in the Cases Are list. This merely means that you have defined date variables with command syntax that cannot be shown in the dialog box. The date variables will "work" everywhere else just fine.

See DATE in the *SPSS Base System Syntax Reference Guide* for a more complete description of date variables.

Using Date Variables

Once you have created date variables with Define Dates (or with command syntax), you can use them like any other variables.

- *date_* is a string variable with preassigned values. Its length depends on how many variables you requested.

- The other date variables are numeric variables with preassigned values. Remember that their names all end with underscores.

When you specify a time interval in a dialog box, pairs of text boxes will be available in the dialog box to let you enter starting and ending values for each of the numeric date variables you have defined. If you have not defined date variables, there will be text boxes for observation numbers.

Automatic Creation of New Series

Many of the analytical commands in Trends can automatically generate new series containing such things as predicted values and residuals. Each command reports the names of any new series that it creates. The first three letters of the series name indicate the type of series:

- *fit* contains the predicted value according to the current model.
- *err* is a residual or error series. (Normally the *fit* series plus the *err* series equals the original series.)
- *ucl* and *lcl* contain upper and lower confidence limits.
- *sep* is the standard error of the fit or predicted series.
- *sas*, *saf*, and *stc* are series components extracted by the Seasonal Decomposition and X11 ARIMA procedures.

Special Considerations for ARIMA. Because the error series from ARIMA is so important, an error series from a log-transformed ARIMA model contains the log-transformed errors to permit the proper residuals analysis. However, the fit and confidence-limit series are in the original metric. For ARIMA with a log transformation, therefore, it is not true that the fit plus the error equals the original series.

Controlling the Creation of New Series

You can control whether new series are created using the Save dialog box. Choices are:

- **Add to file.** All new series are created and added to file. This alternative carries a performance cost; see "Performance Considerations" on p. 20 for discussion.
- **Replace existing.** New series generated by the most recent procedure are added to the file. Any existing series that were created in this way by Trends procedures are dropped.
- **Do not create.** No new series are created.

For most Trends procedures, you cannot choose to have only one type of series, such as *err*, added to your file. If a command creates three new series, you either get all three or none. The X11 ARIMA procedure does allow you to choose which new series are saved.

New Series Names

The name of a series created automatically consists of:

- The prefix indicating what type of series it is, as listed above.
- An underscore (_) if the Add to file alternative was selected, or a pound sign (#) if the Replace existing alternative was selected.
- A sequential number.

Consult "New Variables" on p. 253 for more details on naming conventions.

Reusing Models

When you click on OK or Paste in SPSS for Windows, current dialog box settings are saved. When you return to a dialog box you have used once, all of your previous specifications are still there (unless you have opened a different data file). This *persistence* of dialog box settings is especially helpful as you develop models for time series data, since you can selectively modify model specifications as needed:

- You can change one or more specifications in the dialog box, or on any subdialog box, and repeat the analysis with the new specifications.
- You can switch variables to repeat your analysis or chart with different variables but with the same specifications.
- You can use the Select Cases facility to restrict analysis to a range of cases, or to process all cases instead of restricting analysis to a previously specified range. You can then repeat an analysis or chart with identical specifications but a different range of observations.
- You can use a transformation command such as Remove Missing Values, or edit data values (responsibly!) in the Data Editor, and then repeat an analysis or chart with identical specifications but modified data.

Reusing Command Syntax

If you are using command syntax instead of the dialog boxes, you can still reuse and selectively modify models using the APPLY subcommand. When it is used, the APPLY subcommand is usually the first specification after the name of the command or after the name of a command and a series. It means *Run this command as before, with the following changes*. If you want to change any specifications from the previous model, continue the command with a slash and enter only those specifications you want to add or change.

For commands that estimate coefficients that you can apply to prediction (ARIMA and AREG), you have the option of applying the coefficients estimated for a previous model to a new model, either as initial estimates or as "final" coefficients to be used in calculating predicted values and residuals.

You can also apply specifications or coefficients from an earlier model rather than from the previous specification of the same command by specifying the model name.

See "APPLY Subcommand" on p. 256 for a complete discussion of the APPLY subcommand and models.

Handling Missing Data

Missing data are particularly troublesome in time series analysis. Some procedures cannot work with missing data at all, since their algorithms depend upon new information at every point. The extent to which different Trends commands can handle missing data is discussed in "Missing Data" on p. 12.

If missing data are a problem, you can use the Replace Missing Values procedure from the Base system. This procedure replaces some or all of the missing data in a series using any of several plausible algorithms. It can either replace missing data in an existing series or create a copy of an existing series with missing data replaced. For more information on Replace Missing Values, see the *SPSS Base System User's Guide*.

Case Weighting

The Weight Cases facility, which simulates case replication, is ignored by most Trends commands, since it makes no sense to replicate cases in a time series.

Changing Settings with Command Syntax

Several SPSS commands determine settings that affect the operation of Trends procedures. In particular, the TSET, USE, and PREDICT commands modify the operation of most subsequent analytical commands in Trends. If you execute such commands from a syntax window and later execute Trends commands from the dialog boxes, you cannot necessarily assume that the settings you established in the syntax window remain in effect. The following are areas where this might occur:

- The Select Cases dialog box can generate a USE command.
- The Save dialog box for any Trends procedure and for Curve Estimation in the Base system can generate a PREDICT command.
- Trends dialog boxes routinely generate a TSET command to reflect settings that are specified in the dialog box. Never assume that your TSET specifications survive the use of a dialog box without inspecting the journal file for a TSET command generated by the dialog box.

The existence and name of the journal file can be verified from the Preferences dialog box.

Performance Considerations

Time series analysis sometimes requires lengthy calculations at places where you may not expect it. The following sections bring these places to your attention and suggest ways of speeding up your work.

ARIMA

ARIMA analysis uses sophisticated iterative algorithms to solve problems that were computationally intractable until recent years. If you are new to ARIMA analysis, you will find that these calculations can require more processing time than non-iterative techniques. Processing time is particularly dependent upon the type of model specified and the presence of imbedded missing data.

Type of Model. You can expect seasonal ARIMA models, ARIMA models that include moving-average components, and especially models with seasonal moving-average components to require somewhat more time than other models.

Imbedded Missing Data. The SPSS Trends ARIMA procedure uses a state-of-the-art maximum-likelihood estimation algorithm that is unique in being able to handle imbedded missing data. It does so with a technique called *Kalman filtering,* which requires considerably more calculation than the simpler technique used when no imbedded missing data are present. Even a single imbedded missing value increases ARIMA processing time greatly—in extreme cases, by a factor of 10.

If you want to use ARIMA on a series that contains imbedded missing data, you can use the following procedure to reduce processing time:

1. Make a copy of the series with valid data interpolated in place of the imbedded missing data (see "Handling Missing Data" on p. 19).

2. Identify the correct model and estimate the coefficients for the series without missing data. ARIMA can use a much faster algorithm when no imbedded missing data are present.

3. Once you have found the correct model, run ARIMA on the original series to get the best possible estimates for the coefficients, using Kalman filtering to handle the missing data. This time, open the ARIMA Options dialog box and select Apply from previous model for Initial Values. This should reduce the number of iterations needed this time.

Most ARIMA packages allow only the first two steps. You can always stop there with Trends ARIMA too, but you have the option of using the Kalman filtering algorithm to get the best possible estimates.

Note that the results obtained by following the steps above are the same as the results you would obtain if you used the ARIMA procedure directly on the series with imbedded missing data, without first estimating initial values from interpolated data. The only difference is processing time.

Autoregression with Maximum-Likelihood Estimation

When you request maximum-likelihood estimation with the Autoregression procedure, Trends uses the same algorithms as in ARIMA. This means that Autoregression can process series with imbedded missing data when maximum-likelihood estimation is requested, but it may take a while.

To reduce processing time when your series has imbedded missing data, you can follow the same steps outlined for ARIMA above. However, since the Autoregression Options dialog box does not have controls for initial values, you need to use command syntax to apply initial estimates the second time you run the Autoregression procedure (step 3 above). The command is:

```
AREG /APPLY INITIAL.
```

Again, if processing time is not a consideration you can simply use the Autoregression procedure directly on the series with imbedded missing data. Alternatively, if you do not need the best-quality estimates, you can stop after step 2 and get results as good as most other packages give.

PACF

Displaying partial autocorrelations (an option in the Autocorrelations dialog box) requires the solution of a system of equations whose size grows with the number of lags. Be careful about requesting partial autocorrelations to a high number of lags (over 24). Even on a fast machine this will take much longer than the autocorrelations. The maximum number of lags can be set in the Autocorrelations Options dialog box.

If you have a series with seasonal effects and need to look at high lags, look at the autocorrelations alone until you are sure the series is stationary. Then ask for the partials as well.

New Series

As described in "Automatic Creation of New Series" on p. 17, many Trends procedures automatically generate new series. This facility can be a great aid—but not always. Possible difficulties with saving new series include:

- Trends must read and write the entire file an extra time to add the new series.
- Your file becomes larger—in some cases, dramatically so—and subsequent processing therefore takes longer.
- Most of the time you do not need most of the new series. Merely keeping track of their names becomes a problem.

When you use commands in the

Statistics
  Time Series ▶

submenu, it's a good idea always to open the Save subdialog box and give a moment's thought to the creation of new variables. The default for these commands is to add new variables permanently to your data file. If you are doing preliminary analysis and are not yet certain of the models you want to use, the Replace existing alternative for new variables gives you the benefits of residuals and predicted values, but does not keep all of them around. Once you have settled on a model, you may want to go back into the Save subdialog box and choose the Add to file alternative.

General Techniques for Efficiency

For any iterative procedures in Trends, you may find it useful to:

1. Relax the convergence criteria for the procedure. These are specified in the Options dialog box for the specific procedure.

2. Perform exploratory analysis to determine the best model.

3. Restore the stricter convergence criteria for the final estimation of your coefficients.

The general point is that some estimation algorithms used in Trends require a lot of processing and will take a long time if you use them blindly. Take advantage of the interactive character of Trends. Loosen things up for speed while you are exploring your data, and then—when you are ready to estimate your final coefficients—exploit the full accuracy of the Trends algorithms.

3 Notes on the Applications

Chapter 4 through Chapter 14 contain examples that show you how the different Trends commands work together in solving real problems. All but one are based on real data, and all the data are included on your system diskettes. You can compare the analyses presented here with published analyses (cited in the Bibliography) and—if you like— with the results you get on your own PC.

- We have not attempted original or profound analysis but rather have tried to show how the commands in Trends work together in analyzing typical time series data.

- When repeating a published analysis we have generally followed the strategy used by the original author rather than exploring alternatives. Doing so makes it easier for you to compare the Trends commands and output with the published analysis.

- We have not attempted to write a textbook in time series analysis. We do try to give a reliable, intuitive explanation of important techniques such as exponential smoothing, ARIMA analysis, intervention analysis, weighted least squares, and two-stage least squares, but our discussion cannot replace more formal training in time series analysis.

Generally speaking, the applications progress from easier to harder, but you should feel free to browse through them as they fit your needs. At the end of this chapter you will find an index to which applications use particular Trends commands.

Working Through the Applications on Your PC

If you would like to work through the analysis in any of the following chapters, you will find the SPSS data files on your Trends disk. If you intend to work through the applications, copy these data files to your hard disk, and open the appropriate data file before beginning each chapter.

The Data Files

The names of the data files are *chap4.sav*, *chap5.sav*, etc. Each data file contains one line per observation. Some of the data files contain series that are not used in the application chapters.

Command Index

Table 3.1 shows which analytical procedures in the Trends option are used in each applications chapter. Many of these chapters also illustrate the use of Base system procedures that analyze time series data. Chapter 11 uses the Weighted Least Squares procedure from the Professional Statistics option.

Table 3.1   Index of procedures by chapter

Procedure	Chapters
Autoregression	9
ARIMA	6, 7, 8, 10, 12
Exponential Smoothing	4, 6, 7
Seasonal Decomposition	11
Spectral Plots	13
X11 ARIMA	14

4 An Inventory Problem: Exponential Smoothing

In this chapter we apply the simple, intuitive method known as *exponential smoothing* to a series of inventory records. Inventory management is typical of the problems to which exponential smoothing is appropriate. It often requires the routine forecasting of many series on a regular basis. With elaborate forecasting techniques, the sheer quantity of calculations would be overwhelming. With exponential smoothing, once you have determined a satisfactory model, the calculations needed to make forecasts are simple and fast.

For a technical discussion of exponential smoothing, see the review article by Gardner (1985).

The Inventory Data

Inventory records are a common type of time series. The stock of an item rises and falls, and you want to make sure it never drops to zero on the one hand, but never rises too high on the other. And since there is usually some lead time needed to acquire new stock, you need accurate projections of the next month's inventory so you can order new stock in advance. If your forecast is too large you may order too little, and later have to place a rush order at extra cost. If your forecast is too small you may order too much, which ties up your capital in inventory and locks you in to a particular set of specifications for the item.

In this chapter we will analyze a series named *amount*, which contains daily inventory totals of power supplies used in computer printers.

Plotting the Series

The first step in analyzing a time series is to plot it. A plot gives you a general idea of how the series behaves:

- Does it have an overall **trend** (a persistent tendency to increase or decrease over time)?
- Does it show **seasonality** (a cyclical pattern that repeats over and over, typically every year)?

- Does it vary smoothly from one period to the next, or is it choppy?
- Is there a break or sudden change in the behavior of the series, or does it look much the same from beginning to end?
- Is the short-term variation about the same throughout the series? Does short-term variation increase or decrease with time? With the overall level of the series?
- Are there **outliers**—points that are far out of line? (Such points are often due to unique events, and must be excluded when you search for the process underlying the series as a whole.)

To plot a time series, from the menus choose

Graphs
  Sequence...

This opens the Sequence Charts dialog box, as shown in Figure 4.1. A sequence plot shows the values of one or more numeric variables in the sequential order of the cases.

Figure 4.1   Sequence Charts dialog box

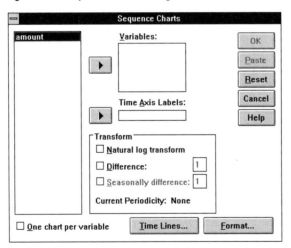

Highlight the variable *amount* in the source list and click on the ▶ pushbutton to move it into the Variables list. To obtain a sequence plot, click on OK. The result is shown in Figure 4.2.

Figure 4.2   Sequence plot

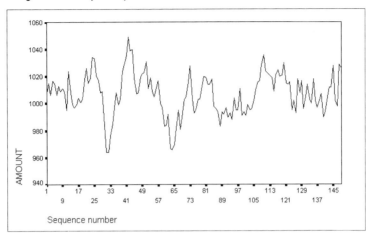

As you can see from the plot:

- The series does not show any trend, but varies randomly around its mean level.
- No seasonality is apparent. For daily data one might expect periods of 7, 30, or 365. We will see in Chapter 11 how to use the Seasonal Decomposition procedure to extract the seasonal component of a series. Most of the time you can tell from the plot whether or not the series shows periodic variation.
- The series has a "memory" in the sense that each value tends to be close to the preceding value. This phenomenon is quite common in time series data, and is called **positive autocorrelation.**

Series that show memory or autocorrelation are good candidates for smoothing techniques. Smoothing techniques emphasize the regularity of a series by removing some of the random variation. Once you have identified this regularity, you can use it to make forecasts.

Smoothing the Series

The purpose of smoothing a series is to strip away the random fluctuations. This allows you to capitalize on any pattern that is evident in the observed series, and to use that pattern to predict new values.

Among the things you might want to consider in predicting the next value in a series are:

- The most recent value. Many (perhaps most) time series show positive autocorrelation, which means that each value tends to be positively correlated with the preceding value.

- The overall average so far. This is sometimes your best guess when you can't find any pattern in the series.

- The trend. If inventory has been decreasing by 10 units a day, you should adjust your forecast to reflect this trend. (However, you would expect this trend to level off sooner or later—certainly when inventory reached 0.)

- The seasonal averages. If you predict inventory of toys in the fall, you must take note of the seasonal patterns that precede and follow Christmas.

Based on the criteria in the above list, you can see that there are two extreme approaches to predicting a value that might be taken:

1. Forget the history of the series and predict that it will hold steady at the most recent value. This approach is justified when positive serial correlation overwhelms any prior patterns, as is often true when the time period used is very short. For example, inventory at 10:31 is likely to be very close to inventory at 10:30, even for toys in December.

2. Forget the most recent value and base your prediction on the mean of the series and any trend or seasonality you can find. This approach makes sense when the time period is long enough to "wash out" the serial correlation. The most recent value isn't much more useful than any other, so you rely on the patterns established in the observed history of the time series: the mean, trend, and seasonality.

In more typical circumstances you want to combine these approaches. You want to use the observed mean, trend, and seasonality, but you want to give extra weight to more recent observations. This strategy is the basis for a technique called **exponential smoothing**.

The strategy of giving extra weight to recent observations can be applied to estimates of the series level, its trend, and its seasonality. In general, recent observations are a more reliable guide to:

- Level, if the overall level of a series is changing slowly.

- Trend, if the trend of a series is changing slowly.

- Seasonality, if the intensity of seasonal variation is changing. (If the holiday effect is growing stronger or weaker, you should give extra weight to recent holiday seasons.)

Depending on whether or not your series shows trend and seasonality, you can provide as many as four values to control the relative importance given to recent observations. All four of these parameters range from 0 to 1:

1. The general parameter, called alpha, controls the weight given to recent observations in determining the overall level and is used for all series. When alpha = 1, the single most recent observation is used exclusively; when alpha = 0, old observations count just as heavily as recent ones.

2. The trend parameter, gamma, is used only when the series shows a trend. When gamma is high, the forecast is based on a trend that has been estimated from the most recent points in the series. When gamma is low, the forecast uses a trend based on the entire series with all points counting equally.

3. The seasonality parameter, delta, is used only when the series shows seasonality. Models with a high delta value estimate seasonality primarily from recent time points; models with a low delta value estimate seasonality from the entire series with all points counting equally.

4. Phi is used in place of gamma when the series shows a trend *and* that trend is **damped,** or dying out. When phi is high the model responds rapidly to any indication that the trend is dying out. When phi is low the estimated damping of the trend is based on the entire series.

All four parameters specify how quickly the exponential-smoothing model reacts to changes in the process that generates the time series. The exponential smoothing algorithm starts at the beginning of the series and works its way through, one period at a time. At each step, it takes the most recent value and adjusts its estimate of the mean value of the series and (if appropriate) its estimates of the trend, seasonality, and damping of the trend. When the parameters alpha, gamma, delta, and phi are near 0, the estimates are inflexible and remain about the same until a good deal of evidence accumulates that they need to change. When the parameters are near 1, the estimates are very flexible and respond to any indication that the level, trend, seasonality, or damping seem to be changing.

Estimating the Parameter Values

You are unlikely to look at a series and guess the value of alpha that fits it best, and less likely still to guess all the values of all parameters needed for a series with seasonality and a damped trend. In practice you must try several values to see which one fits the series best. Start by determining which parameters are not needed at all. For the inventory series *amount*, the plots showed no trend (hence gamma and phi are unnecessary) and no seasonality (hence delta is unnecessary). You need only estimate alpha, the overall smoothing parameter.

You can do this most easily with what is called a "grid search." When a grid is specified, SPSS uses a sequence of equally spaced values for alpha and for each value calculates a measure of how well the predictions agreed with the actual values. The actual statistic is the **sum of squared errors,** or **SSE.** The parameters that produce the smallest

SSE are "best" for the series. By default, SPSS displays the ten best-fitting sets of parameters and the SSE associated with each of them.

The default grid values for alpha start with 0 and end with 1, incrementing by 0.1. Thus, the default grid generates 11 models, with values of alpha ranging from 0, 0.1, 0.2, and so on up to 1. If you specify a grid search for more than one parameter, a model is evaluated for each *combination* of values across all parameters. When your model contains trend and seasonality, using the default grid for each parameter will smooth the series and evaluate the SSE several hundred times for each series analyzed! For this reason, you should be careful not to use more parameters than you need.

Estimating a Simple Model

Let's see how all this works. From the menus choose

Statistics
  Time Series...
    Exponential Smoothing

The Exponential Smoothing dialog box appears, as shown in Figure 4.3.

Figure 4.3   Exponential Smoothing dialog box

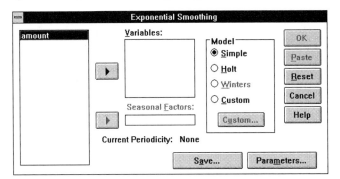

Select *amount* from the source list and move it into the Variables list. Since this series showed no trend and no seasonal variation, leave Simple selected in the Model group. Click on Parameters... to indicate that you want a grid search for the best value of the alpha parameter. The Exponential Smoothing Parameters dialog box is shown in Figure 4.4.

Figure 4.4   Exponential Smoothing Parameters dialog box

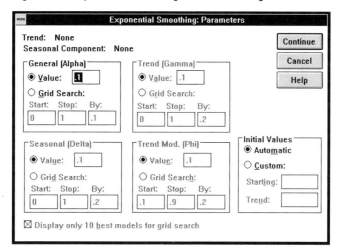

This dialog box has a group of controls for each possible parameter, and a separate group in case you want to specify an initial value or an initial trend parameter. (Most of the time, you can let SPSS determine the initial values.) Since the simple model was select-ed in the main dialog box, only one group of parameter controls is active: those for the general smoothing parameter, alpha. Click on the Grid Search alternative. To accept the default grid from 0 to 1 by increments of 0.1, click on Continue.

Back at the main Exponential Smoothing dialog box, click on OK. Figure 4.5 shows the results.

Figure 4.5   Exponential smoothing, no trend or seasonality

```
Results of EXSMOOTH procedure for Variable AMOUNT
MODEL=NN (No trend, no seasonality)

   Initial values:          Series            Trend
                          1006.90004         Not used

DFE = 148.

The 10 smallest SSE's are:          Alpha                 SSE
                                    .8000000        17291.25233
                                    .9000000        17435.96280
                                    .7000000        17470.24396
                                   1.000000         17879.19675
                                    .6000000        18033.12401
                                    .5000000        19089.28926
                                    .4000000        20820.58960
                                    .3000000        23510.67242
                                    .2000000        27541.47917
                                    .1000000        32919.01373
```

When you do a grid search for the best smoothing parameters, Trends displays the best parameter value (or combinations of parameter values when your model includes trend or seasonality). You can see that the SSE measure of error is lowest when alpha is 0.8. This is a high value, indicating that inventory is best predicted when the most recent observation is weighted quite heavily in comparison to older observations. (Today's inventory is probably close to yesterday's.)

As shown in Figure 4.6, SPSS has added two new series to your file. The series *fit_1* contains the predicted values from the exponential smoothing, and *err_1* contains the errors. These new variables are automatically assigned variable labels describing their type, the series and procedure from which they were generated, and other information including the parameter (*A 0.8*).

Figure 4.6   FIT and ERROR series from exponential smoothing

```
The following new variables are being created:

   NAME          LABEL

   FIT_1         Fit for AMOUNT from EXSMOOTH, MOD_4 NN A .80
   ERR_1         Error for AMOUNT from EXSMOOTH, MOD_4 NN A .80
```

Plotting the Results

Now you can use the Sequence Charts procedure to compare the original series *amount* with the forecasts generated by Exponential Smoothing. As before, from the menus choose

Graphs
　Sequence...

This time, move both *amount* and the new smoothed series *fit_1* into the Variables list and click on OK. The resulting high-resolution plot is shown in . The original series *amount* and the forecast series *fit_1* both appear. The legend indicates the line pattern used for each; you can change these patterns if you wish in the Chart Editor. As you can see, the forecasts track the original series closely. They are always a bit "behind" when the original series changes rapidly, but they stay with it surprisingly well. This is because the Exponential Smoothing algorithm bases each forecast on all the preceding data, and because an alpha value of 0.8 allows just the right flexibility in the forecasts.

Predictions from exponential smoothing

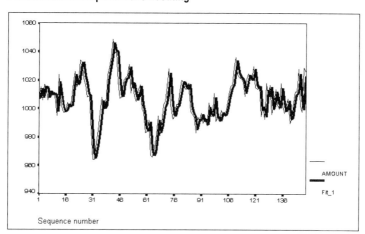

Plotting Residuals

The *err_1* variable created by the Exponential Smoothing procedure contains the **residual,** or **error.** The residual is simply the difference between the actual value and the prediction. It's always a good idea to plot residuals. From the menus choose

Graphs
  Sequence...

Move *err_1* into the Variables list and click on OK. Figure 4.8 shows the residual plot.

Figure 4.8   Residuals from exponential smoothing

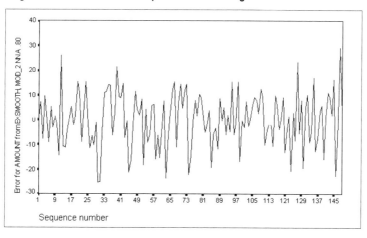

The universal rule for residuals is that they should be randomly distributed, without any discernible pattern. If the residuals from any model show a pattern, the model is inadequate. The residuals in Figure 4.8 show no pattern.

Using the Wrong Parameter Value

To see the importance of finding a good value for alpha, you can force alpha to equal 0.1 and plot the results. Select the Exponential Smoothing command from the menus again, make sure that *amount* is in the Variables list and that the Simple model is selected, and click on Parameters.... This time, select the Value alternative for the general parameter, and specify 0.1 as the value for alpha. Click Continue, and then from the main dialog box click OK to smooth the *amount* series with this inappropriate value for alpha. Figure 4.9 shows a plot of the *amount* with the fitted values from this analysis.

Figure 4.9   Exponential smoothing with a bad alpha

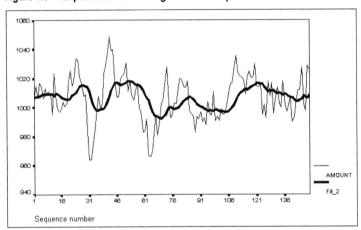

The low value of alpha has made the predictions inflexible. They stay close to the center (the mean) and are unable to respond quickly to rapid fluctuations in the data. The optimal value of alpha is a characteristic of each particular series. You must find it empirically.

Forecasting with Exponential Smoothing

The Exponential Smoothing procedure is best used for short-term forecasting, or what are known as "one-period-ahead" or **one-step-ahead forecasts.** That is what it is designed to do. When you choose the right values for its parameters it extracts a lot of useful information from the most recent observation, somewhat less from the next-most-recent, and so on, and usually makes a good forecast. As it moves into the future, how-ever, making **n-step-ahead forecasts,** it quickly runs out of the recent information on which it thrives.

Generally speaking:

- You get one-step-ahead forecasts in the period for which you have data, because data from the previous observation(s) are available for use in making the forecasts.

- You get *n*-step-ahead forecasts if you ask SPSS to predict past the end of your data, creating observations for which data from the previous observation(s) are not avail-able.

To see the result of predicting far beyond the available data, go back into the Exponential Smoothing dialog box. Select *amount* and the Simple model, if they are not already se-lected. Since you already know that an alpha of 0.8 works best for this series, click on Parameters. . ., choose the Value alternative for alpha and specify 0.8 as the desired val-ue. (A grid search would only waste time, since the series hasn't changed. The result would be the same.) Click on Continue to return to the Exponential Smoothing dialog box.

To predict cases past the end of the file, click on Save..., select the Predict through: option, and enter 180 into the Observation text box. This adds observations 150 through 180 to the original series, which contained 149 observations.

When you execute the procedure and plot the resulting *fit_3* series alongside *amount*, you see the result shown in Figure 4.10.

Figure 4.10 Long-range forecasting with Exponential Smoothing

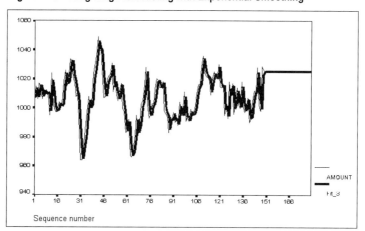

The forecasts from period 150 on remain "stuck" at their last value. With this high value of alpha, the Exponential Smoothing algorithm relies heavily on recent data, and the most recent data point available remains (and will always remain) the one at observation 149. With other parameters the algorithm may behave differently, but its predictions inevitably get worse as it runs out of available data.

When to Use Exponential Smoothing

Exponential smoothing is not based on a theoretical understanding of the data. It forecasts one point at a time, adjusting its forecasts as new data come in. It is often a useful technique, however, particularly when:

- You are satisfied with forecasting one period at a time.
- You are routinely forecasting many series over and over (as is often the case with inventory data).

Once you have determined the best parameters for a series, exponential smoothing is computationally inexpensive. This makes a difference when you forecast next month's inventory for a hundred different items. If the model ceases to perform well and you have to do frequent grid searches for the best parameters, the computational requirements are much heavier.

How to Use Exponential Smoothing

The Exponential Smoothing procedure smooths one or more series by predicting each value using the overall series mean, with recent observations given extra weight as determined by the general parameter alpha. In models with seasonality, trend, or damped trend, coefficients are similarly estimated case-by-case using a combination of overall series values and values from recent cases, as determined by the parameters for seasonality, trend, or damped trend.

The minimum specification is one or more numeric variables to smooth.

To apply Exponential Smoothing to your data, from the menus choose:

Statistics
  Time Series
    Exponential Smoothing...

This opens the Exponential Smoothing dialog box, as shown in Figure 4.11.

Figure 4.11   Exponential Smoothing dialog box

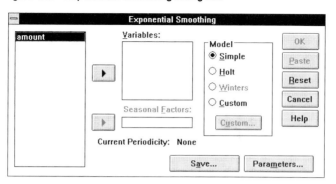

The numeric variables in your data file appear in the source variable list. Select one or more variables and move them into the Variables list. To smooth the series using the default simple model with the default value of 0.1 for the smoothing parameter alpha, click on OK.

Model. Four model types are available in the Model group. You can select one model:

○ **Simple.** The series has no overall trend and shows no seasonal variation.

○ **Holt.** The series has a linear trend but shows no seasonal variation.

○ **Winters.** The series has a linear trend and shows multiplicative seasonal variation. You cannot select this option unless you have defined seasonality with the Define Dates command.

○ **Custom.** You can specify the form of the trend component and the way in which the seasonal component is applied, as described below.

Seasonal Factors. For models with seasonal components (the Winters model and any custom model for which you specify a seasonal component), you can optionally move a variable containing seasonal factors into the Seasonal Factors box. The Seasonal Decomposition procedure creates such variables.

Parameters

Usually you will either request a grid search for the best parameter values or specify particular values for the parameters. To do so, click on Parameters... in the Exponential

Smoothing dialog box. This opens the Exponential Smoothing Parameters dialog box, as shown in Figure 4.12.

Figure 4.12   Exponential Smoothing Parameters dialog box

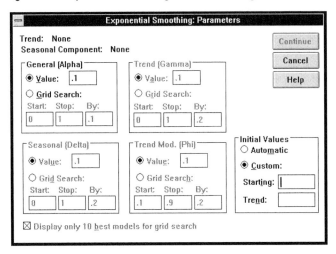

This dialog box has four control groups for model parameters and one for initial values. Parameter controls are disabled if they do not apply to the model specified in the main Exponential Smoothing dialog box. The parameter control groups are:

General (Alpha). Alpha controls the relative weight given to recent observations, as opposed to the overall series mean. It ranges from 0 to 1, with values near 1 giving higher weight to recent values. These controls are always available.

Seasonal (Delta). Delta controls the relative weight given to recent observations, as opposed to the overall series, in estimating the present seasonality. It ranges from 0 to 1, with values near 1 giving higher weight to recent values. These controls are available for the Winters model and for custom models with a seasonal component.

Trend (Gamma). Gamma controls the relative weight given to recent observations, as opposed to the overall series, in estimating the present series trend. It ranges from 0 to 1, with values near 1 giving higher weight to recent values. These controls are available for the Holt and Winters models, and for custom models with a linear or exponential trend component.

Trend Modification (Phi). Phi controls the rate at which a trend is "damped," or reduced in magnitude over time. It ranges from 0 to 1 (but cannot equal 1), with values near 1 representing more gradual damping. These controls are available for custom models with a damped trend component.

For each control group you can choose between two alternatives:

○ **Value.** The parameter is assigned a single value. Enter the value after selecting this alternative. It must be between 0 and 1; the value of phi should not equal 1.

○ **Grid Search.** The parameter is assigned a starting value in the Start text box, an increment value in the By text box, and ending value in the Stop text box. Enter these values after selecting this alternative. The ending value must be greater than starting value, and the increment value must be less than their difference.

If you specify a grid search, smoothing is carried out for each value of the parameter. If you specify grid searches for more than one parameter, smoothing is carried out for each combination of parameter values. You can use the following to control the amount of output displayed:

❏ **Display only 10 best models for grid search.** When this is selected, the parameter value(s) and sum of squared errors (SSE) are displayed only for the 10 parameter combinations with the lowest SSE, regardless of the number of parameter combinations tested. If this option is not selected, all tested parameter combinations are displayed.

Initial Values. You can specify the starting and trend values used in smoothing the series by selecting one of the following:

○ **Automatic.** SPSS calculates suitable starting and trend values from the data. This is usually desirable.

○ **Custom.** If you select Custom, enter a number in the Starting text box and, for models with a trend, a number in the Trend text box. Poor choice of initial values can result in an inferior solution.

Saving Predicted Values and Residuals

To save smoothed values and residuals as new variables, or to produce forecasts past the end of your data, click on Save... in the Exponential Smoothing dialog box. This opens the Exponential Smoothing Save dialog box, as shown in Figure 4.13. The current estimation period is shown at the bottom of this dialog box.

Figure 4.13   Exponential Smoothing Save dialog box

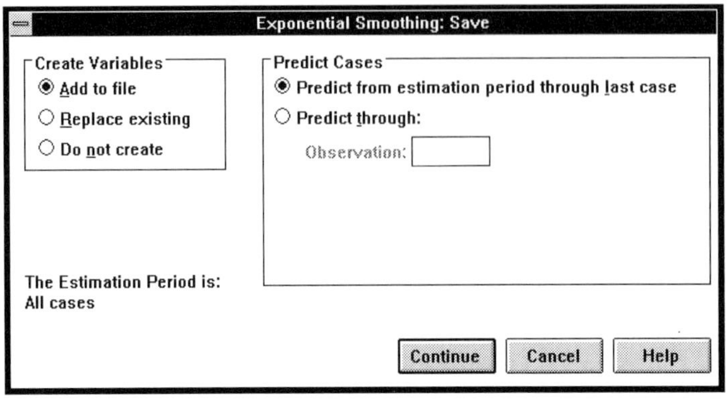

Create Variables. To control the creation of new variables, you can choose one of these alternatives:

○ **Add to file.** The new series created by Exponential Smoothing are saved as regular variables in your working data file. Variable names are formed from a three-letter prefix, an underscore, and a number. This is the default.

○ **Replace existing.** The new series created by Exponential Smoothing are saved as temporary variables in the working data file and any existing temporary variables created by Trends commands are dropped. Variable names are formed from a three-letter prefix, a pound sign (#), and a number.

○ **Do not create.** The new series are not added to the working data file.

Predict Cases. If you select either Add to file or Replace existing above, you can specify a forecast period:

○ **Predict from estimation period through last case.** Predicts values for all cases from the estimation period through the end of the file but does not create new cases. If you are analyzing a range of cases that starts after the beginning of the file, cases prior to that range are not predicted. The estimation period, displayed at the bottom of this dialog box, is defined in the Range dialog box available through the Select Cases option on the Data menu. If no estimation period has been defined, all cases are used to predict values. This is the default.

○ **Predict through.** Predicts values through the specified date, time, or observation number, based on the cases in the estimation period. This can be used to forecast values beyond the last case in the time series. The text boxes that are available for specifying the end of the prediction period depend on the currently defined date variables. (Use the Define Dates option on the Data menu to create date variables.) If there are no defined date variables, you can specify the ending observation (case) number.

New cases created as forecasts have missing values for all series in the original data file and for new series (such as residuals) whose definition requires an existing value. For Exponential Smoothing, only the smoothed series *fit* has valid values past the end of the original data.

Custom Models

If you select Custom in the Model group in the Exponential Smoothing dialog box, you must click on Custom... to specify your custom model. This opens the Exponential Smoothing Custom Model dialog box, as shown in Figure 4.14.

Figure 4.14   Exponential Smoothing Custom Model dialog box

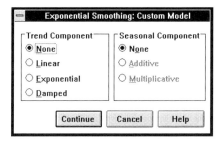

Select an alternative from the Trend Component group:

❍ **None.** The series has no overall trend.

❍ **Linear.** The mean level of the series increases or decreases linearly with time.

❍ **Exponential.** The mean level of the series increases or decreases exponentially with time.

❍ **Damped.** The mean level of the series increases or decreases with time, but the rate of change declines.

If you have defined the periodicity of your data with Define Dates on the Data menu, you can also specify a Seasonal Component:

❍ **None.** The series has no variation at the seasonal periodicity specified in Define Dates.

❍ **Additive.** The series has seasonal variation that is additive: the magnitude of seasonal variation does not depend on the overall level of the series.

○ **Multiplicative.** The series has seasonal variation that is multiplicative: the magnitude of seasonal variation is proportional to the overall level of the series.

The Holt model in the main Exponential Smoothing dialog box is equivalent to selecting Linear for Trend Component and None for Seasonal Component in the Custom dialog box. The Winters model is equivalent to selecting Linear for Trend Component and Multiplicative for Seasonal Component.

Additional Features Available with Command Syntax

You can customize your exponential smoothing if you paste your selections to a syntax window and edit the resulting EXSMOOTH command syntax. The additional feature is:

- Seasonal factors can be specified numerically by providing as many additive or multiplicative numbers as the seasonal periodicity.

See the Syntax Reference section of this manual for command syntax rules and for complete EXSMOOTH command syntax.

5

Forecasting Sales with a Leading Indicator: Regression Forecasting

Methods based on regression analysis are widely applied to time series and forecasting. In this chapter we apply two different regression-based techniques to the common problem of forecasting sales.

The Sales Data

One of the examples in Box and Jenkins' classic book *Time Series Analysis: Forecasting and Control*, called "Series M," studies sales data with a leading indicator. A *leading indicator* is a series that helps predict the values of another series one or more time periods later.

In this chapter we will examine the sales data using two different regression-based methods. First we will use the Curve Estimation procedure to try to extrapolate the series; then we will see how to use the leading indicator and the Linear Regression procedure to get better predictions. (Both of these procedures are in the Base system.)

This example will be the first of several that illustrate the important technique of dividing a time series into two periods: a **historical** or **estimation period** and a **validation period**. Data from the validation period are sometimes called the **hold-out sample**. As mentioned in Chapter 2, a common technique is to split a series in this way, develop a model or models using only the data in the historical period, and then apply the models to the data in the validation period as a test.

Plotting the Sales Data

We will use the first 100 points in the *sales* series as the historical period for this analysis. From the menus choose:

Data
  Select Cases...

This opens the Select Cases dialog box, as shown in Figure 5.1.

Figure 5.1   Select Cases dialog box

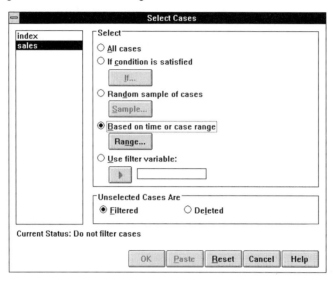

Select Based on time or case range and then click on the Range... pushbutton. This opens the Select Cases Range dialog box, as shown in Figure 5.2.

Figure 5.2   Select Cases Range dialog box

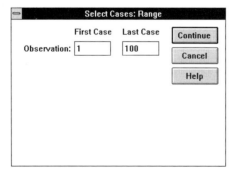

If you have defined date variables for your data, this dialog box contains fields in which you can specify a range of cases by date. Since no date variables are defined for this file, the range is specified by observation number. Type 1 under First Case, tab to Last Case, and type 100 there. Click on Continue to return to the Select Cases dialog box. Make sure that Filtered is specified for Unselected Cases, so that cases after 100 will be available later for use in the validation period. Click OK to establish the historical period for the next few commands.

Now let's take a look at the series. From the menus choose:

Graphs
  Sequence...

This opens the familiar Sequence Charts dialog box. Move *sales* into the Variables list and click on OK. The plot of *sales* is shown in Figure 5.3.

Figure 5.3   Sales data (historical period)

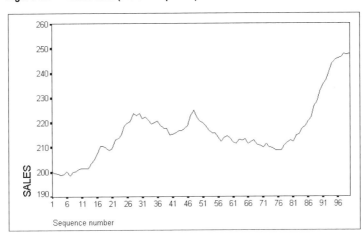

Extrapolation with Curve Estimation

Over the first 100 points, the *sales* series shows an irregular increase, particularly at the end. Like the inventory series in Chapter 4, it is positively autocorrelated: each point is close to the previous point, as if the series had a memory. A straightforward way to forecast such a series is to draw a simple curve that passes close to the existing points, and extend the curve to make forecasts.

The Curve Estimation procedure does just that: it determines the best way to draw any of about a dozen simple types of curves through your data and reports how well each curve fits. It also generates four new time series showing the fitted value, or prediction; the error; and upper and lower confidence limits around the fitted value. You can plot these new series and analyze them to see how well the model works.

Fitting Quadratic and Cubic Curves

It is unclear what type of curve would best fit the series plotted in Figure 5.3. We will estimate coefficients for the quadratic and cubic curves from the first 100 points in the series (the historical period established above is still in effect). We will then calculate forecasts based on these curves through the validation period and compare the two models.

Curve Estimation is one of the family of related techniques known as regression analysis. To fit the quadratic curve to the *sales* series, from the menus choose:

Statistics
  Regression
    Curve Estimation...

This opens the Curve Estimation dialog box, as shown in Figure 5.4.

Figure 5.4   Curve Estimation dialog box

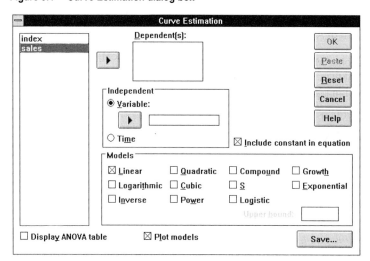

Select *sales* and move it into the Dependent(s) list.

In the Independent group, select the Time alternative. In the Models group, deselect Linear, and select the Quadratic and Cubic models. To compare the predictions of these models with the *sales* series itself, click on Save.... This opens the Curve Estimation Save dialog box, as shown in Figure 5.5.

Figure 5.5   Curve Estimation Save dialog box

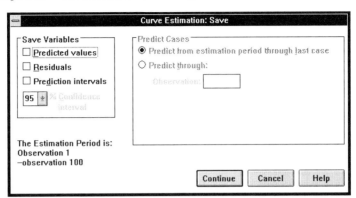

We will examine the predictions from the quadratic and cubic models first, so select Predicted values in the Save group. The estimation period, from observation 1 through observation 100, is displayed at the bottom of this dialog box. To get predicted values through the last case in the data file, leave the default Predict from estimation period through last case selected in the Predict Cases group. Click on Continue to return to the main Curve Estimation dialog box. Make sure both Include constant in equation and Plot models are still selected. Then click on OK to carry out the analysis.

First look at the statistical summary displayed in the output window (Figure 5.6).

Figure 5.6   Quadratic and cubic curve estimation

```
Dependent Mth   Rsq  d.f.      F  Sigf     b0      b1      b2     b3

   SALES    QUA  .462    97  41.73  .000 206.517   .0593   .0021
   SALES    CUB  .877    96 227.80  .000 185.507  2.4952  -.0579   .0004

The following new variables are being created:

  Name      Label

  FIT_1     Fit for SALES from CURVEFIT, MOD_2 QUADRATIC
  FIT_2     Fit for SALES from CURVEFIT, MOD_2 CUBIC
```

The quadratic model is summarized on the first line, the line with QUA in the method (*Mth*) column. The coefficients of the equation appear in the columns labeled *b0* (the constant), *b1* (the linear term), and *b2* (the quadratic term). The best-fitting quadratic curve is given by

$$\text{sales} = 206.517 + (0.0593 \times \text{case}) + (0.0021 \times \text{case}^2)$$

where case is the sequential case number. The quadratic term is quite small; this quadratic curve is almost a straight line. Now look at the cubic model summarized on the next line, with *CUB* in the method column. In addition to *b0*, *b1*, and *b2*, this model has a *b3* coefficient for the cubic term. The cubic coefficient *b3* is quite small. This makes sense, because the cubed values of the observation number (which are multiplied by *b3*) range from 1 to 1,000,000. When multiplied by a million, even a coefficient of 0.0004 makes a difference of 400 in the predicted sales.

The best cubic equation, then, is:

$$\text{sales} = 185.507 + (2.4952 \times \text{case}) - (0.0579 \times \text{case}^2) + (0.0004 \times \text{case}^3)$$

Which model is best? The R^2 for the cubic equation is larger, but that is a foregone conclusion. A quadratic equation *can't* have a larger R^2 than a cubic equation estimated with the same data. The cubic equation can always do as well as the quadratic equation by setting *b3* to 0, and for real data there's sure to be some value of *b3* that does even better. In general, you can always obtain a better fit by using a more complex model specification—but that does not always mean the complex model is more appropriate. A much better comparison is the performance of the two models during the validation period.

Plotting the Curves

The Curve Estimation procedure generated predicted values for each of the two models. As reported in the output in Figure 5.6, the new variables are named *fit_1* and *fit_2*. Figure 5.7 shows a sequence plot of these predicted values with the original series.

During the historical period (through observation 100), the predictions from the cubic model stay closer to *sales* than the predictions from the quadratic model. The more complex cubic model seems to work better. In the validation period, however, it wanders away from the actual sales.

Figure 5.7   Sequence plot of predicted values with sales

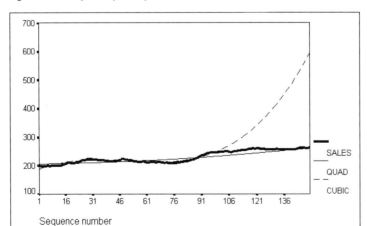

Unlimited Growth?

The cubic curve will continue to increase rapidly. Although you cannot see it yet, the quadratic curve will do the same, less rapidly. In the long run it is unlikely that sales could keep up with either. Be wary of n-step-ahead forecasts based on models that show exploding growth—sooner or later the real data will level off. Most of the models in the Curve Estimation procedure, including the quadratic model and even the linear model, suffer from this problem when extended too far.

Regression with a Leading Indicator

The Curve Estimation procedure performs regression analysis, which is discussed in detail in the *SPSS Base System User's Guide*. We have been using time as the predictor (independent) variable. Used in this way, Curve Estimation finds a curve that fits the shape of a time series plot, without regard to why the plot has that shape. If you have another series, an indicator, that does a good job of predicting the series you are interested in, you can get much better forecasts. To be of practical use, the indicator must be a **leading indicator.** That is, it must predict future levels of your series.

The Leading Indicator

Box and Jenkins' sales data contain an indicator series known to be a good predictor of *sales* at some later date. (They do not specify what it is; we shall call it *index*.) To use it you must first determine how far it leads the sales series. If this month's index predicts sales four months from now, you may not get very far trying to predict next month's sales.

Sometimes you know from experience how far one series leads another. When you do not, you can use the Cross-Correlations procedure to look at the **cross-correlation function,** or CCF. The cross-correlation function shows the correlation between two series at the same time and also with each series leading by one or more lags. By inspecting the CCF between two series, you can often see the lag at which they are most highly correlated.

Stationary and Nonstationary Series

You should use the Cross-Correlations procedure only on series that are **stationary.** A series is stationary if its mean and variance stay about the same over the length of the series. (Stationary series play a very important role in time series analysis. We shall discuss them more in Chapter 6 and throughout the remainder of the book.) Looking at the plot in Figure 5.3, you can see that the *sales* series is not stationary. It begins around 200, drifts up between 210 and 220, wanders there for a while, and eventually ends up at about 250.

Differencing

The most effective way to make a drifting series stationary is to **difference** it. Taking differences simply means replacing the original series by the differences between adjacent values in the original series.

For example, Table 5.1 shows the first few values of series *sales* and their differences. The second differences are the differences of the differences. Notice that a differenced series always begins with as many missing values as the order of differencing.

Table 5.1   Sales and differences

sales	First differencing	Second differencing
200.1	(not defined)	(not defined)
199.5	−0.6	(not defined)
199.4	−0.1	0.5
198.9	−0.5	−0.4
199.0	0.1	0.6
200.2	1.2	1.1

Differencing a nonstationary series once, or occasionally twice, usually makes it stationary. Since the differencing operation is so useful in time series analysis, many of the commands used for analyzing time series can do it on the fly, analyzing the differences rather than the original series. The Cross-Correlations procedure is one that offers this option.

The Cross-Correlations Procedure

The Cross-Correlations procedure calculates cross-correlation coefficients. It is simple to use. From the menus choose:

Graphs
  Time Series
    Cross-Correlations...

This opens the Cross-Correlations dialog box, as shown in Figure 5.8.

Figure 5.8   Cross-Correlations dialog box

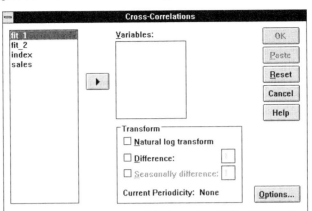

Select both *index* and *sales* and move them into the Variables list. Since the series are not stationary, select Difference in the Transform group. Leave the degree of differencing at 1 and click on OK. The resulting plot is shown in Figure 5.9.

Figure 5.9   Cross-correlations of index and sales

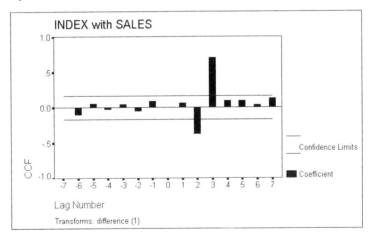

As shown in the plot, most of the correlations are small. There is a fairly large negative correlation of –0.345 at lag 2, and a very large positive correlation of 0.715 at lag 3. (The numerical values of the coefficients are displayed, along with a low-resolution character plot, in the output window.) Note that the plot displays correlations at both negative and positive lags. A negative lag indicates that the first series specified, *index, follows* the second series, *sales*. A positive lag indicates that the first series *leads* the second series. We conclude that the leading indicator *index* really is a leading indicator, and that it works best at predicting the value of *sales* three periods later.

Creating the Indicator

The observations in the data file have a value for *sales* and a value for *index*, both measured at the same time. However, to predict *sales* you need to generate a series where each observation contains the value of the index from three periods ago—the value that you know is a good predictor. In other words, you want to *lag* the indicator by three periods so that each value of *sales* is associated with the value of *index* from three periods before it. Trends performs this operation easily. From the menus choose:

Transform
  Create Time Series...

The Create Time Series dialog box is shown in Figure 5.10.

Figure 5.10   Create Time Series dialog box

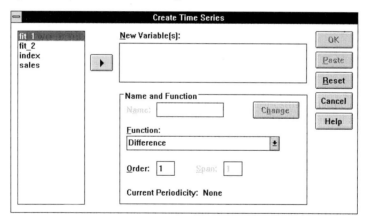

Select index and press ▶. Trends then generates the following assignment statement, which appears in the New Variable(s) list:

```
index_1=DIFF(index,1)
```

If you clicked on OK, this expression would create a new variable named *index_1*, containing the differences for series *index*. Trends chooses differencing by default, since this is one of the most common time series transformations. To use other transformations, you use the controls in the Name and Function group:

- Highlight the contents of the Name text box (*index_1*) and type a name that you want to replace it. In the rest of this chapter we will use the name *lead3ind*, since the new series is going to be a leading indicator with a lag of three cases.

- Choose the Lag function from the Function drop-down list. Since *index* leads the series of interest, a lagged copy of index will be correlated with that series.

- The Order text box shows a value of 1. Highlight this and type 3 to lag the value of index by three cases.

- Click on the Change pushbutton. The New Variables list should now contain:

  ```
  lead3ind=LAG(index,3)
  ```

- Click on OK to create the new time series.

If you go to the Data Editor, you will see a new column containing the new variable *lead3ind*. The first three observations will have a period, representing a missing value, since the file lacks information about the index prior to observation 1. Other observations will equal the value of *index* three rows higher.

Simple Regression

The Linear Regression procedure, which is part of the Base system, can be used to generate regression predictions. Since the historical period defined above is still in effect, you can proceed by choosing the following from the menus:

Statistics
  Regression ▶
    Linear...

This opens the Linear Regression dialog box, as shown in Figure 5.11.

Figure 5.11   Linear Regression dialog box

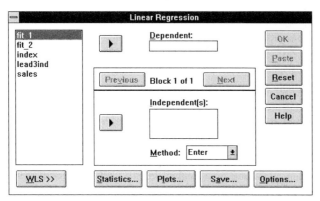

Move *sales* into the Dependent box and *lead3ind* into the Independent(s) list, and click on OK. The results are shown in Figure 5.12.

Figure 5.12   Linear regression with leading indicator

```
Analysis of Variance
                       DF       Sum of Squares      Mean Square
Regression              1          11238.47698      11238.47698
Residual               95           1380.93622         14.53617

F =      773.13876       Signif F =   .0000


----------------- Variables in the Equation -----------------

Variable              B         SE B       Beta        T   Sig T

LEAD3IND      14.685254      .528144    .943700   27.805   .0000
(Constant)    54.406312     5.861806              9.281   .0000


End Block Number    1    All requested variables entered.
```

   The regression coefficients in the column labeled B show that the best prediction equation is:

$$sales = 54.4 + (14.7 \times \text{lead3ind})$$

Linear Regression displays other statistics too—standard errors, t tests, R^2 (not shown), and an analysis of variance table. These statistics from Linear Regression are often not valid in time series analysis because the assumptions of ordinary least-squares regression analysis sometimes do not hold.

Regression Assumptions

One of the assumptions made in ordinary regression analysis is that the residuals or errors from the regression are uncorrelated among themselves. The most common cause of autocorrelated errors is failure to include in the equation an important explanatory variable which itself is autocorrelated. Because of the difficulty of including all the important explanatory variables, time series regression frequently violates the assumption of uncorrelated errors. When this happens the significance levels and goodness-of-fit statistics reported by Linear Regression are unreliable. You will see in later chapters how to detect and measure autocorrelation in residuals, and how to use the Trends command Autoregression, which corrects for autocorrelated residuals.

You *can,* however, use the regression equation to make forecasts on the basis of a leading indicator. The regression coefficients themselves are not biased by the autocorrelated errors, and Linear Regression requires much less processing than Autoregression. Of course, you need to know the values of your leading indicator. If you plan to forecast a dependent series value for which a leading indicator does not exist, you must first forecast the indicator and then use it to help forecast your series.

Forecasts from Linear Regression

The Linear Regression procedure is able to create new series containing predictions and residuals, but it does so only for the observations that it analyzes. To make forecasts for both the historical and validation sample periods, you must first compute the predicted values yourself from the regression equation. This is easy to do with the Compute procedure on the Transform menu. From the menus choose:

Transform
  Compute...

In the Compute Variable dialog box, type *predict* into the Target Variable text box. Click in the Numeric Expression text box and type 54.4 + 14.7*lead3ind. (If you like, you can click on buttons in the dialog box to build this expression. Typing is usually faster, though.) Click on OK to compute the new variable *predict*.

Now you can plot the new series *predict* along with the original series *sales*. From the menus choose

Data
  Select Cases

and click on All cases. Figure 5.13 shows the plot.

Figure 5.13   Linear regression forecasts

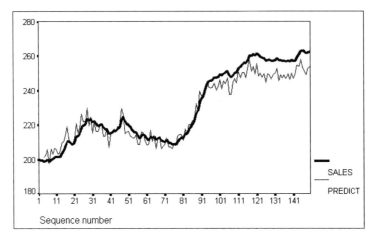

The forecasts look pretty good. In the validation period (past case 100), the forecasts are consistently low but do continue to track the *sales* series reasonably well.

6 A Quality-Control Chart: Introduction to ARIMA

Quality control in manufacturing offers an application of time-series methods in which the object is to determine if and when random fluctuations exceed their usual levels. A certain amount of variation is inevitable in production processes, but when excessive variation occurs you suspect a problem that can be corrected. If you do not catch a problem quickly, you will produce defective products, but if you stop the line for every random variation that occurs, your plant will be paralyzed.

Various types of **control charts** such as the X-bar and range chart are commonly used to provide an approximate answer to the question of whether random variation is exceeding its usual bounds. Trends lets you derive a more accurate model for the random variation in your data, so that your control chart will be more reliable.

The Quality-Control Data

The quality-control series used here consists of print-quality scores taken at regular intervals at a plant that manufactures computer printers. Excessively high or low scores indicate something is amiss with the production process.

Plotting the Series

To build a model of the typical variation in the print-quality scores, you begin by plotting the series during a period of normal operation. Figure 6.1 shows the plot. The analysis has been restricted to the first 100 points with the Select Cases Range dialog box available through the Select Cases option on the Data menu. As you can see in the plot, the series shows neither trend nor seasonality.

Figure 6.1   Quality-control data

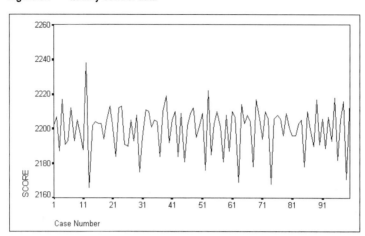

Exponential Smoothing

If you use exponential smoothing on this series, you find that the best-fitting value of alpha is 0 (Figure 6.2). To verify this, from the menus choose:

Statistics
  Time Series ▶
    Exponential Smoothing

This opens the Exponential Smoothing dialog box. As in Chapter 4, move *score* into the Variables list. Leaving the model set at Simple, click on Parameters... and request a grid search for alpha. Click on Continue to return to the main Exponential Smoothing dialog box, and click on Save.... From the Create Variables group, select Do not create, since the purpose here is not to create a smoothed series.

Click on Continue again, and then click on OK to carry out the exponential smoothing. The results are shown in Figure 6.2.

Figure 6.2   Exponential smoothing of quality data

```
Results of EXSMOOTH procedure for Variable SCORE
MODEL= NN (No trend, no seasonality)

 Initial values:        Series              Trend
                    2200.21000           Not used

DFE = 99.

The 10 smallest SSE's are:        Alpha              SSE
                                .0000000        16640.59000
                                .1000000        18371.71939
                                .2000000        20283.01731
                                .3000000        22425.62140
                                .4000000        24849.88356
                                .5000000        27609.29659
                                .6000000        30766.92829
                                .7000000        34400.65016
                                .8000000        38608.21333
                                .9000000        43513.74357
```

With alpha=0, exponential smoothing does not use information from the most recent observation in its forecasts. It simply predicts the overall mean, and hence is of little use. You need a more sophisticated modeling technique for this series: ARIMA.

ARIMA Models: An Overview

ARIMA models are flexible and widely used in time-series analysis. ARIMA stands for *Auto*Regressive *I*ntegrated *M*oving *A*verage, after the three components of the general ARIMA model. These "Box-Jenkins" models (after Box and Jenkins, 1976) work well for a large variety of time series. The methods used to solve for the parameters of ARIMA models require quite a lot of computation; for practical use you need computer software such as Trends.

The methods used in identifying, estimating, and diagnosing ARIMA models are quite involved. If you are going to use ARIMA, you should read one of the standard texts on the subject, such as Box and Jenkins (1976) or McCleary and Hay (1980). In this section we give only a brief overview of ARIMA modeling.

ARIMA models combine as many as three types of processes: autoregression (AR); differencing to strip off the integration (I) of the series; and moving averages (MA). All three are based on the simple concept of random **disturbances** or **shocks**. Between two observations in a series, a disturbance occurs that somehow affects the level of the series. These disturbances can be mathematically described by ARIMA models. Each of the three types of processes has its own characteristic way of responding to a random disturbance.

The most general ARIMA model involves all three processes. Each is described by a small integer. The general model, neglecting seasonality, is traditionally written as ARIMA(p,d,q), where p is the order of autoregression, d is the degree of differencing, and q is the order of moving average involved. Although they are related, each aspect of the model can be examined separately.

Autoregression

The first of the three processes included in ARIMA models is **autoregression**. In an autoregressive process each value in a series is a linear function of the preceding value or values. In a first-order autoregressive process only the single preceding value is used; in a second-order process the two preceding values are used; and so on. These processes are commonly indicated by the notation AR(n), where the number in parentheses indicates the order. Thus, AR(1) is a first-order autoregressive process, where:

$$\text{Value}_t = \text{disturbance}_t + \Phi \times \text{Value}_{t-1}$$

The coefficient Φ is estimated from the observed series and indicates how strongly each value depends on the preceding value. Since the order of autoregression is the first ARIMA parameter, an AR(n) model is the same as an ARIMA(n,0,0) model.

Conceptually, an autoregressive process is one with a "memory," in the sense that each value is correlated with all preceding values. In an AR(1) process the current value is a function of the preceding value, which is a function of the one preceding it, and so on. Thus, each shock or disturbance to the system has a diminishing effect on all subsequent time periods. When the coefficient Φ is greater than -1 and less than +1, as is usually the case, the influence of earlier observations dies out exponentially. (In this respect autoregressive forecasts are similar to those made with exponential smoothing. The algorithm used in ARIMA is quite different, however, from that used in exponential smoothing.)

Differencing

Time series often reflect the cumulative effect of some process. The process is responsible for *changes* in the observed level of the series but is not responsible for the level itself. Inventory levels, for example, are not determined by receipts and sales in a single period. Those activities cause changes in inventory levels. The levels themselves are the cumulative sum of the changes in each period.

A series that measures the cumulative effect of something is called **integrated.** In the long term, the average level of an integrated series might not change, but in the short term values can wander quite far from the average level purely by chance. You can study an integrated series by looking at the changes, or **differences,** from one observation to the next. When a series wanders, the difference from one observation to the next is often small. Thus, the differences of even a wandering series often remain fairly constant. This steadiness, or **stationarity,** of the differences is highly desirable from a statistical point of view.

The standard shorthand for integrated models, or models that need to be differenced, is I(1) or ARIMA(0,1,0). Occasionally you will need to look at differences of the differences; such models are termed I(2) or ARIMA(0,2,0).

One way of looking at an I(1) process is that it has a *perfect* memory of the previous value—but only the previous value. Except for random fluctuations, each value equals the previous value. This type of I(1) process is often called a **random walk** because each value is a (random) step away from the previous value. You can also think of an I(1) or ARIMA(0,1,0) model as an autoregressive model—AR(1) or ARIMA(1,0,0)—with a regression coefficient Φ of 1.0. It is always easier to look at differences than to work with regression coefficients near 1.0.

Moving Averages

The last type of process used in ARIMA models, and the most difficult to visualize, is the **moving average.** In a moving-average process, each value is determined by the average of the current disturbance and one or more previous disturbances. The order of the moving average process specifies how many previous disturbances are averaged into the new value. The equation for a first-order moving average process is:

$$\text{Value}_t = \text{disturbance}_t - \theta \times \text{disturbance}_{t-1}$$

In the standard notation, an MA(n) or ARIMA(0,0,n) process uses n previous disturbances along with the current one.

The difference between an autoregressive process and a moving-average process is subtle but important. Each value in a moving-average series is a weighted average of the most recent *random disturbances,* while each value in an autoregression is a weighted average of the recent *values* of the series. Since these values in turn are weighted averages of the previous ones, the effect of a given disturbance in an autoregressive process dwindles as time passes. In a moving-average process, a disturbance affects the system for a finite number of periods (the order of the moving average) and then abruptly ceases to affect it.

Steps in Using ARIMA

Since the three types of random processes in ARIMA models are closely related, there is no computer algorithm that can determine the correct model. Instead, there is a model-building procedure, described by Box and Jenkins (1976), that allows you to construct the best possible model for a series. This procedure consists of three steps—*identification, estimation,* and *diagnosis*—which you repeat until your model is satisfactory.

Identification

The first and most subjective step is the identification of the processes underlying the series. You must determine the three integers $p, d,$ and q in the ARIMA(p,d,q) process generating the series. (Seasonal models also require another set of parameters, analogous to these, to describe seasonal variation. As described in Chapter 12, ARIMA models can be extended to handle seasonal variation, but the discussion here assumes that no seasonal variation is present.)

To identify the process underlying a series, you first determine from a plot whether or not the series is stationary, since the identification process for the AR and MA components *requires* stationary series. A stationary series has the same mean and variance throughout. Autoregressive and moving-average processes are inherently stationary, given certain sensible constraints on their parameters; integrated series are typically not stationary.

When a series is not stationary—when its average level varies in the short term or when the short-term variation is greater in some places than in others—you must transform the series until you obtain a series that is stationary. The most common transformation is differencing, which replaces each value in the series by the difference between that value and the preceding value. Logarithmic and square-root transformations are useful in the relatively frequent situation in which there is more short-term variation where the actual values are large than where they are small.

Once you have obtained a stationary series, you know the second ARIMA parameter d: it is simply the number of times you had to difference the series to make it stationary. Usually it is 0 or 1. Next you must identify p and q, the orders of autoregression and of moving average. In nonseasonal processes:

- Both p and q are usually small: 0, 1, or 2 at most.
- The autocorrelation function (ACF) and partial autocorrelation function (PACF) of a series usually reveal the correct values of p and q.

The **autocorrelation function** simply gives the autocorrelations calculated at lags 1, 2, and so on; the **partial autocorrelation function** gives the corresponding partial autocorrelations, controlling for autocorrelations at intervening lags.

- AR(p) models have exponentially declining values of the ACF (possibly with alternating positive and negative values), and have precisely p spikes in the first p values of the PACF.
- MA(q) models have precisely q spikes in the first q values of the ACF, and exponentially declining values of the PACF.
- If the ACF declines very slowly, you need to take differences before identifying the model.
- Mixed AR and MA models have more complex ACF and PACF patterns. Identifying them often takes several cycles of identification-estimation-diagnosis.

Appendix B shows plots of the theoretical ACF and PACF functions for the most common AR and MA models.

Estimation

The Trends ARIMA procedure estimates the coefficients of the model you have tentatively identified. You supply the parameters p, d, and q, and ARIMA performs the iterative calculations needed to determine maximum-likelihood coefficients and adds new series to your file representing the fit or predicted value, the error (residual), and the confidence limits for the fit. You use these new series in the next step, the diagnosis of your model.

Diagnosis

The final step in the ARIMA modeling procedure, diagnosis, is discussed in detail in most textbooks that cover ARIMA. The following checks are essential:

- The ACF and PACF of the error series should not be significantly different from 0. One or two high-order correlations may exceed the 95% confidence level by chance; but if the first- or second-order correlation is large you have probably misspecified the model. ARIMA adds the residuals to your file as a new series. Always check their ACF and PACF.

- The residuals should be without pattern. That is, they should be **white noise.** A common test for this is the Box-Ljung Q statistic, also called the modified Box-Pierce statistic. You should look at Q at a lag of about one quarter of the sample size (but no more than 50). This statistic should not be significant. The Trends Autocorrelation procedure displays the Box-Ljung statistic and its significance level at each lag alongside the low-resolution version of the ACF plot in the output window, so you can check it easily.

A traditional Box-Jenkins analysis also estimates the standard error of the coefficients and verifies that each is statistically significant. When the identification of the model is uncertain, a complex model is "overfit" and the coefficients that are not statistically significant are dropped.

Many statisticians today prefer to use other criteria to identify the form of the model and accept the best-fitting model even if it includes coefficients that are not significant according to simple univariate tests. The ARIMA procedure in Trends provides several criteria for choosing among models.

Using ARIMA with the Quality-Control Data

To apply this procedure to the quality-control series, you begin by examining a plot (Figure 7.1) to determine whether the series is stationary. The mean of the series appears to be about 2200 from beginning to end, and likewise the variance does not noticeably change. Evidently there is no need to take differences, nor to transform it in any other way.

Identifying the Model

The next step is always to obtain plots of the ACF and PACF. From the menus choose:

Graphs
  Time Series
    Autocorrelations...

This opens the Autocorrelations dialog box, as shown in Figure 6.3.

Figure 6.3   Autocorrelations dialog box

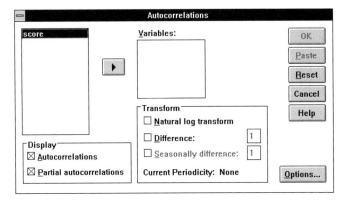

Move *score* into the Variables list and click on OK to get a plot of the autocorrelations and partial autocorrelations for this series. Figure 6.4 shows the high-resolution plots.

Figure 6.4   ACF and PACF plots

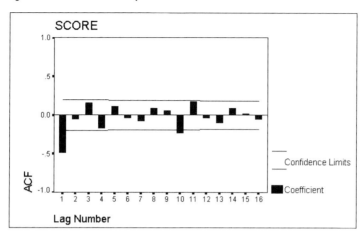

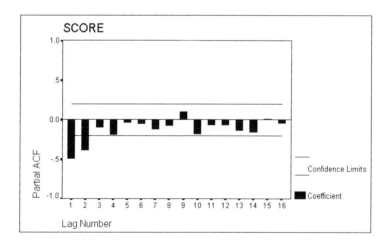

In addition to the correlation coefficients, the ACF and PACF plots show 95% confidence limits, which serve as rough guides to which correlations should be taken seriously. The ACF shows a strong negative "spike" at lag 1, with a few marginally significant correlations scattered through the rest of the plot. The PACF shows rapidly declining values at the first few lags. If you compare these plots with those in Appendix B, the nearest pattern is ARIMA(0,0,1), which has a spike at lag 1 in the ACF and an exponential decline in the PACF. You should try the ARIMA(0,0,1) model—which is the same as MA(1)—as a first attempt.

Estimating with ARIMA

To estimate parameters for a simple ARIMA(0,0,1) model for the *score* series, from the menus choose:

Statistics
  Time Series ▶
    ARIMA...

This opens the ARIMA dialog box, as shown in Figure 6.5.

Figure 6.5   ARIMA dialog box

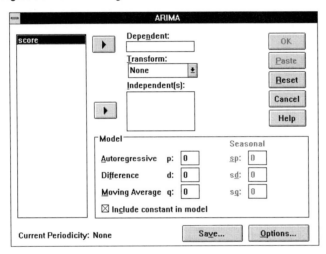

Move *score* into the Dependent box. In the Model group, type 1 in the Moving Average (q) text box. Make sure that Include constant in model is selected and click on OK. The results are shown in Figure 6.6.

Figure 6.6   An ARIMA(0,0,1) model

```
Split group number: 1  Series length: 100
No missing data.
Melard's algorithm will be used for estimation.

Termination criteria:
Parameter epsilon: .001
Maximum Marquardt constant: 1.00E+09
SSQ Percentage: .001
Maximum number of iterations: 10

Initial values:

MA1        .64081
CONSTANT 2200.166

Marquardt constant = .001
Adjusted sum of squares = 10681.408

              Iteration History:

  Iteration   Adj. Sum of Squares    Marquardt Constant

          1            10431.585            .00100000
          2            10426.464            .00010000
          3            10425.782            .00001000
          4            10425.675            .00000100

Conclusion of estimation phase.
Estimation terminated at iteration number 5 because:
   Sum of squares decreased by less than .001 percent.

FINAL PARAMETERS:

Number of residuals  100
Standard error       10.265823
Log likelihood       -374.23949
AIC                  752.47899
SBC                  757.68933

              Analysis of Variance:

             DF  Adj. Sum of Squares   Residual Variance
Residuals    98           10425.658           105.38713

              Variables in the Model:

                     B          SEB    T-RATIO   APPROX. PROB.
MA1             .78105    .06411139    12.1828        .0000000
CONSTANT    2200.16919    .23323983  9433.0765        .0000000

The following new variables are being created:

   Name       Label

   FIT_1      Fit for SCORE from ARIMA, MOD_3 CON
   ERR_1      Error for SCORE from ARIMA, MOD_3 CON
   LCL_1      95% LCL for SCORE from ARIMA, MOD_3 CON
   UCL_1      95% UCL for SCORE from ARIMA, MOD_3 CON
   SEP_1      SE of fit for SCORE from ARIMA, MOD_3 CON
```

ARIMA reports how many iterations were required (5), summarizes each iteration, and explains why it stopped iterating (the sum of squared errors decreased by less than 0.001% after the last iteration). The ARIMA procedure in Trends gives you a great deal of control over the iterative search for a solution. The tradeoff is simple: more iterations take longer but yield more accurate coefficients. The default criteria were chosen as a reasonable compromise, but you are free to relax them (for faster solutions) or tighten them (for more accurate estimates).

When ARIMA has obtained a solution, it reports its final parameters (see Figure 6.6), which include several statistics describing how well the model fits your data, an analysis of variance table, and the coefficients of the model. Among the goodness-of-fit statistics are two labeled *AIC* and *SBC*. These are the Akaike information criterion (AIC) and the Schwartz Bayesian criterion (SBC). They measure how well the model fits the series, taking into account the fact that a more elaborate model is expected to fit better. Generally speaking, the AIC is for autoregressive models while the SBC is a more general criterion. You can use these in choosing between different models for a given series. The model with the lowest AIC or SBC is the best.

As in regression output, the actual coefficients appear in a column labeled B, along with their estimated standard errors, *t* ratios, and significance levels. For the simple model in Figure 6.6, an MA1 coefficient and a constant are calculated and displayed. The MA1 coefficient is called θ in the ARIMA literature. For this model $\theta=0.78$. Books on ARIMA modeling discuss the algebraic interpretation of θ; for this model, each value in the series equals the current random disturbance minus 0.78 times the previous disturbance.

Diagnosing the MA(1) Model

Before leaving the ARIMA output in Figure 6.6 you may want to check the statistical significance of the estimated coefficients. These significance levels are given on the same lines as the estimated coefficients themselves. As you can see, both *t* ratios are statistically significant.

The main way of diagnosing an ARIMA model is with the residual series. To check the residuals, plot the ACF and PACF of the error series created by ARIMA. The error series contains the residuals from the model and is listed along with the other new series in Figure 6.6. Each new series is given a label describing the type of series it is, the original series being analyzed, the model name of the analysis, and whether or not a constant was estimated.

To check the ACF and PACF of the residuals from the above analysis, from the menus choose:

Graphs
  Time Series ▶
    Autocorrelations...

This opens the Autocorrelations dialog box again. If *score* is still in the Variables list, select it and move it out. Then select *err_1* (the error or residual variable reported by ARIMA) and move it into the Variables list. Click on OK to see the plots.

Figure 6.7 shows the autocorrelation and partial autocorrelation plots of the residuals in high resolution. Figure 6.8 shows the ACF plot in low resolution. We show the low-resolution plot because it includes the values for the Box-Ljung statistic.

Figure 6.7   ACF and PACF plots of residuals

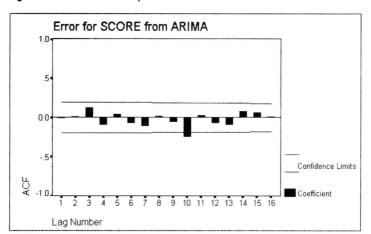

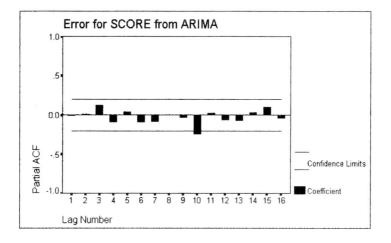

Figure 6.8   ACF in low-resolution

```
Autocorrelations:    ERR_1          Error for SCORE from ARIMA, MOD_5 CON

      Auto- Stand.
 Lag  Corr.  Err.  -1  -.75  -.5 -.25   0   .25  .5   .75  1   Box-Ljung  Prob.
                   +----+----+----+----+----+----+----+----+
   1  -.002  .099                        *   .                   .000     .985
   2   .009  .098                   .    *   .                   .008     .996
   3   .125  .098                   .    |**  .                 1.639     .651
   4  -.086  .097                   .  **|   .                  2.426     .658
   5   .040  .097                   .    |*  .                  2.596     .762
   6  -.068  .096                   .   *|   .                  3.100     .796
   7  -.102  .095                   .  **|   .                  4.237     .752
   8   .017  .095                   .    *   .                  4.271     .832
   9  -.052  .094                   .   *|   .                  4.573     .870
  10  -.239  .094                   *.***|   .                 11.053     .353
  11   .030  .093                   .    |*  .                 11.159     .430
  12  -.067  .093                   .   *|   .                 11.672     .472
  13  -.090  .092                   .  **|   .                 12.616     .478
  14   .077  .092                   .    |** .                 13.323     .501
  15   .065  .091                   .    |*  .                 13.829     .539
  16   .013  .091                   .    *   .                 13.851     .610

Plot Symbols:      Autocorrelations *     Two Standard Error Limits .

Total cases:   100     Computable first lags:  99
```

The ACF and PACF appear to be randomly distributed—only a few scattered correlations exceed the 95% confidence limits, which appear as dotted lines on the plots. Furthermore, the Box-Ljung statistic for the ACF function is not statistically significant at any lag. This is consistent with the null hypothesis that the population autocorrelation function is 0. You can accept the ARIMA(0,0,1) model with the MA(1) parameter θ equal to 0.78.

Applying the Control Chart

As shown in Figure 6.6, ARIMA produces new series containing predictions (*fit_1*), residuals (*err_1*), standard errors (*sep_1*), and the upper and lower confidence limits (*ucl_1* and *lcl_1*) for the original series. To make a control chart, you need to predict the upper and lower bounds for the variation of the series beyond the end of the data you used to estimate the model. From the menus choose:

Statistics
  Time Series
    ARIMA...

Your previous variable selection (*score*) and model specification (q=1) should still be showing in the ARIMA dialog box. Click on Save... to display the ARIMA Save dialog box, as shown in Figure 6.9.

Figure 6.9   ARIMA Save dialog box

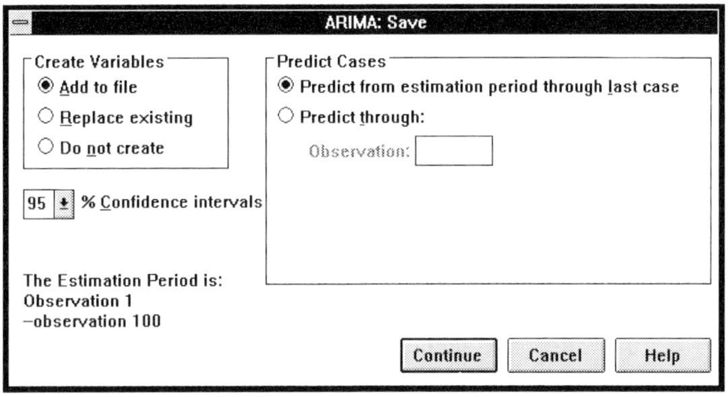

The only thing you need to do here is change from 95% to 99% confidence limits. The 99% limits are typically used in control charts. Click on the ⬇ arrow next to % Confidence Intervals to open the drop-down list and from it select 99. Back at the main ARIMA dialog box, click on OK to generate the 99% confidence limits. Before requesting the plot, restore the cases in the forecast period. From the menus choose:

Data
  Select Cases...

In the Select Cases dialog box, choose All Cases. Then obtain the plot by choosing

Graphs
  Sequence...

In the Sequence Charts dialog box, move *score*, *fit_2*, *lcl_2*, and *ucl_2* into the Variables list. Make sure that One chart per variable is *not* selected and click on OK. The resulting plot is shown in Figure 6.10.

Figure 6.10   N-step-ahead ARIMA forecasts

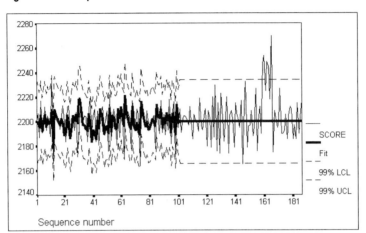

Sequence number

Superimposed on the plot of the original series you have ARIMA predictions (*fit_2*), as well as the confidence limits *lcl_2* and *ucl_2*. During the first 100 observations, the period used to estimate the model, these three ARIMA series bounce around with the original series. During the forecast period, the predictions and the confidence limits are *constant,* because the model had no seasonal component or trend and because no current data are being used to update the moving average. However, the confidence limits accurately capture the amount of variation that you should expect from this first-order moving average model. They are in fact a control chart—and a reliable one, because they are based on a good model. As long as the underlying process remains the same, you should expect 99% of the series to remain between the upper and lower confidence limits.

A Real-Life Ending

As you can see, the observed series begins to exceed the confidence limits around point 160. For several periods the quality-control scores were higher than they should have been if the process had remained the same. Quality-control engineers noticed the excess variation and stopped the production line for a detailed examination. Inspection revealed that bad print wheels had been introduced at about the time where the series went out of its control bounds. When the faulty components were replaced, the series returned to normal. The identification of the process underlying this series enabled the engineers to detect the change in that process and hence to correct the underlying cause.

How to Obtain ARIMA Analysis

The first step in ARIMA analysis is to identify the model using plots of the autocorrelation and partial autocorrelation functions.

- Determine if the series is stationary, that is, if it is without overall trend.
- If it is not, difference the series once or perhaps twice until a stationary series results. You can difference the series within the Autocorrelations procedure, as discussed in the SPSS Base system documentation.
- Compare the ACF and PACF of the stationary series to the idealized versions in Appendix B to determine the parameters *p, d,* and *q* of the model.

The next step is to estimate the coefficients of the model. From the menus choose:

Statistics
  Time Series ▶
    ARIMA...

This opens the ARIMA dialog box, as shown in Figure 6.11.

Figure 6.11   ARIMA dialog box

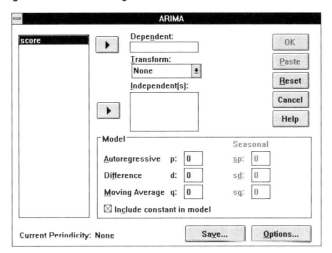

The numeric variables in your data file appear in the source list. To obtain a nonseasonal ARIMA analysis, select one variable as the Dependent variable and specify at least one positive integer for the parameters in the Model group, as determined by the results of the model identification step.

◆ **Transform.** To analyze the dependent variable in a logarithmic scale, select one of the alternatives on the Transform drop-down list. If you select a log transformation, ARIMA transforms the predicted values (*fit*) and confidence limits (*lcl* and *ucl*) that it creates back into the original metric, but leaves the residuals (*err*) in the log metric for diagnostic purposes.

None. The untransformed variable is analyzed.

Natural log. The logarithm to base e of the variable is analyzed.

Log base 10. The logarithm to base 10 of the variable is analyzed.

Independent(s). You can move one or more numeric variables into the Independent(s) list. These are used as regressors or predictor variables.

Model. The Model group contains six text boxes, each of which can contain 0 or a positive integer, usually 1. You must specify at least one of the six; in practice, you must specify at least one of the autoregressive or moving-average orders. The parameters in the first column are for nonseasonal model components. For a nonseasonal model, you can specify one, two, or all three parameters:

Autoregressive. The autoregressive order p of the process.

Difference. The number of times d that the series must be differenced to make it stationary.

Moving Average. The order q of moving average in the process.

If the seasonality of the data has been defined in the Define Dates dialog box, three analogous text boxes let you specify the corresponding parameters $sp, sd,$ and sq of the process at seasonal lags. For seasonal models, you can specify these parameters in addition to the parameters in the first column. Again, these values can be 0 or a positive integer, usually 1. Identification of seasonal ARIMA models is discussed in Chapter 12.

❏ **Include constant in model.** Deselect this option if you can assume that the constant in the model equals 0.

Saving Predicted Values and Residuals

To save predicted values, confidence limits, or residuals as new variables, or to produce forecasts past the end of your data, click on Save... in the ARIMA dialog box. This opens the ARIMA Save dialog box (see Figure 6.12). The current estimation period is shown at the bottom of the box.

Figure 6.12   ARIMA Save dialog box

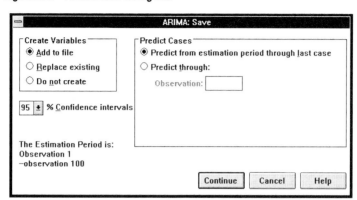

Create Variables. To control the creation of new variables, you can choose one of these alternatives:

○ **Add to file.** The new series ARIMA creates are saved as regular variables in your working data file. Variable names are formed from a three-letter prefix, an underscore, and a number. This is the default.

○ **Replace existing.** The new series ARIMA creates are saved as temporary variables in your working data file. At the same time, any existing temporary variables created by Trends commands are dropped when you execute the ARIMA procedure. Variable names are formed from a three-letter prefix, a pound sign (#), and a number.

○ **Do not create.** The new variables are not added to the working data file.

If you select either Add to file or Replace existing above, you can select:

⬇ **% Confidence intervals.** Select either 90, 95, or 99% from the drop-down list.

Predict Cases. If you select Add to file or Replace existing above, you can specify a forecast period:

○ **Predict from estimation period through last case.** Predicts values for all cases from the estimation period through the end of the file but does not create new cases. If you are analyzing a range of cases that starts after the beginning of the file, cases prior to that range are not predicted. The estimation period, displayed at the bottom of this dialog box, is defined with the Range dialog box available through the Select Cases option on the Data menu. If no estimation period has been defined, all cases are used to predict values. This is the default.

○ **Predict through.** Predicts values through the specified date, time, or observation number, based on the cases in the estimation period. This can be used to forecast values beyond the last case in the time series. The text boxes that are available for specifying the end of the prediction period depend on the currently defined date variables. (Use the Define Dates option on the Data menu to create date variables.) If there are no defined date variables, you can specify the ending observation (case) number.

New cases created as forecasts have missing values for all series in the original data file, and for new series (such as residuals) whose definition requires an existing value. For ARIMA, only the predicted values *(fit)*, the standard errors *(sep)*, and the confidence limits *(lcl* and *ucl)* have valid values past the end of the original data.

ARIMA Options

To control convergence criteria and initial values used in the iterative algorithm, or to specify the amount of output to be displayed, click on Options... in the ARIMA dialog box. This opens the ARIMA Options dialog box, as shown in Figure 6.13.

Figure 6.13   ARIMA Options dialog box

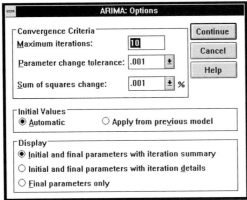

Convergence Criteria. The convergence criteria determine when the iterative algorithm stops and the final solution is reported.

Maximum iterations. By default, iteration halts after 10 iterations, even if the algorithm has not converged. You can specify a positive integer here.

⬇ **Parameter change tolerance.** By default, iteration stops if no parameter changes by more than 0.001 from one iteration to the next. You can choose a smaller or larger value for more or less precision in the parameter estimates. For greater precision it may also be necessary to increase the maximum iterations.

⬇ **Sum of squares change.** By default, iteration stops if the adjusted sum of squares does not decrease by 0.001% from one iteration to the next. You can choose a smaller or larger value for more or less precision in the parameter estimates. For greater precision it may also be necessary to increase the maximum iterations.

Initial Values. Choose one of these alternatives:

○ **Automatic.** ARIMA chooses initial values.

○ **Apply from previous model.** The parameter estimates from the previous execution of ARIMA (in the same session) are used as initial estimates. This can save time if the data and model are similar to the last one used.

Display. Choose one of these alternatives to indicate how much detail you want to see.

○ **Initial and final parameters with iteration summary.** ARIMA displays initial and final parameter estimates, goodness-of-fit statistics, the number of iterations, and the reason that iteration terminated.

○ **Initial and final parameters with iteration details.** In addition to the above, ARIMA displays parameter estimates after each iteration.

○ **Final parameters only.** ARIMA displays final parameters and goodness-of-fit statistics.

Additional Features Available with Command Syntax

You can customize your ARIMA analysis if you paste your selections to a syntax window and edit the resulting ARIMA command. The additional features are:

• Constrained models in which autoregressive or moving average parameters (either regular or seasonal) are estimated only for specified orders. For example, you can request a second-order autoregressive parameter, while constraining the first-order parameter to 0.

• More precise control over convergence criteria.

See the Syntax Reference section of this manual for command syntax rules and for complete ARIMA command syntax.

7 A Random Walk with Stock Prices: The Random-Walk Model

One of the most important processes sometimes found to underlie time series data is the *random walk*. A random-walk process is inherently unpredictable but serves as a standard of comparison for series with more structure. In this chapter we will use both exponential smoothing and ARIMA to study a series that is expected, on theoretical grounds, to follow a random walk.

Johnson & Johnson Stock Prices

Financial theory predicts that stock prices should fluctuate randomly if the stock market is efficient. Since the market should have already adjusted for any public information that might affect the future price of the stock, daily price fluctuations appear, in theory, as random *white noise*. A process that generates random *changes* in the level of a series is known as a **random walk.** In this chapter we will examine the stock prices of Johnson & Johnson during 1984 and 1985 to see if they do indeed show the characteristics of a random walk.

Dating the Stock Series

Stocks are not traded on weekends or holidays. At first glance this seems to violate the basic time series requirement that observations be taken at regularly spaced intervals. The requirement, however, is that the time intervals be regularly spaced in terms of the process underlying the series. Here the underlying process is the trading of stock, so that prices at the end of each business day are perfectly appropriate.

If stocks were traded every weekday, we could create date variables for a five-day work week by selecting Weeks, work days(5) in the Define Dates dialog box. This almost works—but holidays such as the Fourth of July and Labor Day are not trading days and hence are absent from the data. We will forego the use of Define Dates, therefore, and identify observations simply by sequential position in the series.

Plotting the Series

The *stock* series includes 251 observations. We will use the first 200 observations for the historical period and the last 51 for the validation period. From the menus choose:

Data
  Select Cases...

This opens the Select Cases dialog box. Select Based on time or case range and click on Range.... This opens the Select Cases Range dialog box. Type 1 in the First Case text box and 200 in the Last Case text box. Click on Continue to return to the Select Cases dialog box and click on OK.

To plot the stock prices, from the menus choose:

Graphs
  Sequence...

This opens the Sequence Charts dialog box. Move *stock* from the source list to the Variables list. Click on Format... to open the Sequence Charts Format dialog box. Select Reference line at mean of series and click on Continue. To obtain the sequence chart, click on OK. This produces the chart shown in Figure 7.1.

Figure 7.1   Johnson & Johnson stock prices, historical period

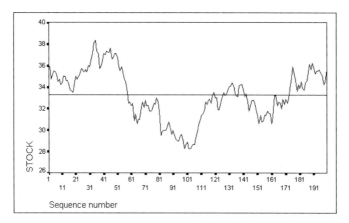

The data appear to drift above and below the mean value (where the reference line is), indicating that the series is not stationary. Other than this, the series shows no apparent pattern. If the stock prices are indeed based on a random-walk process, we will be driven to quite a simple model. Let us apply exponential smoothing first.

Exponential Smoothing of the Stock Series

To request exponential smoothing, from the menus choose:

Statistics
  Time Series ▶
  Exponential Smoothing...

In the Exponential Smoothing dialog box, move *stock* to the Variables list. The chart in Figure 7.1 shows no evidence of trend or seasonality, so leave Simple selected in the Model group.

To define the smoothing parameters, click on Parameters.... This opens the Exponential Smoothing Parameters dialog box. Since a grid search will find the best value of the general smoothing parameter alpha, select Grid Search in the General (Alpha) group and click on Continue and OK. The output is shown in Figure 7.2.

Figure 7.2   Exponential smoothing with no trend or seasonality

```
Results of EXSMOOTH procedure for Variable STOCK
MODEL= NN (No trend, no seasonality)

 Initial values:        Series          Trend
                        33.29125      Not used

DFE = 199.

The 10 smallest SSE's are:      Alpha            SSE
                               1.000000       72.73826
                                .9000000       74.01562
                                .8000000       76.70986
                                .7000000       81.05149
                                .6000000       87.53897
                                .5000000       97.18905
                                .4000000      112.22474
                                .3000000      138.20934
                                .2000000      192.32206
                                .1000000      352.34995

The following new variables are being created:

   NAME        LABEL

   FIT_1       Fit for STOCK from EXSMOOTH, MOD_2 NN A1.00
   ERR_1       Error for STOCK from EXSMOOTH, MOD_2 NN A1.00
```

The best-fitting model—the one with the smallest sum of squared errors, or SSE—is the one where alpha equals 1.0. An alpha of 1.0 represents an extreme model, where the best prediction is simply the most recent value. Earlier values in the series are given no weight at all in the predictions. This is, in fact, the model for a pure random walk. If fluctuations in stock prices are random, the best prediction for tomorrow's price is today's price.

Plotting the Residuals

The exponential smoothing procedure adds two new series to the file for the best prediction, one holding the prediction and one holding the error or residual (the observed value minus the prediction). As you can see in Figure 7.2, the residuals for the model with alpha=1.0 are in a series named *err_1*. To test whether these residuals really are white noise, you can plot the autocorrelations. From the menus choose:

Graphs
  Time Series ▶
    Autocorrelations...

Move *err_1* to the Variables list, deselect Partial autocorrelations in the Display group, and click on OK. Figure 7.3 shows the low-resolution plot, which includes the actual values of the autocorrelation function as well as the Box-Ljung statistic (the low-resolution plot appears in the output window).

- The plotted autocorrelations all fall within the dotted lines, which show the 95% confidence intervals. Since the actual values and standard errors appear at the left of the plot, you can confirm that none of the values is twice as large as its standard error.

- The Box-Ljung statistics to the right of the plot are never statistically significant (the probability is always substantially greater than 0.05). As you recall from Chapter 6, this statistic estimates the probability that autocorrelations as large or larger than those observed could have been the result of random variation. The probability at lag 16 is 0.932, which means that white noise would generate autocorrelations as large or larger than these sixteen values over 93% of the time.

Figure 7.3   ACF for exponential smoothing residuals (low resolution)

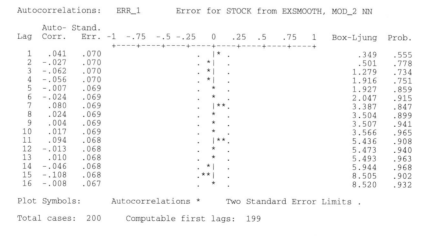

```
Autocorrelations:    ERR_1         Error for STOCK from EXSMOOTH, MOD_2 NN

      Auto- Stand.
Lag   Corr.  Err.  -1  -.75  -.5 -.25   0   .25   .5   .75   1   Box-Ljung  Prob.
                   +----+----+----+----+----+----+----+----+
  1   .041   .070                       . |* .                     .349     .555
  2  -.027   .070                       . *| .                     .501     .778
  3  -.062   .070                       . *| .                    1.279     .734
  4  -.056   .070                       . *| .                    1.916     .751
  5  -.007   .069                       . * .                     1.927     .859
  6  -.024   .069                       . * .                     2.047     .915
  7   .080   .069                       . |**.                    3.387     .847
  8   .024   .069                       . * .                     3.504     .899
  9   .004   .069                       . * .                     3.507     .941
 10   .017   .069                       . * .                     3.566     .965
 11   .094   .068                       . |**.                    5.436     .908
 12  -.013   .068                       . * .                     5.473     .940
 13   .010   .068                       . * .                     5.493     .963
 14  -.046   .068                       . *| .                    5.944     .968
 15  -.108   .068                       .**| .                    8.505     .902
 16  -.008   .067                       . * .                     8.520     .932

Plot Symbols:      Autocorrelations  *      Two Standard Error Limits .

Total cases:  200      Computable first lags:  199
```

Exponential smoothing seems to confirm the random-walk theory of stock prices, at least for this stock. The best model simply predicts the most recent value, and the residuals from that model appear to be white noise.

An ARIMA Model for Stock Prices

Perhaps the pattern in these prices is too subtle for exponential smoothing. A more sophisticated technique such as ARIMA might detect a deviation from the random-walk pattern.

Identifying the Model

Figure 7.4 shows the autocorrelations and partial autocorrelations for the Johnson & Johnson stock prices in high resolution. The ACF dies out quite slowly, confirming our earlier observation that this series is nonstationary. (Compare this plot with those in Appendix B.)

To properly identify the ARIMA model, we need to first difference the series and then check the ACF and PACF plots. However, if you did not recognize the fact that the series was nonstationary, you might erroneously interpret the fading ACF and spiked PACF as evidence of an AR(1) autoregressive model. Let's go ahead and estimate this model without differencing to see what happens when we use a nonstationary series. From the menus choose:

Statistics
  Time Series ▶
    ARIMA...

This opens the ARIMA dialog box. Move *stock* to the Dependent box and type 1 in the Autoregressive text box in the Model group. Click on Options... and select Final parameters only in the Display group. Click on Continue and then on OK. Figure 7.5 shows the results of the AR(1) model.

Figure 7.4   ACF and PACF for stock prices

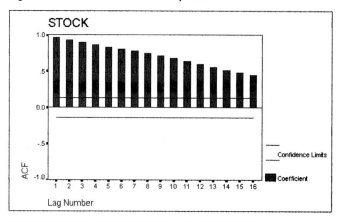

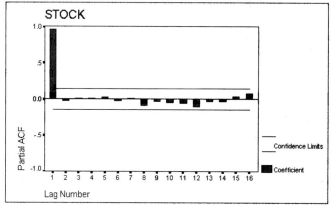

Figure 7.5   ARIMA(1,0,0) on stock prices

```
Split group number: 1  Series length: 200
No missing data.
Melard's algorithm will be used  for estimation.


Conclusion of estimation phase.
Estimation terminated at iteration number 2 because:
   Sum of squares decreased by less than .001 percent.

FINAL PARAMETERS:

Number of residuals  200
Standard error        .5744063
Log likelihood       -173.30938
AIC                   350.61876
SBC                   357.21539

            Analysis of Variance:

            DF  Adj. Sum of Squares   Residual Variance
Residuals   198         66.255997            .32994259


          Variables in the Model:

                 B        SEB     T-RATIO   APPROX. PROB.
AR1         .969712    .0163268  59.393801      .0000000
CONSTANT  33.887538   1.1671238  29.035084      .0000000

The following new variables are being created:

   Name        Label

   FIT_2       Fit for STOCK from ARIMA, MOD_4 CON
   ERR_2       Error for STOCK from ARIMA, MOD_4 CON
   LCL_2       95% LCL for STOCK from ARIMA, MOD_4 CON
   UCL_2       95% UCL for STOCK from ARIMA, MOD_4 CON
   SEP_2       SE of fit for STOCK from ARIMA, MOD_4 CON
```

The autoregressive coefficient ϕ (labeled *AR1* in Figure 7.5) equals 0.97, which is very close to its **limit of stationarity,** 1.0. Autoregressive models with the absolute value of ϕ greater than or equal to 1.0 are not stationary. When $\phi = 1.0$ exactly, the AR(1) model is identical to a random-walk model. This is easy to see. The AR(1) model is

$$\text{Value}_t = \phi \times \text{Value}_{t-1} + \text{disturbance}_t$$

When $\phi = 1.0$, this becomes

$$\text{Value}_t = \text{Value}_{t-1} + \text{disturbance}_t$$

or

$$\text{Value}_t - \text{Value}_{t-1} = \text{disturbance}_t$$

The changes from one observation to the next are a random disturbance or shock. This is the definition of a random-walk model.

Differencing the Series

Since the φ coefficient estimated above is very nearly equal to 1, the differences between stock prices from one observation to the next should be distributed as white noise. To plot the differences, from the menus choose:

Graphs
  Sequence...

Move *stock* to the Variables list and in the Transform group select Difference. The default value is 1. (Specifying 2 for Difference indicates second differences, which are simply the differences of the differences. You rarely need to take second or higher differences.) Click on Format..., and in the Sequence Chart Format dialog box select Reference line at mean of series. Click on Continue and OK. The sequence chart is shown in Figure 7.6.

Figure 7.6   Differenced Johnson & Johnson stock prices

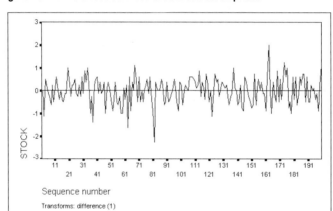

As shown in Figure 7.6, the differenced series is stationary. Its short-term average is always about the same. In fact, it is always around 0.

It is possible for the differenced series to be stationary and to have a mean value other than 0. If the mean of the differenced stock prices were about 1, for example, that would indicate that the average difference from one observation to the next was +1—in other words, that stock prices were steadily rising. Since the plot of the original series (Figure 7.1) shows no long-term trend, you know that the average change is near 0. Figure 7.6 confirms this.

Comparing Differences to White Noise

To verify that the differenced stock prices in Figure 7.6 are essentially white noise, you can plot ACF and PACF. From the menus choose:

Graphs
  Time Series ▶
    Autocorrelations...

In the Transform group, select Difference to indicate that you want autocorrelations of the differences in the stock prices rather than the prices themselves. In the Display group, select Autocorrelations and Partial autocorrelations. Figure 7.7 shows the ACF and PACF of the differenced stock prices.

Figure 7.7   ACF and PACF for differenced stock prices

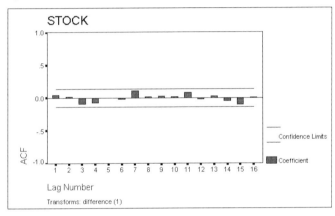

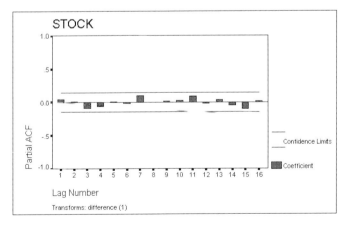

None of the values of the ACF or PACF equals twice its standard error (they do not exceed the confidence limits on the plots). If you looked at the low-resolution plot in the output window, you would see that the probability value of the Box-Ljung statistic is high at all lags, indicating that this ACF could easily be generated by a white-noise process. Since the differences are white noise, the original series is accurately described as a random walk.

When differencing a series reduces it to white noise, the ARIMA modeling procedure is complete. The model is simply an ARIMA(0,1,0) model.

Comparing the Two Models

We began analyzing the Johnson & Johnson stock prices by developing an exponential smoothing model with alpha=1.0. When alpha=1.0, the model's prediction always equals the previous observation, without regard to prior observations. The residuals or errors from that model equal the difference between the prediction—which is the previous observation—and the current observation. In Figure 7.3 we found these errors to be white noise.

Using ARIMA methodology we then developed an ARIMA(0,1,0) model. We did not use the ARIMA command itself with this model because an ARIMA(0,1,0) model has no coefficients to estimate. If you use the ARIMA procedure with a (0,1,0) model, it terminates processing after 0 iterations!

In fact, the differenced series is *identical* to the error series from the exponential-smoothing model with alpha=1.0. You can verify that the residual autocorrelations from exponential smoothing (Figure 7.3) are virtually the same as the autocorrelations for the differenced series (Figure 7.7). Models for a random walk all look about the same.

Forecasting a Random Walk

In "Dating the Stock Series" on p. 79, we established the historical period as the first 200 observations. To generate forecasts for the validation period (the remaining 51 observations), follow these steps. From the menus choose:

Statistics
  Time Series ▶
    ARIMA...

Select *stock* as the Dependent variable. In the Model group, specify 0 for p, 1 for d, and 0 for q. Click on Options..., which opens the ARIMA Options dialog box. In the Display group, select Final parameters only. Click on Continue to return to the ARIMA dialog box, and then click on Save.... You can see that Predict from estimation period through last case is selected by default. Click on Continue and then on OK. Figure 7.8 shows the output from this procedure. Notice that:

- ARIMA displays a message saying that estimation was terminated after 0 iterations because there were no ARMA (autoregressive or moving average) parameters to estimate.

- The value estimated for the constant is very close to 0, as we noticed from the plot of the differenced series in Figure 7.6.

- The new series containing forecasts is named *fit_3*, and the series containing confidence limits are named *lcl_3* and *ucl_3*.

Figure 7.8   N-step-ahead forecasts from random-walk model

```
Split group number: 1  Series length: 200
No missing data.
Melard's algorithm will be used  for estimation.


Conclusion of estimation phase.
Estimation terminated at iteration number 0 because:
  No ARMA parameters were available for estimation.

FINAL PARAMETERS:

Number of residuals  199
Standard error        .5776222
Log likelihood       -172.65054
AIC                   347.30109
SBC                   350.59439

          Analysis of Variance:

            DF  Adj. Sum of Squares    Residual Variance
Residuals   198           66.062186            .33364740

          Variables in the Model:

                 B        SEB      T-RATIO    APPROX. PROB.
CONSTANT   -.00125628  .04094655  -.03068101      .97555494

The following new variables are being created:

  Name      Label

  FIT_3     Fit for STOCK from ARIMA, MOD_8 CON
  ERR_3     Error for STOCK from ARIMA, MOD_8 CON
  LCL_3     95% LCL for STOCK from ARIMA, MOD_8 CON
  UCL_3     95% UCL for STOCK from ARIMA, MOD_8 CON
  SEP_3     SE of fit for STOCK from ARIMA, MOD_8 CON
```

To plot the stock price series along with the forecasts and confidence limits for the validation period, from the menus choose:

Data
  Select Cases...

In the Select Cases dialog box, select Based on time or case range and click on Range.... In the Select Cases Range dialog box, specify 201 in the First Case text box and 250 in the Last Case text box. Click on Continue and then on OK. From the menus choose:

Graphs
  Sequence...

This opens the Sequence Charts dialog box. Move *stock*, *fit_3*, *lcl_3*, and *ucl_3* to the Variables list and click on OK. Figure 7.9 shows the chart.

Figure 7.9   Stock forecasts in the validation period

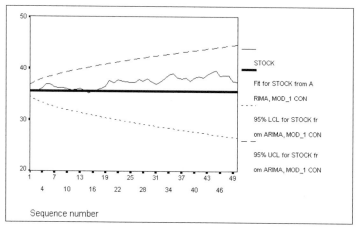

Note in Figure 7.9 that the forecasts remain "stuck" on the last value in the historical period, while the confidence limits expand as our confidence in the forecasts dwindles with time. Since the changes in stock prices are completely random in this model, we can do no better than to predict that the price will be somewhere around where it was the last time we knew it.

This conclusion may be disappointing, but it is not surprising. If you could predict that a stock was going to rise on the basis of its recent history, so could other people. They would buy the stock, driving its price up, until the prediction method said that it would rise no further. This implies that most of the time *any* good prediction method based on public information must predict that a stock will remain at the same price. In greatly simplified form, this is the theoretical argument for why stock prices are expected to follow a random-walk pattern.

Why Bother with the Random Walk?

The random walk is an important class of time series, not because there is much to say about it—there is not—but because it has characteristics to which we can compare other series.

- A random walk is defined as the *cumulative sum of random disturbances*. If the mean of the random disturbances is 0, as is often the case, the random walk will show no overall trend; but it can and often does drift far away from its long-term mean.
- The differences between successive observations in a random walk are white noise.
- When the mean of the disturbances is 0, the best forecast for a random walk is simply the most recent observation.

Tracking the Inflation Rate: Outliers in ARIMA Analysis

8

Most time series are not as simple as the stock prices we analyzed in Chapter 7. In this chapter we use ARIMA techniques once again on a more difficult series. This series is also afflicted with an *outlier*—an observation far out of line with those around it.

The Inflation Rate Data

In this example we follow the monthly inflation rate from January 1970 through December 1985. These data are contained in a series named *inflat*. To create appropriate date variables for the series, from the menus choose:

Data
  Define Dates...

This opens the Define Dates dialog box. Scroll to the top of the Cases Are list and select Years, months. Specify 1970 in the Year text box in the First Case Is group, as shown in Figure 8.1.

Figure 8.1   Define Dates dialog box

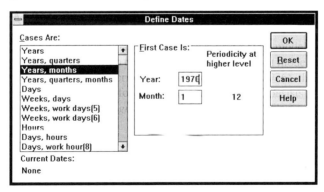

Click on OK and Trends calculates each observation's value for the new variables *year_*, *month_*, and *date_*. (Trends puts an underscore at the end of these names so that they are less likely to conflict with similarly named variables in your data.) Now plot the series. From the menus choose:

Graphs
  Sequence...

In the Sequence Charts dialog box, move *inflat* into the Variables list. Move *date_* into the Time Axis Labels box, and click on OK. The resulting chart is shown in Figure 8.2.

Figure 8.2   Monthly inflation rates 1970–1985

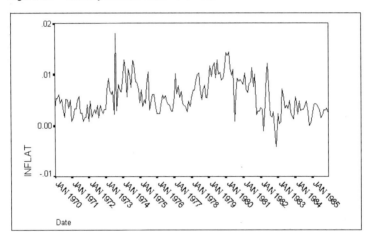

As you can see in Figure 8.2, the inflation rate varied considerably, with one exceptionally high point in the summer of 1973. The fact that the series wanders tells us that it is not stationary. In other words, the short-term mean level is not constant but varies over the course of the series. We must remember this when identifying a model.

The Outlier

The *monthly* inflation rate in August 1973 was 1.8%, which if continued would have produced an annual rate of over 23%. This was far higher than any other monthly rate. Extreme observations such as this are called **outliers.** You should always note outliers when you plot a series, since they can seriously affect your analysis.

It is easy to assign a cause to this particular outlier. Wage and price controls had recently been lifted, and the OPEC oil consortium had just imposed an oil embargo. The embargo affected the inflation statistics very suddenly in August.

When you know what causes an outlier, as you do here, you can always remove it and model the process underlying the normal behavior of the series. It is revealing, however, to see how the presence of an outlier affects an analysis. We therefore begin by analyzing the inflation series as it is, including the outlier.

ARIMA with an Outlier

We will try to develop an ARIMA model for the inflation series. Like the series in Chapter 8, this one is nonstationary. There is more pattern to the inflation rates, however, than the random walk we found in stock prices.

Historical and Validation Periods

We will use the period 1970 through 1980 as a historical or estimation period and the period 1981 through 1985 as a validation period. To restrict the analysis to the historical period, first restore the SPSS main menu bar by selecting:

Window
   !Output1

This activates the SPSS output window and the main menu bar. Now from the menus choose:

Data
   Select Cases...

In the Select Cases dialog box, choose Based on time or case range. Click on Range... to open the Select Cases Range dialog box, as shown in Figure 8.3.

Figure 8.3   Select Cases Range dialog box

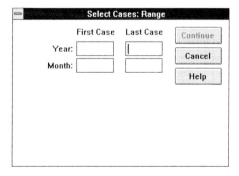

There is no need to specify values for Year and Month for the first case you want to use, since Trends assumes, if you do not indicate otherwise, that you want to start at the beginning of your data. Click in the Year text box for Last Case and type 1980, and then click in (or tab to) the Month text box and type 12. Click on Continue to return to the Select Cases dialog box, and then click on OK to establish the historical period for the following analysis.

Identifying the Model

The sequence chart of the inflation series suggested that the series was not stationary. To verify this you can inspect the ACF plot. From the menus choose:

Graphs
    Time Series ▶
        Autocorrelations...

Move *inflat* into the Variables list. Deselect Partial autocorrelations in the Display group to save time; partial autocorrelations require quite a bit of calculation and aren't needed yet. Click on OK. The resulting ACF plot is shown in Figure 8.4.

Figure 8.4   ACF of inflation series

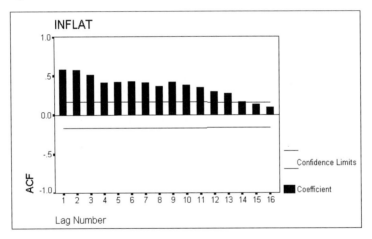

Like the ACF of the *stock* series in Chapter 7, this autocorrelation plot starts out with large positive values, which die out very slowly at increasing lags. This pattern confirms that the series is not stationary, and that we must take differences when analyzing it. Rather than creating a new series containing the differences in inflation rates, we can simply request differencing in the Autocorrelations dialog box. This time we also ask for the PACF also, since we need both plots to identify an ARIMA model. Return to the output or data window to restore the main menu bar. From the menus, once again choose:

Graphs
  Time Series ▶
    Autocorrelations...

The Variables list should still contain *inflat*. Select Difference in the Transform group, leaving the degree of differencing set to 1. Select Partial autocorrelations, if you deselected it before, and click on OK. The resulting ACF and PACF plots of the differences in *inflat* are shown in Figure 8.5.

Figure 8.5   ACF and PACF for differenced series

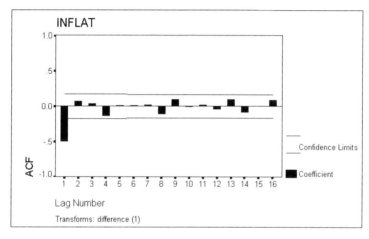

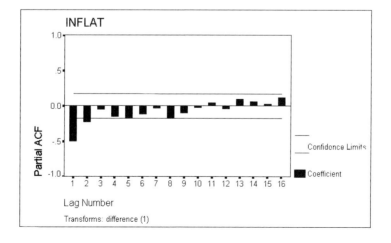

The ACF of the differenced series shows a spike at lag 1, while the PACF shows rapid attenuation from its initial value. These patterns suggest an MA(1) process. (Refer to Appendix B for the characteristic patterns exhibited by common ARIMA processes.) Since we differenced the original series to obtain the MA(1) patterns, our ARIMA identification includes one degree of differencing and a first-order moving average. In conventional ARIMA notation, we have tentatively identified an ARIMA(0,1,1) model.

Estimating the Model

You took differences in the inflation series to make it stationary (although there are instances when a differenced series is still nonstationary). Taking differences often has another consequence: the mean of a differenced series is frequently 0.

It is easy to see why this is so. Although the original inflation series was not stationary, it did not seem to show a long-term trend. It wandered around a long-term average that stayed about the same. From this fact you know that the differences in the series average out to 0—increases in the inflation rate roughly balance out decreases in the inflation rate over the whole period.

The Constant in an ARIMA Model

The general ARIMA model includes a constant term, whose interpretation depends on the model you are using:

- In MA models the constant is the mean level of the series.
- In AR(1) models the constant is a trend parameter.
- When a series has been differenced, the above interpretations apply to the differences.

Our ARIMA(0,1,1) model is an MA model of a differenced series. Therefore, the constant term will represent the mean level of the differences. Since you know that the mean level of the differences is about 0 for the inflation series, the constant term in the ARIMA model should be 0. The Trends implementation of ARIMA lets you suppress the estimation of the constant term. This speeds up the computation, simplifies the model, and yields slightly smaller standard errors on the other estimates.

To estimate the ARIMA(0,1,1) model, from the main menu bar select:

Statistics
  Time Series ▶
    ARIMA...

This opens the ARIMA dialog box, as shown in Figure 8.6.

Figure 8.6   ARIMA dialog box

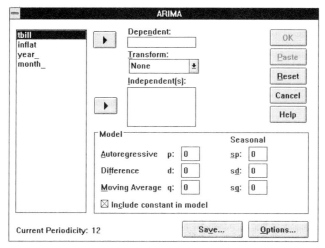

Move *inflat* into the Dependent box. In the Model group:

- Specify 1 for the Difference parameter *d*.
- Specify 1 for the Moving Average parameter *q*.
- Leave the Autoregressive parameter *p* and all three of the Seasonal parameters at 0.
- Deselect Include constant in model.

Now click on Save..., which opens the ARIMA Save dialog box, as shown in Figure 8.7.

Figure 8.7   ARIMA Save dialog box

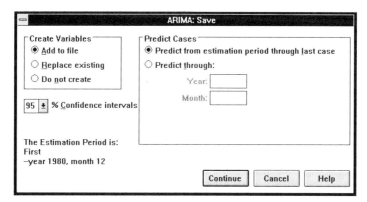

In the Create Variables group, select Replace existing and click on Continue. This keeps Trends from adding a lot of variables to the working data file while you are still searching for the best model.

The output from the ARIMA analysis appears in Figure 8.8. In the historical period (January 1970 through December 1980), the first differences in monthly inflation rates followed an MA(1) process with θ=0.685.

Figure 8.8   ARIMA(0,1,1) for the inflation series

```
Split group number: 1  Series length: 132
No missing data.
Melard's algorithm will be used for estimation.

Termination criteria:
Parameter epsilon: .001
Maximum Marquardt constant: 1.00E+09
SSQ Percentage: .001
Maximum number of iterations: 10

Initial values:

MA1          .65199

Marquardt constant = .001
Adjusted sum of squares = .00089164

                Iteration History:

   Iteration   Adj. Sum of Squares    Marquardt Constant
           1            .00089041            .00100000
           2            .00089035            .00010000

Conclusion of estimation phase.
Estimation terminated at iteration number 3 because:
   Sum of squares decreased by less than .001 percent.

FINAL PARAMETERS:

Number of residuals  131
Standard error       .00261071
Log likelihood       593.5097
AIC                  -1185.0194
SBC                  -1182.1442

          Analysis of Variance:

              DF  Adj. Sum of Squares   Residual Variance
Residuals    130           .00089035           .00000682

          Variables in the Model:

            B          SEB     T-RATIO    APPROX. PROB.
MA1    .68464518   .06432286  10.643886        .0000000

The following new variables are being created:

    Name       Label

    FIT_1      Fit for INFLAT from ARIMA, MOD_4 NOCON
    ERR_1      Error for INFLAT from ARIMA, MOD_4 NOCON
    LCL_1      95% LCL for INFLAT from ARIMA, MOD_4 NOCON
    UCL_1      95% UCL for INFLAT from ARIMA, MOD_4 NOCON
    SEP_1      SE of fit for INFLAT from ARIMA, MOD_4 NOCON
```

Because you indicated in the Define Dates dialog box that this series is monthly, ARIMA is aware of the seasonal period of twelve observations. Since the specified model contains no seasonal component, ARIMA displays a warning (not shown) that it is ignoring the seasonality in the data. In Chapter 13 we will see a series that requires us to specify a seasonal ARIMA model.

Diagnosing the Model

Before proceeding it is wise to check that the residuals are *white noise*. From the menus choose:

Graphs
  Time Series ▶
    Autocorrelations...

Move *inflat* out of the Variables list, and move *err#1* (the name of the residual variable created by the ARIMA command) into the list. Deselect Difference in the Transform group, and make sure both Display options are selected. Click on OK.

Figure 8.9 shows the autocorrelation function for the ARIMA residuals in high resolution. None of the residual autocorrelations exceeds the confidence limits around 0. With residuals it's also a good idea to look at the low-resolution ACF plot, so that you can see the Box-Ljung statistics. Return to the output window, where the end of the PACF plot is visible. Scroll up to the ACF plot, as shown in Figure 8.10. (You can do this quickly by clicking the button on the icon bar with two upward-pointing wedges.) You may need to scroll the output window to the right in order to see the significance levels for the Box-Ljung statistic. It is not statistically significant at any lag, so you cannot reject the null hypothesis that the residuals are white noise.

Figure 8.9   Autocorrelation function for residuals in high resolution

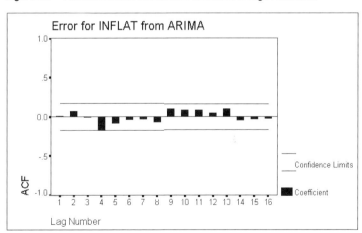

Figure 8.10   Autocorrelation function for residuals

```
Autocorrelations:    ERR_1        Error for INFLAT from ARIMA, MOD_6 NOCON

     Auto- Stand.
Lag  Corr.  Err.  -1 -.75  -.5 -.25   0   .25  .5   .75   1   Box-Ljung   Prob.
                   +----+----+----+----+----+----+----+----+
  1   .012  .086                     . * .                      .019      .891
  2   .074  .086                     . |* .                     .757      .685
  3  -.005  .086                     . * .                      .761      .859
  4  -.165  .085                   ***| .                      4.482      .345
  5  -.079  .085                    .**| .                      5.349      .375
  6  -.038  .085                     . *| .                      5.551      .475
  7  -.028  .084                     . *| .                      5.659      .580
  8  -.068  .084                     . *| .                      6.319      .612
  9   .102  .084                     . |**.                      7.797      .555
 10   .089  .083                     . |**.                      8.938      .538
 11   .088  .083                     . |**.                     10.064      .525
 12   .053  .083                     . |* .                     10.481      .574
 13   .100  .082                     . |**.                     11.962      .531
 14  -.046  .082                     . *| .                     12.271      .585
 15  -.030  .082                     . *| .                     12.408      .648
 16  -.022  .081                     . * .                      12.481      .710

Plot Symbols:      Autocorrelations *     Two Standard Error Limits .

Total cases:  132     Computable first lags:  130
```

Plotting Residuals

Figure 8.11 shows a sequence chart of the ARIMA residuals. In general the residuals show no pattern, although the large outlier of August 1973 is still present. Let's see what happens if we remove the outlier.

Figure 8.11   Residuals from ARIMA including outlier

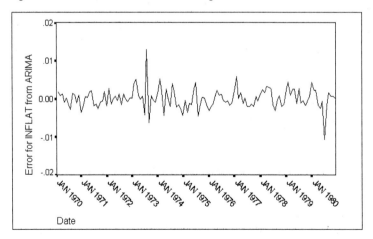

ARIMA without the Outlier

The main problem with the above analysis is that we have included the outlier from August 1973. We developed an ARIMA model for a random process that supposedly produced the entire series, yet we know that the prominent bounce in 1973 was due to the oil embargo and associated one-time events. Let's see what happens when we exclude the observation from August 1973 from the analysis. We can do this in two ways:

- Assign a *missing value* to the observation. The Trends ARIMA command handles imbedded missing data, so this is a feasible alternative. ARIMA with missing data, however, uses an algorithm that is computationally intensive and requires a lot of processing time. Until you are certain of the model you want, you are better off taking the other route.

- Interpolate a value for August 1973. This value would probably be closer to the typical value of the series and therefore would influence estimation of ARIMA coefficients less than the outlier did.

Removing the Outlier

The Data Editor in SPSS makes it easy to assign a missing value to the observation for August 1973. Activate the Data Editor window and scroll down to the observation for that month. Click in the cell for *inflat*, which contains the value of 0.018086. Press the Del key followed by ↵Enter to delete this unusually large value. The August value is replaced by a period, and the highlight moves to the next cell. The period stands for the *system-missing value,* a value that can never occur in real data and that all SPSS commands recognize. If you analyze the inflation series after the above command, ARIMA discovers a gap in the series at August 1973—as if the inflation rate for that month were unknown—and carefully works around it.

To interpolate a substitute value for August 1973, you can use the Replace Missing Values procedure. From the menus choose:

Transform
  Replace Missing Values...

This opens the Replace Missing Values dialog box, as shown in Figure 8.12.

Figure 8.12 Replace Missing Values dialog box

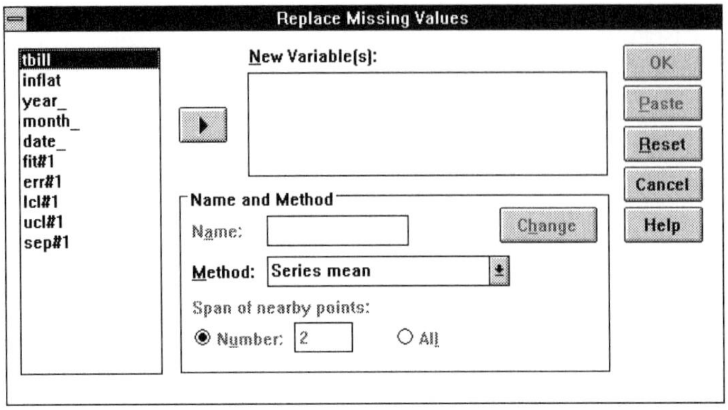

Highlight *inflat* in the source variable list and move it into the New Variable(s) list, where it appears in an expression:

```
inflat_1=SMEAN(inflat)
```

If it is executed, this expression create a new series, named *inflat_1*, which is identical to *inflat* except that missing values have been replaced by the overall series mean (SMEAN). In a series with positive autocorrelation, like this one, you can do better by interpolating between the neighboring values. Click on the ⬇ arrow next to the Method drop-down list and select the Linear interpolation method. Then click on Change.

The expression in the New Variable(s) list now shows the LINT function. When you click on OK, Trends creates a new series *inflat_1* that is identical to *inflat* except that any missing values in *inflat* are replaced using a linear interpolation of the neighboring valid values. This replaces the system-missing value (which we substituted above for the actual value of 1.8%) with a more typical monthly rate of 0.26%, which is midway between the rates for July and September. If you scroll the Data Editor to the far right, you can see the new series with its interpolated value for August 1973. (To keep track of which case you are interested in, click on the case number (44) to highlight the entire row.)

We do not insist that the interpolated value is a particularly good estimate of what the inflation rate would have been if the oil embargo had not taken place. It is, however, an unobtrusive estimate, one that will not have any great effect on the analysis of the series as a whole. For this modest purpose a simple linear interpolation is quite adequate.

Identifying the Model

To identify the model after replacing the outlier, you simply plot the ACF and PACF of *inflat_1*, remembering to take differences since the series is not stationary (see "Identifying the Model" on p. 96). The resulting plots are shown in Figure 8.13.

Figure 8.13 ACF plots with outlier replaced

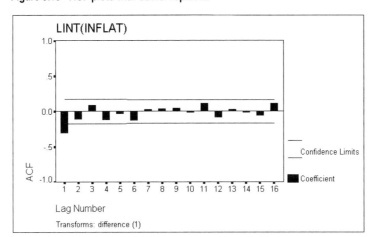

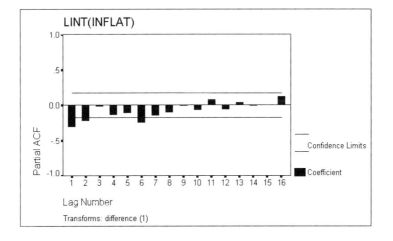

Comparing these plots with Figure 8.5, you see that removing the outlier has reduced the size of the negative ACF at lag 1. There is an unexpected peak in the PACF at lag 6, which we will ignore for the time being, in the absence of any explanation of why inflation rates might follow a six-month seasonal pattern. Aside from the peak, both ACF and PACF show declines from their initial value at lag 1, rather than spikes. This suggests a model with both autoregressive and moving-average components. Since the series was differenced for the ACF plots, we have an ARIMA(1,1,1) model.

By removing a single outlier from this series, we have changed the identification of the model! Even when an outlier does not affect the type of model, it can affect estimates of the coefficients drastically. If you estimated the ARIMA(0,1,1) model without the outlier, you would find the fit improves and the θ parameter decreases noticeably.

Estimating the Model

Figure 8.14 shows the estimation of an ARIMA(1,1,1) model for the inflation series after removing the outlier. (To obtain this analysis, you would open the ARIMA dialog box, move *inflat* out of the Dependent box, move *inflat_1* into the Dependent box, and change the Autoregressive parameter p from 0 to 1.)

Compare these results with Figure 8.8. The log-likelihood has increased, and the AIC and SBC have decreased. The standard error of the estimate is smaller. The model estimated without the outlier seems to be much better on all of these statistical grounds. That is not surprising, since the outlier was due to factors that are ignored in these models.

Figure 8.14   ARIMA(1,1,1) after replacing outlier

```
Split group number: 1  Series length: 132
No missing data.
Melard's algorithm will be used for estimation.

Termination criteria:
Parameter epsilon: .001
Maximum Marquardt constant: 1.00E+09
SSQ Percentage: .001
Maximum number of iterations: 10

Initial values:

AR1        .33674
MA1        .72357

Marquardt constant = .001
Adjusted sum of squares = .00067359

                Iteration History:

   Iteration   Adj. Sum of Squares   Marquardt Constant
         1            .00066685             .00100000
         2            .00066584             .00010000
         3            .00066577             .00001000


Conclusion of estimation phase.
Estimation terminated at iteration number 4 because:
   Sum of squares decreased by less than .001 percent.

FINAL PARAMETERS:

Number of residuals  131
Standard error       .0022672
Log likelihood       612.54406
AIC                  -1221.0881
SBC                  -1215.3377

              Analysis of Variance:

             DF  Adj. Sum of Squares   Residual Variance
Residuals    129         .00066577            .00000514

              Variables in the Model:

            B          SEB       T-RATIO   APPROX. PROB.
AR1   .40987963    .12585801    3.256683      .00144044
MA1   .83249607    .07776481   10.705305      .00000000


The following new variables are being created:

    Name       Label

    FIT_3      Fit for INFLAT_1 from ARIMA, MOD_13 NOCON
    ERR_3      Error for INFLAT_1 from ARIMA, MOD_13 NOCON
    LCL_3      95% LCL for INFLAT_1 from ARIMA, MOD_13 NOCON
    UCL_3      95% UCL for INFLAT_1 from ARIMA, MOD_13 NOCON
    SEP_3      SE of fit for INFLAT_1 from ARIMA, MOD_13 NOCON
```

Diagnosing the Final Model

As the low-resolution plot in Figure 8.15 shows, the residual ACF for this last model is acceptable. A couple of the autocorrelations are marginally significant considered alone, but the Box-Ljung statistic is not statistically significant at any lag.

Figure 8.15   Residual ACF

```
Autocorrelations:   ERR_4        Error for INFLAT1 from ARIMA, MOD_13 NOC

      Auto- Stand.
Lag   Corr.  Err. -1  -.75  -.5 -.25   0   .25  .5   .75   1    Box-Ljung  Prob.
                  +----+----+----+----+----+----+----+----+
  1    .030   .072                   .  |* .                      .177     .674
  2   -.018   .072                   .  * .                       .243     .885
  3    .040   .071                   .  |* .                       .556     .907
  4   -.068   .071                   . *|  .                      1.466     .833
  5   -.048   .071                   .  *| .                      1.930     .859
  6   -.171   .071                   ***|  .                      7.745     .257
  7   -.040   .071                   .  *| .                      8.069     .327
  8    .042   .070                   .  |* .                      8.425     .393
  9    .126   .070                   .  |*** .                   11.644     .234
 10    .052   .070                   .  |* .                     12.205     .272
 11    .186   .070                   .  |**.*                    19.258     .057
 12    .038   .070                   .  |* .                     19.556     .076
 13    .017   .069                   .  |* .                     19.616     .105
 14   -.088   .069                   .**|  .                     21.243     .096
 15    .035   .069                   .  |* .                     21.494     .122
 16    .073   .069                   .  |* .                     22.627     .124

Plot Symbols:      Autocorrelations *      Two Standard Error Limits .

Total cases:   192    Computable first lags:   190
```

ARIMA with Imbedded Missing Values

If you prefer, you can use the ARIMA procedure without replacing the missing data. A technique known as Kalman filtering allows the generation of maximum-likelihood estimates for series with missing data.

For some models, the Kalman filtering algorithm takes much longer to reach its solution. However, you can minimize the time by applying a solution obtained with interpolated values as an initial estimate. (This and similar performance considerations are discussed in Chapter 2.) For example, to apply the solution obtained in Figure 8.14, which was estimated using a smoothed value for the outlier, as an initial estimate, select:

Statistics
  Time Series ▶
    ARIMA...

This opens the ARIMA dialog box, as before. Move *inflat_1* out of the Dependent box, and move *inflat* (which still has the missing value) in. Leaving the Model specifications as they are, click on Options. This opens the ARIMA Options dialog box, as shown in Figure 8.16.

Figure 8.16   ARIMA Options dialog box

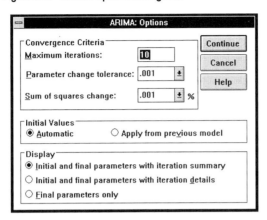

In the Initial Values group, select Apply from previous model. This means that ARIMA should use the final solution of the most recent ARIMA command (that in Figure 8.14) as an initial estimate. Since the *inflat* series is almost identical to *inflat_1*, this a good initial estimate and ARIMA will converge on a solution more quickly.

Execute the ARIMA command. A portion of the output is shown in Figure 8.17. ARIMA reports that an imbedded missing value is present, and that Kalman filtering will be used for estimation. The estimates in Figure 8.17 are close to those in Figure 8.14. Sometimes the discrepancies will be larger. In general, estimates with Kalman filtering will take longer but will be more reliable because they use all the data.

The Validation Period

At this point you are ready to see how well the model performs in the validation period. From the menus choose:

    Data
      Select Cases

Click on All Cases and then repeat the ARIMA analysis. As you can see, the model continues to fit the series well in the validation period.

Figure 8.17   ARIMA with missing data

```
Split group number: 1  Series length: 132
Number of cases containing missing values: 1
Kalman filtering will be used for estimation.

Termination criteria:
Parameter epsilon: .001
Maximum Marquardt constant: 1.00E+09
SSQ Percentage: .001
Maximum number of iterations: 10

Initial values:

AR1       .38924
MA1       .82392

Marquardt constant = .001
Adjusted sum of squares = .00066588

Conclusion of estimation phase.
Estimation terminated at iteration number 1 because:
   Sum of squares decreased by less than .001 percent.

FINAL PARAMETERS:

Number of residuals  130
Standard error       .00227366
Log likelihood       607.36132
AIC                  -1210.7226
SBC                  -1204.9876

            Analysis of Variance:

             DF  Adj. Sum of Squares    Residual Variance
Residuals    128         .00066588            .00000517

          Variables in the Model:

              B         SEB      T-RATIO    APPROX. PROB.
AR1     .38909849    .12830115   3.032697      .00293489
MA1     .82383779    .07980484  10.323155      .00000000

The following new variables are being created:

    Name        Label

    FIT_5       Fit for INFLAT from ARIMA, MOD_15 NOCON
    ERR_5       Error for INFLAT from ARIMA, MOD_15 NOCON
    LCL_5       95% LCL for INFLAT from ARIMA, MOD_15 NOCON
    UCL_5       95% UCL for INFLAT from ARIMA, MOD_15 NOCON
    SEP_5       SE of fit for INFLAT from ARIMA, MOD_15 NOCON
```

Another Approach

In this chapter we simply removed an observation that was due to factors beyond those normally influencing the series. In Chapter 11 we will see how to include such factors explicitly in a model—a technique known as *intervention analysis*.

9

Consumption of Spirits: Correlated Errors in Regression

In this chapter we use regression methods, as we did in Chapter 5. This time we will look more closely at the assumption underlying regression analysis and particularly at the problem of *autocorrelated errors*.

The Durbin-Watson Data

The Durbin-Watson data (Durbin & Watson, 1951) consist of three log-transformed series: the consumption of alcoholic spirits in England between 1870 and 1938, real percapita income, and an inflation-adjusted price index. Our goal is to develop a regression model in which income and price predict consumption of spirits. First we apply some smoothing techniques to the spirit-consumption series.

Smoothing the Series

The initial step is always to plot the time series. First we will create a date variable, so we can label the plot with dates. From the menus choose:

Data
  Define Dates...

Scroll to the top of the Cases Are list and select the first item, Years. The data were recorded for each year, starting with 1870, so type 1870 in the Year text box in the First Case Is group. Click on OK. This creates two new variables, *year_* and *date_*. To obtain a sequence plot, from the menus choose:

Graphs
  Sequence...

Move *consump* to the Variables list and the variable *date_* to the Time Axis Labels box. Figure 9.1 shows the resulting chart.

Figure 9.1   Initial plot: Consumption of spirits

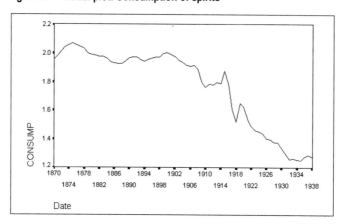

The data points in Figure 9.1 are not scattered randomly across the plot. With the exception of the years around World War I, consumption of spirits in each year was close to that in the previous year. Over the longer period a decline in consumption seems to begin sometime around 1910. The most striking pattern is that the points line up into a squiggly line across the plot, with only occasional jumps. In other words, the value of *consump* acts as if it has a memory—it does not change much from one year to the next. In statistical terms, the consumption of spirits is **positively autocorrelated.**

Autocorrelation is typical of time series analysis. It reflects the fact that most things you measure turn out to be about what they were the last time you measured them. If they are not—perhaps because too long a period intervenes between measurements— the time series degenerates into the random pattern called white noise.

Fitting a Curve to the Data: Curve Estimation

The Curve Estimation procedure, which we used in Chapter 5, determines how best to draw any of about a dozen simple types of curves through your data. It then reports how well this best curve fits and generates new time series showing the fitted value, or prediction; the error; and confidence limits around the fitted value.

The simplest kind of curve is a straight line. To restore the main menu bar, select the Output1 window or the Data Editor window from the Window menu. Then, to fit a straight line to the *consump* series, from the menus choose:

Statistics
  Regression ▶
    Curve Estimation...

Move *consump* to the Dependent(s) list, and in the Independent group select Time. In the Models group, Linear is selected by default. Since we will be plotting a detailed chart by using the Sequence Charts dialog box, deselect Plot models. Click on Save... to open the Curve Estimation Save dialog box. In the Save Variables group, select Predicted values, Residuals, and Prediction intervals.

Figure 9.2 shows the output. The prediction intervals are *lcl_1* and *ucl_1*.

Figure 9.2   Fitting a straight line

```
Dependent Mth   Rsq  d.f.      F   Sigf     b0      b1

  CONSUMP  LIN  .820   67  305.97  .000  2.1989  -.0122

The following new variables are being created:

  Name         Label

  FIT_1        Fit for CONSUMP from CURVEFIT, MOD_2 LINEAR
  ERR_1        Error for CONSUMP from CURVEFIT, MOD_2 LINEAR
  LCL_1        95% LCL for CONSUMP from CURVEFIT, MOD_2 LINEAR
  UCL_1        95% UCL for CONSUMP from CURVEFIT, MOD_2 LINEAR
```

To plot the original series, the linear model, and the prediction intervals all on one plot, from the menus choose:

Graphs
  Sequence...

In the Sequence Charts dialog box, move *consump*, *fit_1*, *lcl_1*, and *ucl_1* to the Variables list. Move *date_* to the Time Axis Labels box, if it is not already there. The chart is shown in Figure 9.3.

Figure 9.3   Sequence plot with prediction intervals

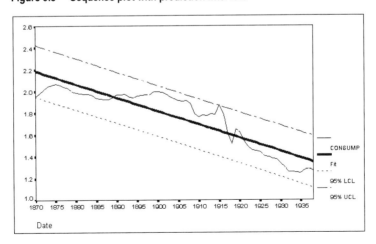

Although the values of *consump* shown in Figure 9.3 all lie within the confidence limits, the straight line is *not* an acceptable model for the series because of the pronounced pattern in the residuals. For the first couple of decades consumption is below the linear prediction; then consumption rises above the line and remains there until about 1920; and from then on consumption remains below the line.

Whenever there is a pattern in the residuals, you should try to improve your model so that it explains the pattern. A parabola, or quadratic curve, might fit the consumption series rather well. To find out, open the Curve Estimation dialog box again and in the Models group deselect Linear and then select Quadratic. Click on Save..., and make sure that Predicted values, Residuals, and Prediction intervals are still selected. The output is shown in Figure 9.4.

Figure 9.4   Fitting a quadratic curve (parabola)

```
Dependent Mth   Rsq   d.f.        F   Sigf       b0       b1       b2

  CONSUMP  QUA   .952     66  649.97   .000   1.9710    .0070   -.0003

The following new variables are being created:

  Name          Label

  FIT_2         Fit for CONSUMP from CURVEFIT, MOD_4 QUADRATIC
  ERR_2         Error for CONSUMP from CURVEFIT, MOD_4 QUADRATIC
  LCL_2         95% LCL for CONSUMP from CURVEFIT, MOD_4 QUADRATIC
  UCL_2         95% UCL for CONSUMP from CURVEFIT, MOD_4 QUADRATIC
```

To plot the quadratic model and its prediction intervals, from the menus choose:

Graphs
  Sequence...

In the Sequence Charts dialog box, leave *consump* in the Variables list, but move *fit_1*, *lcl_1*, and *ucl_1* out, replacing them with *fit_2*, *lcl_2*, and *ucl_2*. Move *date_* to the Time Axis Labels box, if it is not already there. The plot is shown in Figure 9.5.

Figure 9.5   Plot of quadratic model

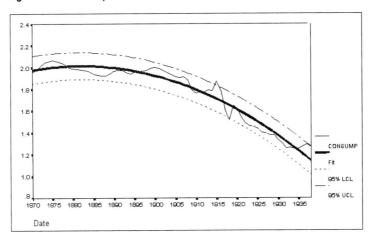

The fit is reasonably good. The *consump* series stays close to the *fit_2* series throughout the period. You have made no attempt to understand the factors affecting consumption of spirits in the years 1870–1938, but you have found a simple curve—a parabola—that comes reasonably close to fitting the data.

Forecasting with Curve Estimation

Once you have found a curve that fits the series well, you can use it to forecast. With the Curve Estimation procedure there is no theory behind the forecast—the program simply extends the curve. When the curve fits well, this is a very straightforward method of short-term forecasting. It's not reliable for more than a few time periods unless you have good reason to believe that the series really is following the kind of curve that you specified.

To get forecasts with the Curve Estimation procedure, restore the main menu bar and from the menus choose:

Statistics
  Regression ▶
    Curve Estimation...

The variable *consump* is probably already in the Variables list from the previous Curve Estimation procedure, and Quadratic is selected. Click on Save... to open the Curve Estimation Save dialog box. In the Predict Cases group, select Predict through year and type 1945 in the Year box. Predicted Values, Residuals, and Prediction intervals should all be selected as before. Then return to the Sequence Charts dialog box and request a plot of *consump*, *fit_3*, *lcl_3*, and *ucl_3*. The plot is shown in Figure 9.6.

Figure 9.6   Forecasting with Curve Estimation

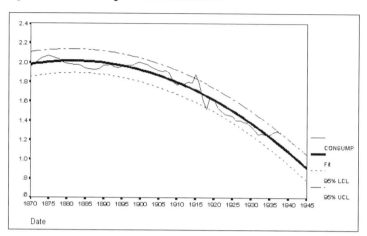

Notice that the forecast simply continues the same curve that seemed to fit the existing data. The quadratic curve is sloping down sharply in 1938, so the Curve Estimation procedure predicts that consumption of spirits will continue to decline at an ever-increasing rate. Sooner or later any forecast of this type will become obviously wrong—the prediction may drop below zero, for example. And if anything were to happen during the forecast years 1939–1945 that affected consumption of spirits, the series might deviate far from your prediction.

Regression Methods

The Curve Estimation procedure looked for patterns in the spirit-consumption data as if consumption were an unexplained process, having a life of its own. Often you know that other variables affect the level of a time series and you want to use them in a regression analysis to understand or predict it. Time series data present special problems for regression analysis because the statistical assumptions underlying regression analysis are frequently invalid for time series.

Note: this section assumes a basic understanding of ordinary regression. If you are unfamiliar with regression analysis, consult the SPSS Base system documentation.

Ordinary Least-Squares Regression

Durbin and Watson's data on the consumption of spirits include two explanatory variables, real per-capita income and the adjusted price level of the spirits in question. To run an ordinary regression model with residuals analysis, from the menus choose:

Statistics
  Regression ▶
    Linear...

This opens the Linear Regression dialog box. Move the variable *consump* to the Dependent box and *income* and *price* to the Independent(s) list, as shown in Figure 9.7.

Figure 9.7   Linear Regression dialog box

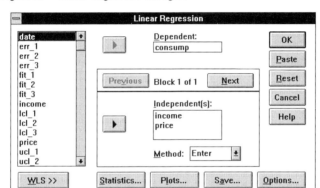

Click on Plots... and in the Standardized Residual Plots group, select Normal probability plot, Casewise plot, and All cases. Click on Continue to return to the Linear Regression dialog box and click on Save.... Select Unstandardized in both the Predicted Values and the Residuals groups. Return to the Linear Regression dialog box, click on Statistics... and select Durbin-Watson in addition to the default selections.

Some of the output from this regression appears in Figure 9.8. *price* has a statistically significant regression coefficient ($T = -24.5$), but *income* does not ($T = -1.1$). R^2 is very high, as is typical of regression with time series. However, residuals analysis reveals that the assumptions underlying these statistics are violated.

Figure 9.8   Output from ordinary regression

```
* * * *    M U L T I P L E    R E G R E S S I O N    * * * *

Listwise Deletion of Missing Data

Equation Number 1    Dependent Variable..    CONSUMP

Beginning Block Number  1.  Method:  Enter      INCOME    PRICE


Variable(s) Entered on Step Number
     1..    PRICE
     2..    INCOME


Multiple R            .97766
R Square              .95581
Adjusted R Square     .95447
Standard Error        .05786

Analysis of Variance
                    DF      Sum of Squares      Mean Square
Regression           2           4.77917          2.38959
Residual            66            .22095           .00335

F =      713.78788     Signif F =  .0000


----------------- Variables in the Equation -----------------

Variable          B          SE B        Beta          T  Sig T

INCOME        -.120141      .108436     -.042713    -1.108  .2719
PRICE        -1.227648      .050052     -.945573   -24.527  .0000
(Constant)    4.606734      .152035                 30.301  .0000


End Block Number   1   All requested variables entered.

From Equation   1:   2 new variables have been created.

   Name        Contents
   ----        --------

   PRE_1    Predicted Value
   RES_1    Residual
```

Residuals Analysis

Figure 9.9 shows the residuals analysis produced by the regression analysis. The Durbin-Watson statistic is 0.24878. Values of this statistic range from 0 to 4, with values less than 2 indicating positively correlated residuals and values greater than 2 indicating negatively correlated residuals. From the table in Appendix A you can see that this value is significant at the 0.01 level. The residuals are positively autocorrelated.

Figure 9.9   Residuals analysis

```
         * * * *   M U L T I P L E   R E G R E S S I O N   * * * *

Equation Number 1    Dependent Variable..    CONSUMP


Residuals Statistics:

                    Min         Max    Mean  Std Dev   N
*PRED           1.2822      2.0922  1.7704    .2651  69
*RESID          -.1352       .1154   .0000    .0570  69
*ZPRED         -1.8413      1.2138   .0000  1.0000  69
*ZRESID        -2.3372      1.9951   .0000    .9852  69

Total Cases =        69


Durbin-Watson Test =     .24878
```

The normal probability plot shown in Figure 9.10. indicates that the residuals are normally distributed, as they should be. (This plot shows the residuals on the vertical axis and the expected value—if the residuals were normally distributed—on the horizontal axis. If the residuals *are* normally distributed the cases fall near the diagonal, as they do here.)

Figure 9.10   Normal probability plot

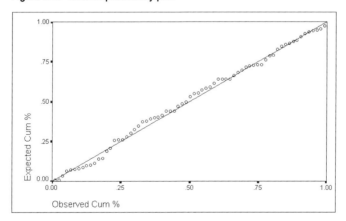

The main problem uncovered by residuals analysis so far is the indication from the Durbin-Watson statistic of positively autocorrelated residuals. The casewise output in Figure 9.11 confirms this problem. The residuals snake back and forth across the center line and are obviously not randomly distributed.

Figure 9.11   Casewise plot of residuals from Linear Regression

```
          -3.0      0.0      3.0
 Case #   O:.......:........:O     CONSUMP     *PRED       *RESID
    1     .     *    .          .   1.9565     2.0403      -.0838
    2     .    *     .          .   1.9794     2.0535      -.0741
    3     .    *     .          .   2.0120     2.0856      -.0736
    4     .     *  . .          .   2.0449     2.0922      -.0473
    5     .        *.          .   2.0561     2.0580   -1.9394E-03
    6     .        .*          .   2.0678     2.0401       .0277
    7     .        .*          .   2.0561     2.0353       .0208
    8     .        *.          .   2.0428     2.0355    7.2622E-03
    9     .        .*          .   2.0290     2.0044       .0246
   10     .        *           .   1.9980     1.9903    7.6955E-03
   11     .       *.           .   1.9884     2.0108      -.0224
   12     .       *.           .   1.9835     1.9983      -.0148
   13     .       *.           .   1.9773     1.9913      -.0140
   14     .       *.           .   1.9748     1.9905      -.0157
   15     .        *           .   1.9629     1.9633   -3.7952E-04
   16     .        .*          .   1.9396     1.9272       .0124
   17     .        .*          .   1.9309     1.9139       .0170
   18     .        .*          .   1.9271     1.9063       .0208
   19     .        .*          .   1.9239     1.9033       .0206
   20     .        . *         .   1.9414     1.9069       .0345
   21     .         . *        .   1.9685     1.9047       .0638
   22     .         . *        .   1.9727     1.9058       .0669
   23     .         . *        .   1.9736     1.9138       .0598
   24     .         .*         .   1.9499     1.9088       .0411
   25     .         . *        .   1.9432     1.8807       .0625
   26     .         .  *       .   1.9569     1.8649       .0920
   27     .         .  *       .   1.9647     1.8644       .1003
   28     .         .  *       .   1.9710     1.8770       .0940
   29     .         .  *       .   1.9719     1.8953       .0766
   30     .         .   *      .   1.9956     1.8802       .1154
   31     .         .  *       .   2.0000     1.9112       .0888
   32     .         . *        .   1.9904     1.9060       .0844
   33     .         . *        .   1.9752     1.9061       .0691
   34     .         .*         .   1.9494     1.9136       .0358
   35     .         .*         .   1.9332     1.9198       .0134
   36     .        .*          .   1.9139     1.9180   -4.0622E-03
   37     .       *.           .   1.9091     1.9214      -.0123
   38     .       *.           .   1.9139     1.9317      -.0178
   39     .       *.           .   1.8886     1.9226      -.0340
   40     .   *    .           .   1.7945     1.9280      -.1335
   41     .      *.            .   1.7644     1.8464      -.0820
   42     .      *.            .   1.7817     1.8509      -.0692
   43     .     *  .           .   1.7784     1.8659      -.0875
   44     .      *.            .   1.7945     1.8755      -.0810
   45     .      *.            .   1.7888     1.8667      -.0779
   46     .     *  .           .   1.8751     1.9805      -.1054
   47     .   *    .           .   1.7853     1.9205      -.1352
   48     .      * .           .   1.6075     1.6584      -.0509
   49     .      * .           .   1.5185     1.5801      -.0616
   50     .        . *         .   1.6513     1.6050       .0463
   51     .        . *         .   1.6247     1.5916       .0331
   52     .        *           .   1.5391     1.5477   -8.5632E-03
   53     .        . *         .   1.4922     1.4565       .0357
   54     .        .  *        .   1.4606     1.4056       .0550
   55     .        . *         .   1.4551     1.4082       .0469
   56     .        . *         .   1.4425     1.4076       .0349
   57     .        . *         .   1.4023     1.3726       .0297
   58     .        .*          .   1.3991     1.3785       .0206
   59     .        *           .   1.3798     1.3751    4.7159E-03
   60     .        .*          .   1.3782     1.3677       .0105
   61     .        *           .   1.3366     1.3453   -8.7389E-03
   62     .        *           .   1.3026     1.3110   -8.4091E-03
   63     .       *.           .   1.2592     1.2966      -.0374
   64     .       *.           .   1.2635     1.2822      -.0187
   65     .       *.           .   1.2549     1.2846      -.0297
   66     .       *.           .   1.2527     1.2898      -.0371
   67     .       *.           .   1.2763     1.3027      -.0264
   68     .       *.           .   1.2906     1.3275      -.0369
   69     .      *  .          .   1.2721     1.3347      -.0626
 Case #   O:.......:........:O     CONSUMP     *PRED       *RESID
          -3.0      0.0      3.0
```

Autocorrelated residuals commonly occur when you have omitted important explanatory variables from the regression analysis. When the residuals from a regression analysis are strongly autocorrelated, you cannot rely on the results. The significance levels reported for the regression coefficients are wrong, and the R^2 value does not accurately summarize the explanatory power of the independent variables.

Plotting the Residuals

It is always a good idea to plot the residuals from a regression analysis against the predicted values and also against each of the predictor variables. You can get plots of the residuals, predicted values, and the dependent variable within the Linear Regression procedure by specifying scatterplots in the Linear Regression plots dialog box.

You can also create scatterplots of any saved variables. After you have run the Linear Regression procedure and saved the variables, from the menus choose:

Graphs
  Scatter...

Specify the variables you want to plot. For more information on scatterplots, see the SPSS Base system documentation.

Figure 9.12 shows the plots of the residuals (*res_1*) versus the predicted values (*pre_1*), residuals versus *income*, and residuals versus *price*.

Figure 9.12   Residual scatterplots

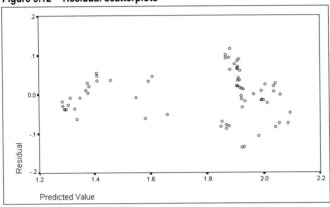

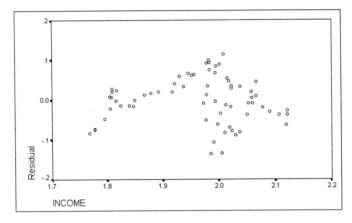

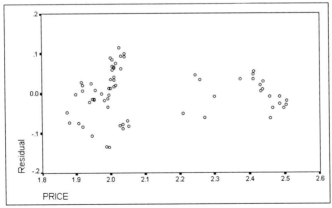

The plot shows that the variance of the residuals (their vertical "spread") increases as the predicted values increase. Residuals should show no pattern, and this violates one of the assumptions of regression analysis. In addition, the other two plots reveal that the variance of the residuals increases with increasing *income* and decreases with increasing *price*.

Autocorrelation Plots

The most glaring problem revealed by the residuals analysis is the autocorrelation of the residuals. Autocorrelation is common in time series analysis, so SPSS provides procedures to calculate and plot the sample autocorrelation function (ACF) and others like it. You have seen these procedures in earlier chapters. To produce autocorrelations and partial autocorrelations, from the menus choose:

Graphs
  Time Series ▶
    Autocorrelations...

- When Autocorrelations is selected in the Display group, the Autocorrelations procedure calculates and plots the autocorrelation function, which gives the correlation between values of the series and lagged values of the series, for different lags.
- When Partial autocorrelations is selected in the Display group, the Autocorrelations procedure calculates and plots the partial autocorrelation function, which gives the autocorrelations controlling for intervening lags.

Figure 9.13 shows autocorrelations and partial autocorrelations of the variable *res_1*, which was created by the Linear Regression procedure, in low resolution. As you can see, the low-resolution plot shows the actual values of the ACF and the Box-Ljung statistic, which tests whether an observed ACF could come from a population in which the autocorrelations were 0 at all lags.

Figure 9.13 Autocorrelations of residuals

```
Autocorrelations:    RES_1      Residual

       Auto- Stand.
Lag   Corr.  Err.  -1  -.75  -.5 -.25   0   .25  .5  .75   1   Box-Ljung  Prob.
                   +----+----+----+----+----+----+----+----+
  1    .851  .118                       |****.************     52.156    .000
  2    .738  .117                       |****.**********       91.932    .000
  3    .629  .116                       |****.********        121.281    .000
  4    .500  .115                       |****.*****           140.155    .000
  5    .392  .114                       |****.***             151.896    .000
  6    .284  .113                       |****.*               158.172    .000
  7    .149  .112                     . |***.                 159.932    .000
  8    .005  .112                     .   *   .               159.934    .000
  9   -.081  .111                     .  **|   .              160.464    .000
 10   -.199  .110                     ****|   .               163.750    .000
 11   -.255  .109                    *.***|   .               169.235    .000
 12   -.308  .108                    **.***|   .              177.367    .000
 13   -.395  .107                  ****.***|   .              191.010    .000
 14   -.432  .106                 *****.***|   .              207.602    .000
 15   -.431  .105                 *****.***|   .              224.427    .000
 16   -.389  .104                  ****.***|   .              238.404    .000

Plot Symbols:      Autocorrelations *     Two Standard Error Limits .

Total cases:  69    Computable first lags:  68


Partial Autocorrelations:   RES_1     Residual

      Pr-Aut- Stand.
Lag   Corr.  Err.  -1  -.75  -.5 -.25   0   .25  .5  .75   1
                   +----+----+----+----+----+----+----+----+
  1    .851  .120                       |****.************
  2    .049  .120                     .   |*    .
  3   -.035  .120                     .  *|     .
  4   -.133  .120                     . ***|    .
  5   -.027  .120                     .   *|    .
  6   -.064  .120                     .   *|    .
  7   -.177  .120                     .****|    .
  8   -.180  .120                     .****|    .
  9    .074  .120                     .   |*    .
 10   -.174  .120                     . ***|    .
 11    .089  .120                     .   |**   .
 12   -.076  .120                     .  **|    .
 13   -.189  .120                     .****|    .
 14    .020  .120                     .   *    .
 15    .059  .120                     .   |*   .
 16    .131  .120                     .   |*** .

Plot Symbols:      Autocorrelations *     Two Standard Error Limits .

Total cases:  69    Computable first lags:  68
```

The autocorrelations start quite high and fade. The first-order autocorrelation is 0.851, the second-order is 0.738, and the third-order is 0.629. They die out by the eighth lag, then become negative, and then start to die out again. There is a single spike in the PACF plot. This pattern indicates that the regression residuals are those of a first-order autoregressive process. (You know it is a first-order process from the PACF, which is nearly 0 from lag 2 on. After removing the effect of the first-order autocorrelation, no autocorrelation remains at lag 2. Refer to Appendix B for the typical ACF and PACF plots of various types of process.)

Plotting the Regression Results

To see how well ordinary regression did, you can produce a sequence plot of *consump* together with the regression predictions (*pre_1*), as in Figure 9.14.

Figure 9.14   Predictions from Linear Regression

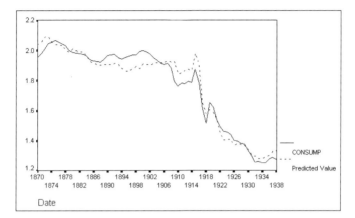

The predictions from the Linear Regression procedure, using the two predictor variables *price* and *income*, are noticeably better than those from the Curve Estimation procedure. These fitted values do a good job of tracking the "bounce" in consumption during the First World War, 1914–1918. (There was also a dip in the relative price of spirits during those years, which partially explains the bounce in consumption.)

However, ordinary regression with serially correlated time series is unreliable. It isn't hard to understand why this is true. Most time series have some trend, either up or down, and any two trending time series will correlate simply because of the trends, regardless of whether they are causally related or not. An increasing trend will likely continue to increase, but that doesn't mean you should use just any other trend to predict that it will continue to increase. When you regress one time series on another, you want estimates of the linear relationship apart from accidental similarities resulting from autocorrelation. Trends provides a procedure, Autoregression, that allows you to do this.

Regression with Autocorrelated Error

The Autoregression procedure estimates true regression coefficients from time series with first-order autocorrelated errors. It offers three algorithms. Two algorithms (Prais-Winsten and Cochrane-Orcutt) transform the regression equation to remove the autocorrelation. The third (maximum likelihood), shown here, uses the same algorithm that the ARIMA procedure uses for estimating autocorrelation. Maximum likelihood, or ML, estimation is more demanding computationally but gives better results—and it can tolerate missing data in the series. To use the Autoregression procedure, from the menus choose:

Statistics
  Time Series ▶
    Autoregression...

This opens the Autoregression dialog box, as shown in Figure 9.15.

Figure 9.15   Autoregression dialog box

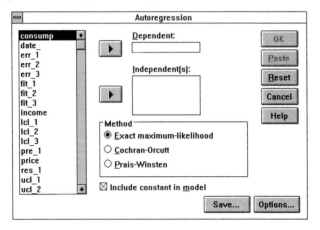

Move *consump* to the Dependent box and *income* and *price* to the Independent(s) list. The method Exact maximum-likelihood is selected by default. With this method, the Autocorrelations procedure performs many calculations. This takes a while, but it gives the best possible estimates. Figure 9.16 shows some of the output.

Figure 9.16   Maximum-likelihood regression with autocorrelated errors

```
Split group number: 1  Series length: 69
Number of cases skipped at end because of missing values: 7
Melard's algorithm will be used  for estimation.



Conclusion of estimation phase.
Estimation terminated at iteration number 5 because:
   All parameter estimates changed by less than .001

FINAL PARAMETERS:

Number of residuals  69
Standard error       .02266242
Log likelihood       163.29783
AIC                  -318.59566
SBC                  -309.65925


              Analysis of Variance:

              DF  Adj. Sum of Squares    Residual Variance
Residuals     65            .03554182            .00051359


           Variables in the Model:

                    B         SEB      T-RATIO    APPROX. PROB.
AR1          .9933525    .01169890   84.909921      .00000000
INCOME       .6233058    .14689313    4.243260      .00007154
PRICE       -.9280837    .07816891  -11.872797      .00000000
CONSTANT    2.4488569    .37368189    6.553320      .00000000

The following new variables are being created:

   Name       Label

   FIT_4      Fit for CONSUMP from AREG, MOD_10
   ERR_4      Error for CONSUMP from AREG, MOD_10
   LCL_4      95% LCL for CONSUMP from AREG, MOD_10
   UCL_4      95% UCL for CONSUMP from AREG, MOD_10
   SEP_4      SE of fit for CONSUMP from AREG, MOD_10
```

Compare the Autocorrelation regression coefficients in Figure 9.16 with those from the Linear Regression procedure in Figure 9.8. Ordinary regression showed a small negative relationship between *income* and *consump*, one that was not statistically significant. The Autoregression procedure shows a statistically significant *positive* relationship. Both ordinary regression and the Autoregression procedure show a strong and significant negative relationship between *price* and *consump*. The estimates from the Autoregression procedure are much more likely to represent the true relationships among these variables, because they take the correlated errors into account.

Plotting the Fit from Autoregression

Figure 9.17 shows a sequence plot of the *fit_4* values from the above Autoregression procedure, along with the confidence limits. Notice how closely the predicted values track the original series, and how narrow the confidence limits are. That is because this regression model, unlike the previous one, takes note of the autocorrelation in the consumption series. Each year's consumption of spirits is very close to that of the previous year, with changes that may be due to changes in price and income. This is a common situation in time series analysis, and one to which the Autoregression procedure is particularly suited.

Figure 9.17   Fitted values and confidence limits from the Autoregression procedure

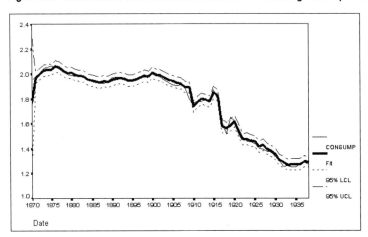

Forecasting with the Autoregression Procedure

In "Forecasting with Curve Estimation" on p. 115, we defined the years 1939–1945 as the forecast period in the Curve Estimation Save dialog box. Yet the Autoregression procedure did not produce forecasts. There is a simple reason for this. Autoregression models are based not only on the main series but also on information in the predictor variables. To forecast with the Autoregression procedure, you need to know the values of the predictor variables for the forecast period.

Since we have no data for the prediction period, we must first extend the *price* and *income* series. One way to do this is with the Curve Estimation procedure. From the menus choose

Statistics
  Regression ▶
    Curve Estimation...

This opens the Curve Estimation dialog box, as shown in Figure 9.18.

Figure 9.18   Curve Estimation dialog box

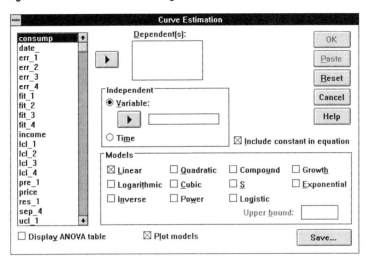

Move *income* and *price* into the Dependent(s) box. For Independent, select Time. Select the Linear model, and deselect Plot Models. Click on Save.... This opens the Curve Estimation Save dialog box, as shown in Figure 9.19. In the Save Variables group, select Predicted values. Then click on Continue and OK. Curve Estimation creates variables *fit_5*, which contains predicted values for *income*, and *fit_6*, which contains predicted values for *price*.

Figure 9.19   Curve Estimation Save dialog box

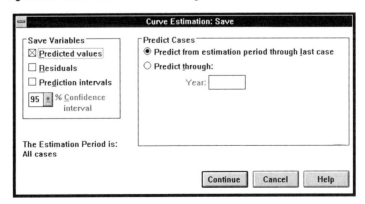

In this example, we use the linear model. You can extend a series any way you like—as long as you believe the results.

Because forecasts for *consump* through 1945 were created earlier with Curve Estimation (Figure 9.6), the series *income* and *price* have already been extended to include the forecast period 1939–1945. However, the observations in this period were assigned system-missing values for these two variables. To replace the missing values in the forecast period with predicted values for *income* and *price*, from the menus choose:

Transform
  Compute...

This displays the Compute Variable dialog box. Type income into the Target Variable list, spelling it exactly as shown here. You want to modify the values of this existing variable, not create a new variable. Now select *fit_5*, the forecast values for *income*, in the source variable list, and move it into the Numeric Expression box. Click on If... to open the Compute Variable If Cases dialog box, as shown in Figure 9.20.

Figure 9.20   Compute Variable If Cases dialog box

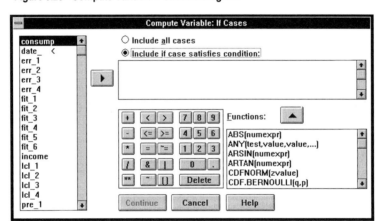

Select Include if case satisfies condition. Scroll the Functions list until you see SYSMIS(numvar). This function returns the logical value True if the numeric variable within its parentheses has the system-missing value. Click on SYSMIS(numvar), and then click on the [▲] button to move it into the box above the Functions list. It appears in that box with a question mark highlighted within its parentheses. Select *income* in the source variable list (to the left) and click on [▶]. The variable name *income* replaces the question mark to form the expression SYSMIS(income). Click on Continue to return to the Compute Variable dialog box, and notice that the conditional expression is now displayed next to the If... button. Click on OK to execute the command.

Before changing values of an existing variable, such as *income*, SPSS asks if it is OK to do so, in case you typed an existing variable name by mistake. Click on OK. Then go back into the Compute Variable dialog box and do the same transformation for *price*:

- Replace *income* with *price* in the Target Variable box.
- Replace *fit_5* with *fit_6* in the Numeric Expression list.
- Click on If.... Highlight *income* in the expression, and then select *price* in the source variable list and move it into the expression, replacing *income*. (Make sure the parentheses are intact. If necessary, you can delete the entire expression, move the SYSMIS function back in, and then move *price* into the parentheses.)

When you execute this transformation, you must again confirm that it is OK to replace the values of the existing variable *price*.

Now you are ready to predict *consump* with the Autoregression procedure: the predictor variables *price* and *income* both have projected values through the forecast period. From the menus choose:

Statistics
  Time Series ▶
    Autoregression...

This opens the Autoregression dialog box, with your previous specifications intact. You do not need to change any of the specifications; the two independent variables, *income* and *price*, now have nonmissing values through the forecast period. Click on OK to run the command again.

Figure 9.21 shows a sequence plot of *consump*, the new forecast series *fit_7* from the Autoregression procedure, and the extended independent variables *income* and *price*.

Figure 9.21 Sequence chart of consump, fit_7, income, and price

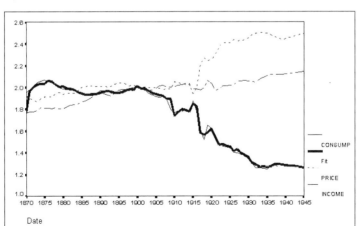

The projections are not startling. Both *income* and *price* have been projected to show a small positive trend in the forecast period 1939-1945, based on their trend in the historical period. In Figure 9.16, the negative coefficient of *price* is greater (in absolute value) than the positive coefficient of *income*, so the model predicts slowly declining consumption during the forecast years.

This projection depends upon both the model developed with the Autoregression procedure and the projections we made for *income* and *price* using the Curve Estimation procedure. Either of these could turn out to be unreliable during the forecast period. Nevertheless, the Autoregression projections—based on realistic estimates of the effect of price and income upon consumption—are much better than those from the Curve Estimation procedure or from Linear Regression.

Summary of Regression Methods

The ordinary least-squares (OLS) regression algorithm used by the Linear Regression procedure gave inaccurate results because the autocorrelation in the time series violated its assumption of independence in the residuals:

- It overestimated the influence of price on consumption, because during this period price showed a more consistent trend that could be matched to the trend in consumption. OLS regression with time series data often gives undue importance to trends that arise from other causes.

- It underestimated the influence of income on consumption. There was no statistically significant relationship between these two variables with OLS (Figure 9.8), but there was one when the Autoregression procedure corrected for autocorrelation (Figure 9.16).

- It underestimated the standard errors of the coefficients, which indicate the precision with which b's are estimated.

The Trends procedure Autoregression corrected these problems and gave more reliable estimates.

How to Obtain an Autoregression Analysis

To estimate the parameters and goodness-of-fit of a first-order autoregressive model, from the menus choose:

Statistics
  Time Series ▶
    Autoregression...

This opens the Autoregression dialog box, as shown in Figure 9.22.

Figure 9.22   Autoregression dialog box

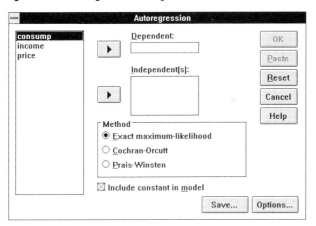

The numeric variables in your data file appear in the source list. Move one variable into the Dependent box and one or more variables into the Independent(s) list.

Method. You can select one of three alternatives for the method by which the autoregressive model is estimated:

○ **Exact maximum-likelihood.** This method can handle missing data within the series, and can be used when one of the independent variables is the lagged dependent variable.

○ **Cochran-Orcutt.** This is a simple and widely used method for estimating a first-order autoregressive model. It cannot be used when a series contains imbedded missing values.

○ **Prais-Winsten.** This is a generalized least-squares method. It cannot be used when a series contains imbedded missing values.

You can also specify the following:

❏ **Include constant in model.** The regression model includes a constant term. This is the default. To suppress this term and obtain regression through the origin, deselect this item.

Saving Predicted Values and Residuals

To save predicted values, confidence limits, or residuals as new variables, or to produce forecasts past the end of your dependent series, click on Save... in the Autoregression dialog box. This opens the Autoregression Save dialog box (see Figure 9.23). The current estimation period is shown at the bottom of this box.

Figure 9.23   Autoregression Save dialog box

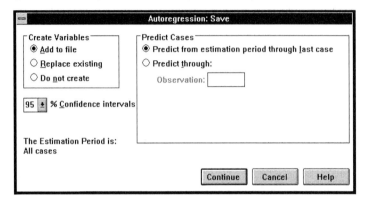

Create Variables. The Autoregression procedure can create five new variables: fitted (predicted) values, residuals, the standard errors of the prediction, and the lower and upper confidence limits of the prediction. To control the creation of new variables, you can choose one of these alternatives:

○ **Add to file.** The five new series Autoregression creates are saved as regular variables in your working data file. Variable names are formed from a three-letter prefix, an underscore, and a number. This is the default.

○ **Replace existing.** The five new series Autoregression creates are saved as temporary variables in your working data file. At the same time, any existing temporary variables created by time series commands are dropped when you run the Autoregression procedure. Variable names are formed from a three-letter prefix, a pound sign (#), and a number.

○ **Do not create.** The new variables are not added to the working data file.

If you select either Add to file or Replace existing above, you can select:

⬇ **% Confidence intervals.** Select either 90, 95, or 99% from the drop-down list.

Predict Cases. If you select either Add to file or Replace existing above, you can specify a forecast period. Autoregressive forecasts require valid (nonmissing) data for all of the independent variables.

○ **Predict from estimation period through last case.** Predicts values for all cases with valid data for the independent variable(s), from the estimation period through the current end of the file, but does not create new cases. If you are analyzing a range of cases that starts after the beginning of the file, cases prior to that range are not predicted. The estimation period, displayed at the bottom of this box, is defined with the Range dialog box available through the Select Cases option on the Data Menu. If no estimation period has been defined, all cases are used to predict values. This is the default.

○ **Predict through.** Predicts values through the specified date, time, or observation number, based on the cases in the estimation period. This can be used to forecast values beyond the last case in the time series. The text boxes that are available for specifying the end of the prediction period depend on the currently defined date variables. (Use the Define Dates option on the Data menu to create date variables.) If there are no defined date variables, you can specify the ending observation (case) number.

New cases created as forecasts have missing values for residuals, whose definition requires an existing value.

Autoregression Options

To control convergence criteria and initial values used in the iterative algorithm, or to specify the amount of output to be displayed, click on Options... in the Autoregression dialog box. This opens the Autoregression Options dialog box, as shown in Figure 9.24.

Figure 9.24   Autoregression Options dialog box

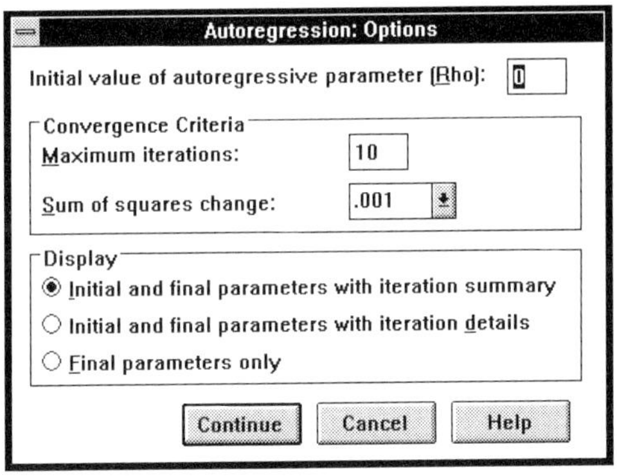

Initial value of autoregressive parameter (Rho). This is the value from which the iterative search for the optimal value of rho begins. You can specify any number less than 1 and greater than -1, although negative values of rho are uncommon in this procedure. The default is 0.

Convergence Criteria. The convergence criteria determine when the iterative algorithm stops and the final solution is reported.

> **Maximum iterations.** By default, iteration stops after 10 iterations, even if the algorithm has not converged. You can specify a positive integer in this text box.

⬇ **Sum of squares change.** By default, iteration stops if the adjusted sum of squares does not decrease by 0.001% from one iteration to the next. You can choose a smaller or larger value for more or less precision in the parameter estimates. For greater precision it may also be necessary to increase the maximum iterations.

Display. Choose one of these alternatives to indicate how much detail you want to see.

○ **Initial and final parameters with iteration summary.** The Autoregression procedure displays initial and final parameter estimates, goodness-of-fit statistics, the number of iterations, and the reason that iteration terminated.

○ **Initial and final parameters with iteration details.** In addition to the above, the Autoregression procedure displays parameter estimates after each iteration.

○ **Final parameters only.** The Autoregression procedure displays final parameters and goodness-of-fit statistics.

Additional Features Available with Command Syntax

You can customize your analysis if you paste your selections to a syntax window and edit the resulting AREG command syntax. The additional features are:

• Use of the final estimate of Rho from a previous execution of Autoregression as the initial estimate for iteration.

• More precise control over convergence criteria.

See the Syntax Reference section of this manual for command syntax rules and for complete AREG command syntax.

10 An Effective Decay-Preventive Dentifrice: Intervention Analysis

The examples so far have tried to produce models for the typical behavior of a time series. A technique called **intervention analysis** concentrates instead on a disruption in the normal behavior of a series. Intervention analysis was first applied to this series by Wichern and Jones (1977), and we will follow their analysis.

The Toothpaste Market Share Data

In this chapter we analyze a pair of series containing the weekly market shares of Colgate and Crest toothpastes during the years 1958 through 1963. At the beginning of this period Colgate held a substantial lead in market share. On August 1, 1960, the Council on Dental Therapeutics of the American Dental Association made an unprecedented endorsement of Crest as an aid in preventing tooth decay. As some of you may remember, Procter and Gamble, the makers of Crest, advertised this endorsement heavily for two weeks (and less heavily thereafter). The effect upon the market shares of both Crest and Colgate was immediate and dramatic.

We will use the technique of intervention analysis, introduced by Box and Tiao (1975), to assess the impact of the ADA endorsement and the subsequent advertising campaign. The two series we will analyze are *crest* and *colgate*, which contain the market shares of the two toothpastes.

Plotting the Market Shares

Figure 10.1 shows the two series around the time of the endorsement, which occurred in week 135. The impact of the endorsement is evident.

137

Figure 10.1   Market shares of Colgate and Crest

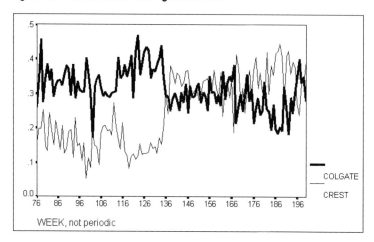

Intervention Analysis

The basic strategy of intervention analysis is:

- Develop a model for the series before intervention.
- Add one or more dummy variables that represent the timing of the intervention.
- Reestimate the model, including the new dummy variables, for the entire series.
- Interpret the coefficients of the dummy variables as measures of the effect of the intervention.

We will carry out this strategy for both the *crest* and the *colgate* data. As a first step, then, we must develop a model for each series using the first 134 observations. From the menus choose

Data
  Select Cases...

In the Select Cases dialog box, select Based on time or case range and click on Range.... In the Select Cases Range dialog box, enter 1 in the text box for First Case and 134 in the text box for Last Case. This establishes the range of cases from which the model will be identified.

Identifying the Models

The first step is to identify the ARIMA model using the ACF and PACF plots. Since we assume that the underlying process is similar for the two toothpaste series, we will show the ACF plot just for one (*colgate*) (Figure 10.2).

Figure 10.2   ACF for COLGATE

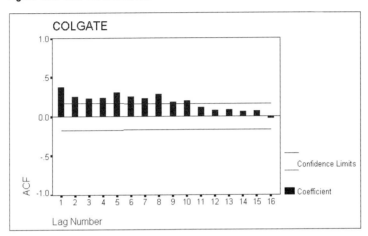

Figure 10.2 shows that the autocorrelations do not die out rapidly, indicating that the series is not stationary and must be differenced. Figure 10.3 shows the ACF and PACF of the differenced series.

- The ACF shows a spike at lag 1.
- The PACF attenuates rapidly (if not altogether neatly) from lag 1.

These plots indicate an MA(1) process. Since the series has been differenced, the overall identification is ARIMA(0,1,1).

Figure 10.3   ACF and PACF for COLGATE (differenced)

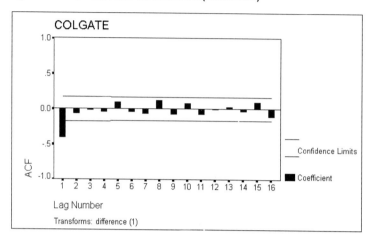

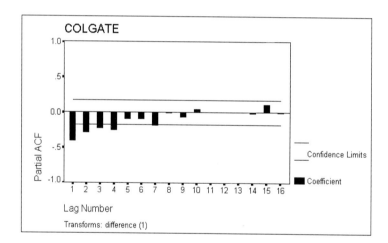

More ARIMA Notation

To see how intervention analysis works, you must understand how to express an ARIMA model as an equation. The only novelty is the "backshift operator" B.

- For any series, say *crest*, *B(crest)* is the series shifted back in time by one observation. If you index the series, $B(crest_t)$ means exactly the same as $crest_{t-1}$.

- The differences between $crest_t$ and $crest_{t-1}$ are simply $crest - B(crest)$. It is convenient, for the sake of notation, to "factor" this expression:

$$crest - B(crest) = (1 - B)\, crest$$

Using this notation, a random-walk model is simply

$$(1 - B)\, crest_t = disturbance_t$$

An MA(1), or ARIMA(0,0,1), model states that an observation is an average of the current disturbance and some proportion of the previous disturbance. The proportion is given by a number θ, which must be between -1 and $+1$. This translates into the formula

$$crest_t = disturbance_t - \theta\, disturbance_{t-1}$$

$$crest_t = disturbance_t - \theta\, B\, (disturbance_t)$$

$$crest_t = (1 - \theta\, B)\, disturbance_t$$

When you get used to this standard notation it is not hard to read. The value of *crest* at time t equals the disturbance at time t minus θ times the backshifted disturbance—which is the disturbance at time $t-1$. (The minus sign before θ is conventional in ARIMA analysis.)

To get an equation for the ARIMA(0,1,1) model that describes the toothpaste market shares, you simply substitute the expression for the differences in the *crest* series into the MA(1) equation:

$$(1 - B)\, crest_t = (1 - \theta\, B)\, disturbance_t \qquad \text{Equation 10.1}$$

That is the equation for an ARIMA(0,1,1) model, as you might find it in an ARIMA textbook. It says that the change in Crest market share at time t—the left side of the equation—equals the disturbance at time t minus some fraction (θ) of the disturbance at time $t-1$.

Creating Intervention Variables

Now that you have a linear equation for the market share at any time prior to the ADA endorsement, you must figure out a way to incorporate a term for the endorsement itself—the "intervention," as it is called. Figure 10.4 shows values of the market-share series around the time of the endorsement.

Figure 10.4   Data values for weeks 130 through 140

	week_	crest	colgate
130	130	.141	.369
131	131	.145	.364
132	132	.127	.386
133	133	.171	.406
134	134	.152	.439
135	135	.211	.345
136	136	.309	.291
137	137	.242	.292
138	138	.380	.249
139	139	.362	.283
140	140	.328	.301

You would like to pinpoint precisely when the effect of the endorsement showed up in the market shares of both toothpastes. The endorsement was advertised most heavily in weeks 135 and 136. From the listing of the two series you can see that the Crest market share was volatile during this period; it jumped up in week 135 and again in week 136, seemed to settle back, and then resumed its high level. The Colgate share dropped sharply in week 135 and again in week 136, and then basically remained at its new, low level. A simple model would say that the effect showed up over the two weeks 135 and 136, perhaps in two stages.

Dummy Variables

A variable or series that has only the values 0 or 1 is called a **dummy variable.** It represents the presence or absence of something. You can easily include a dummy variable in a model—just write it into the equation, with a coefficient of its own. Here we call the coefficient β:

Market share = rest of model + β (dummy)

You want a dummy variable that reflects the presence or absence of the intervention. Prior to week 135, then, the dummy variable *dummy* should equal 0. Then $\beta \times$ *dummy* equals 0 and the predicted market share is given by the rest of the model. Starting with week 135, *dummy* should equal 1 and the prediction becomes (rest of the model) + β. By using the dummy variable you can thus produce a "step" in the prediction—regardless of what the rest of the model involves.

The coefficient β must be estimated along with all the rest of the coefficients in the model. When β is positive the step goes up (like Crest market share in week 135); when β is negative the step goes down (like Colgate market share in week 135).

To represent the ADA endorsement, whose effect occurred over a two-week period, you need two dummy variables, one for week 135 and one for week 136. Each will have a coefficient β that indicates the effect of the endorsement in that week. The equation for the model becomes

$$(1 - B)\,\text{crest}_t \ = \ (1 - \theta B)\,\text{disturbance}_t + \beta_1\,\text{dummy1} \ + \beta_2\,\text{dummy2} \qquad \textbf{Equation 10.2}$$

Before you can estimate the coefficients of the dummy variables, you must decide how to build them. In order to work as described above, they must equal 0 when the intervention is not present and 1 when the intervention is present.

Steps and Pulses

The most common types of dummy variables in time series analysis are step functions and pulse functions. The names are descriptive. A **step function** is 0 until some crucial moment comes, when it "steps" immediately to 1. It remains at 1 thereafter. A **pulse function** similarly jumps to 1 at a crucial moment but then returns immediately to 0 and remains there. When you represent step and pulse functions by the values of a time series, the relationship between the two is clear:

- The differences in a step variable form a pulse variable. (All the differences are 0 except when the step occurs, and that difference is 1—so the differences are a pulse variable.)
- The cumulative total of a pulse variable makes a step variable. (The cumulative total starts as 0, becomes 1 at the time of the pulse, and then never changes.)

You can easily create variables representing steps or pulses in SPSS using the Compute Variable dialog box. Here we will create step variables; in "Alternative Methods" on p. 150 we will create pulse variables.

First, restore all cases. From the menus choose:

Data
  Select Cases...

Select All Cases and click on OK.

Next, create the step variables. From the menus choose:

Transform
  Compute...

This opens the Compute Variable dialog box, as shown in Figure 10.5.

Figure 10.5   Compute Variable dialog box

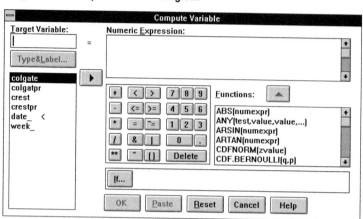

- In the Target Variable text box, type *step135*.
- Click in the Numeric Expression text box and type `week_ >= 135`.

When you click on OK, SPSS calculates the values of the new variable *step135*. This is a **logical variable**: it has the value 1 for cases in which it is true that *week_* is greater than or equal to 135, and the value 0 for cases in which that expression is false. Now repeat this process, creating another logical variable, *step136*, with the expression *week_* >= 136.

A Model for the ADA Endorsement

For the toothpaste market-share series, the "rest of the model" was an ARIMA(0,1,1) process (Equation 10.1). In other words, the differences in market share followed a first-order moving average, or MA(1), model. The effect of the intervention on market share had the shape of a double step function. Crest market share stepped up on week 135 and again on week 136, while Colgate market share stepped down on each of the two weeks. You can approach this intervention in either of two ways:

1. Use two step functions as dummy predictor variables for the original series, using an ARIMA(0,1,1) model.

2. Use two pulse functions as dummy predictor variables for the *differences* in the series, using an ARIMA(0,0,1) model.

The two approaches are equivalent, as explained above. A step function in the market-share series is the same as a pulse function in the differences of the market-share series. Here we choose the first approach. At the end of the chapter we will discuss the second method also.

We have created two dummy variables, as described above. The series *step135* takes its step at week 135; *step136* takes its step the following week. After week 136, both of these dummy variables contribute to the level of the series.

Specifying Predictor Variables in ARIMA

The Trends ARIMA procedure allows you to specify one or more **predictor variables** (also called **regressors**) for the series you are analyzing. ARIMA treats these predictors much like predictor variables in regression analysis: it estimates the coefficients for them that best fit the data.

We will use the same two predictor variables, *step135* and *step136*, for both Crest market share and Colgate market share. We expect positive coefficients for both predictor variables in the Crest model, and negative coefficients in the Colgate model. The sum of the Crest coefficients will represent the total increase in Crest market share over the two-week period, and the sum of the Colgate coefficients will represent the total decrease in Colgate market share.

Estimating the Models

To estimate the intervention analysis model, from the menus choose:

Statistics
  Time Series ▶
    ARIMA...

This opens the ARIMA dialog box, as shown in Figure 10.6.

Figure 10.6 ARIMA dialog box

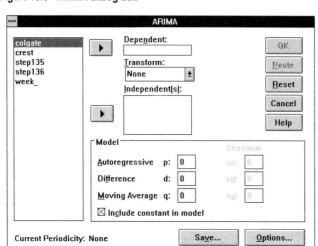

- Move *colgate* into the Dependent box.
- Move *step135* and *step136* into the Independent(s) list.
- Specify 1 for the Difference parameter *d*, and specify 1 for the Moving Average parameter *q*. Leave all the other parameters 0.
- Deselect Include constant in model. Since an ARIMA(0,1,1) model analyzes differences and neither series showed a long-term trend (aside from the effect of the intervention), we expect the average differences to be 0.
- Click on OK.

To obtain the same analysis for *crest*, you can simply go to the ARIMA dialog box, move *colgate* out of the Dependent box, and move *crest* in. (If you want to reduce processing time for this second analysis, click on Options and, in the Initial Values group in the ARIMA Options dialog box, select Apply from previous model, as explained in Chapter 8.) Figure 10.7 and Figure 10.8 show the results for the intervention analysis.

Figure 10.7   Intervention analysis for Colgate

```
Split group number: 1  Series length: 276
No missing data.
Melard's algorithm will be used for estimation.

Termination criteria:
Parameter epsilon: .001
Maximum Marquardt constant: 1.00E+09
SSQ Percentage: .001
Maximum number of iterations: 10

Initial values:

MA1        .57105
STEP135   -.06619
STEP136   -.06061

Marquardt constant = .001
Adjusted sum of squares = .63460269

                Iteration History:

  Iteration   Adj. Sum of Squares   Marquardt Constant
          1            .59567279            .00100000
          2            .59430370            .00010000
          3            .59427067            .00001000

Conclusion of estimation phase.
Estimation terminated at iteration number 4 because:
   Sum of squares decreased by less than .001 percent.

FINAL PARAMETERS:

Number of residuals  275
Standard error       .04665299
Log likelihood       453.65255
AIC                 -901.3051
SBC                 -890.45479

              Analysis of Variance:

              DF  Adj. Sum of Squares   Residual Variance
Residuals    272         .59426928           .00217650

              Variables in the Model:

                    B          SEB      T-RATIO    APPROX. PROB.
MA1          .80588760    .03671173    21.951775     .00000000
STEP135     -.05245968    .04665299    -1.124466     .26180685
STEP136     -.06085701    .04665299    -1.304461     .19317882


The following new variables are being created:

   Name       Label

   FIT_1      Fit for COLGATE from ARIMA, MOD_8 NOCON
   ERR_1      Error for COLGATE from ARIMA, MOD_8 NOCON
   LCL_1      95% LCL for COLGATE from ARIMA, MOD_8 NOCON
   UCL_1      95% UCL for COLGATE from ARIMA, MOD_8 NOCON
   SEP_1      SE of fit for COLGATE from ARIMA, MOD_8 NOCON
```

Figure 10.8 Intervention analysis for Crest

```
Split group number: 1  Series length: 276
No missing data.
Melard's algorithm will be used for estimation.

Termination criteria:
Parameter epsilon: .001
Maximum Marquardt constant: 1.00E+09
SSQ Percentage: .001
Maximum number of iterations: 10

Initial values:

MA1        ..63926
STEP135    .06103
STEP136    .10316

Marquardt constant = .001
Adjusted sum of squares = .53437524

                 Iteration History:

  Iteration   Adj. Sum of Squares   Marquardt Constant
         1          .51922627              .00100000
         2          .51921252              .00010000

Conclusion of estimation phase.
Estimation terminated at iteration number 3 because:
  Sum of squares decreased by less than .001 percent.

FINAL PARAMETERS:

Number of residuals  275
Standard error       .04361667
Log likelihood       472.2175
AIC                  -938.43499
SBC                  -927.58468

           Analysis of Variance:

              DF  Adj. Sum of Squares   Residual Variance
Residuals    272         .51921166            .00190241

           Variables in the Model:

                 B          SEB      T-RATIO   APPROX. PROB.
MA1        .77839041   .03816927   20.393119     .00000000
STEP135    .06539159   .04361667    1.499234     .13497251
STEP136    .11187739   .04361667    2.565014     .01085377


The following new variables are being created:

   Name        Label

   FIT_2       Fit for CREST from ARIMA, MOD_9 NOCON
   ERR_2       Error for CREST from ARIMA, MOD_9 NOCON
   LCL_2       95% LCL for CREST from ARIMA, MOD_9 NOCON
   UCL_2       95% UCL for CREST from ARIMA, MOD_9 NOCON
   SEP_2       SE of fit for CREST from ARIMA, MOD_9 NOCON
```

As reported in the ARIMA output, the residuals for the analysis of Colgate market share are in the new series *err_1*, and those for the analysis of Crest market share are in *err_2*.

Diagnosis

Figure 10.9 shows the residual autocorrelations from the two models estimated above. There are no significant values of the ACF, and the Box-Ljung statistic indicates that the observed autocorrelations are quite consistent with the hypothesis that these residuals are white noise. Both models fit well.

Figure 10.9 Diagnosis of intervention models

```
Autocorrelations:     ERR_1          Error for COLGATE from ARIMA, MOD_5 NOCO

      Auto- Stand.
Lag   Corr.  Err.  -1  -.75  -.5 -.25   0   .25   .5   .75    1   Box-Ljung  Prob.
                    +----+----+----+----+----+----+----+----+
  1    .055  .060                          . |*.                    .834     .361
  2   -.002  .060                          . * .                    .835     .659
  3   -.048  .060                          .*| .                   1.493     .684
  4   -.094  .060                         **| .                    3.964     .411
  5    .053  .060                          . |*.                   4.751     .447
  6   -.001  .059                          . * .                   4.752     .576
  7   -.004  .059                          . * .                   4.757     .690
  8    .078  .059                          . |**                   6.494     .592
  9    .003  .059                          . * .                   6.496     .689
 10   -.022  .059                          . * .                   6.636     .759
 11   -.005  .059                          . * .                   6.644     .827
 12   -.070  .059                          .*| .                   8.074     .779
 13   -.064  .059                          .*| .                   9.274     .752
 14   -.073  .059                          .*| .                  10.848     .698
 15    .011  .058                          . * .                  10.882     .761
 16   -.051  .058                          .*| .                  11.655     .767

Plot Symbols:      Autocorrelations *     Two Standard Error Limits .

Total cases:  276     Computable first lags:  274


Autocorrelations:     ERR_2          Error for CREST from ARIMA, MOD_6 NOCON

      Auto- Stand.
Lag   Corr.  Err.  -1  -.75  -.5 -.25   0   .25   .5   .75    1   Box-Ljung  Prob.
                    +----+----+----+----+----+----+----+----+
  1   -.012  .060                          . * .                    .037     .847
  2   -.004  .060                          . * .                    .041     .980
  3    .046  .060                          . |*.                    .629     .890
  4   -.029  .060                          .*| .                    .872     .929
  5    .061  .060                          . |*.                   1.918     .860
  6    .030  .059                          . |*.                   2.173     .903
  7   -.054  .059                          .*| .                   2.988     .886
  8   -.004  .059                          . * .                   2.994     .935
  9   -.078  .059                         **| .                    4.749     .856
 10   -.031  .059                          .*| .                   5.034     .889
 11   -.096  .059                         **| .                    7.690     .741
 12   -.015  .059                          . * .                   7.758     .804
 13   -.068  .059                          .*| .                   9.111     .765
 14   -.082  .059                         **| .                   11.080     .680
 15   -.014  .058                          . * .                  11.137     .743
 16   -.026  .058                          .*| .                  11.331     .789

Plot Symbols:      Autocorrelations *     Two Standard Error Limits .

Total cases:  276     Computable first lags:  274
```

Assessing the Intervention

Figure 10.8 shows that the coefficient for the dummy variable *step135* was 0.065 in the Crest model. This means that the Crest market share jumped up by about 6.5% at week 135. Likewise, the coefficient for *step136* indicates an additional increase of 11.2% in week 136, on top of the existing level. In all, then, Crest market share increased by about 17.7% in those two weeks, and stayed at the new high level. The endorsement by the ADA, and the heavy publicity given to it by Proctor and Gamble, had a strong and lasting effect on the market share of Crest toothpaste.

The corresponding coefficients for the Colgate model in Figure 10.7 show a decrease of 5.2% in week 135 and 6.1% in week 136, for a total drop of about 11.3%. About two-thirds of Crest's gain in market share came at the expense of Colgate.

These estimates of the effect of the intervention are based on the entire series of market shares, not on a simple comparison of a few weeks' data.

Alternative Methods

As explained above, a model using step functions for the intervention dummy variables is equivalent to one using pulse functions with the *differences* in the series. A permanent step in the level of a market-share series shows up as a one-time pulse in the differences of market share from one period to the next.

An ARIMA(0,1,1) model is, in fact, a moving-average model for the differences of the original series. The expression on the left-hand side of Equation 10.2 represents differences in the level of *crest*. The ARIMA procedure works by taking differences in the original series and estimating a (0,0,1) model on those differences. In order to preserve the "shape" of the intervention you specified, *ARIMA also took differences in the predictor series.* You specified a step function as the predictor for market share. ARIMA took differences in both series and used a pulse function as the predictor for changes in market share.

You can take the differences in market share yourself if you prefer and specify an ARIMA(0,0,1) model for the differences. When you do this you are "hiding" the differencing from ARIMA. From the menus choose:

Transform
  Create Time Series...

Move *colgate* and *crest* into the New Variable(s) list. The DIFF function is already selected, so you can simply click OK to create new series *colgat_1* and *crest_1*, containing the differences in the original series.

You must supply dummy variables to describe the effect of the intervention on the series ARIMA analyzes, which is now the differences in market share. The intervention produced pulses in these differences, so you create two series to represent pulse functions. From the menus choose:

Transform
  Compute...

Type `pulse135` into the Target Variable text box. Click in the Numeric Expression text box and type (or paste) `week_ = 135`. Click OK to create this variable; then repeat the operation with `pulse136` and the expression `week_ = 136`.

To repeat the ARIMA analysis for *crest*, go back to the ARIMA dialog box, which still shows your previous specifications. Move *crest* out of the Dependent box, and put *crest_1* in its place. Move the step variables *step135* and *step136* out of the Independent(s) list, and move the pulse variables *pulse135* and *pulse136* in their place. Change the order of differencing, *d*, from 1 to 0. You have already taken differences in *crest*, *colgate*, and the intervention variables, so you do not want ARIMA to take differences again.

The output from this analysis is equivalent to that from the one performed earlier in the chapter. The *fit* series that ARIMA generates is not the same, however, because it contains predicted values for the differences in *crest*.

Predictors in Differenced ARIMA Models

The above discussion brings up a consideration worth noting:

- When the ARIMA procedure takes differences in the series you are analyzing (when the Difference parameter *d* is greater than 0), it also takes differences in any independent (predictor) variables that you specify.

Sometimes this is a feature; sometimes it is a nuisance. With intervention models this behavior is often what you want. You can set up an intervention variable that gives the effect of the intervention on the original series. If your ARIMA model requires differencing, ARIMA takes differences in your intervention variable so that it will correspond to the same type of intervention.

When you do not want ARIMA to difference your predictor variables you must take charge of the differencing yourself. If you want to specify an ARIMA model in which the dependent variable is differenced but *not* the predictor, you must do all the differencing prior to ARIMA, in the Create Time Series dialog box. Since ARIMA does not have to take differences in the dependent variable (because you used Create Time Series to do so), it will leave the independent variable or variables undifferenced also. As noted above, the *fit_* values, when the series is differenced outside of ARIMA, will be for the differenced series, not the original series.

11

Trends in the Ozone: Seasonal Regression and Weighted Least Squares

Some scientists have found that chemicals called chlorofluorocarbons (CFC's), widely used in refrigeration and other industrial processes, promote chemical reactions in the upper atmosphere that destroy the ozone that protects the earth from ultraviolet radiation. Consequently, CFC's are no longer used as aerosol propellants, and industries that use them are under pressure to convert to some other kind of technology.

In this chapter we use regression techniques to analyze a series of ozone readings from a study of this problem. Many of the problems that can occur in time-series regression analysis turn up in this series:

• Missing data.

• Strong seasonal variation.

• A change in measurement technique.

• Outliers.

• Heteroscedasticity.

Ozone Readings at Churchill

The series we are concerned with includes monthly measurements of the ozone level taken from weather balloons 15 kilometers above a weather station at Churchill, Manitoba, on Hudson Bay. The series runs from October 1973 through September 1983, although several observations are missing. A plot of the series shows the seasonal variation in the ozone readings (Figure 11.1).

Figure 11.1 Ozone readings (partial)

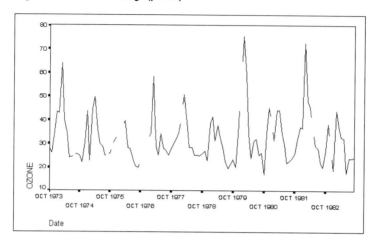

The original study of these ozone readings (Tiao et al., 1986) included data from several altitudes at many stations. In this chapter we will analyze the single series from 15 kilometers at Churchill.

We want to know whether or not the Churchill ozone readings show a trend. To do this we build a regression model, expressing the ozone level as a linear combination of other variables, including time. If the model is satisfactory, the coefficient of time indicates the trend. A negative coefficient indicates a decreasing ozone level, as predicted by environmentalists.

Defining the Seasonal Periodicity

Since the ozone readings show seasonal variation, our analysis will need to take into account the twelve-month period of seasonality. From the menus choose:

Data
  Define Dates...

This opens the Define Dates dialog box, as shown in Figure 11.2.

Figure 11.2   Define Dates dialog box

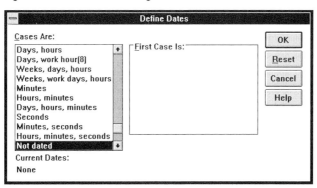

Since the dating of the series has not been defined, the Cases Are list shows Not dated. Scroll to the top of the list and click on Years, months. Text boxes appear in the First Case Is group, into which you can enter the year and month of the first case. (Notice that Trends recognizes that the periodicity of monthly data is 12.) Select the contents of the Year text box and enter 1973, and then select the contents of the Month text box and enter 10. Click on OK to define the date variables and establish the length of the seasonal period.

Replacing the Missing Data

First we must deal with the missing data. There are two considerations:

- In time series analysis, you cannot have any missing time periods, since observations must be evenly spaced. In a monthly series like this one, you must have an observation for every month—even if the observation contains missing data. You must address this question before you begin analysis with Trends.

- Once the series has a complete set of time periods, the next step is to decide how to deal with any missing observations within the series. Some Trends procedures cannot process a series that contains missing data. Seasonal Decomposition, which we use below, is one of them. Before using one of the procedures that require valid data, you must fill in reasonable values in place of the missing data, either by hand or with the Replace Missing Values procedure on the Transform menu.

The sample data file for this chapter includes a complete set of time periods for every month from October 1973 to September 1983. Suppose, however, that a month was missing from the ozone file. For example, if part of the data file looked like this (here we show year, month, and ozone level)

```
74  6  24.0
74  7  24.4
74  9  25.6
74  10 24.8
```

you would have to insert another line for the missing month, August 1974, *prior to using Trends:*

```
74  6  24.0
74  7  24.4
74  8
74  9  25.6
74  10 24.8
```

In the SPSS Data Editor, a missing value (such as that for ozone in example above) appears as a period, which represents the system-missing value. (Missing values in the Data Editor are discussed in the *SPSS Base System User's Guide.*)

We now need to decide how to handle the missing observations. From the menus choose:

Transform
  Replace Missing Values...

This opens the Replace Missing Values dialog box, as shown in Figure 11.3.

Figure 11.3   Replace Missing Values dialog box

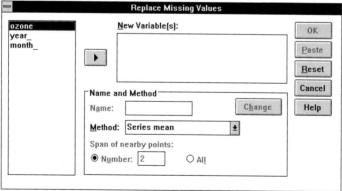

Move *ozone* into the New Variable(s) list. By default, Trends uses the series mean function, which appears as SMEAN in the New Variable(s) list. Since the ozone data are so seasonal, a value midway between the preceding and following months is likely to be a better guess, so we will use linear interpolation instead.

⬇ Select Linear interpolation from the Method drop-down list and click on Change. Then click on OK to remove the missing values in the new series *ozone_1*.

For the data above, linear interpolation supplies a value of 25 for August 1974, which is midway between the values for July and September. You can verify this and other interpolated values for *ozone_1* in the Data Editor.

Calculating a Trend Variable

We are trying to determine if there is a trend in the ozone data. Since the trend per month would be quite small, we would prefer to see the trend per year. To express the trend in parts per year, we need a variable to indicate how many years each observation is from the beginning of the study. There are several ways to compute such a variable; perhaps the simplest is to use the system variable *$casenum*, which automatically gives the sequential number of each monthly observation in the data file. Dividing it by 12 gives the number of years since the first observation. From the menus choose:

Transform
  Compute...

This opens the Compute Variable dialog box. Type `trend` in the Target Variable text box, and type `$casenum/12` in the Expression text box. Click on OK to compute the new variable.

A Change in Measurement Technique

Starting in September 1979, a newer and more sensitive measuring instrument was used to record ozone levels. We take account of this change in measurement technique with a "dummy variable," much as we did in the intervention analysis of Chapter 10. There are various ways to create this dummy variable. The most straightforward is to use two steps. Once again, from the menus choose:

Transform
  Compute...

Type techniq in the Target Variable text box. Clear the contents of the Expression text box and enter 0. Click on OK to create the variable *techniq*, which now equals 0 for all cases.

To set *techniq* equal to 1 for cases starting in September 1979, open the Compute Variable dialog box again. Select the 0 in the Numeric Expression box with the mouse, and type 1 to replace it. Then, to specify the condition under which *techniq* should be set equal to 1, click on If.... This opens the If Cases dialog box, as shown in Figure 11.4.

Figure 11.4   If Cases dialog box

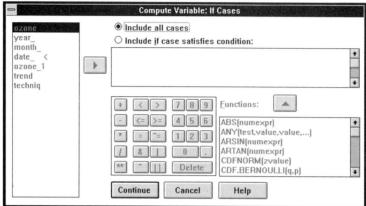

First, at the top of the dialog box select Include if case satisfies condition. Then click in the large text box and carefully build the condition, either by typing this expression:

```
year_ > 1979 | (year_ = 1979 & month_ >=9)
```

or by copying variable names and symbols, as discussed in the *SPSS Base System User's Guide*:

1. Select the variable *year_* and click on ▶ to move it into the condition box.

2. Click on the > symbol on the keypad.

3. Type 1979, or click on the numeric keys 1 9 7 9.

4. Click on the vertical bar (|), which means "or."

5. Click on the parentheses, which are immediately below the vertical bar. Notice that the cursor is inside the parentheses.

6. Select *year_* again, if it is not still selected, and move it into the expression. It will show up within the parentheses, where the cursor was positioned.

7. Continue by typing, or clicking on, the equals sign (=), 1979, and the ampersand (&).

8. Select *month_* and move it to follow the ampersand.

9. Click on the >= key, which means "greater than or equal to."

10. Finally, type (or click on) 9.

Compare the condition that you have built with that given above and correct it, if you need to. When it looks right, click on Continue and then on OK. SPSS will ask if it's OK to change the values of an existing variable, since *techniq* is already present in the data file (it equals 0 for all cases). That is what you want to do, so click on OK.

The intervention variable *techniq* is now 1 for observations where *year_* is greater than 1979 or where *year_* equals 1979 and *month_* is greater than or equal to 9. That includes all observations starting with September, 1979, when the ozone measurements began to be made with the new technique. It's a good idea to activate the Data Editor at this point and verify that the intervention variable was created correctly. It should be 0 for all the cases at the beginning of the data file, and change to 1 starting in September, 1979. If there is a problem, reopen the Compute Variable dialog box—your specifications will still be there—and set things right.

We will include *techniq* in the model not because we are interested in the effect of the intervention (as we were in Chapter 10), but because we want to evaluate the trend apart from the effect of the intervention. The dummy variable *techniq* will capture the effect of changing instruments, and the trend variable *trend* will capture any trend excluding the effect of changing instruments.

Removing Seasonality

In order to uncover any real trend in the ozone levels, we first need to account for the variation in the readings that is due to seasonal effects. For example, if ozone levels are always higher in the winter than in the summer, this would confound our estimate of the trend.

The Seasonal Decomposition procedure decomposes a seasonal series into a seasonal component, a combined trend and cycle component, and an "error" component (Makridakis, Wheelwright, & McGee, 1983). It creates four new series containing these components or combinations of them. The prefixes used in creating series names are shown in Table 11.1.

Table 11.1 Series names created by Seasonal Decomposition

Prefix	Contents	Components
saf	Seasonal Adjustment Factor	Seasonal
sas	Seasonally Adjusted Series	Original minus seasonal
stc	deSeasoned Trend and Cycle	Trend plus cycle
err	Error	Error

The Seasonal Decomposition procedure normally treats the series as the product of the seasonal, trend, and cycle components. This **multiplicative model** is appropriate when seasonal variation is greater at higher levels of the series. For series such as this one, where seasonality does not increase with the level of the series, an alternative **additive model** is available.

To carry out seasonal decomposition, Trends needs to know the periodicity (how many observations there are in a season) of the series. It takes this periodicity, 12, from the date variables defined above for the series.

To apply seasonal decomposition to *ozone_1*, the ozone series with missing data interpolated, from the menus choose:

Statistics
  Time Series ▶
    Seasonal Decomposition...

This opens the Seasonal Decomposition dialog box, as shown in Figure 11.5.

Figure 11.5   Seasonal Decomposition dialog box

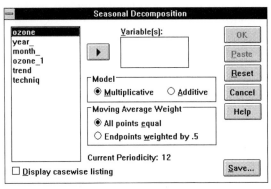

Move *ozone_1* into the Variable(s) list. Select the Additive model, and click on OK. This produces the output shown in Figure 11.6.

Figure 11.6   Output from Seasonal Decomposition

```
Results of SEASON procedure for variable OZONE_1
Additive Model.  Equal weighted MA method.  Period = 12.

                    Seasonal
           Period    index
             1      -7.522
             2      -3.253
             3        .395
             4       4.898
             5      12.652
             6      13.914
             7       7.120
             8      -1.215
             9      -3.299
            10      -6.456
            11      -8.607
            12      -8.627

The following new variables are being created:

   Name          Label

   ERR_1         Error for OZONE_1 from SEASON, MOD_2  ADD EQU 12
   SAS_1         Seas adj ser for OZONE_1 from SEASON, MOD_2  ADD EQU 12
   SAF_1         Seas factors for OZONE_1 from SEASON, MOD_2  ADD EQU 12
   STC_1         Trend-cycle for OZONE_1 from SEASON, MOD_2  ADD EQU 12
```

The seasonal index shown in the figure is the average deviation of each month's ozone level from the level that was due to the other components that month. Period 1 (which is October, since this series began in October, 1973) averaged about 7.5 units below the deseasonalized ozone level. As you can see, periods 5 and 6 (February and March) had the highest ozone levels, while periods 11 and 12 (August and September) had the lowest levels.

If you used the multiplicative model with the Seasonal Adjustment procedure, the seasonal index would be expressed as a percentage. Indexes for high-ozone months such as February and March would be above 100, while indexes for low-ozone months such as August and September would be below 100. You cannot convert directly between the additive and multiplicative seasonal indexes, since the type of model used determines how the observations for each month are averaged.

One of the new series created by Seasonal Decomposition, *saf_1*, contains these seasonal adjustment factors. Another, *sas_1*, contains the deseasonalized or seasonally adjusted series (the original levels minus the seasonal adjustment factor). We can use *sas_1* to try to determine whether there is a significant trend in ozone level.

Predicting Deseasonalized Ozone

Our next step is to estimate a regression model predicting the deseasonalized ozone level. First, change the name of the seasonally adjusted series (*sas_1*) to something that is easier to remember:

1. Activate the Data Editor window by clicking in it or by selecting the name of the data file from the Window menu.

2. Double-click on the column heading for *sas_1*. This opens the Define Variable dialog box with the variable name *sas_1* highlighted.

3. Type deseas to assign the new name, and click on OK.

Now for the regression analysis. From the menus choose:

Statistics
  Regression ▶
    Linear...

This opens the Linear Regression dialog box, as shown in Figure 11.7.

Figure 11.7   Linear Regression dialog box

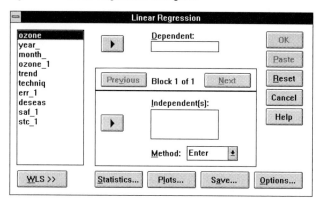

Move *deseas* into the Dependent box, and move *trend* and *techniq* into the Independent(s) list. The results of the regression analysis are shown in Figure 11.8.

Figure 11.8   Regression on deseasonalized ozone levels

```
Listwise Deletion of Missing Data

Equation Number 1    Dependent Variable..   DESEAS   Seas adj ser for OZONE_1 fr

Block Number  1.  Method:  Enter      TREND     TECHNIQ


Variable(s) Entered on Step Number
   1..    TECHNIQ
   2..    TREND


Multiple R          .23819
R Square            .05673
Adjusted R Square   .04061
Standard Error     6.95559

Analysis of Variance
                 DF      Sum of Squares      Mean Square
Regression        2           340.45174       170.22587
Residual        117          5660.48633        48.38023

F =      3.51850      Signif F =  .0328

----------------- Variables in the Equation -----------------

Variable            B         SE B        Beta        T  Sig T

TREND         -.882926      .419332    -.360412    -2.106  .0374
TECHNIQ       6.499065     2.462670     .451729     2.639  .0094
(Constant)   33.943468     1.504648               22.559  .0000
```

From Figure 11.8 you can see that:

- The coefficient of *trend*, about −0.88, represents the annual trend. Deseasonalized ozone readings declined slowly over this ten-year period. This effect is statistically significant at the 0.037 level.

- The coefficient of *techniq*, representing the effect of changing the measurement instrument, is about 6.5. Ozone readings taken with the new instrument averaged over 6 units higher than those taken with the old instrument. If you had not included an intervention variable to capture the effect of changing instruments, the decline in ozone level would have been completely masked by this artificial "increase."

- The model does not explain much of the variation. The R^2, adjusted for the number of cases and variables, is only about 0.04.

Evaluating Trend and Seasonality Simultaneously

Seasonally adjusting a series prior to evaluating the model, as done above, was once almost the only practical way of analyzing seasonal data. Modern software such as SPSS Trends enables you to build seasonal effects into a larger model so that you can evaluate *simultaneously* the seasonal effects, the trend, and the change in measuring instrument.

Dummy-Variable Regression

One way to include seasonal effects in a regression model without seasonally adjusting the data is to use dummy variables for the seasons. In our example, we use 11 dummy variables for 11 of the 12 months. The 12th month is reserved as a baseline for comparison. If you used all 12 months, the 12th one would add no information that you couldn't figure out from the first 11.

You can calculate the 11 dummy variables in several ways. The most direct way is probably to use logical expressions. Since there are so many transformations, first ask SPSS to hold all of the transformations and execute them when they're needed. From the menus choose:

Edit
  Preferences...

In the Preferences dialog box, select Calculate values before used in the Transformation & Merge Options group and click on OK. Now SPSS will collect all of your transformations and process them together, rather than reading through the data file after you enter each one. (These settings are remembered across sessions. If you usually prefer to see the results of your transformations immediately in the Data Editor, remember to go back to the Preferences dialog box later and restore that setting.)

Now create the 11 dummy variables for the effect of each month (except one). From the menus choose:

Transform
  Compute...

In the Compute Variable dialog box, the expression you used to calculate *techniq* is probably still displayed in the box beside the If... button. To clear it, click on If... and select Include all cases. Click on Continue to return to the Compute Variable dialog box, and type jan into the Target Variable text box. Select the variable *month_* and copy it into the Numeric Expression text box; then click on the equals sign (=) and on 1 on the keypad. When you click on OK, SPSS closes the dialog box.

Now it is easy to create the rest of the dummy variables. For each of them:

- Open the Compute Variable dialog box again.

- Type a variable name that corresponds to the next month in sequence—for example, *february*, *march*, *april*, and so on. Stop after *november*—you always have to omit one possibility from a set of dummy variables.

- Edit the numeric expression to indicate the correct month number for each variable: 2 for *february*, 3 for *march*, 4 for *april*, and so on.

- Click on OK for each variable in turn.

After completing the specifications for *november*, tell SPSS to go ahead and create the variables. From the menus choose:

Transform
  Run Pending Transforms

This group of transformations creates a set of 11 dummy variables that equal 1 for observations in a particular month and 0 for observations in other months.

Using the 11 dummy variables, you can analyze *ozone_1*, the original *ozone* series with missing values interpolated, and evaluate seasonality, trend, and instrument change simultaneously. From the menus choose:

Statistics
  Regression ▶
    Linear...

In the Linear Regression dialog box (Figure 11.7), move *deseas* out of the Dependent box (if it is still there), replacing it with *ozone_1*. Leave *trend* and *techniq* in the Independent(s) list, and add all 11 of the dummy month variables created above into the list as well.

Next, click on Plots... to open the Linear Regression Plots dialog box, as shown in Figure 11.9. In the Standardized Residual Plots group, select all three options: Histogram, Normal probability plot, and Casewise plot. Change the 3 to 2 to see Outliers outside 2 std. deviations.

Figure 11.9   Linear Regression Plots dialog box

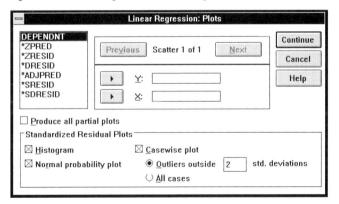

Finally, click on Save... in the main Linear Regression dialog box to open the Linear Regression Save New Variables dialog box, as shown in Figure 11.10. In the Residuals group, select Standardized.

Figure 11.11 shows the goodness-of-fit statistics and parameter estimates from this regression analysis.

Figure 11.10 Linear Regression Save New Variables dialog box

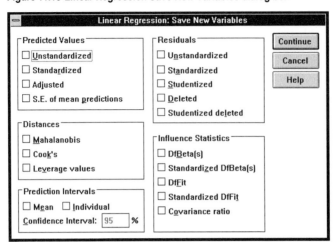

The output shows that:

- The R^2 is much higher than in Figure 11.8. Over 52% of the variation in ozone readings is predicted by this model, even after adjusting for the number of variables and cases. This improvement is largely due to the fact that the seasonal variation is included in the model and "explained" by the dummy variables, rather than being removed prior to the analysis.

- The standard error of the estimate in Figure 11.11 (7.28) is slightly higher than that in Figure 11.8 (6.96). It was easier to fit a model for the deseasonalized ozone levels. (The dummy-variable regression actually did much the same thing as Seasonal Decomposition but gave up degrees of freedom in doing so, which led to larger standard errors.)

- The coefficient of the intervention variable *techniq* has increased slightly to 6.6.

- The coefficient of the *trend* variable has increased in magnitude to about −0.91, and its t statistic of −2.04 has a significance level of 0.0438.

- Each of the dummy month variables shows the seasonal effect of that month *compared to December,* the omitted month. Since the December seasonal effect (period 3) was quite small in Figure 11.6, the coefficients of these dummy variables are pretty close to the effects estimated by Seasonal Decomposition.

- The constant term of 33.99 is the predicted ozone level at the beginning of the time period, after removing the seasonal factors.

Figure 11.11 Regression with dummy month variables

```
Listwise Deletion of Missing Data

Equation Number 1    Dependent Variable..   OZONE_1    LINT(OZONE__2) on 08 Jun 9

Block Number  1.  Method:  Enter
    TREND     TECHNIQ   JAN       FEB       MAR       APR       MAY       JUN
    JUL       AUG       SEP       OCT       NOV


Variable(s) Entered on Step Number
    1..    NOV
    2..    TECHNIQ
    3..    OCT
    4..    AUG
    5..    JUL
    6..    JUN
    7..    MAY
    8..    APR
    9..    MAR
   10..    FEB
   11..    JAN
   12..    SEP
   13..    TREND


Multiple R            .75989
R Square              .57744
Adjusted R Square     .52561
Standard Error       7.27977

Analysis of Variance
                  DF     Sum of Squares      Mean Square
Regression        13        7676.32697        590.48669
Residual         106        5617.47395         52.99504

F =      11.14230      Signif F =  .0000


        * * * *   M U L T I P L E   R E G R E S S I O N   * * * *

Equation Number 1    Dependent Variable..   OZONE_1    LINT(OZONE__2) on 08 Jun 9


----------------- Variables in the Equation -----------------

Variable          B         SE B       Beta         T    Sig T

TREND        -.908037     .445098    -.249037    -2.040   .0438
TECHNIQ      6.628768    2.605100     .309560     2.545   .0124
JAN          5.084670    3.255823     .133519     1.562   .1213
FEB         12.094340    3.256457     .317587     3.714   .0003
MAR         15.405009    3.257513     .404523     4.729   .0000
APR          7.075679    3.258991     .185802     2.171   .0322
MAY          -.743651    3.260890    -.019528     -.228   .8200
JUN         -3.902981    3.263209    -.102489    -1.196   .2343
JUL         -6.067312    3.265949    -.159323    -1.858   .0660
AUG         -8.151642    3.269107    -.214055    -2.494   .0142
SEP         -8.718849    3.260326    -.228950    -2.674   .0087
OCT         -7.694340    3.256457    -.202047    -2.363   .0200
NOV         -4.039670    3.255823    -.106070     1.241   .2174
(Constant)  33.988670    2.662917                12.764   .0000


End Block Number   1   All requested variables entered.
```

Residuals Analysis

Figure 11.12 shows the residuals analysis for the above regression. It includes a list of the outliers, giving their case numbers, ozone levels, predicted values, and residuals. Three of the residuals (cases 17, 77, and 101) are fairly large, greater than 3 times 7.28, which is the standard error of the estimate in Figure 11.11. That is more than you would expect from only 120 observations. Consequently, the histogram of standardized residuals in Figure 11.13 shows noticeable departures from normality. (Specifically, it shows **positive kurtosis:** too many observations in the extreme tails, which therefore inflate the standard deviation and create the impression of too many observations close to the mean.)

Figure 11.12 Residuals analysis

```
                * * * *   M U L T I P L E   R E G R E S S I O N   * * * *

     Equation Number 1    Dependent Variable..   OZONE_1   LINT(OZONE__2) on 08 Jun 9


     Casewise Plot of Standardized Residual

     Outliers = 2.     *: Selected   M: Missing

             -5.     -2.  2.     5.
      Case #  O:.......: :.......:O   OZONE_1      *PRED      *RESID
         6   .         ..*         .    64.00     48.9397     15.0603
        17   .      *  ..          .    22.70     44.7966    -22.0966
        76   .         ..*         .    54.55     39.9512     14.5988
        77   .         ..     *    .    75.20     46.8852     28.3148
       101   .         ..     *    .    72.50     45.0691     27.4309
       112   .       * ..          .    18.80     37.2271    -18.4271


           6 Outliers found.


                * * * *   M U L T I P L E   R E G R E S S I O N   * * * *

     Equation Number 1    Dependent Variable..   OZONE_1   LINT(OZONE__2) on 08 Jun 9


     Residuals Statistics:

                   Min      Max    Mean   Std Dev    N

     *PRED      20.4645  50.1202  32.1458   8.0316  120
     *RESID    -22.0966  28.3148    .0000   6.8706  120
     *ZPRED     -1.4544   2.2380    .0000   1.0000  120
     *ZRESID    -3.0353   3.8895    .0000    .9438  120

     Total Cases =      120
```

Figure 11.13 Histogram of standardized residuals

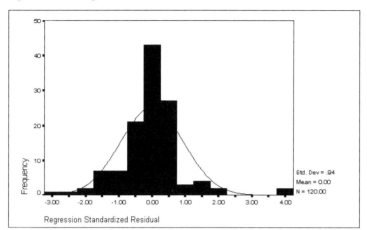

Figure 11.14 Normal probability plot

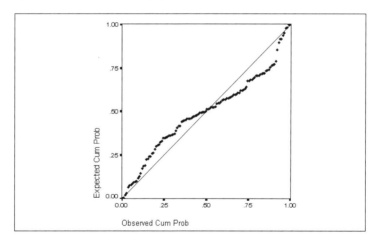

The normal probability plot in Figure 11.14 also shows that observed values of the residuals at the top end of the distribution are greater than those expected if the residuals were normally distributed.

Outliers can have a disproportionate influence on trend estimates. Significance tests on regression coefficients depend on the assumption of normally distributed residuals and hence are also sensitive to outliers. Since we are primarily interested in estimating the trend and testing its significance, we will smooth out the outliers and reestimate the regression equation.

Regression with Smoothed Outliers

The residuals from this last regression model were saved in the working data file as a new series named *zre_1*, so it is easy to identify the observations that are outliers. We first substitute the system-missing value for the outliers and then use the Remove Missing Values procedure to fill in values using linear interpolation, as before. Then we repeat the regression, requesting some additional plots of the residuals.

You could use the procedures on the Transform menu to delete the problematic cases. Instead, we'll do so directly in the Data Editor. (Tampering with data like this is not something that should be done without good cause. You might, for example, take a look at the original data and discover that there had been problems recording data for the outlying cases. In order to proceed with the demonstration of time series analysis with Trends, we will assume that a good reason has been discovered for deleting the outlying data values.)

Activate the Data Editor window, by clicking in it or selecting the name of the data file from the Window menu. Click on the horizontal scroll bar at the bottom of the window until the column containing the residuals, *zre_1*, is visible. Now scroll down through the cases by clicking on the vertical scroll bar. If you want to replicate the analysis in the rest of this chapter, look for cases where the value of *zre_1* is greater than 2.5 or less than –2.5. (These are cases 17, 77, 101, and 112, as reported in Figure 11.12.) Each time you find such a case, click on its case number at the left side of the Data Editor window. This highlights the entire case and scrolls the window back to the far left. Click in the highlighted case's cell for *ozone_1*, and press (Del) and (↵Enter) to delete the offending value.

Once you have deleted the bad data values, you can interpolate more reasonable values in their place. From the menus choose:

Transform
  Replace Missing Values...

Scroll to the bottom of the source variable list, highlight *ozone_1*, and click on [▶] to move it into the New Variable(s) list. The expression that appears there is not what you want, so you must fix things up in the Name and Method group. First, the name:

- To simplify the next round of regression analysis (and to avoid unattractive variable names), delete one of the two underscores in the Name text box, leaving only the original variable name, *ozone_1*. (Choose a different name entirely if you like.)

- Select Linear interpolation from the Method drop-down list.

- Click on Change. The resulting dialog box is shown in Figure 11.15.

Figure 11.15 Replace Missing Values dialog box

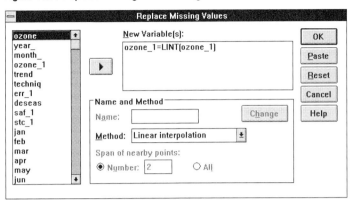

When you click on OK to execute this transformation, Trends asks you to confirm that it is OK to change the existing variable (*ozone_1*). When you confirm, it reports the number of missing values that it has replaced.

Now repeat the regression analysis. From the menus choose:

Statistics
  Regression ▶
    Linear...

Your previous specifications are still in the Linear Regression dialog box. The Dependent variable is still *ozone_1*, so if you used *ozone_1* as the new variable name in the Replace Missing Values procedure, as suggested, you can leave it alone. (If you chose a new variable name, move it into the Dependent box in place of *ozone_1*.)

Before running the Linear Regression procedure, click on Plots... to open the Linear Regression Plots dialog box, as shown in Figure 11.9. Select **zresid* in the source variable list and move it into the Y box, and then select **adjpred* and move it into the X box. This will produce a scatterplot of the standardized residuals with the adjusted predicted values.

Figure 11.16 shows the basic output from the regression analysis after smoothing the outliers. It is similar to that from the previous regression analysis (Figure 11.11), but notice that:

- The R^2 for the equation has improved markedly, as you should expect when you remove the cases that are farthest from the regression line.

- The coefficient of the intervention variable *techniq* is slightly smaller, but its standard error is much smaller. The effect of changing measurement technique is now statistically significant at the 0.01 level.

- The coefficient of *trend* is slightly smaller, but its standard error is much smaller. It is now statistically significant at the 0.01 level.

Figure 11.16 Regression with smoothed outliers

```
Listwise Deletion of Missing Data

Equation Number 1    Dependent Variable..   OZONE_1   LINT(OZONE_1) on 09 Jun 93

Block Number  1.  Method:  Enter
    TREND    TECHNIQ  JAN       FEB       MAR       APR       MAY       JUN
    JUL      AUG      SEP       OCT       NOV


Variable(s) Entered on Step Number
    1..    NOV
    2..    TECHNIQ
    3..    OCT
    4..    AUG
    5..    JUL
    6..    JUN
    7..    MAY
    8..    APR
    9..    MAR
   10..    FEB
   11..    JAN
   12..    SEP
   13..    TREND


Multiple R            .83152
R Square              .69143
Adjusted R Square     .65359
Standard Error       5.50728

Analysis of Variance
                    DF      Sum of Squares      Mean Square
Regression          13         7204.14374        554.16490
Residual           106         3214.99449         30.33014

F =      18.27110      Signif F =  .0000


        * * * *   M U L T I P L E   R E G R E S S I O N   * * * *

Equation Number 1    Dependent Variable..   OZONE_1   LINT(OZONE_1) on 09 Jun 93


----------------- Variables in the Equation -----------------

Variable           B         SE B       Beta         T    Sig T

TREND        -.884673     .336725    -.274064    -2.627   .0099
TECHNIQ     5.567655    1.970806     .293693     2.825   .0056
JAN         6.825223    2.463090     .202445     2.771   .0066
FEB         9.382945    2.463570     .278310     3.809   .0002
MAR        15.399168    2.464369     .456759     6.249   .0000
APR         7.067891    2.465487     .209643     2.867   .0050
MAY         -.753386    2.466924    -.022346     -.305   .7607
JUN        -3.914664    2.468678    -.116114    -1.586   .1158
JUL        -6.080941    2.470751    -.180368    -2.461   .0155
AUG        -8.167218    2.473140    -.242250    -3.302   .0013
SEP        -8.630261    2.466497    -.255985    -3.499   .0007
OCT        -7.690445    2.463570    -.228108    -3.122   .0023
NOV        -4.037723    2.463090    -.119764    -1.639   .1041
(Constant) 34.302134    2.014546                17.027   .0000


End Block Number   1   All requested variables entered.
```

Residuals Analysis

Figure 11.17 through Figure 11.20 show the residuals analysis for the regression after the outliers were smoothed. The histogram in Figure 11.18 and the normal probability plot in Figure 11.19, although not perfect, look much better than in the previous analysis, prior to smoothing of the outliers.

Figure 11.17 Residuals analysis with smoothed outliers

```
            * * * *   M U L T I P L E   R E G R E S S I O N   * * * *

Equation Number 1    Dependent Variable..   OZONE_1   LINT(OZONE_1) on 09 Jun 93


Casewise Plot of Standardized Residual

Outliers = 2.    *: Selected   M: Missing

          -5.    -2.  2.    5.
  Case #   O:.......: :.......:O   OZONE_1      *PRED      *RESID
       6   .           .. *     .    64.00    49.2590     14.7410
      42   .           ..*      .    58.30    46.6049     11.6951
      66   .        * ..        .    31.10    44.8356    -13.7356
      76   .           .. *     .    54.55    41.0921     13.4579
      77   .           .. *     .    56.88    43.5761     13.2989
      87   .           ..*      .    45.10    33.4559     11.6441
      89   .         *..        .    31.50    42.6914    -11.1914


       7 Outliers found.



            * * * *   M U L T I P L E   R E G R E S S I O N   * * * *

Equation Number 1    Dependent Variable..   OZONE_1   LINT(OZONE_1) on 09 Jun 93


Residuals Statistics:

                Min      Max     Mean  Std Dev    N

*PRED       20.9006  49.5186  32.0654   7.7807  120
*ZPRED      -1.4349   2.2431    .0000   1.0000  120
*SEPRED      1.7970   1.9773   1.8801    .0605  120
*ADJPRED    20.7335  49.2138  32.0624   7.8054  120
*RESID     -13.7356  14.7410    .0000   5.1978  120
*ZRESID     -2.4941   2.6766    .0000    .9438  120
*SRESID     -2.6722   2.8679    .0003   1.0047  120
*DRESID    -15.7681  16.9223    .0030   5.8907  120
*SDRESID    -2.7540   2.9719    .0011   1.0183  120
*MAHAL      11.6784  14.3475  12.8917    .8970  120
*COOK D       .0000    .0869    .0095    .0163  120
*LEVER        .0981    .1206    .1083    .0075  120

Total Cases =     120
```

Figure 11.18 Histogram of standardized residuals after smoothing of outliers

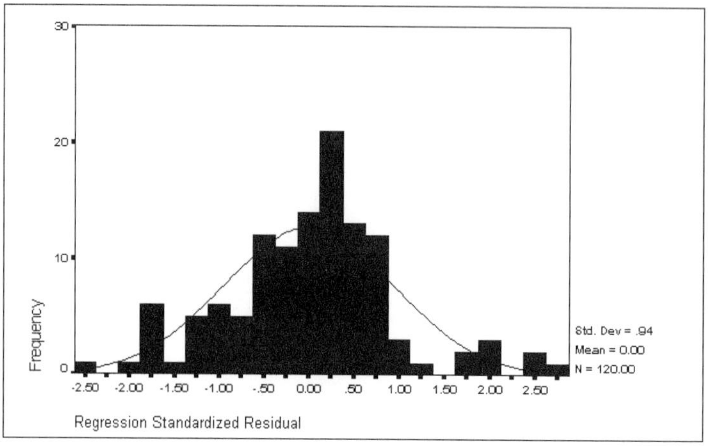

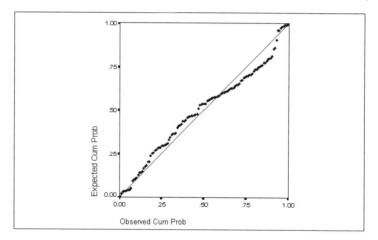

Figure 11.19 Normal probability plot of standardized residuals after smoothing of outliers

The scatterplot in Figure 11.20 compares the residuals (on the vertical axis) with the pre-dicted values (on the horizontal axis). The plot shows a funnel shape: the variance of the points at the right is more than the variance of the points at the left.

The shape of the plot of the residuals with the predicted values indicates that the re-siduals for observations with high predicted ozone levels have more variance than the residuals for observations with low predicted ozone levels. Ordinary regression analysis assumes that the residuals have constant variance. This regression model evidently violates that assumption—in technical language, the model shows **heteroscedasticity.**

Figure 11.20 Scatterplots of residuals with predicted values

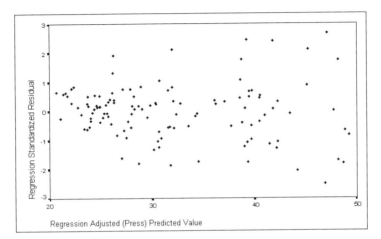

Heteroscedasticity

The variance of the regression errors increases with the predicted value. The components of the predicted value are *trend*, the intervention variable *techniq* and the 11 dummy month variables. We have already seen that ozone levels vary with the seasons, averaging roughly 20 points higher in February and March than in August and September. (This is from the coefficients in Figure 11.16.) We know from experience that weather patterns are more variable in winter—when ozone levels are high—than in summer. Perhaps the pattern in the scatterplot is due to greater variance in ozone levels during the winter months. This is easy to check.

Plotting Residuals by Month

The residuals from this last regression were saved in the series *zre_2*. Figure 11.21 shows these residuals plotted against the month of the observation. This is not a time series plot; all the Januaries are plotted together, all the Februaries, and so on, so that you can evaluate the *variance* of the residuals in each month. To obtain such a plot, from the menus choose:

Graphs
  Scatter...

In the Scatterplot dialog box, select Simple and click on Define to open the Simple Scatterplot dialog box. Move *zre_2* into the Y Axis box, move *month_* into the X Axis box, and click on OK.

Figure 11.21 Residual variance by month

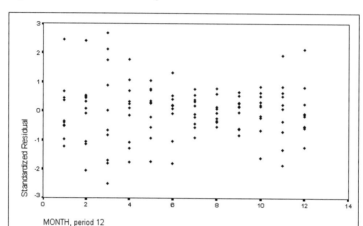

This plot shows a dramatic sideways hourglass pattern. The residuals are spread out vertically in the early months, squeezed together during the summer months 7–9, and spread out again at the end of the year. Ozone levels at Churchill fluctuated more in the winter—when they were generally high—than in the summer.

The heteroscedasticity of the residuals violates one of the assumptions of ordinary least-squares regression, so some of the statistical results of the analysis above may not be reliable. To obtain reliable results, you must use *weighted least squares.*

Weighted Least Squares

Weighted least squares, a procedure in the SPSS Professional Statistics option, performs regression analysis for observations (not necessarily time series) that are measured with varying precision. In the current example, you assume that ozone levels really are a linear function of *trend, techniq,* and the dummy month variables, and that the residuals have a different variance in each month due to transient conditions or measurement problems. Observations from August, a month with small residual variance, will count more heavily in determining the regression equation than observations from March, a month with large residual variance. This is reasonable, since the observations from

March are likely to be farther from the typical March value than observations from August are from the typical August value.

Calculating Residual Variance by Month

The plot in Figure 11.21 shows that the error variance differs according to the month of the observation. **Weighted least squares** (WLS) is a technique that uses this information, giving more weight to the precise observations and less weight to the highly variable observations. To use WLS, you must form a series that shows how much error you expect in each observation. The first step is to calculate how widely the ozone levels are spread within each month. From the menus choose:

Data
  Aggregate...

This opens the Aggregate Data dialog box, as shown in Figure 11.22.

Figure 11.22 Aggregate Data dialog box

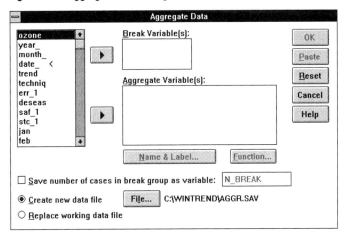

- Select *month_* and move it into the Break Variable(s) list.
- Select the residual variable from the last regression, *zre_2*, and move it into the Aggregate Variable(s) list. It appears within an expression involving the MEAN function, which is not what you want; but first take care of the new variable name.
- Click on Name & Label.... In the Name and Label dialog box, type `sdozone` into the Name text box. If you wish, type `Standard Deviation of Ozone Residuals` into the Label text box. Click on Continue.

- Click on Function..., and in the Aggregate Function dialog box, select Standard deviation. Click on Continue.
- The expression in the Aggregate Variable(s) list now reads sdozone=sd(zre_2).
- Be sure that the Create new data file option is selected in the Aggregate Data dialog box. Notice the default filename beside the File... button. It should say *aggr.sav*, possibly with a path preceding the name. Click on OK.

SPSS quickly calculates the standard deviation of the residuals within each month and saves them in a data file named *aggr.sav*. To use them, you need to combine them with the ozone series in the Data Editor. First, sort the data in the Data Editor. From the menus choose:

Data
  Sort Cases...

In the Sort Cases dialog box, select *month_* and move it into the Sort By list. Click on OK to sort the data file. Next, from the menus choose:

Data
  Merge Files ▶
    Add Variables...

This opens the Add Variables Read File dialog box, from which you select the data file (*aggr.sav*) containing the variable or variables that you want to add to the Data Editor. Locate and select it, and then click on Continue. This opens the Add Variables From dialog box.

- Select Match cases on key variables in sorted files.
- Below that option, select External file is keyed table.
- Select *month_* in the Excluded Variables list, and click on the lower ▶ button to move it onto the Key Variable(s) list.

If you like, you can scroll through the variables that appear in the New Working Data File list. Except for *sdozone*, all of the variables are marked with an asterisk (*) to indicate that they come from the working data file—that is, the file in the Data Editor. The variable *sdozone* is marked with a plus sign (+) to indicate that it comes from *aggr.sav*, the file named in the Aggregate Data dialog box.

When you click on OK, SPSS displays a warning that it will fail to add the variables if the data files are not sorted. Since they are sorted, click on OK. SPSS then asks if it should save your working data file before merging in the new variable. There is no need to do so; click on No.

If you changed your preferences above, as suggested, to Calculate values before used, all the cells in the Data Editor will be cleared at this point. Now, from the menus choose:

Transform
  Run Pending Transforms

to merge in the new variable. (You may want to switch your preference back.)

Once SPSS has added the new variable *sdozone* to your data file, it is a good idea to sort the observations back into their natural order. From the menus choose:

Data
  Sort Cases...

Scroll down the source variable list, select *year_*, and move it into the Sort By list. Then select *month_* and move it into the Sort By list below *year_*. Both variable names should be followed by (A) on that list. Click on OK to sort the cases back into chronological order. It is always wise to keep time series observations in order by date, since many Trends procedures assume that the file is in order.

These file-manipulation procedures are explained fully and examples are given in the SPSS Base system documentation.

The Weight Estimation Procedure

The Weight Estimation procedure in the SPSS Professional Statistics option helps you estimate the power to which a source variable should be raised in order to measure the precision of each observation. Specifically, it seeks to measure the variance of the measurement of the dependent variable for each observation.

Since the series *sdres* contains the estimated standard deviation of each month's residuals, the best power should be about 2.0 (the variance of the residuals is the second power of our estimates of their standard deviation). To be safe, we specify a search range from 1.0 to 2.6, increasing delta by 0.2 each time. From the menus choose:

Statistics
  Regression ▶
    Weight Estimation...

This opens the Weight Estimation dialog box, as shown in Figure 11.23.

Figure 11.23 Weight Estimation dialog box

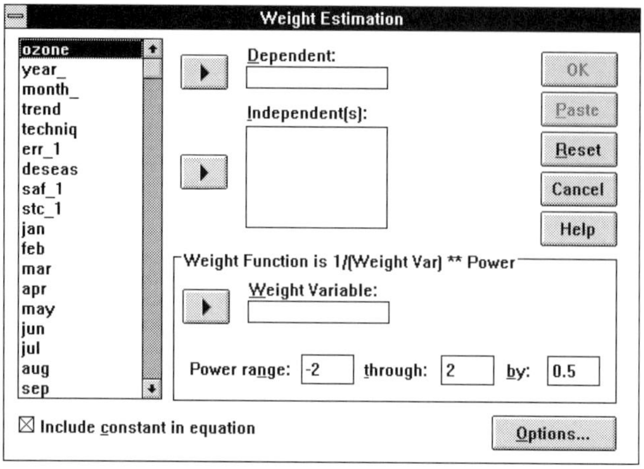

Move *ozone_1* into the Dependent box. Move *trend*, *techniq*, and the 11 dummy month variables into the Independent(s) list. Move *sdozone* into the Weight Variable box, since we suspect that the variance of the ozone measurements is some power of this variable. In the Power range text boxes, specify 1 through 2.6 by 0.2. This specification causes Trends to estimate the regression equation nine times, using exponents of 1.0, 1.2, ..., 2.4, 2.6.

   With all the calculations, this procedure will take a while to run. Before running it, click on Options..., and in the Weight Estimation Options dialog box, select Save best weight as new variable and click on Continue. Make sure that Include constant in equation is checked in the Weight Estimation dialog box, and click on OK. Some of the results are shown in Figure 11.24.

Figure 11.24 Weighted least-squares estimation

```
Source variable.. SDOZONE              Dependent variable.. OZONE_1

Log-likelihood Function = -354.636609    POWER value =  1.000
Log-likelihood Function = -352.851120    POWER value =  1.200
Log-likelihood Function = -351.381577    POWER value =  1.400
Log-likelihood Function = -350.236678    POWER value =  1.600
Log-likelihood Function = -349.424992    POWER value =  1.800
Log-likelihood Function = -348.954770    POWER value =  2.000
Log-likelihood Function = -348.833703    POWER value =  2.200
Log-likelihood Function = -349.068632    POWER value =  2.400
Log-likelihood Function = -349.665231    POWER value =  2.600

The Value of POWER Maximizing Log-likelihood Function =  2.200


Source variable..    SDOZONE            POWER value =  2.200

Dependent variable.. OZONE_1

Listwise Deletion of Missing Data

Multiple R           .83007
R Square             .68901
Adjusted R Square    .65087
Standard Error      5.56823

              Analysis of Variance:

               DF    Sum of Squares    Mean Square

Regression     13       7281.5659       560.12045
Residuals     106       3286.5541        31.00523

F =     18.06536      Signif F =   .0000

------------------ Variables in the Equation ------------------

Variable        B         SE B        Beta        T   Sig T

TREND       -.546957     .239348    -.240705   -2.285  .0243
TECHNIQ     3.045785    1.398132     .228900    2.178  .0316
JAN         6.797080    2.465532     .193685    2.757  .0069
FEB         9.326660    2.709015     .228904    3.443  .0008
MAR        15.314739    3.717634     .246239    4.119  .0001
APR         6.955319    2.526084     .190546    2.753  .0069
MAY         -.894101    2.198795    -.031509    -.407  .6851
JUN        -4.083521    2.190418    -.145173   -1.864  .0651
JUL        -6.277942    1.840909    -.353733   -3.410  .0009
AUG        -8.392362    1.757325    -.568371   -4.776  .0000
SEP        -8.631361    1.820996    -.502824   -4.740  .0000
OCT        -7.634160    2.023948    -.323250   -3.772  .0003
NOV        -4.009580    2.540083    -.108782   -1.579  .1174
(Constant) 33.706733    1.764436                19.103  .0000

Log-likelihood Function = -348.833703

The following now variables are being created:

   Name       Label

   WGT_2      Weight for OZONE_1 from WLS, MOD_4  SDOZONE** -2.200
```

The output shows that:

- The best-fitting equation used a power of 2.2, about what we expected.
- The adjusted R^2 is still about 0.65.

- The estimated effect of changing measurement technique is now only 3.04, somewhat smaller than with ordinary least squares.
- The trend estimate is now only about −0.55 points per year, which has a statistical significance of 0.0243.
- The constant—the estimated value at the beginning of the time period, with seasonal effect removed—is 33.71.

The estimates have changed again, this time showing a smaller trend and a smaller increase due to the new measurement technique. Evidently, less reliable observations made in the highly variable winter months had contributed to the trend and intervention estimates from ordinary least squares (Figure 11.16). We should expect the weighted least-squares estimates to be the better ones.

Our conclusion, then, is that over this decade the ozone level at 15 kilometers over Churchill was decreasing by about 0.55 points (about 1 1/2%) each year.

Residuals Analysis with Weighted Least Squares

You can take the regression weights from the Weight Estimation procedure and use them with the powerful facilities for residual analysis in the Linear Regression procedure. The steps are:

1. Run Weight Estimation, as above, specifying a power range to find the best value. Note the name of the series created by Weight Estimation (*wgt_2* in Figure 11.24).

2. Open the Linear Regression dialog box and specify the dependent variable *ozone_1* and the independent variables *trend*, *techniq*, and *january* through *november*.

3. Click on WLS>> and move the newly created weighting variable (*wgt_2*) into the WLS Weight box.

4. Click on Save..., and in the Linear Regression Save New Variables dialog box, select Unstandardized in both the Predicted Values group and the Residuals group.

5. Run the procedure.

The output from the Linear Regression procedure is not shown. The regression statistics are identical to those reported by the Weight Estimation procedure.

For residual analysis, you must transform the residuals (saved in variable *res_1*) and the predicted values (saved in variable *pre_1*) before generating diagnostic plots (Draper & Smith, 1981; Montgomery & Peck, 1982). From the menus choose:

Transform
  Compute...

In the Compute Variable dialog box, type `pred` in the Target Variable text box. To build the expression for the necessary transformation:

1. Select *pre_1* from the source variable list and move it into the Numeric Expression box.

2. Click on the asterisk (*) on the keypad.

3. Scroll down the Functions list to SQRT(numexpr). Select it and then click on ▲ to move it into the Numeric Expression box.

4. With the question mark in parentheses highlighted, select *wgt_2* from the source variable list and click on ▶ so that it replaces the question mark.

The numeric expression for *pred* now reads pre_1 * SQRT(wgt_2). Click on OK to calculate the weighted predicted values.

Now it is easy to calculate the weighted residuals. Open the Compute Variable dialog box again and type `resid` in the Target Variable text box. Select the variable name *pre_1* in the Numeric Expression box; then select *res_1* from the source variable list and click on ▶ so that it replaces *pre_1*. The numeric expression for *resid* now reads res_1 * SQRT(wgt_2). Click on OK. If necessary, from the menus choose:

Transform
  Run Pending Transforms

to calculate the weighted residuals.

To check the normality of the transformed residuals, from the menus choose:

Graphs
  Normal P-P...

In the Normal P-P Plots dialog box, move *resid* into the Variables list. The resulting plot is shown in Figure 11.25. It is noticeably better than the plot of residuals from the ordinary least-squares analysis shown in Figure 11.19.

Figure 11.25 Normal probability plot of transformed residuals

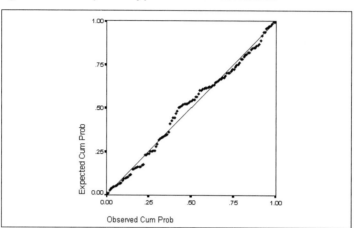

Finally, to check that weighted least squares has solved the problem of heteroscedasticity observed in Figure 11.20, from the menus choose:

Graphs
  Scatter...

In the Scatterplot dialog box, select Simple. Put *resid* on the Y axis and *pred* on the X axis. The resulting chart (Figure 11.26) does not show the heteroscedasticity observed earlier, despite the irregular distribution of *pred*.

Figure 11.26 Scatterplot of residuals against predicted values

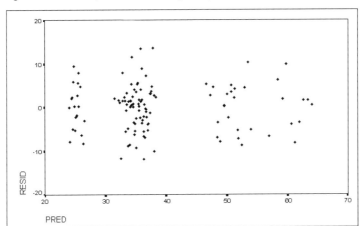

It is also a good idea to plot residuals against important independent variables. Figure 11.27 shows a plot of *resid* against *trend*, the independent variable whose effect we are primarily interested in. Once again, there is no apparent pattern in this plot.

Figure 11.27 Scatterplot of residuals against trend

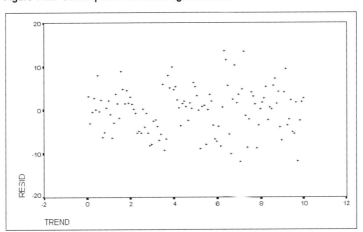

How to Obtain Seasonal Decomposition

The Seasonal Decomposition procedure splits the variation in a periodic time series into a seasonal component, a combined trend and cycle component, and a residual. It normally creates new variables containing these components, plus a variable containing the seasonally adjusted series (the original series minus the seasonal component).

The minimum specification is one or more numeric variables for which a seasonal periodicity has been defined. You must define the periodicity (with the Define Dates procedure on the Data menu, or by using the command syntax for DATE) before you can use this procedure.

- The series cannot contain any missing values. You must substitute nonmissing for missing data to use this procedure, perhaps with the Replace Missing Values procedure on the Transform menu.

To apply Seasonal Decomposition to your data, from the menus choose:

Statistics
  Time Series ▶
    Seasonal Decomposition...

If the periodicity of the working data file is defined, this menu selection opens the Seasonal Decomposition dialog box, as shown in Figure 11.28. The current periodicity is displayed in the dialog box.

Figure 11.28 Seasonal Decomposition dialog box

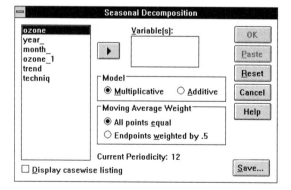

The numeric variables in your data file appear in the source variable list. Select one or more variables and move them into the Variable(s) list. To analyze the seasonal variation in the selected variables with the default multiplicative model, treating all points equally, click on OK. This creates four new series for each selected variable, adding them to your working data file.

To see the decomposition for each observation, select Display casewise listing. This produces a one-line summary listing the four new series along with some intermediate steps in calculating them.

To specify the model by which seasonal and nonseasonal components are combined, select one of the Model alternatives:

○ **Multiplicative.** The seasonal component is a factor by which the seasonally adjusted series is multiplied to yield the original series. In effect, Trends estimates seasonal components that are proportional to the overall level of the series. Observations without seasonal variation have a seasonal component of 1. This is the default.

○ **Additive.** The seasonal component is a term that is added to the seasonally adjusted series to yield the original series. In effect, Trends estimates seasonal components that do not depend on the overall level of the series. Observations without seasonal variation have a seasonal component of 0.

The Moving Average Weight group controls the calculation of moving averages for series with odd periodicity:

○ **All points equal.** Moving averages are calculated with a span equal to the periodicity and with all points weighted equally. This method is always used if the periodicity is odd.

○ **Endpoints weighted by .5**. Moving averages for series with even periodicity are calculated with a span equal to the periodicity plus 1, and with the endpoints of the span weighted by 0.5.

Saving Seasonal Components and Residuals

By default, the Seasonal Decomposition procedure creates four new series for each selected variable, adding them to your working data file as new variables. The new series have names beginning with the following prefixes:

saf   Seasonal adjustment factors, representing seasonal variation. For the multiplicative model, the value 1 represents the absence of seasonal variation; for the additive model, the value 0 represents the absence of seasonal variation.

sas   Seasonally adjusted series, representing the original series with seasonal variation removed.

stc   Smoothed trend-cycle component, a smoothed version of the seasonally adjusted series which shows both trend and cyclic components.

err   The residual component of the series for a particular observation.

To suppress the creation of these new series, or to add them to the working data file as temporary variables only, click on Save... in the Seasonal Decomposition dialog box. This opens the Season Save dialog box, as shown in Figure 11.29.

Figure 11.29 Season Save dialog box

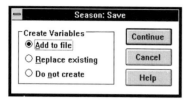

Create Variables. To control the creation of new variables, you can choose one of the following alternatives:

○ **Add to file.** The new series created by Seasonal Decomposition are saved as regular variables in your working data file. Variable names are formed from a three-letter prefix, an underscore, and a number. This is the default.

○ **Replace existing.** The new series created by Seasonal Decomposition are saved as temporary variables in your working data file. At the same time, any existing temporary variables created by Trends procedures are dropped. Variable names are formed from a three-letter prefix, a pound sign (#), and a number.

○ **Do not create.** The new variables are not added to the working data file.

Additional Features Available with Command Syntax

You can customize your seasonal decomposition if you paste your selections to a syntax window and edit the resulting SEASON command syntax. As an additional feature, you can specify any periodicity within the SEASON command, rather than select one of the alternatives offered by the Define Dates procedure. See the Syntax Reference section of *SPSS Professional Statistics* for command syntax rules and for complete WLS command syntax.

12 Telephone Connections in Wisconsin: Seasonal ARIMA

In Chapter 11, we used dummy variables to estimate a regression model that included seasonal variation. Here we will extend our earlier work with ARIMA models to include seasonal variation.

Seasonal ARIMA models, particularly those involving seasonal moving averages, require significantly more computation than nonseasonal models. Calculation of the partial autocorrelation function (PACF) is also slow at the large lags that are needed to identify seasonal ARIMA models. Commands in the example session for this chapter take somewhat more time than those in the sessions for other chapters.

The Wisconsin Telephone Series

The customer base of the Wisconsin Telephone Company varies from month to month as new customers are connected and old customers are disconnected. The numbers of connections and disconnections are a matter of public record and have been analyzed by Thompson and Tiao (1971). Connections always exceed disconnections; our goal is to predict the growth in the customer base.

We will develop a model based on the 190 observations from January 1951 through October 1966, reserving an additional 25 observations through November 1968 as a validation period for the model. First, we define the dates and periodicity of the data. From the menus choose:

Data
  Define Dates...

In the Define Dates dialog box, scroll to the top of the Cases Are list and select Years, months. In the First Case Is group, specify 1951 as the year, leaving the month set to 1. Click on OK.

Next, define the estimation period for the analysis. From the menus choose:

Data
  Select Cases...

In the Select Cases dialog box, select Based on time or case range, and click on Range... to open the Select Cases Range dialog box, as shown in Figure 12.1.

Figure 12.1   Select Cases Range dialog box

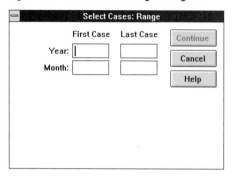

Leave the text boxes for First Case blank; click in the Year text box for Last Case, or simply press (Tab→) twice. Type 1966, and then click in (or tab to) the Month text box and type 10. This establishes the estimation period.

Plotting the Series

The two series are named *connect* and *dsconect*. Figure 12.2 shows a plot of both series.

Figure 12.2   Connections and disconnections

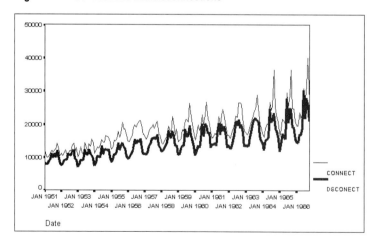

Several things are evident from the plot:

- Both series have distinct seasonal patterns, with peaks around September and valleys around January or February.
- The series follow one another; they are not independent.
- The series show a long-term upward trend.
- Variability of the series increases as the level of the series rises.

Stationary Variance and the Log Transformation

The techniques of ARIMA modeling assume stationarity—that is, over the course of the series, both the short-term mean and the short-term variance are constant. When the mean is not constant, you can usually stabilize it by taking differences in the series, but differencing will not stabilize the variance. For series such as this one, in which the variance is larger when the mean is larger, a log transformation often makes the variance constant. Most SPSS Trends procedures can perform log transformations "on the fly," leaving the original series unchanged, so you do not have to transform the data permanently.

Calculating the Growth Ratio

To analyze growth, we will compute a single series representing the ratio of connections to disconnections. From the menus choose:

Transform
  Compute...

In the Compute Variable dialog box, type `ratio` in the Target Variable text box. Select connect from the source variable list and click on ▶. Then type a slash (/), or click on the slash (/) on the keypad. Finally, select disconnect and click on ▶. Click on OK to compute the new variable *ratio* as the ratio of telephone connections to disconnections.

Figure 12.3 shows a plot of the *ratio* series.

Figure 12.3   Ratio of connections to disconnections

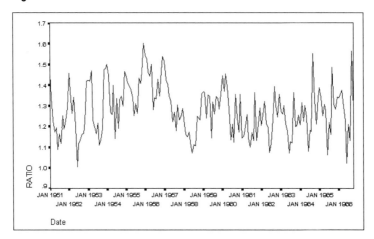

Like the *connect* and *dsconect* series, *ratio* is seasonal—although not as dramatically as the two separate series—and it also shows increasing variability in those years when the ratio of connections to disconnections is higher. The trend is less pronounced, but it appears likely that some form of differencing will be required to achieve a stationary mean.

You might think, incidentally, that the net difference between connections and disconnections would be easier to interpret than the ratio. We analyze the ratio primarily because Thompson and Tiao did so.

Seasonal ARIMA Models

Seasonal ARIMA is more complex than nonseasonal ARIMA, but it has the same components as regular ARIMA:

- A seasonal autoregressive model expresses the current observation as a linear function of the current disturbance and one or more previous observations.

- Seasonal differencing transforms the data by subtracting the observation lagged by the seasonal period. For monthly data, you subtract the observation from the same month of the previous year. Just as regular differencing reduces the length of a series by 1, seasonal differencing reduces the series by one period.

- A seasonal moving average model expresses the current observation as a linear function of the current disturbance and one or more previous disturbances.

For a seasonal ARIMA model, you must specify the period. A monthly series such as *ratio* usually has a seasonal period of 12, although other periods are possible. Since the Define Dates procedure specified year and month, Trends assumes a periodicity of 12 for *ratio*.

The traditional notation for seasonal ARIMA models places the length of the seasonal period after the set of parentheses containing p, d, and q. Thus, a model with a period of 12 that is a first-order seasonal moving average after it has been seasonally differenced once is termed seasonal ARIMA(0,1,1) 12.

The precise form of a seasonal ARIMA model is best expressed in equations with the "backshift" operator B we used in Chapter 10. The form of the equations is virtually identical to that for nonseasonal models. Recall that B simply means to look at the series shifted back to the previous time point. Thus, for a series *ratio*, $B(ratio_t)$ means $ratio_{t-1}$. To get seasonal backshifts, simply "multiply" the operator as many times as necessary. $B^2(ratio)$ is a backshift of $B(ratio)$, so it is the value of *ratio* two observations earlier. For monthly data, then, $B^{12}(ratio)$ is the value of *ratio* twelve observations earlier—the seasonal backshift.

To express a seasonal ARIMA(0, 0, 1) 12 (seasonal moving average model with period 12), you simply use B^{12} in place of B in the equation for a regular moving average model:

$$series_t = (1 - \theta B^{12}) disturbance_t \qquad \text{Equation 12.1}$$

Here θ is the seasonal moving average coefficient and is exactly analogous to θ for nonseasonal moving averages. Similarly for seasonal ARIMA(0,1,1) 12, the equation is

$$(1 - B^{12}) series_t = (1 - \theta B^{12}) disturbance_t \qquad \text{Equation 12.2}$$

Interpreting an equation like this is easier than it may look. The series minus its seasonal backshift—the change over the seasonal period, in other words—equals a combination of the current disturbance and some fraction (θ) of the disturbance one seasonal period ago.

Seasonal ARIMA effects are (unfortunately) usually mixed with nonseasonal effects. The mixed form is normally taken to be multiplicative—the seasonal and nonseasonal effects are multiplied in the equation. A multiplicative first-order moving average with a first-order seasonal moving average, written ARIMA(0,0,1) (0,0,1) 12, is represented by

$$series_t = (1 - \theta B)(1 - \theta B^{12}) disturbance_t \qquad \text{Equation 12.3}$$

If you work out the algebra, you find that the usual multiplicative model predicts some non-zero autocorrelations (for example, at lag 13) that would be 0 in an additive model. This makes sense: if the current observation is affected by the observations 1 and 12 months ago, logically it should be affected by the one 13 months ago. If you know enough to be sure that you want an additive model, you can constrain the unwanted coefficients to 0 by using SPSS command syntax. Consult ARIMA in the Syntax Reference for information on specifying a constrained model.

Problems in Identifying Seasonal Models

Although seasonal ARIMA models are conceptually similar to nonseasonal models, they can be more difficult to identify.

Length of the Series

You need a longer series to develop a seasonal model. With a period of 12, as in the present example, you identify the form of the model on the basis of the ACF and PACF at lags 12, 24, 36, and so on. You must calculate these functions to an unusually large number of lags, as specified in the Autocorrelations Options dialog box. Note that the calculation of the PACF to so many lags requires a great deal of processing time. Do not specify so many lags unless you are estimating a seasonal model.

To estimate the coefficients for a seasonal ARIMA model, you should have at least enough data for seven or eight seasonal periods. Models based on shorter series are likely to be unreliable.

Confounding of Seasonal and Nonseasonal Effects

The characteristic ACF and PACF patterns produced by seasonal processes are the same as those shown in Appendix B for nonseasonal processes, except that the patterns occur in the first few *seasonal* lags rather than the first few lags. It is easy to determine that a seasonal process is present: if the ACF, PACF, or both show significant values at lags that are multiples of the seasonal period, you know that there is a seasonal process. It is less easy to identify the processes involved.

The principal problem in identifying seasonal ARIMA models is the complexity of the ACF and PACF plots. These plots arise from the combination of the seasonal and nonseasonal ARIMA processes with random noise and are rarely as clean as textbook illustrations. In practice, you often have to identify some of the model, estimate the coefficients, obtain a residual series, and then inspect the ACF and PACF of the residuals for clues about components you need to add to your tentative model. The ARIMA cycle of identification, estimation, and diagnosis takes longer when seasonal processes are present.

A Seasonal Model for the Telephone Series

We begin analysis of the ratios of connections to disconnections by generating an ACF plot. As explained in "Stationary Variance and the Log Transformation" on p. 191, we use a log transformation to make the variance of the series constant. To obtain this plot, from the menus choose:

Graphs
  Time Series ▶
    Autocorrelations...

This opens the Autocorrelations dialog box, as shown in Figure 12.4.

Figure 12.4 Autocorrelations dialog box

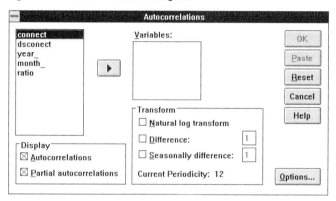

Move *ratio* into the Variables list. To save processing time, deselect Partial autocorrelations in the Display group. This takes a long time to calculate and we have not yet even determined whether the series is stationary. The Transform group should show the current periodicity as 12. In that group, select Natural log transform. Click on Options... to open the Autocorrelations Options dialog box, as shown in Figure 12.5.

Figure 12.5 Autocorrelations Options dialog box

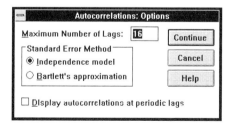

In the text box for Maximum Number of Lags, type 36. This will provide three seasonal lags (at 12, 24, and 36) for identification of the seasonal model. Click on OK to see the autocorrelation function for the *ratio* series.

We do not request the PACF plot at this point, since it takes a long time to calculate and we have not yet even determined whether the series is stationary.

Figure 12.6   ACF plot with log transformation

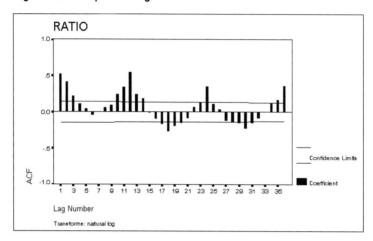

Identifying the Seasonal Model

The ACF plot in Figure 12.6 above shows large values at lags 12, 24, and 36. The slowness with which values at these seasonal lags decline confirms our suspicion that seasonal differencing is required to achieve a stationary mean. To do so, reopen the Autocorrelations dialog box. Select Seasonally difference in the Transform group, and select Partial autocorrelations in the Display group. You will notice that the calculation of the PACF requires a long time at high lags. Figure 12.7 shows plots after seasonal differencing.

Figure 12.7   Seasonally differenced plots

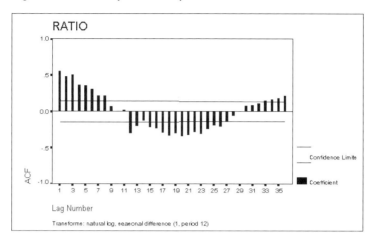

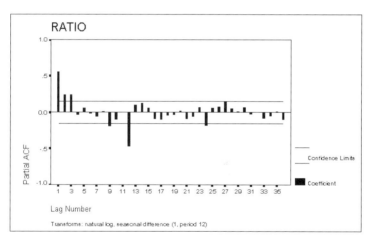

Seasonal differencing has smoothed out the rapid seasonal fluctuations. The ACF still shows a lot of nonseasonal action, with a single seasonal spike emerging at lag 12. The PACF shows a large spike at 12, a smaller one at 24, and possibly a hint of one at 36.

Checking Appendix B, you find that the pattern "one spike in ACF, rapidly declining PACF" indicates an MA(1) process, in this instance a *seasonal* MA(1) process, since the pattern appears at the seasonal lags.

These plots were from a seasonally differenced series, so the tentative seasonal model is (0,1,1). The next step is to estimate the MA(1) coefficient in the seasonal model, so we can plot the ACF of the residuals and get a cleaner look at the type of nonseasonal model involved.

Estimating the Seasonal Coefficient

To estimate the seasonal model, from the menus choose:

Statistics
  Time Series ▶
    ARIMA...

This opens the ARIMA dialog box, as shown in Figure 12.8.

Figure 12.8   ARIMA dialog box

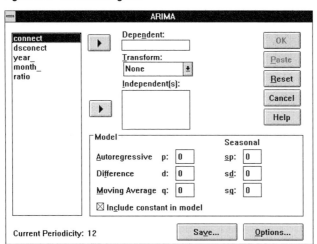

- Move *ratio* into the Dependent box.
- Select Natural log on the Transform drop-down list. The log transformation is included in the model to stabilize the variance, as discussed above.
- In the Model group, deselect Include constant in model. The mean seasonal difference should be about 0.
- Specify the parameters of the seasonal model: set *sd* to 1 and *sq* to 1. Leave the other four parameters at 0.
- Click on Options... and, in the ARIMA Options dialog box, select Final parameters only. We are not interested in the details of this model, but in the residuals.

This is only a preliminary estimation of the seasonal model. We know from the plots above that nonseasonal processes are also involved. By estimating the seasonal model, we hope to obtain a residual series free of seasonal effects. The results of the preliminary analysis are shown in Figure 12.9.

Figure 12.9 Estimation of seasonal (0,1,1) model

```
Split group number: 1  Series length: 190
No missing data.
Melard's algorithm will be used for estimation.

Conclusion of estimation phase.
Estimation terminated at iteration number 6 because:
   Sum of squares decreased by less than .001 percent.

FINAL PARAMETERS:

Number of residuals  178
Standard error        .07520585
Log likelihood       205.85675
AIC                 -409.7135
SBC                 -406.53172

            Analysis of Variance:

            DF  Adj. Sum of Squares    Residual Variance

Residuals    177            1.0310954              .00565592

          Variables in the Model:

            B        SEB      T-RATIO   APPROX. PROB.

SMA1    .59551885   .06601872   9.0204542      .0000000

The following new variables are being created:

  Name      Label

  FIT_1      Fit for RATIO from ARIMA, MOD_6 LN NOCON
  ERR_1      Error for RATIO from ARIMA, MOD_6 LN NOCON
  LCL_1      95% LCL for RATIO from ARIMA, MOD_6 LN NOCON
  UCL_1      95% UCL for RATIO from ARIMA, MOD_6 LN NOCON
  SEP_1      SE of fit for RATIO from ARIMA, MOD_6 LN NOCON
Note: The error variable is in the log metric.
```

Identifying the Nonseasonal Model from Residuals

The series *err_1* contains residuals of the log-transformed *ratio* series from the seasonal model estimated above. If our identification of the seasonal model was correct, these residuals show the nonseasonal portion of the model. (If it was incorrect, they will still show autocorrelations at the seasonal lags.) To identify the nonseasonal components of the model, from the menus choose:

Graphs
 Time Series ▶
  Autocorrelations...

In the Autocorrelations dialog box, move *ratio* out of the Variables list and *err_1* in. Make sure that both Display options are selected. Deselect Natural log transform and Seasonally difference in the Transform group. Figure 12.10 and Figure 12.11 show the ACF and PACF plots of the residuals from the seasonal ARIMA model.

Figure 12.10 ACF plot of residuals from seasonal model

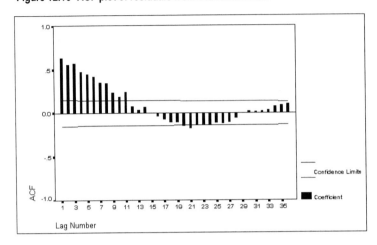

Figure 12.11 PACF plot of residuals from seasonal model

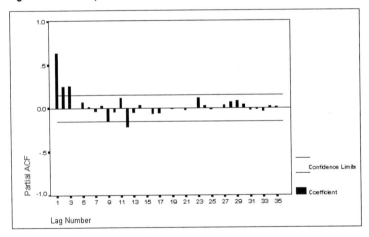

Since the option specified earlier for maximum lags is still in effect, Trends displays autocorrelations to 36 lags. (We still want to see high-order lags in case there is any seasonal variation remaining in the residuals.) Calculating the higher-order lags of the PACF takes a while. In the figure, we observe the following:

- The ACF starts large and then dies out.

- The PACF also dies out, somewhat more quickly.

Comparing this pattern to those inAppendix B, we decide that the nonseasonal model may be ARIMA(1,0,1). The relatively slow attenuation of the ACF indicates that the autoregressive coefficient will be large. (Remember from Chapter 7 that a slowly declining ACF can mean an integrated series—which is equivalent to an AR(1) model with a coefficient of 1.0.)

Before estimating coefficients for the combined model, let us pause to emphasize an important feature of the way Trends ARIMA handles log-transformed data.

Residuals in Log-Transformed ARIMA

The log-transformation options of the ARIMA procedure allow you to analyze a log-transformed series while retaining the untransformed data in your file. To evaluate such a model, you need the residuals of the series that was analyzed—the transformed data, in other words. Thus, if you select either of the two log transforms in the ARIMA dialog box, the residual series (with the prefix *err*) is created in the log-transformed metric.

However, other series generated by ARIMA (with prefixes *fit*, *lcl*, *ucl*, and *sep*) are transformed back so that they will be comparable to the series analyzed. Therefore, when you use a log transformation in ARIMA, it is *not* true—as it otherwise would be—that the *fit* series plus the *err* series equals the original series. The *fit* series is not transformed and is suitable for comparison with the original series; the *err* series is transformed for diagnostic purposes.

Note that we did not specify a log transformation for the ACF plot in Figure 12.10, as we did earlier. The series *err_1* (unlike the series *ratio* in Figure 12.7) is in the logged metric.

Estimating the Complete Model

The tentative model, incorporating both seasonal and nonseasonal effects, is (1,0,1)(0,1,1)12. To estimate this model, from the menus choose:

Statistics
    Time Series ▶
        ARIMA...

In the ARIMA dialog box, make sure that *ratio* is specified as the dependent variable, and that Natural log is selected for Transform. Specify 1 for p and 1 for q. Leave d equal to 0, and leave the three seasonal parameters equal to 0, 1, and 1, respectively. Make sure Include constant in model is not selected.

Click on Save... to check the options for creating new variables. The default options, Add to file and Predict from estimation period through last case, should be selected. Click on Continue and then on Options... in the ARIMA dialog box. In the ARIMA Options dialog box, select the first Display option, Initial and final parameters with iteration summary.

Figure 12.12 shows the estimation of this model. All coefficients are statistically significant and, as expected, the AR(1) coefficient is nearly 1.

Figure 12.12 The complete model

```
Split group number: 1  Series length: 190
No missing data.
Melard's algorithm will be used for estimation.


Conclusion of estimation phase.
Estimation terminated at iteration number 5 because:
   Sum of squares decreased by less than .001 percent.

FINAL PARAMETERS:

Number of residuals  178
Standard error       .05363987
Log likelihood       266.10097
AIC                  -526.20195
SBC                  -516.6566

             Analysis of Variance:

             DF  Adj. Sum of Squares   Residual Variance
Residuals    175            .52400402           .00287724

             Variables in the Model:

             B          SEB        T-RATIO    APPROX. PROB.
AR1    .91658654    .03955866    23.170311       .0000000
MA1    .52165306    .08352885     6.245184       .0000000
SMA1   .65676324    .06741673     9.741844       .0000000


The following new variables are being created:

   Name        Label

   FIT_2       Fit for RATIO from ARIMA, MOD_8 LN NOCON
   ERR_2       Error for RATIO from ARIMA, MOD_8 LN NOCON
   LCL_2       95% LCL for RATIO from ARIMA, MOD_8 LN NOCON
   UCL_2       95% UCL for RATIO from ARIMA, MOD_8 LN NOCON
   SEP_2       SE of fit for RATIO from ARIMA, MOD_8 LN NOCON
Note: The error variable is in the log metric.
```

Diagnosis

The residuals from the above analysis are in the series *err_2*, as reported in Figure 12.12. As before, this error series remains in the logged metric and is suitable for diagnostic analysis. Figure 12.13 shows the ACF plot of *err_2* in low resolution, including the values of the Box-Ljung statistic and its significance levels.

Figure 12.13 ACF of residuals from complete model

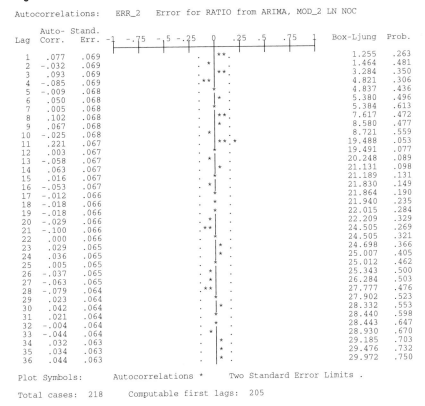

```
Autocorrelations:    ERR_2    Error for RATIO from ARIMA, MOD_2 LN NOC

      Auto- Stand.
Lag   Corr.  Err.  -1  -.75  -.5 -.25   0   .25  .5   .75   1   Box-Ljung  Prob.

  1    .077  .069                           **.                 1.255    .263
  2   -.032  .069                        .  *  .                1.464    .481
  3    .093  .069                           **.                 3.284    .350
  4   -.085  .069                        .**                    4.821    .306
  5   -.009  .068                           *                   4.837    .436
  6    .050  .068                        .  |*  .               5.380    .496
  7    .005  .068                           *                   5.384    .613
  8    .102  .068                        .  **.                 7.617    .472
  9    .067  .068                        .  |* .                8.580    .477
 10   -.025  .068                        . *|                   8.721    .559
 11    .221  .067                        .  |**.*               19.488   .053
 12    .003  .067                        .  *                   19.491   .077
 13   -.058  .067                        . *|  .                20.248   .089
 14    .063  .067                        .  |* .                21.131   .098
 15    .016  .067                        .  *                   21.189   .131
 16   -.053  .067                        . *|  .                21.830   .149
 17   -.012  .066                        .  *                   21.864   .190
 18   -.018  .066                        . *|                   21.940   .235
 19   -.018  .066                        . *|                   22.015   .284
 20   -.029  .066                        . *|                   22.209   .329
 21   -.100  .066                        .**|  .                24.505   .269
 22    .000  .066                        .  *                   24.505   .321
 23    .029  .065                        .  |* .                24.698   .366
 24    .036  .065                        .  |* .                25.007   .405
 25    .005  .065                        .  *                   25.012   .462
 26   -.037  .065                        . *|  .                25.343   .500
 27   -.063  .065                        . *|  .                26.284   .503
 28   -.079  .064                        .**|  .                27.777   .476
 29    .023  .064                        .  *                   27.902   .523
 30    .042  .064                        .  |* .                28.332   .553
 31    .021  .064                        .  *                   28.440   .598
 32   -.004  .064                        .  *                   28.443   .647
 33   -.044  .064                        . *|  .                28.930   .670
 34    .032  .063                        .  |* .                29.185   .703
 35    .034  .063                        .  |* .                29.476   .732
 36    .044  .063                        .  |* .                29.972   .750

Plot Symbols:      Autocorrelations *      Two Standard Error Limits .

Total cases:  218    Computable first lags:  205
```

The ACF shows a significant spike at lag 11. We have no reason to expect a lag-11 autocorrelation, and we have plotted enough values so that one or two should be significant by chance alone, so we can safely ignore this spike. The Box-Ljung statistics do not indicate significant departures from white noise in the residual autocorrelations.

Checking the Validation Period

To check the performance of the model during the validation period (the 25 observations not used to estimate the coefficients), we plot the observations along with the new *fit_2* series for the entire data file. From the menus choose:

Data
  Select Cases...

Figure 12.14 Time Axis Reference Lines dialog box

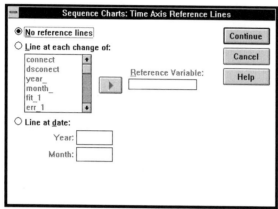

In the Select Cases dialog box, click on Range... and set the First Case text box for Year to 1959 and for Month to 1. Clear the values in the text boxes for Last Case. This provides a short enough range to see the detail in a sequence plot.

Now, from the menus choose:

Graphs
  Sequence...

Move *ratio* and *fit_2* into the Variables list, and move *date_* into the Time Axis Labels box. Click on Time Lines... to open the Time Axis Reference Lines dialog box, as shown in Figure 12.14.

Select the option Line at date, and enter the date marking the end of the estimation period: Year 1966, Month 10. This will make it easier to see where the validation period begins in the plot. The results are shown in Figure 12.15.

Figure 12.15 Sequence plot of ratio and predicted ratio

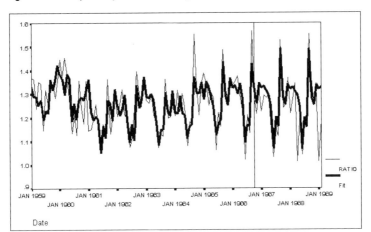

With a couple of exceptions, the *fit* series from the ARIMA model with both seasonal and nonseasonal components does a good job of tracking the ratio of connections to disconnections.

13 Cycles of Housing Construction: Introduction to Spectral Analysis

The rate at which new houses are constructed is an important barometer of the state of the economy. Housing starts are thought to respond to changes in interest rates, to expectations about the strength of the economy, to changes in family income and birth and marriage rates, as well as to seasonal factors. Much longer cycles, based on the rate at which housing wears out, may also exist.

The Housing Starts Data

Series *hstarts* records the number of permits issued per month for new, single-unit residential dwelling construction in thousands in the United States from January 1965 through December 1975.

A sequence plot of *hstarts* is shown in Figure 13.1. The plot shows a strong seasonal effect dominating all other variation, but there appears to be a slower cycle in the data as well.

Figure 13.1 Housing starts 1965–1975

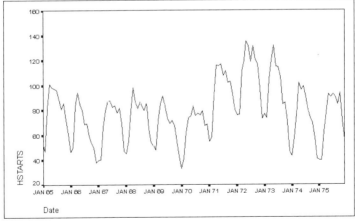

Seasonally differencing this series helps to reveal the nonseasonal cyclical variation. Because these are monthly data with a defined periodicity of 12, we can use the Create Time Series procedure (on the Transform menu) to calculate the differences of observations 12 months apart. From the menus choose:

Transform
  Create Time Series...

In the Create Times Series dialog box:

1. Select *hstarts* and click on ▶. The expression hstart_1=DIFF(hstarts 1) appears in the New Variable(s) list.

2. Press Tab→ to highlight the Name text box in the Name and Function group. Type sdhstart to make it easier to remember that this variable represents the seasonal differences in housing starts.

3. Select Seasonal difference from the Function drop-down list.

4. Click on Change. The expression in the New Variable(s) list should now read sdhstart=SDIFF(hstarts 1).

When you click on OK, Trends creates the seasonally differenced series *sdhstart*, containing 12 fewer nonmissing observations than the original series. Figure 13.2 shows the seasonally differenced housing starts series as well as the original.

Figure 13.2 Housing starts, raw and seasonally differenced

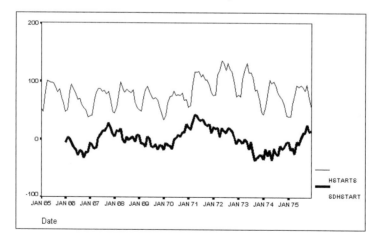

After a brief introduction to the methods of spectral analysis, we will study the components of this series further.

Spectral Analysis: An Overview

Spectral analysis is about rhythms. It is used to find various kinds of periodic behavior in series, although it can be used for nonperiodic data. A spectral analysis of a series yields a description of that series in terms of the cycles of different period (length) or frequency that generate the series. This is portrayed in a graph called the **periodogram**, which shows an estimate of the amount of variance of the series accounted for by cycles of each frequency. You can also apply spectral analysis to pairs of series to examine their covariation at each frequency.

Although spectral descriptions are given in terms of frequencies or periods of the component cycles, there is an exact (but complicated) relationship between the frequency representation and the autocorrelations of the series. The same information is portrayed in different ways by the periodogram and the ACF plot.

Often you will have expectations about what periodicities are present in the data; at other times your analysis will be purely exploratory. Determining the relative magnitude and phase (how far one cycle leads or lags another) of various periodic variations is often of interest. Sometimes the periodicities in the data are immediately obvious and a spectral description will only confirm what is visually apparent. When several different frequencies occur together, however, or when there is a considerable amount of random noise or static in the data, spectral analysis is more fruitful.

Model-Free Analysis

Spectral analysis is almost entirely model free. It analyzes a series into sine and cosine waves, but this analysis is purely mathematical and is not based on any theory about a process underlying the series. In contrast to other time series techniques, you don't determine a parametric model of your data and then estimate it, not even implicitly. Instead, you estimate the spectrum without any *a priori* constraints—although you may tune the estimators according to the properties of your series and what you want to learn about the data. Consequently, spectral methods are not worth doing if you have only a small amount of data. A short series has so little information in it that you cannot analyze it without a model. Spectral analysis is usually done with hundreds of observations.

The Periodogram

To produce a periodogram of the housing-starts series *hstarts,* from the menus choose:

Graphs
  Time Series ▶
    Spectral...

This opens the Spectral Plots dialog box, as shown in Figure 13.3.

Figure 13.3   Spectral Plots dialog box

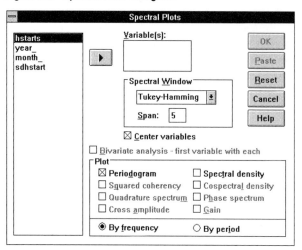

Move *hstarts* onto the Variable(s) list. Make sure that the Center variables option is selected. (Centering adjusts the series to have a mean of 0 before calculating the spectrum. It usually improves the periodogram display by removing the relatively large term associated with the mean, so you can focus your attention on variation in the series.) Click on OK to generate the default periodogram, which is shown in Figure 13.4.

Figure 13.4   Periodogram of housing starts

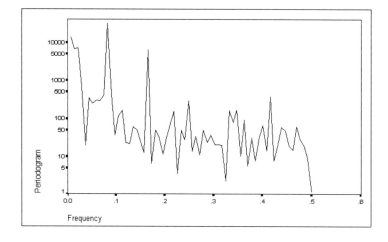

The horizontal axis shows the frequencies into which Spectral Plots has decomposed the series, and the vertical axis shows the relative weight, or importance, of each frequency. (The periodogram weight is plotted on a logarithmic scale, which allows you to see more detail. If the periodogram were plotted on a linear scale, the large differences between periodogram values would obscure detail.) We observe two high spikes and a great many other small jagged spikes.

All the plots in this chapter are displayed by frequency. If you prefer, you can select By period in the Spectral Plots dialog box to display the periodogram by period instead. Frequency and period are reciprocals of one another, so both forms of the plot contain the same information. Choose whichever you find easier to understand. For monthly data with a cycle lasting exactly one year, the period is 12 months and the frequency is 1/12 cycle per month. The frequencies plotted in a periodogram are equally spaced, but the periods corresponding to them are not, since the periods are the reciprocals of the frequencies. When you select the By period option, Trends uses the logarithms of the periods so that the plotted points do not bunch up at the left end of the plot.

The Frequency Domain

Most time series techniques are carried out "in the time domain." That is, they describe the relationship of observations in a series at different *points in time*. Spectral analysis is carried out "in the frequency domain." It describes the variations in a series in terms of cycles of sines and cosines at different *frequencies*. For example, in a time-domain description, you might say that the series x at time t is approximately equal to its value at time $t-12$ plus 0.2 times its value at time $t-1$. In the frequency domain, you might report that x is approximately composed of a sine wave of frequency of 1/12 cycles per month plus 0.3 times a sine wave of frequency of 1/20 cycles per month. Descriptions of real series, of course, are likely to be more complicated than this.

Fourier Frequencies

To model cycles of different length, you express the series in terms of sine and cosine functions having different frequencies. The actual frequencies are chosen so that the length of the series contains a whole number of cycles at each frequency. These are called the **Fourier frequencies**, after the mathematician who discovered their properties.

The lowest Fourier frequency has zero cycles. This represents a "cycle" that does not vary; that is, a constant. The next lowest completes one cycle during the whole observed length of the series. The highest, or most rapid, frequency that you can observe has half as many cycles as the number of observations. For example, if you have 100 observations, you cannot possibly observe more than 50 complete cycles, because it takes two observations (a high and a low) to complete the smallest recognizable cycle. Aside from the constant, the Fourier frequencies consist of a **fundamental frequency** (one long cycle in the entire observed series) and its **overtones** (two cycles in the series, three cycles in the series, and so on).

Frequencies are measured in terms of cycles per time period. In SPSS Trends, the frequencies are expressed as cycles per observation, since each observation represents a point in time. Such frequencies are always fractional, since a single observation makes up only a portion of a cycle. The highest Fourier frequency is 1/2, because its cycles are half as frequent as the observations themselves. In general, the jth Fourier frequency is expressed as

$$\text{Frequency}_j = \frac{j}{N}$$

Equation 13.1

where j is the number of times the cycle repeats in the sample and N is the number of observations. (In the equations in the Syntax Reference, you will see these frequencies multiplied by 2π, since that makes the periods of the sine and cosine functions equal to those of the corresponding cycles.)

Notice that the Fourier frequencies depend entirely upon the length of the series. If you know of a periodicity in your series and you want to make sure it shows up cleanly as a single term in spectral analysis, make sure that the length of the series is an exact multiple of the length of the period.

For example, the housing-starts data have 132 monthly observations. In Figure 13.1, there was a strong annual cycle. This annual cycle repeats exactly 11 times in the observed series of 132 observations, so it corresponds to $j=11$ in Equation 13.1, and its frequency is 11/132, or 1/12. (The annual cycle is 1/12 as frequent as the observations themselves, in other words.) The periodogram in Figure 13.4 does, in fact, show its largest spike at a frequency of 1/12, or about 0.08. If the sample size had been 126 or some other number that is not a multiple of 12, there would have been no single Fourier frequency that corresponded exactly to an annual cycle. The annual cycle would be "smeared" over several of the Fourier frequencies.

Figure 13.5 shows the periodogram of a sine wave with period 0.085, which is not a Fourier frequency in a sample of 128 cases. Instead of producing a single point at frequency 0.085, the effect is spread out over all the frequencies, even though it is highly concentrated at the frequencies nearest to 0.085 (0.078 and 0.086). The appearance of non-zero weights in the periodogram for cycles with frequencies different from the exact series frequency is called **leakage.** It can make reading the periodogram more difficult, but its effect is attenuated by the use of spectral windows, as discussed on pp. 218–221.

Figure 13.5 Leakage in a periodogram

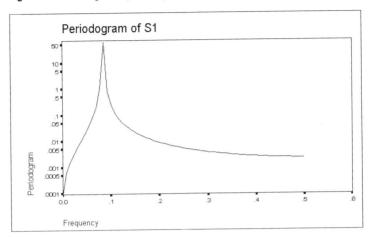

The Fourier frequencies for a series can be adjusted by padding the end of the series with either zeros or the series mean, thus changing the length of the series. While these extra points are not valid data, their addition will have little effect on the interesting parts of the periodogram.

Interpreting the Periodogram

The smoothest possible series is one that varies only at frequency 0: a constant. Its periodogram just has a single spike at frequency 0. Such a series is white noise, as described in Chapter 7. A white noise series with a mean of 0 will have no spikes at all. The roughest series, in contrast, is one with a spike only at frequency 1/2. Its cycle occurs half as often as the observations themselves: high, low, high, low, and so forth. Every two observations make a cycle. Generally speaking,

- The smoother the series, the more variation is accounted for by low-frequency variation.
- The rougher the series, the more variation is accounted for by high-frequency variation.

In time-domain analysis, such as we have discussed in earlier chapters, smoothness is measured by autocorrelation. The Durbin-Watson statistic is one measure used in the time domain for autocorrelation or smoothness. The Durbin-Watson statistic has a value near 0 for a very smooth series, or one with positive autocorrelation. In the frequency domain, such a series shows most of its variation at low frequencies. A series with a Durbin-Watson statistic of about 2, indicating no autocorrelation (such as a white noise series), normally divides its variation among all the Fourier frequencies and has no interesting shape.

A Way to Think about Spectral Decomposition

The periodogram of a series shows its *energy* or *variance* at each of the Fourier frequencies. In order to determine this value, the cyclic pattern in the series is expressed at each frequency as a weighted sum of a sine term and a cosine term having that frequency. Mathematically, it turns out that the sine and cosine functions at the Fourier frequencies can be combined to reproduce the observed series exactly, provided that each of the sine and cosine functions is given the correct weight.

The value plotted in the periodogram, for any given frequency, is the sum of the squares of the two weights (sine and cosine) at that frequency. There are half as many Fourier frequencies as there are observations on the series, and each frequency has two parameters: the weights of the sine and cosine terms. Let us see how this works.

For a series with 100 observations, there are actually 51 Fourier frequencies: the constant (with frequency 0) and the frequencies that repeat 1, 2, 3, . . ., 50 times during the course of the 100 observations. This seems to give 51 sines and 51 cosines, which require a total of 102 coefficients. There are really only 100, however.

- At frequency 0, the sine term is always 0, because the sine of 0 is 0. The cosine of 0 is 1, so the "constant cycle" of frequency 0 can be created by simply giving the cosine weight equal to the constant, or mean, value of the series.

- At frequency 50, the sine function cycles up and down between observations but always equals 0 at the moment of observation. The cosine function, on the other hand, is in sync with the observations. It reaches its highest and lowest values at exactly the moments of observation. It is thus ideally suited to describing the fastest observable cycle.

Thus, a spectral analysis of a series of 100 observations yields 51 cosine terms and 49 sine terms—for a total of exactly 100 terms. The details are slightly different for a series with an odd number of terms, but the idea is the same. You can express n values of a series as exactly n coefficients that apply to sine and cosine functions at the Fourier frequencies.

When you know these coefficients, you can re-create the original series exactly. For example, to get the value at observation 17, you could

- Take one of the Fourier frequencies and figure out where it was in its cycle at exactly the moment of observation 17.

- Look up the values of the sine and cosine functions at that point in the cycle.

- Multiply these values by the coefficients that you have for the sine and cosine functions at the frequency you are working with.

- Repeat all of this for each of the Fourier frequencies, adding up the results as you go.

If you worked your way through all 51 Fourier frequencies and all 100 coefficients like this, you would end up with the value of the original series at observation 17. Note, however, that you don't actually do this when you carry out a spectral analysis. You get the coefficients and analyze them. The fact that you *could* recreate the original series from the spectral coefficients means that you have not lost any information in switching to a spectral point of view. You are looking at the same information that was in the series of values, but you are looking at it as a combination of wavelike oscillations rather than a series of values.

The mathematical theory of Fourier analysis reveals that the correlations among the sine and cosine functions used are all 0. This means that the Fourier coefficients are unique—there is only one set of them that captures all of the information in the original series.

Spectral decomposition is a reexpression of the original series as coefficients of these sines and cosines at the Fourier frequencies. But how should we choose the coefficients? We could use a technique from the time domain: regression. Imagine regressing the series being analyzed on 99 "explanatory" variables consisting of the sine and cosine terms discussed above. (The zero-frequency cosine term is just the constant term in the regression.) In fact, this is equivalent to what spectral decomposition does. The weights for each frequency are just the regression coefficients for the sine and cosine terms at that frequency. Fortunately, there are computational shortcuts so that we don't actually have to compute the decomposition this way.

All of the weights or coefficients are computed on the basis of the entire observed series, so that you *cannot perform spectral analysis if any data are missing,* even at the ends of the series. Use the Replace Missing Values procedure to substitute values for missing data, or use Select Cases with a range of cases that excludes missing data at the beginning or end.

Some Examples of Decompositions

The periodogram for a series consisting of a single sine wave is shown in Figure 13.5. Figure 13.6 and Figure 13.7 show a plot and a periodogram for a series that is the sum of two sine curves at different frequencies. The periodogram has a spike for each component curve.

Figure 13.6   Sum of two periodic oscillations

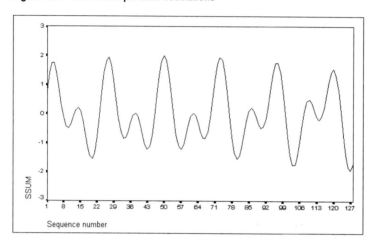

Figure 13.7   Sum of two periodic oscillations (periodogram)

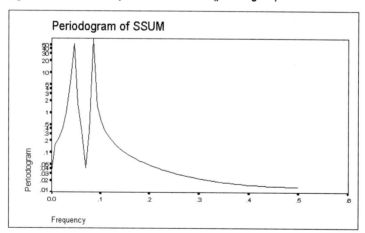

A series consisting simply of a linear trend produces the periodogram in Figure 13.8.

Figure 13.8   Linear trend

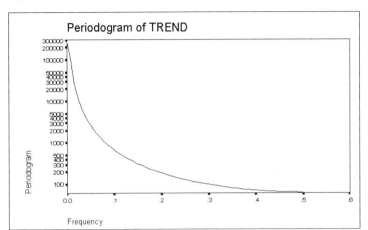

Finally, Figure 13.9 shows a periodogram of a second-order moving average of a series containing nothing but white noise. The appearance of this type of a periodogram depends upon the size and sign of the MA coefficients. This moving average is dominated by high-frequency variation: the general tendency across the plot is one of increasing amplitude with increasing frequency.

Figure 13.9   Second-order moving average

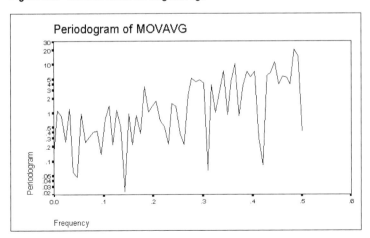

You may find it useful to generate your own series with known statistical properties and display their spectra (periodograms) in order to become more familiar with the shape of typical spectral curves.

Smoothing the HSTARTS Periodogram

In regression analysis, you would be justifiably suspicious of an analysis where the number of cases equaled the number of explanatory variables. You would expect the individual coefficients to be highly unreliable. In fact, the *t* statistics would have zero degrees of freedom! But you would get a perfect fit to the data. The Fourier analysis method produces as many coefficients as there are terms in the series analyzed, and each element in the periodogram is based on the squares of only two coefficients. Individual periodogram terms have large variance and are statistically independent of each other. Therefore, we don't just look at the individual coefficients, because they are very noisy.

Examining the *hstarts* periodogram in Figure 13.4, we see a great deal of irregular variation. It would be unwise, to say the least, to attribute significance to each individual peak. However, we can apply various smoothing transformations to the periodogram terms to reduce their variance (at some cost in resolution and bias). The smoothing process can also reduce leakage.

Smoothing transformations for a periodogram are called **windows.** You define a window by choosing the shape and the number of terms (or **span**) of the group of neighboring points that are to be averaged together. Each of the values in the periodogram is averaged with one or more values on either side of it. To obtain a smoothed periodogram, from the menus select:

Graphs
  Time Series
    Spectral...

The Spectral Plots dialog box still shows your previous specifications. Notice that the Spectral Window group (which did not affect the periodogram in Figure 13.4) shows a Tukey-Hamming window with a span of five. That is, each point in the periodogram will be averaged with two neighbors on each side. In the Plot group, deselect Periodogram and select Spectral density. The smoothed periodogram is called the **spectral density estimate.** The spectral density estimate for *hstarts* appears in Figure 13.10.

Figure 13.10 Smoothed periodogram (spectral density)

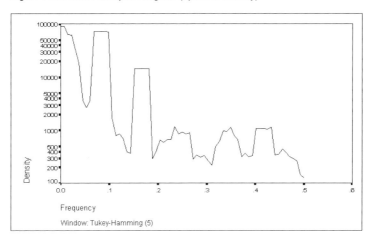

Much of the jaggedness has been removed, revealing two clear peaks at 12 and 6 months (corresponding to plotted frequencies of about 1/12, or about 0.08, and 1/6, or 0.17). These peaks have been smoothed, so they are broader than those shown in the periodogram. The spectral density estimate also shows three possible peaks at higher frequencies.

You can choose from several windows and vary the span using the Spectral Window group (see "Specifying Windows for the Spectral Density" on p. 220). Figure 13.11 shows the *hstarts* spectral density estimated using the Parzen window with a span of 11. The general shape is clearly the same as in Figure 13.10, but the broader window has begun to obscure the shape of the plot.

Figure 13.11 Spectral density with PARZEN(11) window

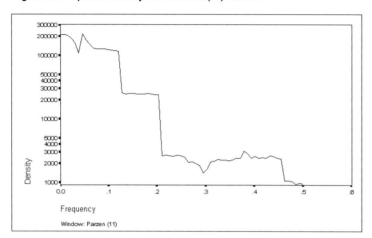

Specifying Windows for the Spectral Density

The windows that Spectral Plots uses to produce spectral density estimates have two characteristics, both of which are under your control: the type (or shape) of the window, and its span. These are specified in the Spectral Window control group in the Spectral Plots dialog box. They affect the spectral density estimate but not the periodogram.

The window shape is specified by choosing an alternative from the drop-down list. **Window shape** refers to the pattern of the weights applied in constructing the moving average. These weights are usually symmetric around the middle point; the span of the window is odd to reflect this. The largest weight is given to the middle point, and the weights fall off smoothly for points further away, except for the Daniell (Unit) window, where they are constant. Smoother windows generally lead to less leakage.

The span parameter indicates the number of points included in the moving average. (For the Tukey and Bartlett windows, the end points in the average turn out to have weights of 0, so the effective span is two less than the number you specify.) A wide data window reduces the effect of random variation in the periodogram. It makes the spectral density plot easier to read, but also blurs it, introducing some bias. If you smooth the periodogram too much, you may miss spikes corresponding to important periodic variation at certain narrow frequency ranges. This is particularly likely to happen if two spikes occur close together. In general, longer spans reduce the variance of the spectral density estimates more than shorter ones, but they also increase the bias in areas where the density function is steep. One rule of thumb is to make the data window span 10%

to 20% of your data. In practice, you will often find it useful to try several different window spans in constructing the spectral density estimate.

An alternative to selecting one of the common window shapes and a span is to construct your own window by giving the weights for the averaging process. See SPECTRA in the Syntax Reference section for information on specifying your own weights.

A window of span 1, that is, no windowing at all, can be specified by selecting None. This makes the spectral density estimate the same as the periodogram.

While the merits of different windows are much analyzed, in practice the span of the window is more important than its precise shape. The Tukey window and the Tukey-Hamming window are perhaps the most popular. The Bartlett window has fallen into disuse.

Transformations in Spectral Analysis

Fourier analysis works best when the periodic behavior of a series has a sinusoidal shape at each important frequency. But real data don't necessarily look this way. The level of a series and the magnitude of its fluctuations may grow over time. In this case, trend removal and power transformations of the data may be helpful. The effects of a trend, being like very low-frequency variation, will load most heavily on the lowest frequencies of the periodogram, but it will be reflected to a smaller degree in higher-frequency terms. The effect of a strong trend on the periodogram can resemble the effect of nonstationarity in an ACF plot. The large spike at low frequencies can overwhelm variation elsewhere—just as large ACF values due to nonstationarity overwhelm any patterns due to AR or MA processes.

Transformations will take care of many of these problems. When a trend or other strong low-frequency phenomenon dominates the periodogram, differencing the series is appropriate. If the short-term variation increases as the level of the series increases, a log or square-root transformation is commonly used. Generally speaking, you should remove the trend from a series before undertaking spectral analysis. You should also deseasonalize the series, unless the seasonality itself is the focus of your investigation. Strong seasonality overwhelms the other variation in a periodogram.

- To detrend a series, you can take differences (or seasonal differences). You can also use the Curve Estimation procedure, usually with a linear model. The *err* series it creates is a detrended series.

- To remove seasonality, you can use the Seasonal Decomposition procedure, which creates a seasonally adjusted series with the prefix *sas*.

A series may be stationary but still fail to look sinusoidal. The shape of the periodic variation may be pinched, or the peaks and troughs may have different shapes. You may be able to solve such problems by raising the series to some power. Exponents greater than 1 stretch out some portions of the series, while exponents between 0 and 1 stretch out others. Use the Compute Variable facility (on the Transform menu) to carry out power transformations.

Leakage

The phenomenon of leakage occurs when variation at one frequency "leaks" into peri-odogram terms at frequencies different from the true frequency of the variation. Spectral analysis only uses the Fourier frequencies, those that complete a whole number of com-plete cycles from the first observation to the last observation. The particular frequencies used depend, therefore, on the length of the series, and it is entirely possible that an im-portant cycle in the data will not be one of the Fourier frequencies. When a cycle that is not at one of the Fourier frequencies accounts for a considerable part of the variation in the series, it shows up at the frequencies closest to its true frequency. This phenomenon, known as **leakage,** can obscure other important frequencies in the data.

Windowing can reduce leakage by smoothing the periodogram in a controlled way. Another useful technique is called **prewhitening.** This simply means reducing the im-portance of variation at a strong frequency by differencing or filtering the data. Since a very smooth series will have large weights on small frequencies, "roughing it up" by re-placing it by its first differences (or seasonal differences) reduces the relative impor-tance of the low (or seasonal) frequencies and leads to a clearer picture of the other variation. To see the effect this can have on the spectral density, compare Figure 13.12, the spectral density of the seasonally differenced housing-starts series created at the be-ginning of this chapter, to the density of the undifferenced series in Figure 13.10.

Figure 13.12 Prewhitened housing starts

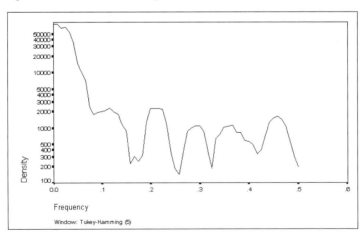

- The annual cycle, at a frequency of 1/12 cycle per observation, is completely gone. You expect this after seasonal differencing.
- The six-month cycle has turned into a dip. After seasonal differencing, almost no variation remains at this frequency.
- The remainder of the spectral density presents a much more regular pattern than in Figure 13.10.

It is important to remember that taking differences in a series can produce peaks or dips in the spectral density as well as remove them (just as differencing too many times causes problems in ARIMA analysis).

Spectral Analysis of Time Series

Analysis in the frequency domain—spectral analysis—never conflicts with analysis in the time domain. It is a different way of formulating the same problems. As you learn about spectral analysis, you will find that your understanding of autoregressive and moving-average processes helps you to interpret the frequency decomposition expressed in a periodogram. It is equally true that the language of frequencies and periodic wave functions will give new insight into the behavior of the sequential models of more traditional time series analysis.

How to Obtain a Spectral Analysis

To perform spectral analysis of time series, from the menus choose:

Graphs
  Time Series ▶
    Spectral...

This opens the Spectral Plots dialog box, as shown in Figure 13.13.

Figure 13.13 Spectral Plots dialog box

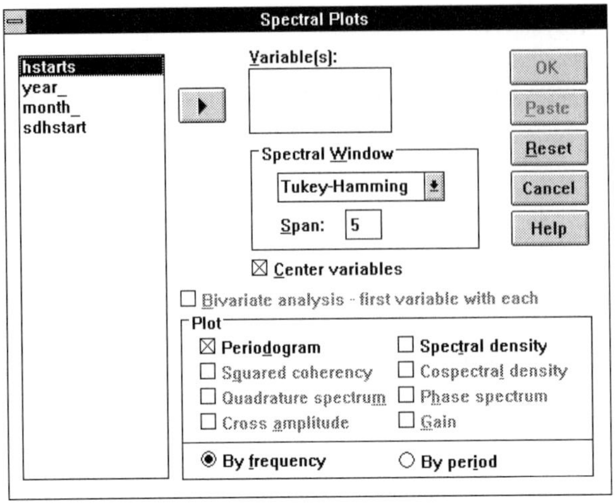

The numeric variables in your data file appear on the source list. To obtain univariate periodograms (with variables centered and frequency on the horizontal axis), move one or more variables into the Variable(s) list and click on OK.

Variables used in this procedure must not contain any missing data, even at the beginning or end of the series. Use the Replace Missing Values procedure, or Select Cases with a range, to ensure that all values are nonmissing.

The Spectral Window group lets you specify the manner in which the periodograms are smoothed to obtain spectral density plots. The formulas used to determine the weights will depend on the window type. They do not affect the periodograms themselves. Available windows are:

⬇ **Tukey-Hamming.** This is the default.

Tukey.

Parzen.

Bartlett.

Daniell (Unit). With this window, all values within the span are weighted equally.

None. If you select this, the spectral density plots are not smoothed and are identical to the periodograms.

For detailed information about window types, see SPECTRA in the Syntax Reference.

In the Span text box you can specify the span, which is the range of consecutive values across which the smoothing is carried out. Specify a positive integer, normally an odd integer. Larger spans smooth the spectral density plot more than smaller spans.

❑ **Center variables**. This option adjusts the series to have a mean of zero before calculating the spectrum and to remove the large term that may be associated with the series mean. To retain the term for the series mean, deselect this option.

By default, each series in the Variable(s) list is analyzed and plotted separately. You can also obtain bivariate spectral plots.

❑ **Bivariate analysis**. The first variable in the Variable(s) list is plotted with each of the other variables on the list. Univariate plots are still produced for each variable.

The Plot group lets you choose which plots are displayed for each variable (or each pair of variables in a bivariate analysis) on the Variable(s) list. Select one or more of the following:

❑ **Periodogram**. An unsmoothed plot of spectral amplitude (plotted on a logarithmic scale) against either frequency or period. This is the default.

❑ **Spectral density**. This plots the periodogram after it has been smoothed according to the specifications in the Spectral Window group.

❑ **Squared coherency**. Available only for bivariate analysis.

❑ **Cospectral density.** Available only for bivariate analysis.

❑ **Quadrature spectrum**. Available only for bivariate analysis.

❑ **Phase spectrum**. Available only for bivariate analysis.

❑ **Cross amplitude**. Available only for bivariate analysis.

❑ **Gain**. Available only for bivariate analysis.

Select one of the alternatives for the horizontal axis of the spectral plots:

○ **By frequency.** All plots are produced by frequency, ranging from frequency 0 (the constant or mean term) to frequency 0.5 (the term for a cycle of two observations).

○ **By period.** All plots are produced by period, ranging from 2 (the term for a cycle of two observations) to a period equal to the number of observations (the constant or mean term). Period is displayed on a logarithmic scale.

Additional Features Available with Command Syntax

You can customize your spectral analysis if you paste your selections into a syntax window and edit the resulting SPECTRA command syntax. The additional features are:

- New variables. You can save the Fourier frequencies, periods and, for the given frequency or period, the sine and cosine values and the values that are plotted in any of the available univariate or bivariate plots. These new series correspond to Fourier frequencies or periods and not to the original observations. Thus, the new variables will be missing for the last half of the observations.

- Display of the values plotted.

- User-specified weights for the spectral windows.

See the Syntax Reference section of this manual for command syntax rules and for complete SPECTRA command syntax.

14 Another Look at Housing Starts: X11 ARIMA

In Chapter 13, we looked at the number of permits issued per month for starting new, privately owned one-unit dwellings. In this chapter, we're going to include multiple-unit dwellings in our measure of housing construction, so the number of permits issued per month is for starts on all new, privately owned dwellings—apartment buildings as well as single-family houses.

This new series of housing starts will help demonstrate the use of X11 ARIMA in making seasonal adjustments. The X11 ARIMA procedure is based on the Statistics Canada modification to the U.S. Bureau of the Census Method II-X-11 seasonal adjustment program, used by many government agencies and businesses worldwide for analyzing time series with seasonal effects.

The Total Housing Starts Data

The series *totalhs* is the number, in thousands, of privately owned housing starts in the United States each month from January 1968 to October 1981. Figure 14.1 presents a plot of the series. The strong monthly seasonal effect and longer cyclical pattern characteristic of housing data that you saw in a similar series in Chapter 13 are evident in this series as well. The monthly periodicity of the data has been established with the Define Dates procedure. A defined periodicity, either monthly or quarterly, is *required* in order to use the specialized X11 ARIMA procedure. Moreover, the observations must all be dated within the twentieth century.

Figure 14.1   Total housing starts 1968–1981 (partial)

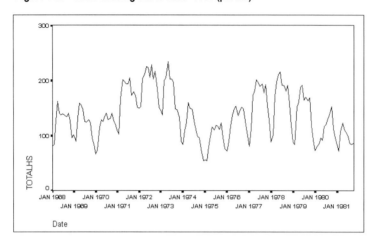

Seasonal Adjustment Methods

As we saw in Chapter 11, we can remove the seasonal effect from a series in order to look at other characteristics of interest that may be "masked" by the seasonal component. This can be done by using the Seasonal Decomposition procedure to break down a series into its seasonal, trend-cycle, and error (irregular) component parts. We could then use the seasonally adjusted series in further analyses, as was done in Chapter 11, or we could use the seasonal adjustment factors in forecasting. Although we saw in that chapter that there are other ways to handle the seasonal effects of a series (seasonal ARIMA, for example), seasonally adjusting a time series by a *decomposition method* continues to be popular in time series analysis.

The Census Methods

The type of decomposition method used in the Seasonal Decomposition procedure is known as the Census Method I or the **ratio-to-moving-averages method** (Makridakis, Wheelwright & McGee, 1983). The method first removes the seasonal and error variance by calculating moving averages whose number of terms equals the periodicity. This removes seasonality, since the high and low points of each season are averaged. The averaging also reduces the unsystematic error throughout the series. The result is the trend-cycle component. The ratio of the original series to this series of moving averages (the trend-cycle component) is then computed. The result is a seasonal-plus-error component, which can be broken down further by computing monthly averages (averaging the Januaries, then the Februaries, and so on) to eliminate the error.

This popular method was the basis for a computer program for seasonally adjusting time series by the Bureau of the Census in 1954 called the Census Method. A revised version of the program, called Census Method II, replaced the original in 1955. Since then, there have been several experimental variants of the program, each one labeled with an *X* and a sequential number. The X-11 version was adopted in 1965 as the standard program of the Bureau of the Census (Shiskin, Young & Musgrave, 1967). Census Method II-X-11, or simply X-11, offers many new refinements over previous versions, such as the ability to adjust for extreme events in the series, new trading-day adjustments, a wider selection of the moving averages computed, and other special adjustment options. The method goes through several phases of trading and seasonal adjustments, each time refining the previous estimates. The standard output from computer programs implementing X-11 includes tables and plots showing the series and derived components at various stages throughout the adjustment process.

The X11 ARIMA Method

Although ratio-to-moving-averages methods like Seasonal Decomposition are adequate for addressing many seasonal adjustment tasks, researchers at Statistics Canada have developed a significant modification to the basic method (Dagum, 1983). They found that when new data become available and are added to the series, in some cases the new seasonal factors computed can be quite different from the old ones. These changes are greatest for the most recent observations but are present even for observations going back several years. This unreliability in seasonal factors, especially the most recent ones, can be troublesome in forecasting if your series has a strong but variable seasonal component. Your forecasts could significantly change every time new data become available. The problem arises because of the inherent limitation of nonsymmetric weights in moving averages; that is, the first and last observations in a series can never have the same weights as the central observations, since averages computed at the ends of a series do not have the same number of terms as those computed in the middle of the series.

The technique the Statistics Canada researchers developed, X11 ARIMA, attempts to reduce the size of these changes in seasonal factors. Essentially, it consists of adding forecasts and backcasts obtained through ARIMA modeling to the ends of the original series and then seasonally adjusting this extended series with X-11. You can see how this helps with the problem of unequal weights at the beginning and end of the series when computing moving averages. The series has been extended at both ends with more data so that the original first and last observations are now treated more like the central observations.

Applying X11 ARIMA to the TOTALHS Series

Since the first step to X11 ARIMA analysis is actually ARIMA modeling, we start by identifying an ARIMA model that will fit the *totalhs* data. (ARIMA modeling is discussed in Chapter 6, Chapter 8, and Chapter 12; see also Box & Jenkins, 1976 and McCleary & Hay, 1980.) The first step involves examining the series and ACF plots.

Identifying the ARIMA Model

In other chapters on ARIMA modeling, we saw the importance of stationarity. In a short run of the series, both the mean and variance should be constant. The plot of the *totalhs* series in Figure 14.1 and the plot of the ACF, shown in Figure 14.2, suggests that this is not the case for *totalhs*. The series exhibits nonstationarity in mean and variance.

Figure 14.2   ACF of the totalhs series

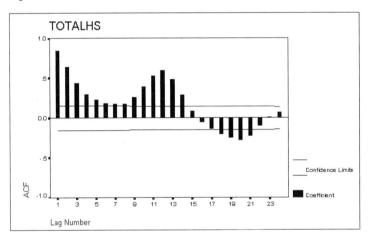

To obtain a new ACF plot, using seasonal and nonseasonal differencing and a natural log transformation to account for the nonstationarity, from the menus choose:

Graphs
  Time Series ▶
    Autocorrelations...

In the Autocorrelations dialog box, move *totalhs* into the Variables list. Note that the defined periodicity, 12, is displayed in the Transform group. Select all three Transform options to stabilize the mean and variance. Make sure that both of the Display options are selected. Figure 14.3 shows how the dialog box should look.

Figure 14.3 Autocorrelations dialog box

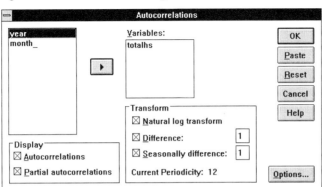

Click on Options... and increase the maximum number of lags to 24, since a seasonal model must be identified. Figure 14.4 and Figure 14.5 show the ACF and PACF plots.

Figure 14.4 ACF after seasonal and nonseasonal differencing

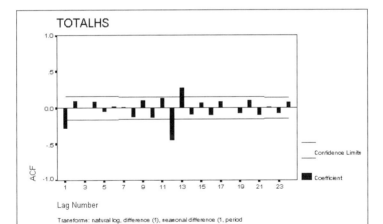

Figure 14.5   PACF after seasonal and nonseasonal differencing

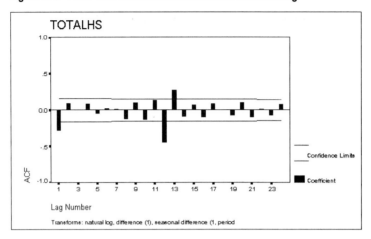

Using conventional ARIMA identification techniques (see Chapter 6, Chapter 12, and Appendix B), a likely ARIMA model for the log-transformed *totalhs* series would seem to be (0,1,1)(0,1,1) or perhaps (1,1,0)(0,1,1). (The two sets of parentheses contain the nonseasonal *p, d,* and *q* parameters and the seasonal *sp, sd,* and *sq* parameters, respectively.) We will use the first of these models.

Identifying ARIMA models can be more difficult than the example presented here. As noted in Chapter 12, identifying seasonal models can be more difficult than identifying nonseasonal models and may require identifying the model in stages.

Additionally, you might want to test the fit of the model with ARIMA before using it to generate forecasts and backcasts in X11 ARIMA. You could follow the ARIMA procedure with an ACF plot of the residuals to make sure that they are essentially white noise. The process of diagnosing the adequacy of a tentative model is discussed in Chapter 8. After following this process, you'll find that the (0,1,1)(0,1,1) model seems to fit the *totalhs* series adequately.

Adjusting with X11 ARIMA

Having identified an ARIMA model, we can estimate it with the X11 ARIMA procedure. From the menus choose:

Statistics
  Times Series ▶
    X11 ARIMA...

This opens the X11 ARIMA dialog box, as shown in Figure 14.6.

Figure 14.6   X11 ARIMA dialog box

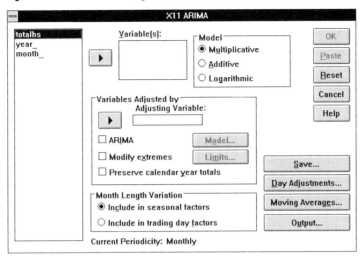

1. Move *totalhs* into the Variable(s) list.

2. Make sure that Multiplicative is selected in the Model group. This controls the application of seasonal adjustments. We want them to be multiplicative, as discussed in Chapter 11.

3. In the Variables Adjusted By group, select ARIMA. Leave the other options unchecked.

4. Click on Model... beside the ARIMA check box. This opens the X11 ARIMA Model dialog box.

5. Select the Custom model option and specify the parameters of the nonseasonal and seasonal ARIMA models identified above: *d, q, sd,* and *sq* should equal 1, while p and sp should remain equal to 0.

6. In the Transform group, select Natural log. Figure 14.7 shows how the X11 ARIMA Model dialog box should look. Click on Continue to close it.

Figure 14.7   Adjusted X11 ARIMA Model dialog box

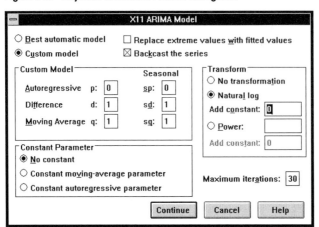

Now click on Day Adjustments... in the X11 ARIMA dialog box to open the X11 ARI-
MA Day Adjustments dialog box. Select Compute trading day regression estimates
and Conditionally adjust series below it. X11 ARIMA computes trading-day regression
estimates to adjust the daily weights for the differences in the number of times each
weekday occurs in each month. (This calendar variation can be very important for some
series.) The procedure already knows the number of times each work day occurred in
each month or quarter of a series for any time period in the twentieth century. The selected option specifies that the weights should be adjusted by the regression estimates in
later tables only if the regression estimates are significant.

In the Day Weights group, select Equal work days. This group lets you assign a special weighting structure to the days of the week. If some days are more important than
others, you can use one of these options to specify how they should be weighted. The
weighting structure specified here is one of the most common. Since building permits
are issued only on Monday through Friday, these days are assigned equal weights and
the weekend days are assigned a weight of 0.

Figure 14.8 shows how the X11 ARIMA Day Adjustments dialog box should now
look. Click on Continue to close it.

Figure 14.8   X11 ARIMA Day Adjustments dialog box

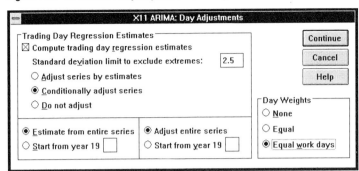

Next, ask for the standard X11 ARIMA output. (There is a lot of it, so you have to ask.) Click on Output... and select Standard set in both the Tables group and the Plots group in the X11 ARIMA Output dialog box. Finally, click on OK to carry out the analysis. Figure 14.9 shows one of the many tables that are produced.

Figure 14.9   X11 ARIMA adjustment of totalhs

D11.   Final seasonally adjusted series

Year	Jan	Feb	Mar	Apr	May	Jun	Jul	Aug	Sep
1968	115	118	121	134	114	124	124	124	131
1969	142	130	131	131	130	129	109	115	123
1970	95	107	109	108	106	115	120	122	125
1971	163	146	158	166	174	165	169	182	169
1972	228	204	190	192	183	187	189	195	200
1973	213	194	194	183	185	175	175	166	151
1974	123	154	125	140	116	132	108	96	96
1975	84	77	83	86	93	95	100	105	104
1976	116	126	116	119	126	126	118	128	140
1977	143	163	168	167	164	163	170	169	156
1978	149	150	166	189	172	174	181	164	163
1979	147	127	153	150	155	163	147	146	153
1980	118	114	91	85	78	101	105	117	121
1981	139	110	109	110	97	89	88	81	73
Avge	141	137	137	140	135	138	136	136	136

Year	Oct	Nov	Dec	Total
1968	131	136	129	1501
1969	114	106	110	1471
1970	134	140	156	1437
1971	175	186	195	2047
1972	206	201	207	2382
1973	137	141	132	2046
1974	87	83	77	1337
1975	108	112	105	1152
1976	133	138	142	1529
1977	176	165	173	1977
1978	162	170	159	2001
1979	140	122	125	1727
1980	124	125	121	1301
1981	72	.	.	966
Avge	136	141	141	.

Table total-   22876   Mean-   138   Std. deviation-   34

The table in Figure 14.9 presents the values of the series after the last iteration of seasonal and trading-day adjustments have been applied. See X11ARIMA in the Syntax Reference for a complete list of available tables.

The amount of output you receive is determined to some extent by the options in the X11 ARIMA Output dialog box. Depending on the selected options, some of your tables might include F tests and other summary measures to help you evaluate such things as whether the seasonal factors are identifiable, whether there is any evidence of residual seasonality after seasonal adjustment, and characteristics of your error and seasonal components. Tables of particular interest are those showing month-to-month percentage changes (E5, E6, E6A) and the F group of summary tables for information on the amount of variation of the original series caused by the different components.

When interpreting your output, you should use Table 14.1 to help interpret some of the symbols used by Statistics Canada.

Table 14.1   Symbols used in X11 ARIMA output

Symbol	Description
O	Original series
C	Trend-cycle variation
I′	Irregular (error) variation[*]
E	Extremes (values outside 2.5 standard deviations)
I	Residual or true irregular variation
P	Prior adjustment factors
Q	Quality control statistic[†]

*Includes unusual and extreme variation (strikes, holidays) as well as true irregular variation.

†Acceptability of irregular and seasonal characteristics (values less than 1 are considered acceptable).

Consult the Statistics Canada manual on X11 ARIMA (Dagum, 1983) and the U.S. Department of Commerce manual on X-11 (Shiskin, Young & Musgrave, 1967) for detailed information on the contents of any particular table.

Along with the many tables, three plots are produced by default. Figure 14.10 shows the legend and Figure 14.11 shows part of the G1 chart, which plots the original series with the ARIMA forecasts and backcasts added, and the original series modified for extremes. Only the beginning and end of the actual plot are shown in the figure.

Figure 14.10 Legend for X11 ARIMA plot of totalhs

```
G 1. Chart
        (X) - B 1. Original series
        (0) - E 1. Original series modified for extremes
                   with zero final weights
        (*) - Coincidence of points
        (E) - ARIMA Extrapolation

        Scale - Semi-log
```

Figure 14.11 X11 ARIMA plot of totalhs

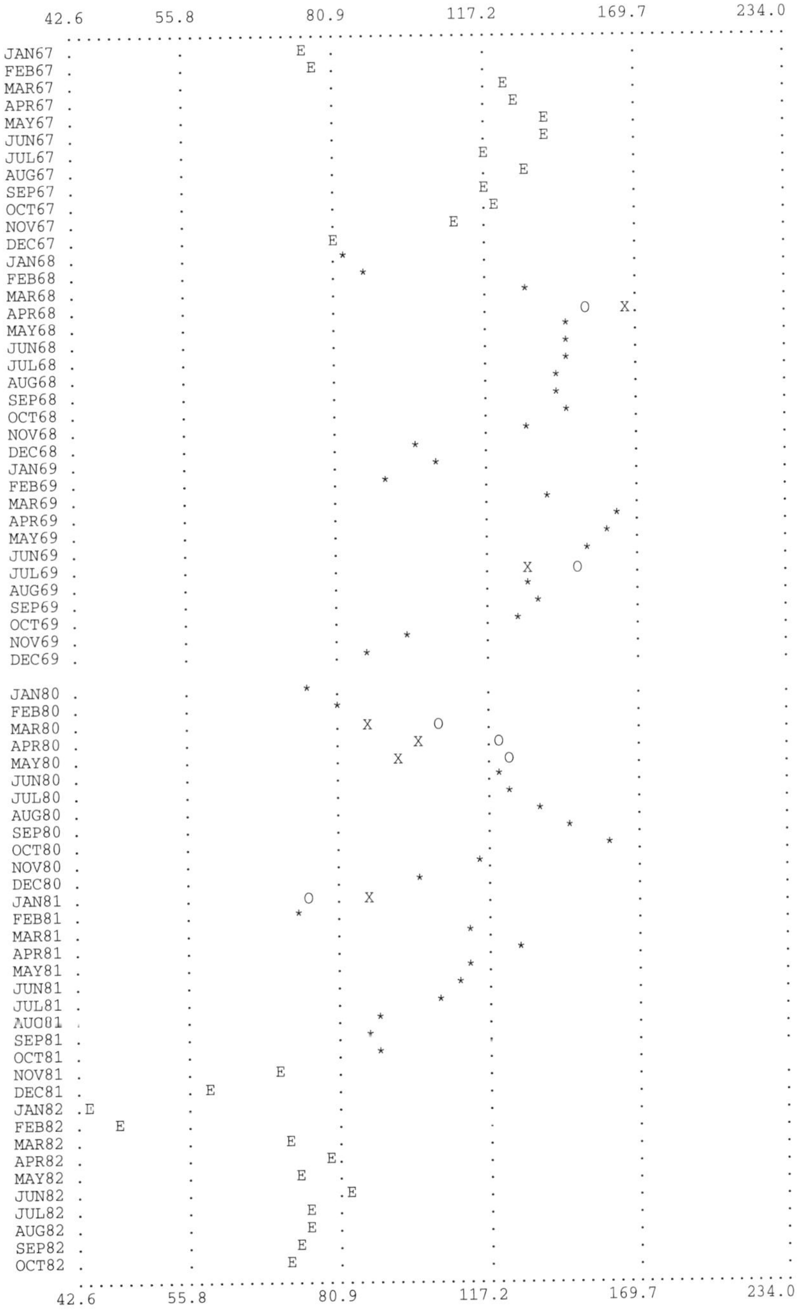

```
            42.6        55.8        80.9        117.2        169.7        234.0
            ...............................................................................
JAN67 .          .          E  .          .          .          .
FEB67 .          .          E  .          .          .          .
MAR67 .          .          .          .   E          .          .
APR67 .          .          .          .    E         .          .
MAY67 .          .          .          .       E      .          .
JUN67 .          .          .          .        E     .          .
JUL67 .          .          .          E          .          .
AUG67 .          .          .          .  E       .          .
SEP67 .          .          .          E          .          .
OCT67 .          .          .          .E          .          .
NOV67 .          .          .       E  .          .          .
DEC67 .          .          E  .          .          .          .
JAN68 .          .          .* .          .          .          .
FEB68 .          .          .  *          .          .          .
MAR68 .          .          .          .          *   .          .
APR68 .          .          .          .          O    X.          .
MAY68 .          .          .          .          *    .          .
JUN68 .          .          .          .          *    .          .
JUL68 .          .          .          .          *    .          .
AUG68 .          .          .          .         *     .          .
SEP68 .          .          .          .          *    .          .
OCT68 .          .          .          .          *    .          .
NOV68 .          .          .          .        *      .          .
DEC68 .          .          .       *  .          .          .
JAN69 .          .          .      *   .          .          .
FEB69 .          .          .    *     .          .          .
MAR69 .          .          .          .       *      .          .
APR69 .          .          .          .          .  *       .
MAY69 .          .          .          .          .  *       .
JUN69 .          .          .          .          .*          .
JUL69 .          .          .          .   X        O          .
AUG69 .          .          .          .       *      .          .
SEP69 .          .          .          .      *       .          .
OCT69 .          .          .          .     *        .          .
NOV69 .          .          .       *  .          .          .
DEC69 .          .          .     *    .          .          .

JAN80 .          .          *  .          .          .          .
FEB80 .          .          *  .          .          .          .
MAR80 .          .          . X       O  .          .          .
APR80 .          .          .       X       .O          .          .
MAY80 .          .          .     X         .O          .          .
JUN80 .          .          .          .*          .          .
JUL80 .          .          .          .  *          .          .
AUG80 .          .          .          .       *      .          .
SEP80 .          .          .          .          *   .          .
OCT80 .          .          .          .     *.          .          .
NOV80 .          .          .          .        *.          .
DEC80 .          .          .       *  .          .          .
JAN81 .          .          O    . X     .          .          .
FEB81 .          .          .*         .          .          .
MAR81 .          .          .          .   *         .          .
APR81 .          .          .          .       *      .          .
MAY81 .          .          .          .    *        .          .
JUN81 .          .          .          .   *         .          .
JUL81 .          .          .          . *          .          .
AUG81 .          .          .       *  .          .          .
SEP81 .          .          .       *  .          .          .
OCT81 .          .          .        * .          .          .
NOV81 .          .   E      .          .          .          .
DEC81 .          . E        .          .          .          .
JAN82 .E         .          .          .          .          .
FEB82 .    E     .          .          .          .          .
MAR82 .          .       E  .          .          .          .
APR82 .          .          E. .          .          .          .
MAY82 .          .       E  .          .          .          .
JUN82 .          .          .E .          .          .          .
JUL82 .          .        E .          .          .          .
AUG82 .          .        E .          .          .          .
SEP82 .          .       E  .          .          .          .
OCT82 .          .       E  .          .          .          .
            ...............................................................................
            42.6        55.8        80.9        117.2        169.7        234.0
```

Like the Seasonal Decomposition procedure, X11 ARIMA also produces four new series and adds them to your working data file. These new series are the seasonally adjusted series, the seasonal factors, the trend-cycle component, and the error component.

The Seasonally Adjusted Series

How does our seasonally adjusted series compare with the original series? Figure 14.12 shows the original series from 1972 to the end of the series. Figure 14.13 shows the seasonally adjusted series for the same period. (X11 ARIMA saves the seasonally adjusted series, by default, in a temporary variable named *sas#1.*) Notice that the frequent peaks and valleys showing the seasonal effect in Figure 14.12 have been smoothed in Figure 14.13 but that the longer cyclical pattern is still present.

Figure 14.12 Unadjusted totalhs series

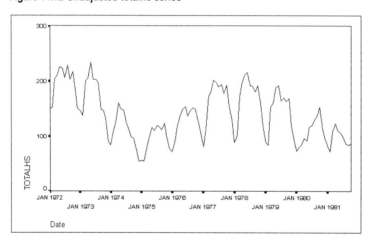

Figure 14.13 Seasonally adjusted totalhs series

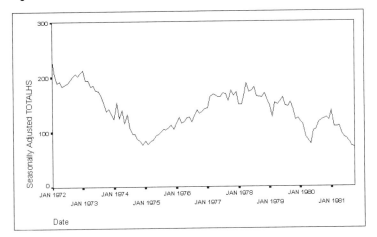

Other X11 ARIMA Options

The example presented in this chapter uses just a few of the many X11 ARIMA subcommands available to fine-tune your adjustments. One of the other capabilities of X11 ARIMA is the option of letting the program select one of three default ARIMA models instead of specifying one yourself. In order to be used to generate forecasts and backcasts for your data, the default model must fit well enough to meet three stringent criteria. If more than one model meets the criteria, X11 ARIMA picks the best-fitting model. If none of the default models fits your data well enough to meet the criteria, the statistics on how well each model fits are reported. This gives you the opportunity to pick one and specify it later as a custom model if you decide the criteria are too conservative for a given series. Models specified as custom models are not subject to meeting these criteria. In fact, the ARIMA model of the *totalhs* series used in this chapter would not have been selected through the default model-fitting routine but was selected based on conventional ARIMA identification and diagnostic techniques.

How to Obtain X11 ARIMA Tables and Plots

To perform X11 ARIMA analysis, from the menus choose:

Statistics
  Time Series ▶
    X11 ARIMA...

This opens the X11 ARIMA dialog box, as shown in Figure 14.14, provided that your working data file has dates defined as either Years, quarters or Years, months. You cannot perform X11 ARIMA analysis unless you have quarterly or monthly data.

Figure 14.14 X11 ARIMA dialog box

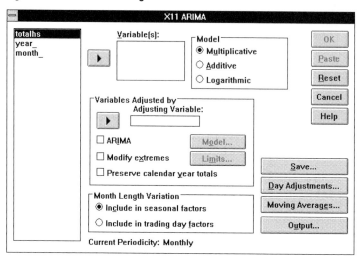

The numeric variables in your data file appear in the source list. To obtain default X11 smoothing with no ARIMA forecasting or backcasting, move one or more variables into the Variable(s) list and click on OK.

The alternatives in the Model group let you choose the way in which seasonal adjustments are applied to the series:

○ **Multiplicative.** The seasonal adjustments are multiplied by the seasonally adjusted series to obtain the observed values.

○ **Additive.** The seasonal adjustments are added to the seasonally adjusted series to obtain the observed values.

○ **Logarithmic.** The seasonal adjustments are added to the seasonally adjusted series in the logarithmic scale. This involves different assumptions about the error term than the multiplicative model.

The options in the Variables Adjusted By group perform various adjustments to the series:

Adjusting Variable. To adjust the observed values prior to seasonal adjustment, select the variable that should be divided into or subtracted from series values and move it into the Adjusting Variable box.

❑ **ARIMA**. To perform ARIMA adjustments, select this option. This activates the Model... button.

❑ **Modify extremes**. To modify extreme values prior to calculating the trend-cycle estimates, select this option. This activates the Limits... button.

❑ **Preserve calendar year totals**. To ensure that yearly totals of the adjusted series are equal to those of the original series, select this option.

The alternatives in the Month Length Variation group control the factors to which differences in the calendar lengths of months are attributed:

○ **Include in seasonal factors**. Attributes these differences to the seasonal adjustments.

○ **Include in trading day factors**. Attributes these differences to the effect of the trading-day adjustments.

X11 ARIMA Model

The X11 ARIMA Model dialog box, shown in Figure 14.15, controls the optional ARIMA forecasts generated by X11 ARIMA. To open this dialog box, select ARIMA in the Variables Adjusted By group in the X11 ARIMA dialog box and click on the Model button.

Figure 14.15 X11 ARIMA Model dialog box

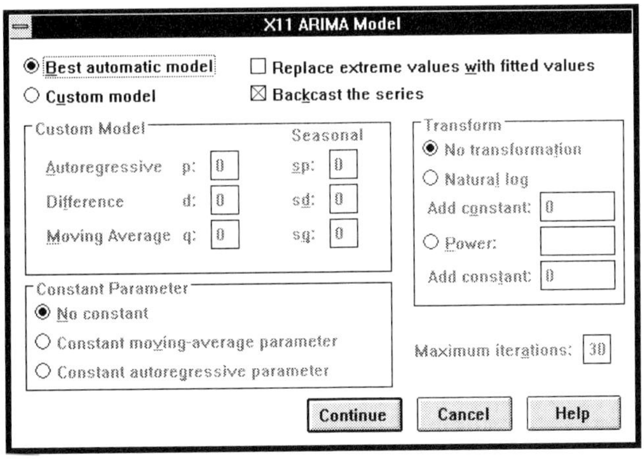

○ **Best automatic model**. X11 ARIMA fits three default models to the series and chooses the one that fits best. If the series is not fit adequately by any of the three, no ARIMA adjustment is done.

○ **Custom model.** X11 ARIMA fits the model described by the specifications in the Custom Model, Transform, and Constant Parameter groups.

Two additional options are available:

❏ **Replace extreme values with fitted values.** Outliers are replaced by fitted values before estimating the parameters used in forecasting, except during the initial observations. The default is not to do this.

❏ **Backcast the series.** Extrapolated values from ARIMA are added to the beginning of the series, as well as the end. The default is to perform backcasting.

Custom Model. The Custom Model group contains six text boxes, each of which can contain 0 or a positive integer, usually 1 or 2. You must specify at least one of the six if you are defining a custom model; in practice, you must specify autoregressive or moving-average orders. The first three parameters describe the nonseasonal model:

Autoregressive. The autoregressive order of the process (p).

Difference. The number of times that the series must be differenced to make it stationary (d).

Moving Average. The order of moving average in the process (q).

The Seasonal column contains text boxes in which you can specify the corresponding parameters sp, sd, and sq of the process at seasonal lags. These values can be 0 or a positive integer, usually 1.

Transform. The Transform group offers three alternatives for transforming of the series before ARIMA modeling:

○ **No transformation.** This is the default.

○ **Natural log.** If you select the log transformation, you can optionally specify a constant to be added to the series before transformation, to ensure that all values are positive.

○ **Power.** If you select the power transformation, you must specify a power to which the series should be raised before ARIMA modeling. You can optionally specify a constant to be added to the series before transformation, for example to prevent taking the square root of negative numbers.

Constant Parameter. You can specify a deterministic parameter for either component of the ARIMA process:

○ **No constant.** This is the default.

○ **Constant moving-average parameter.**

○ **Constant autoregressive parameter.**

Maximum iterations. This text box lets you control how long the ARIMA algorithm iterates in search of a solution. Specify a positive integer.

Limits

If you select the Modify extremes option in the X11 ARIMA dialog box, you can use the X11 ARIMA Limits dialog box, shown in Figure 14.16, to specify the sigma limits for graduating extreme values in estimating the seasonal and trend-cycle components. Enter a number greater than or equal to 0.1 and less than 9.9 into the Lower bound text box, and enter a number greater than the lower bound and less than or equal to 9.9 into the Upper bound text box.

Figure 14.16 X11 ARIMA Limits dialog box

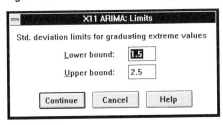

Saving New Variables

By default, X11 ARIMA does not add variables to your working data file. To add variables containing results of the analysis, click on Save... to open the X11 ARIMA Save dialog box.

Figure 14.17 X11 ARIMA Save dialog box

Select one or more of the following options:

❏ **Seasonally adjusted variables**. These are the original variables, smoothed and adjusted for seasonal factors. The variable names begin with *sas*.

❏ **Seasonal factors**. These are the seasonal components of the original variables. The variable names begin with *saf*.

❏ **Trend cycle**. This is the smoothed original series. The variable names begin with *stc*.

❏ **Residuals**. This is the error component of the original series, apart from the trend-cycle component and the seasonal factors. The variable names begin with *err*.

Day Adjustments

To adjust the series by means of trading day regression estimates, click on Day Adjustments... in the X11 ARIMA dialog box to open the X11 ARIMA Day Adjustments dialog box, as shown in Figure 14.18. These adjustments are not available if Additive is selected in the Model group.

Figure 14.18 X11 ARIMA Day Adjustments dialog box

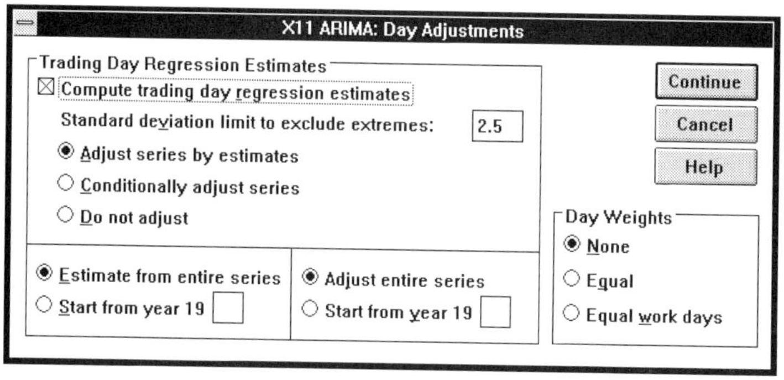

❏ **Compute trading day regression estimates**. Select this option to adjust by trading day regression estimates. This activates the other controls in the group.

Standard deviation limit to exclude extremes. You can specify a value between 0.1 and 9.9 for the number of standard deviations beyond which extreme values are excluded from the regression.

Choose one of three alternatives to adjust the series:

○ **Adjust series by estimates**. Estimates are always used to adjust the series. This is the default.

○ **Conditionally adjust series**. In X11 ARIMA tables of the C series, trading-day regression estimates are used only if they explain significant variation.

○ **Do not adjust.**

Another set of alternatives determines how much of the series is used in carrying out the trading day regressions:

○ **Estimate from entire series**. This is the default.

○ **Start from year 19n**. If you select this alternative, specify a two-digit number in the text box.

A third set of alternatives determines how much of the series is adjusted by the trading day regressions:

○ **Adjust entire series.**

○ **Start from year 19n**. If you select this alternative, specify a two-digit number in the text box.

Day Weights. You can choose one of three alternatives for weighting days:

○ **None**. No weighting of days is used.

○ **Equal**. All days are weighted equally.

○ **Equal work days**. Days from Monday through Friday are weighted equally; Saturday and Sunday are given a weight of 0.

Moving Averages

To control the calculation of moving averages used in smoothing the series, click on Moving Averages... in the X11 ARIMA dialog box. This opens the X11 ARIMA Moving Averages dialog box, as shown in Figure 14.19.

Figure 14.19 X11 ARIMA Moving Averages dialog box

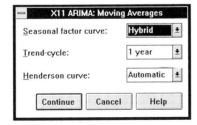

▼ **Seasonal factor curve**. You can choose one of the following alternatives:

Hybrid. A 3×3 average is used for the first estimate and a 3×5 average for the final estimate. This is the default.

3×3. A 3×3 average is used for all estimates.

3×5. A 3×5 average is used for all estimates.

3×9. A 3×9 average is used for all estimates.

Stable. An average of all values is used.

Select. A moving average is chosen for each month on the basis of the I/S ratio.

⬇ **Trend-cycle**. The length of the trend-cycle moving average. You can choose one of the following alternatives:

1 year. This is the default.

2 year.

⬇ **Henderson curve**. The moving average for variable trend-cycles. Alternatives are dependent upon whether the series is monthly or quarterly:

Automatic. An appropriate moving average is selected based on the randomness of the series. This is the default.

Number. For monthly series, 9-, 13-, and 23-term moving averages are available. For quarterly series, 5- and 7-term moving averages are available.

Output

To specify the quantity of tabular and plotted output, click on Output... in the X11 ARIMA dialog box. This opens the X11 ARIMA Output dialog box, as shown in Figure 14.20.

Figure 14.20 X11 ARIMA Output dialog box

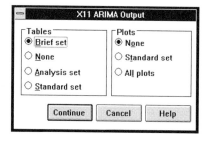

Tables. X11 ARIMA can generate dozens of tables, identified by standard names from A1 to F3. See X11ARIMA in the Syntax Reference for a complete list. Alternatives for tabular output in this dialog box include:

○ **Brief**. Brief output includes a small number of tables, between 3 and 13 depending upon other specifications.

○ **None**. No tabular output.

○ **Analysis set**. Analysis output includes between 7 and 29 tables.

○ **Standard set**. The standard set of tabular output includes between 19 and 40 tables.

Plots. X11 ARIMA also generates a number of plots in low resolution, appearing in the output window as character plots. Available alternatives are:

○ **None**. No plots.

○ **Standard set**. The standard set of plots includes a plot of the original series, the original series with ARIMA extrapolations, the final seasonally adjusted series and trend-cycle components, the seasonal factors, and others. See X11ARIMA in the Syntax Reference for more information.

○ **All plots**. These include the standard set plus a number of less widely used plots.

Additional Features Available with Command Syntax

You can customize your spectral analysis if you paste your selections into a syntax window and edit the resulting X11ARIMA command syntax. Additional features include:

- Prior adjustment by more than one variable.
- Seasonal adjustment of a subset of the specified variables.
- More precise specification of the AR and MA parameters allowed in the ARIMA model.
- Control over the calculation of seasonal moving averages, analogous to that available for nonseasonal moving averages in the Moving Averages dialog box.
- Additional intermediate levels of tabular output.
- Additional flexibility in specifying day weights for trading-day variation.
- Control over the numerical precision of tabular output.

See the Syntax Reference section of this manual for command syntax rules and for complete X11ARIMA command syntax.

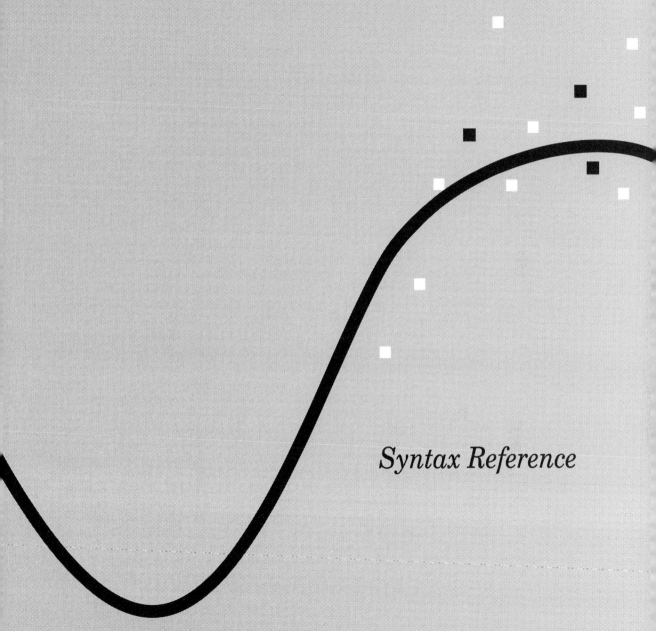

SPSS

Syntax Reference

Universals

Most of the rules described in the Universals section of the *SPSS Base System Syntax Reference Guide* apply to Trends. This section explains some areas that are unique to working with Trends. The topics are divided into five sections:

- *Syntax* provides a quick review of the conventions used in SPSS syntax charts, which summarize command syntax in diagrams and provide an easy reference.

- *Operations* discusses general operating rules, missing values in Trends, and how to control the quantity of output using TSET.

- *New Variables* describes the types of series generated by Trends procedures and their naming conventions.

- *Periodicity* describes the facilities for specifying the periodicity of your series.

- *APPLY Subcommand* discusses the models generated by Trends procedures and how to use the APPLY subcommand as a shorthand method for developing and modifying models.

Syntax

Every effort has been made to keep the language of Trends consistent with that of the SPSS Base system.

Syntax Diagrams

Each Trends command, just like each Base system command, includes a syntax diagram that shows all the subcommands, keywords, and specifications allowed for that command. The rules of the syntax diagram are exactly the same for the Base system and for Trends but are repeated here for your convenience.

- Elements in upper case are subcommands or keywords.
- Elements in lower case describe specifications supplied by the user.
- Elements in boldface type are defaults.
- Elements enclosed in square brackets ([ ]) are optional. When brackets would confuse the format, they are omitted. The command description explains which specifications are required or optional.
- Braces ({ }) indicate a choice among the elements they enclose.
- Special delimiters—such as parentheses, apostrophes, or quotation marks—should be entered as they appear.

Operations

There are a few general operating rules you should be aware of when working with Trends:

- A pass of the data is caused by every Trends command except the following: MODEL NAME, READ MODEL, SAVE MODEL, and TDISPLAY.

- Except when you apply a previous model with the APPLY subcommand, subcommands are in effect only for the current procedure.

- Whenever a subcommand of a procedure performs the same function as a TSET setting, the procedure subcommand, if specified, overrides TSET.

Missing Values

Since time series observations occur at equally spaced intervals and are thus sequentially related in the data file, missing values in a series can present unique problems. There are several ways missing values are handled in Trends.

- In procedures AREG (method ML) and ARIMA, missing values are allowed anywhere in the series and present no problems in estimating parameters but do require extra processing time. AREG methods CO and PW can handle series that have missing values at the beginning or end of the series by dropping those observations but cannot handle series with imbedded missing values.

- Procedures EXSMOOTH, SEASON, SPECTRA, and X11ARIMA cannot handle missing values anywhere in the series. To use one of these procedures when you have missing data, you must first specify either TSET MISSING=INCLUDE to include user-missing values, the RMV procedure to replace missing values, or the USE command to specify a range of non-missing observations.

- The TSET MISSING command allows you to include or exclude user-missing values in Trends procedures. EXCLUDE is the default.

- RMV allows you to replace user-missing and system-missing values with estimates computed from existing values in the series using one of several methods.

Statistical Output

For some Trends procedures, the amount of output displayed can be controlled by the TSET PRINT setting. TSET PRINT can be set to BRIEF, DEFAULT, or DETAILED. The following are some general guidelines used by procedures with multiple iterations.

- For TSET PRINT=BRIEF, no iteration history is shown. Only the final statistics and the number of iterations required are reported.

- For TSET PRINT=DEFAULT, a one-line statistical summary at each iteration plus the final statistics are reported.

- For TSET PRINT=DETAILED, a complete statistical summary at each iteration plus the final statistics are reported.

For details, refer to the individual procedures.

New Variables

Trends procedures AREG, ARIMA, EXSMOOTH, SEASON, and X11ARIMA automatically create, name, and label new variables each time the procedure is executed. These new variables are added to the working data file and can be used or saved like any other variable. The names of these variables consist of the following prefixes, followed by an identifying numeric extension:

FIT   *Predicted values.* When the predictions are for existing observations, the values are called "fitted" values. When the predicted values extend into the forecast period (see PREDICT in the *SPSS Base System Syntax Reference Guide*), they are forecasts. Procedures AREG and ARIMA produce one *FIT* variable for each series list (equation); procedure EXSMOOTH produces one *FIT* variable for each series specified.

ERR   *Residual or "error" values.* For procedures AREG, ARIMA, and EXSMOOTH, these values are the observed value minus the predicted value. These procedures produce one *ERR* variable for each *FIT* variable. Since *FIT* variables are always reported in the original raw score metric and *ERR* might be reported in the natural log metric if such a transformation was part of the model, the reported *ERR* variable will not always equal the observed variable minus the *FIT* variable. (The discussion under each individual procedure will tell you if this is the case.) The *ERR* variable is assigned the system-missing value for any observations in the forecast period that extend beyond the original series.

For procedures SEASON and X11ARIMA, the *ERR* values are what remain after the seasonal, trend, and cycle components have been removed from the series. These procedures produce one *ERR* variable for each series.

LCL   *Lower confidence limits.* These are the lowerbound values of an estimated confidence interval for the predictions. A 95% confidence interval is estimated unless another interval is specified on a subcommand or on a previous TSET CIN command. Procedures AREG and ARIMA produce confidence intervals.

UCL   *Upper confidence limits.* These are the upperbound values of an estimated confidence interval for the predictions. The interval is 95%, unless it is changed on a subcommand or on a previous TSET CIN command.

SEP   *Standard errors of the predicted values.* Procedures AREG and ARIMA produce one *SEP* variable for every *FIT* variable.

SAS   *Seasonally adjusted series.* These are the values obtained after removing the seasonal variation of a series. Procedures SEASON and X11ARIMA produce one *SAS* variable for each series specified.

SAF   *Seasonal adjustment factors.* These values indicate the effect of each period on the level of the series. Procedures SEASON and X11ARIMA produce one *SAF* variable for each series specified.

STC   *Smoothed trend-cycle components.* These values show the trend and cyclical behavior present in the series. Procedures SEASON and X11ARIMA produce one *STC* variable for each series specified.

- If TSET NEWVAR=CURRENT (the default) is in effect, only variables from the current procedure are saved in the working data file, and the suffix #n is used to distinguish variables that are generated by different series on one procedure. For example, if two series are specified on an ARIMA command, the variables automatically generated are *FIT#1*, *ERR#1*, *LCL#1*, *UCL#1*, *SEP#1*, *FIT#2*, *ERR#2*, *LCL#2*, *UCL#2* and *SEP#2*. If these variables already exist from a previous procedure, their values are replaced.

- If TSET NEWVAR=ALL is in effect, all variables generated during the session are saved in the working data file. Variables are named using the extension *_n*, where *n* increments by 1 for each new variable of a given type. For example, if two series are specified on an EXSMOOTH command, the *FIT* variables generated would be *FIT_1* and *FIT_2*. If an AREG command with one series followed, the *FIT* variable would be *FIT_3*.

- A third TSET NEWVAR option, NONE, allows you to display statistical results from a procedure without creating any new variables. This option can result in faster processing time.

TO Keyword

The order in which new variables are added to the working data file dictionary is *ERR*, *SAS*, *SAF*, and *STC* for SEASON and X11ARIMA, and *FIT*, *ERR*, *LCL*, *UCL*, and *SEP* for the other procedures. For this reason, the TO keyword should be used with caution for specifying lists of these generated variables. For example, the specification ERR#1 TO ERR#3 indicates more than just *ERR#1*, *ERR#2*, and *ERR#3*. If the residuals are from an ARIMA procedure, ERR#1 TO ERR#3 indicates *ERR#1*, *LCL#1*, *UCL#1*, *SEP#1*, *FIT#2*, *ERR#2*, *LCL#2*, *UCL#2*, *SEP#2*, *FIT#3*, and *ERR#3*.

Maximum Number of New Variables

TSET MXNEWVAR specifies the maximum number of new variables that can be generated by a procedure. The default is 60.

Periodicity

Trends provides several ways to specify the periodicity of your series.

- Many Trends commands have a subcommand such as PERIOD that can set the periodicity for that specific procedure.
- TSET PERIOD can be used to set the periodicity to be used globally. This specification can be changed by another TSET PERIOD command.
- The DATE command assigns date variables to the observations. Most of these variables have periodicities associated with them.

If more than one of these periodicities are in effect when a procedure that uses periodicity is executed, the following precedence determines which periodicity is used:

- First, the procedure uses any periodicity specified within the procedure.
- Second, if the periodicity has not been specified within the command, the procedure uses the periodicity established on TSET PERIOD.
- Third, if periodicity is not defined within the procedure or on TSET PERIOD, the periodicity established by the DATE variables is used.

If periodicity is required for execution of the procedure (SEASON) or a subcommand of a procedure (SDIFF) and the periodicity has not been established anywhere, the procedure or subcommand will not be executed.

APPLY Subcommand

On most Trends procedures (and on some Base system and Professional Statistics procedures) you can specify the APPLY subcommand. APPLY allows you to use specifications from a previous execution of the same procedure. This provides a convenient shorthand for developing and modifying models. Specific rules and examples on how to use APPLY with a given procedure are described under the individual procedures. The following are some general rules about using the APPLY subcommand:

- In general, the only specification on APPLY is the name of the model to be reapplied in quotes. If no model is specified, the model and series from the previous specification of that procedure is used.

- For procedures AREG and ARIMA, three additional keywords, INITIAL, SPECIFICATIONS, and FIT, can be specified on APPLY. These keywords are discussed under those procedures.

- To change the series used with the model, enter new series names before or after APPLY. If series names are specified before APPLY, a slash is required to separate the series names and the APPLY subcommand.

- To change one or more specifications of the model, enter the subcommands of only those portions you want to change before or after the keyword APPLY.

- Model names are either the default *MOD_n* names assigned by Trends or the names assigned on the MODEL NAME command.

- Models can be applied only to the same type of procedure that generated them. For example, you cannot apply a model generated by ARIMA to the AREG procedure.

- The following procedures can generate models and apply models: AREG, ARIMA, EXSMOOTH, SEASON, SPECTRA, and X11ARIMA in SPSS Trends; ACF, CASEPLOT, CCF, CURVEFIT, NPPLOT, PACF, and TSPLOT in the SPSS Base System; and WLS and 2SLS in SPSS Professional Statistics.

Models

The models specified on the APPLY subcommand are automatically generated by Trends procedures. Models created within a Trends session remain active until the end of the session or until the READ MODEL command is specified.

Each model includes information such as the procedure that created it, the model name assigned to it, the series names specified, the subcommands and specifications used, parameter estimates, and TSET settings.

Four Trends commands are available for use with models:

- TDISPLAY displays information about the active models, including model name, model label, the procedure that created each model, and so forth.

- MODEL NAME allows you to specify names for models.

- SAVE MODEL allows you to save any or all of the models created in a session in a model file.

- READ MODEL reads in any or all of the models contained in a previously saved model file. These models replace currently active models.

Default Model Names

The default model name is *MOD_n*, where *n* increments by 1 each time an unnamed model is created in the session.

- *MOD_n* reinitializes at the start of every session or when the READ MODEL subcommand is specified.
- If any *MOD_n* names already exist (for example, if they are read in using READ MODEL), those numbers are skipped when new names are assigned.
- Alternatively, you can assign model names on the MODEL NAME command.

AREG

```
AREG [VARIABLES=] dependent series name WITH independent series names

[/METHOD={PW**}]
         {CO  }
         {ML  }

[/{CONSTANT† }]
  {NOCONSTANT}

[/RHO={0**  }]
      {value}

[/MXITER={10**}]
         {n   }

[/APPLY [='model name']  [{SPECIFICATIONS}]]
                         {INITIAL       }
                         {FIT           }
```

**Default if the subcommand is omitted.
†Default if the subcommand or keyword is omitted and there is no corresponding specification on the TSET command.

Method definitions:

PW   Prais-Winsten (GLS) estimation
CO   Cochrane-Orcutt estimation
ML   Exact maximum-likelihood estimation

Example:
```
AREG VARY WITH VARX
  /METHOD=ML.
```

Overview

AREG estimates a regression model with AR(1) (first-order autoregressive) errors. (Models whose errors follow a general ARIMA process can be estimated using the ARIMA procedure.) AREG provides a choice among three estimation techniques.

For the Prais-Winsten and Cochrane-Orcutt estimation methods (keywords PW and CO), you can obtain the rho values and statistics at each iteration, and regression statistics for the ordinary least-square and final Prais-Winsten or Cochrane-Orcutt estimates. For the maximum-likelihood method (keyword ML), you can obtain the adjusted sum of squares and Marquardt constant at each iteration and, for the final parameter estimates, regression statistics, correlation and covariance matrices, Akaike's information criterion (AIC) (Akaike, 1974), and Schwartz's Bayesian criterion (SBC) (Schwartz, 1978).

Options

Estimation Technique. You can select one of three available estimation techniques (Prais-Winsten, Cochrane-Orcutt, or exact maximum-likelihood) on the METHOD subcommand. You can request regression through the origin or inclusion of a constant in the model by specifying NOCONSTANT or CONSTANT to override the setting on the TSET command.

Rho Value. You can specify the value to be used as the initial rho value (estimate of the first autoregressive parameter) on the RHO subcommand.

Iterations. You can specify the maximum number of iterations the procedure is allowed to cycle through in calculating estimates on the MXITER subcommand.

Statistical Output. To display estimates and statistics at each iteration in addition to the default output, specify TSET PRINT=DETAILED before AREG. To display only the final parameter estimates, use TSET PRINT=BRIEF (see TSET in the *SPSS Base System Syntax Reference Guide*).

New Variables. To evaluate the regression summary table without creating new variables, specify TSET NEWVAR=NONE prior to AREG. This can result in faster processing time. To add new variables without erasing the values of previous Trends-generated variables, specify TSET NEWVAR=ALL. This saves all new variables generated during the session in the working data file and may require extra processing time.

Basic Specification

The basic specification is one dependent series name, the keyword WITH, and one or more independent series names.

- By default, procedure AREG estimates a regression model using the Prais-Winsten (GLS) technique. The number of iterations is determined by the convergence value set on TSET CNVERGE (default of 0.001), up to the default maximum number of 10 iterations. A 95% confidence interval is used unless it is changed by a TSET CIN command prior to the AREG procedure.
- Unless the default on TSET NEWVAR is changed prior to AREG, five variables are automatically created, labeled, and added to the working data file: fitted values (*FIT#1*), residuals (*ERR#1*), lower confidence limits (*LCL#1*), upper confidence limits (*UCL#1*), and standard errors of prediction (*SEP#1*). (For variable naming and labeling conventions, see "New Variables" on p. 253.)

Subcommand Order

- VARIABLES must be specified first.
- The remaining subcommands can be specified in any order.

Syntax Rules

- VARIABLES can be specified only once.
- Other subcommands can be specified more than once, but only the last specification of each one is executed.

Operations

- AREG cannot forecast beyond the end of the regressor (independent) series (see PREDICT in the *SPSS Base System Syntax Reference Guide*).
- Method ML allows missing data anywhere in the series. Missing values at the beginning and end are skipped and the analysis proceeds with the first non-missing case using Melard's algorithm. If imbedded missing values are found, they are noted and the Kalman filter is used for estimation.
- Methods PW and CO allow missing values at the beginning or end of the series but not within the series. Missing values at the beginning or end of the series are skipped. If imbedded missing values are found, a warning is issued suggesting the ML method be used instead and the analysis terminates. (See RMV in the *SPSS Base System Syntax Reference Guide* for information on replacing missing values.)
- Series with missing cases may require extra processing time.

Limitations

- Maximum 1 VARIABLES subcommand.
- Maximum 1 dependent series in the series list. There is no limit on the number of independent series.

Example

```
AREG VARY WITH VARX
   /METHOD=ML.
```

- This command performs an exact maximum-likelihood (ML) regression using series *VARY* as the dependent variable and series *VARX* as the independent variable.

VARIABLES Subcommand

VARIABLES specifies the series list and is the only required subcommand. The actual keyword VARIABLES can be omitted.

- The dependent series is specified first, followed by keyword WITH and one or more independent series.

METHOD Subcommand

METHOD specifies the estimation technique. Three different estimation techniques are available.

- If METHOD is not specified, the Prais-Winsten method is used.
- Only one method can be specified on the METHOD subcommand.

The available methods are:

PW   *Prais-Winsten method.* This generalized least-squares approach is the default (see Johnston, 1984).

CO   *Cochrane-Orcutt method.* (See Johnston, 1984.)

ML   *Exact maximum-likelihood method.* This method can be used when one of the independent variables is the lagged dependent variable. It can also handle missing data anywhere in the series (see Kohn & Ansley, 1986).

Example

```
AREG VARY WITH VARX
  /METHOD=CO.
```

In this example, the Cochrane-Orcutt method is used to estimate the regression model.

CONSTANT and NOCONSTANT Subcommands

CONSTANT and NOCONSTANT indicate whether a constant term should be estimated in the regression equation. The specification overrides the corresponding setting on the TSET command.

- CONSTANT indicates that a constant should be estimated. It is the default unless changed by TSET NOCONSTANT prior to the current procedure.
- NOCONSTANT eliminates the constant term from the model.

RHO Subcommand

RHO specifies the initial value of rho, an estimate of the first autoregressive parameter.

- If RHO is not specified, the initial rho value defaults to 0 (equivalent to ordinary least squares).
- The value specified on RHO can be any value greater than −1 and less than 1.
- Only one rho value can be specified per AREG command.

Example

```
AREG VAR01 WITH VAR02 VAR03
  /METHOD=CO
  /RHO=0.5.
```

- In this example, the Cochrane-Orcutt (CO) estimation method with an initial rho value of 0.5 is used.

MXITER Subcommand

MXITER specifies the maximum number of iterations of the estimation process.

- If MXITER is not specified, the maximum number of iterations defaults to 10.
- The specification on MXITER can be any positive integer.

- Iteration stops either when the convergence criterion is met or when the maximum is reached, whichever occurs first. The convergence criterion is set on the TSET CNVERGE command. The default is 0.001.

Example

```
AREG VARY WITH VARX
  /MXITER=5.
```

- In this example, AREG generates Prais-Winsten estimates and associated statistics with a maximum of 5 iterations.

APPLY Subcommand

APPLY allows you to use a previously defined AREG model without having to repeat the specifications. For general rules on APPLY, see the APPLY subcommand on p. 256.

- The specifications on APPLY can include the name of a previous model in quotes and one of three keywords. All of these specifications are optional.
- If a model name is not specified, the model specified on the previous AREG command is used.
- To change one or more specifications of the model, specify the subcommands of only those portions you want to change after the APPLY subcommand.
- If no series are specified on the AREG command, the series that were originally specified with the model being reapplied are used.
- To change the series used with the model, enter new series names before or after the APPLY subcommand. If a series name is specified before APPLY, the slash before the subcommand is required.
- APPLY with keyword FIT sets MXITER to 0. If you apply a model that used FIT and want to obtain estimates, you will need to respecify MXITER.

The keywords available for APPLY with AREG are:

SPECIFICATIONS   *Use only the specifications from the original model.* AREG should create the initial values. This is the default.

INITIAL   *Use the original model's final estimates as initial values for estimation.*

FIT   *No estimation.* Estimates from the original model should be applied directly.

Example

```
AREG VARY WITH VARX
   /METHOD=CO
   /RHO=0.25
   /MXITER=15.
AREG VARY WITH VARX
   /METHOD=ML.
AREG VARY WITH VAR01
   /APPLY.
AREG VARY WITH VAR01
   /APPLY='MOD_1'
   /MXITER=10.
AREG VARY WITH VAR02
   /APPLY FIT.
```

- The first command estimates a regression model for *VARY* and *VARX* using the Cochrane-Orcutt method, an initial rho value of 0.25, and a maximum of 15 iterations. This model is assigned the name *MOD_1*.

- The second command estimates a regression model for *VARY* and *VARX* using the ML method. This model is assigned the name *MOD_2*.

- The third command displays the regression statistics for the series *VARY* and *VAR01* using the same method, ML, as in the second command. This model is assigned the name *MOD_3*.

- The fourth command applies the same method and rho value as in the first command but changes the maximum number of iterations to 10. This new model is named *MOD_4*.

- The last command applies the last model, *MOD_4*, using the series *VARY* and *VAR02*. The FIT specification means the final estimates of *MOD_4* should be applied directly to the new series with no new estimation.

References

Akaike, H. 1974. A new look at the statistical model identification. *IEEE Transaction on Automatic Control* AC–19: 716–723.

Harvey, A. C. 1981. *The econometric analysis of time series.* Oxford: Philip Allan.

Johnston, J. 1984. *Econometric methods.* New York: McGraw-Hill.

Kohn, R., and C. Ansley. 1986. Estimation, prediction, and interpolation for ARIMA models with missing data. *Journal of the American Statistical Association* 81: 751–761.

Schwartz, G. 1978. Estimating the dimensions of a model. *Annals of Statistics* 6: 461–464.

ARIMA

```
ARIMA [VARIABLES=] dependent series name [WITH independent series names]

[/MODEL =[(p,d,q)[(sp,sd,sq)[period]]]

            [ {CONSTANT† }] [ {NOLOG†    }]]
              {NOCONSTANT}     {LG10 or LOG}
                               {LN        }

[/P={value       }] [/D=value]  [/Q={value       }]
    {(value list)}                  {(value list)}

[/SP={value       }]  [/SD=value]  [/SQ={value       }]
     {(value list)}                     {(value list)}

[/AR=value list] [/MA=value list]

[/SAR=value list] [/SMA=value list]

[/REG=value list] [/CON=value]

[/MXITER={10**  }] [/MXLAMB={1.0E9**}]
         {value }            {value }

[/SSQPCT={0.001**}] [/PAREPS={0.001†}]
         {value  }            {value }

[/CINPCT={95†  }]
         {value}

[/APPLY [='model name'] [{SPECIFICATIONS}]]
                         {INITIAL        }
                         {FIT            }
```

**Default if the subcommand is omitted.
†Default if the subcommand or keyword is omitted and there is no corresponding specification on the TSET command.

Example:

```
ARIMA SALES WITH INTERVEN
  /MODEL=(0,1,1)(0,1,1).
```

Overview

ARIMA estimates nonseasonal and seasonal univariate ARIMA models with or without fixed regressor variables. The procedure uses a subroutine library written by Craig Ansley that produces maximum-likelihood estimates and can process time series with missing observations.

Options

Model Specification. The traditional ARIMA (p,d,q)(sp,sd,sq) model incorporates nonseasonal and seasonal parameters multiplicatively and can be specified on the MODEL subcommand. You can also specify ARIMA models and constrained ARIMA models by using the separate parameter-order subcommands P, D, Q, SP, SD, and SQ.

Parameter Specification. If you specify the model in the traditional (p,d,q) (sp,sd,sq) format on the MODEL subcommand, you can additionally specify the period length, whether a constant should be included in the model (using keyword CONSTANT or NOCONSTANT), and whether the series should first be log transformed (using keyword NOLOG, LG10, or LN). You can fit single or nonsequential parameters by using the separate parameter-order subcommands to specify the exact lags. You can also specify initial values for any of the parameters using the AR, MA, SAR, SMA, REG, and CON subcommands.

Iterations. You can specify termination criteria using the MXITER, MXLAMB, SSQPCT, and PAREPS subcommands.

Confidence Intervals. You can control the size of the confidence interval using the CINPCT subcommand.

Statistical Output. To display only the final parameter statistics, specify TSET PRINT=BRIEF before ARIMA. To include parameter estimates at each iteration in addition to the default output, specify TSET PRINT=DETAILED.

New Variables. To evaluate model statistics without creating new variables, specify TSET NEWVAR=NONE prior to ARIMA. This could result in faster processing time. To add new variables without erasing the values of Trends-generated variables, specify TSET NEWVAR=ALL. This saves all new variables generated during the current session in the working data file and may require extra processing time.

Forecasting. When used with the PREDICT command, an ARIMA model with no regressor variables can produce forecasts and confidence limits beyond the end of the series (see PREDICT in the *SPSS Base System Syntax Reference Guide*).

Basic Specification

The basic specification is the dependent series name. To estimate an ARIMA model, the MODEL subcommand and/or separate parameter-order subcommands (or the APPLY subcommand) must also be specified. Otherwise, only the constant will be estimated.

- ARIMA estimates the parameter values of a model using the parameter specifications on the MODEL subcommand and/or the separate parameter-order subcommands P, D, Q, SP, SD, and SQ.

- A 95% confidence interval is used unless it is changed by a TSET CIN command prior to the ARIMA procedure.

- Unless the default on TSET NEWVAR is changed prior to ARIMA, five variables are automatically created, labeled, and added to the working data file: fitted values (*FIT#1*), residuals (*ERR#1*), lower confidence limits (*LCL#1*), upper confidence limits (*UCL#1*), and standard errors of prediction (*SEP#1*). (For variable naming and labeling conventions, see "New Variables" on p. 253.)

- By default, ARIMA will iterate up to a maximum of 10 unless one of three termination criteria is met: the change in all parameters is less than the TSET CNVERGE value (the default value is 0.001); the sum-of-squares percentage change is less than 0.001%; or the Marquardt constant exceeds 10^9 (1.0E9).

- At each iteration, the Marquardt constant and adjusted sum of squares are displayed. For the final estimates, the displayed results include the parameter estimates, standard errors, t ratios, estimate of residual variance, standard error of the estimate, log likelihood, Akaike's information criterion (AIC) (Akaike, 1974), Schwartz's Bayesian criterion (SBC) (Schwartz, 1978), and covariance and correlation matrices.

Subcommand Order

- Subcommands can be specified in any order.

Syntax Rules

- VARIABLES can be specified only once.
- Other subcommands can be specified more than once, but only the last specification of each one is executed.
- The CONSTANT, NOCONSTANT, NOLOG, LN, and LOG specifications are optional keywords on the MODEL subcommand and are not independent subcommands.

Operations

- If differencing is specified in models with regressors, both the dependent series and the regressors are differenced. To difference only the dependent series, use the DIFF or SDIFF function on CREATE to create a new series (see CREATE in the *SPSS Base System Syntax Reference Guide*).
- When ARIMA is used with the PREDICT command to forecast values beyond the end of the series, the original series and residual variable are assigned the system-missing value after the last case in the original series.
- The USE and PREDICT ranges cannot be exactly the same; at least one case from the USE period must precede the PREDICT period. (See USE and PREDICT in the *SPSS Base System Syntax Reference Guide*
- If a LOG or LN transformation is specified, the residual (error) series is reported in the logged metric; it is not transformed back to the original metric. This is so the proper diagnostic checks can be done on the residuals. However, the predicted (forecast) values *are* transformed back to the original metric. Thus, the observed value minus the predicted value will not equal the residual value. A new residual variable in the original metric can be computed by subtracting the predicted value from the observed value.
- Specifications on the P, D, Q, SP, SD, and SQ subcommands override specifications on the MODEL subcommand.
- For ARIMA models with a fixed regressor, the number of forecasts and confidence intervals produced cannot exceed the number of observations for the regressor (independent) variable. Regressor series cannot be extended.
- Models of series with imbedded missing observations can take longer to estimate.

Limitations

- Maximum 1 VARIABLES subcommand.
- Maximum 1 dependent series. There is no limit on the number of independent series.
- Maximum 1 model specification.

Example

```
ARIMA SALES WITH INTERVEN
  /MODEL=(0,1,1)(0,1,1).
```

- This example specifies a multiplicative seasonal ARIMA model with a fixed regressor variable.
- The dependent series is *SALES*, the regressor series is *INTERVEN*, and an ARIMA (0,1,1)(0,1,1) model with a constant term is estimated.

VARIABLES Subcommand

VARIABLES specifies the dependent series and regressors, if any, and is the only required subcommand. The actual keyword VARIABLES can be omitted.

- The dependent series is specified first, followed by keyword WITH and the regressors (independent series).

MODEL Subcommand

MODEL specifies the ARIMA model, period length, whether a constant term should be included in the model, and whether the series should be log transformed.

- The model parameters are listed using the traditional ARIMA (p,d,q) (sp,sd,sq) syntax.
- Nonseasonal parameters are specified with the appropriate *p, d,* and *q* values separated by commas and enclosed in parentheses.
- The value *p* is a positive integer indicating the order of nonseasonal autoregressive parameters, *d* is a positive integer indicating the degree of nonseasonal differencing, and *q* is a positive integer indicating the nonseasonal moving-average order.
- Seasonal parameters are specified after the nonseasonal parameters with the appropriate *sp*, *sd*, and *sq* values. They are also separated by commas and enclosed in parentheses.
- The value *sp* is a positive integer indicating the order of seasonal autoregressive parameters, *sd* is a positive integer indicating the degree of seasonal differencing, and *sq* is a positive integer indicating the seasonal moving-average order.
- After the seasonal model parameters, a positive integer can be specified to indicate the length of a seasonal period.
- If the period length is not specified, the periodicity established on TSET PERIOD is in effect. If TSET PERIOD is not specified, the periodicity established on the DATE command is used. If periodicity was not established anywhere and a seasonal model is specified, the ARIMA procedure is not executed.

The following optional keywords can be specified on MODEL:

CONSTANT   *Include a constant in the model.* This is the default unless the default setting on the TSET command is changed prior to the ARIMA procedure.

NOCONSTANT *Do not include a constant.*

NOLOG   *Do not log transform the series.* This is the default.

LG10   *Log transform the series before estimation using the base 10 logarithm.* Keyword LOG is an alias for LG10.

LN   *Log transform the series before estimation using the natural logarithm (base e).*

- Keywords can be specified anywhere on the MODEL subcommand.
- CONSTANT and NOCONSTANT are mutually exclusive. If both are specified, only the last one is executed.
- LG10 (LOG), LN, and NOLOG are mutually exclusive. If more than one is specified, only the last one is executed.
- CONSTANT and NOLOG are generally used as part of an APPLY subcommand to turn off previous NOCONSTANT, LG10, or LN specifications

Example

```
ARIMA SALES WITH INTERVEN
  /MODEL=(1,1,1)(1,1,1) 12 NOCONSTANT LN.
```

- This example specifies a model with a first-order nonseasonal autoregressive parameter, one degree of nonseasonal differencing, a first-order nonseasonal moving average, a first-order seasonal autoregressive parameter, one degree of seasonal differencing, and a first-order seasonal moving average.
- The 12 indicates that the length of the period for *SALES* is 12.
- The keywords NOCONSTANT and LN indicate that a constant is not included in the model and that the series is log transformed using the natural logarithm before estimation.

Parameter-Order Subcommands

P, D, Q, SP, SD, and SQ can be used as additions or alternatives to the MODEL subcommand to specify particular lags in the model and degrees of differencing for fitting single or non-sequential parameters. These subcommands are also useful for specifying a constrained model. The subcommands represent the following parameters:

P   *Autoregressive order.*

D   *Order of differencing.*

Q   *Moving-average order.*

SP   *Seasonal autoregressive order.*

SD   *Order of seasonal differencing.*

SQ   *Seasonal moving-average order.*

- The specification on P, Q, SP, or SQ indicates which lags are to be fit and can be a single positive integer or a list of values in parentheses.
- A single value *n* denotes lags 1 through *n*.
- A single value *in parentheses,* for example *(n)*, indicates that only lag *n* should be fit.
- A list of values in parentheses *(i, j, k)* denotes lags *i, j,* and *k* only.
- You can specify as many values in parentheses as you want.
- D and SD indicate the degrees of differencing and can be specified only as single values, not value lists.
- Specifications on P, D, Q, SP, SD, and SQ override specifications for the corresponding parameters on the MODEL subcommand.

Example

```
ARIMA SALES
  /P=2
  /D=1.
ARIMA INCOME
  /MODEL=LOG NOCONSTANT
  /P=(2).
ARIMA VAR01
  /MODEL=(1,1,4)(1,1,4)
  /Q=(2,4)
  /SQ=(2,4).
ARIMA VAR02
  /MODEL=(1,1,0)(1,1,0)
  /Q=(2,4)
  /SQ=(2,4).
```

- The first command fits a model with autoregressive parameters at lags 1 and 2 (P=2) and one degree of differencing (D=1) for the series *SALES*. This command is equivalent to:

```
ARIMA SALES
  /MODEL=(2,1,0).
```

- In the second command, the series *INCOME* is log transformed and no constant term is estimated. There is one autoregressive parameter at lag 2, as indicated by P=(2).
- The third command specifies a model with one autoregressive parameter, one degree of differencing, moving-average parameters at lags 2 and 4, one seasonal autoregressive parameter, one degree of seasonal differencing, and seasonal moving-average parameters at lags 2 and 4. The 4's in the MODEL subcommand for moving average and seasonal moving average are ignored because of the Q and SQ subcommands.
- The last command specifies the same model as the previous command. Even though the MODEL command specifies no nonseasonal or seasonal moving-average parameters, these parameters are estimated at lags 2 and 4 because of the Q and SQ specifications.

Initial Value Subcommands

AR, MA, SAR, SMA, REG, and CON specify initial values for parameters. These subcommands refer to the following parameters:

AR   *Autoregressive parameter values.*

MA   *Moving-average parameter values.*

SAR   *Seasonal autoregressive parameter values.*

SMA   *Seasonal moving-average parameter values.*

REG   *Fixed regressor parameter values.*

CON   *Constant value.*

- Each subcommand specifies a value or value list indicating the initial values to be used in estimating the parameters.
- CON can be specified only as a single value, not a value list.
- Values are matched to parameters in sequential order. That is, the first value is used as the initial value for the first parameter of that type, the second value is used as the initial value for the second parameter of that type, and so forth.
- Specify only the subcommands for which you can supply a complete list of initial values (one for every lag to be fit for that parameter type).
- If you specify an inappropriate initial value for AR, MA, SAR, or SMA, ARIMA will reset the value and issue a message.
- If MXITER=0, these subcommands specify final parameter values to use for forecasting.

Example

```
ARIMA VARY
  /MODEL (1,0,2)
  /AR=0.5
  /MA=0.8, -0.3.
ARIMA VARY
  /MODEL (1,0,2)
  /AR=0.5.
```

- The first command specifies initial estimation values for the autoregressive term and for the two moving-average terms.
- The second command specifies the initial estimation value for the autoregressive term only. The moving-average initial values are estimated by ARIMA.

Termination Criteria Subcommands

ARIMA will continue to iterate until one of four termination criteria is met. The values of these criteria can be changed using any of the following subcommands followed by the new value:

MXITER   *Maximum number of iterations.* The value specified can be any integer equal to or greater than 0. If MXITER equals 0, initial parameter values become final estimates to be used in forecasting. The default value is 10.

PAREPS   *Parameter change tolerance.* The value specified can be any real number greater than 0. A change in all of the parameters by less than this amount causes termination. The default is the value set on TSET CNVERGE. If TSET CNVERGE is not specified, the default is 0.001. A value specified on PAREPS overrides the value set on TSET CNVERGE.

SSQPCT *Sum of squares percentage.* The value specified can be a real number greater than 0 and less than or equal to 100. A relative change in the adjusted sum of squares by less than this amount causes termination. The default value is 0.001%.

MXLAMB *Maximum lambda.* The value specified can be any integer. If the Marquardt constant exceeds this value, estimation is terminated. The default value is $1,000,000,000 \ (10^9)$.

CINPCT Subcommand

CINPCT controls the size of the confidence interval.

- The specification on CINPCT can be any real number greater than 0 and less than 100.
- The default is the value specified on TSET CIN. If TSET CIN is not specified, the default is 95.
- CINPCT overrides the value set on the TSET CIN command.

APPLY Subcommand

APPLY allows you to use a previously defined ARIMA model without having to repeat the specifications. For general rules on APPLY, see the APPLY subcommand on p. 256.

- The specifications on APPLY can include the name of a previous model in quotes and one of three keywords. All of these specifications are optional.
- If a model name is not specified, the model specified on the previous ARIMA command is used.
- To change one or more of the specifications of the model, specify the subcommands of only those portions you want to change after the subcommand APPLY.
- If no series are specified on the ARIMA command, the series that were originally specified with the model being reapplied are used.
- To change the series used with the model, enter new series names before or after the APPLY subcommand. If a series name is specified before APPLY, the slash before the subcommand is required.
- APPLY with keyword FIT sets MXITER to 0. If you apply a model that used FIT and want to obtain estimates, you will need to respecify MXITER.

The keywords available for APPLY with ARIMA are:

SPECIFICATIONS *Use only the specifications from the original model.* ARIMA should create the initial values. This is the default.

INITIAL *Use the original model's final estimates as initial values for estimation.*

FIT *No estimation.* Estimates from the original model should be applied directly.

Example

```
ARIMA VAR1
  /MODEL=(0,1,1)(0,1,1) 12 LOG NOCONSTANT.
ARIMA APPLY
  /MODEL=CONSTANT.
ARIMA VAR2
  /APPLY INITIAL.
ARIMA VAR2
  /APPLY FIT.
```

- The first command specifies a model with one degree of differencing, one moving-average term, one degree of seasonal differencing, and one seasonal moving-average term. The length of the period is 12. A base 10 log of the series is taken before estimation and no constant is estimated. This model is assigned the name *MOD_1*.

- The second command applies the same model to the same series, but this time estimates a constant term. Everything else stays the same. This model is assigned the name *MOD_2*.

- The third command uses the same model as the previous command (*MOD_2*) but applies it to series *VAR2*. Keyword INITIAL specifies that the final estimates of *MOD_2* are to be used as the initial values for estimation.

- The last command uses the same model but this time specifies no estimation. Instead, the values from the previous model are applied directly.

References

Akaike, H. 1974. A new look at the statistical model identification. *IEEE Transaction on Automatic Control* AC-19: 716–723.

Box, G. E., and G. C. Tiao. 1975. Intervention analysis with applications to economic and environmental problems. *Journal of the American Statistical Association* 70: 70–79.

Cryer, J. D. 1986. *Time series analysis.* Boston: Duxbury Press.

Harvey, A. C. 1981. *The econometric analysis of time series.* Oxford: Philip Allan.

Harvey, A. C. 1981. *Time series models.* Oxford: Philip Allan.

Kohn, R., and C. Ansley. 1985. Regression algorithm. *Biometrika* 81: 751–761.

Kohn, R., and C. Ansley. 1986. Estimation, prediction, and interpolation for ARIMA models with missing data. *Journal of the American Statistical Association* 81: 751–761.

McCleary, R., and R. A. Hay. 1980. *Applied time series analysis for the social sciences.* Beverly Hills, Calif.: Sage Publications.

Melard, G. 1984. A fast algorithm for the exact likelihood of autoregressive-moving average models. *Applied Statistics* 33(1): 104–119.

Schwartz, G. 1978. Estimating the dimensions of a model. *Annals of Statistics* 6: 461–464.

EXSMOOTH

```
EXSMOOTH  [VARIABLES=] series names

  [/MODEL={NN** or SINGLE }]
         {NA              }
         {NM              }

         {LN or HOLT     }
         {LA             }
         {LM or WINTERS  }

         {EN             }
         {EA             }
         {EM             }

         {DN             }
         {DA             }
         {DM             }

  [/PERIOD=n]

  [/SEASFACT={(value list)}]
            {varname      }

  [/ALPHA={0.1**                        }]
         {value                        }
         {GRID ({0,1,0.1              })}
               {start, end, increment }

  [/GAMMA={0.1**                        }]
         {value                        }
         {GRID ({0,1,0.2              })}
               {start, end, increment }

  [/DELTA={0.1**                        }]
         {value                        }
         {GRID ({0,1,0.2              })}
               {start, end, increment }

  [/PHI={0.1**                        }]
       {value                        }
       {GRID ({0.1,0.9,0.2          })}
             {start, end, increment }

  [/INITIAL={CALCULATE**                }]
           {(start value, trend value)}

  [/APPLY[='model name']]
```

**Default if the subcommand is omitted.

Example:

```
EXSMOOTH VAR2
  /MODEL=LN
  /ALPHA=0.2.
```

Overview

EXSMOOTH produces fit/forecast values and residuals for one or more time series. A variety of models differing in trend (none, linear, or exponential) and seasonality (none, additive, or multiplicative) are available (see Gardner, 1985).

Options

Model Specification. You can specify a model with any combination of trend and seasonality components using the MODEL subcommand. For seasonal models, you can specify the periodicity using the PERIOD subcommand.

Parameter Specification. You can specify values for the smoothing parameters using the AL-PHA, GAMMA, DELTA, and PHI subcommands. You can also specify initial values using subcommand INITIAL and seasonal factor estimates using subcommand SEASFACT.

Statistical Output. To get a list of all the SSE's and parameters instead of just the 10 smallest, specify TSET PRINT=DETAILED prior to EXSMOOTH.

New Variables. Because of the number of parameter and value combinations available, EXS-MOOTH can create many new variables (up to the maximum specified on the TSET MXNEW-VARS command). To evaluate the sum of squared errors without creating and saving new variables in the working data file, use TSET NEWVAR=NONE prior to EXSMOOTH. To add new variables without erasing the values of previous Trends-generated variables, specify TSET NEWVAR=ALL. This saves all new variables generated during the current session in the working data file.

Forecasting. When used with the PREDICT command, EXSMOOTH can produce forecasts beyond the end of the series (see PREDICT in the *SPSS Base System Syntax Reference Guide*).

Basic Specification

The basic specification is one or more series names.

- If a model is not specified, the NN (no trend and nonseasonal) model is used. The default value for each of the smoothing parameters is 0.1.
- Unless the default on the TSET NEWVAR is changed prior to the EXSMOOTH procedure, for each combination of smoothing parameters and series specified, EXSMOOTH creates two variables: *FIT#n* to contain the predicted values and *ERR#n* to contain residuals. These variables are automatically labeled and added to the working data file. (For variable naming and labeling conventions, see "New Variables" on p. 253.)
- The output displays the initial values used in the analysis (see Ledolter & Abraham, 1984), the error degrees of freedom (DFE), and an ascending list of the smallest sum of squared errors (SSE) next to the associated set of smoothing parameters, up to a maximum of 10. For seasonal series, initial seasonal factor estimates are also displayed.

Subcommand Order

- Subcommands can be specified in any order.

Syntax Rules

- VARIABLES can be specified only once.

- Other subcommands can be specified more than once, but only the last specification of each one is executed.
- The value list for subcommand SEASFACT and the grid values for the smoothing parameters must be enclosed within parentheses.

Operations

- If a smoothing parameter is specified for an inappropriate model, it is ignored (see "Smoothing Parameter Subcommands" on p. 278).
- EXSMOOTH cannot process series with missing observations. (You can use the RMV command to replace missing values, and USE to ignore missing observations at the beginning or end of a series. See RMV and USE in the *SPSS Base System Syntax Reference Guide* for more information.)
- When EXSMOOTH is used with PREDICT, error series are assigned the system-missing value in the entire PREDICT range. The original series is system-missing beyond the last original case if the series is extended. (See the *SPSS Base System Syntax Reference Guide* for more information on PREDICT.)

Limitations

- Maximum 1 VARIABLES subcommand. There is no limit on the number of series named on the list.
- Maximum 1 model keyword on the MODEL subcommand.

Example

```
EXSMOOTH VAR2
   /MODEL=LN
   /ALPHA=0.2.
```

- This example specifies a linear trend, nonseasonal model for the series *VAR2*.
- The ALPHA subcommand specifies a value of 0.2 for the general smoothing parameter.
- The default value of 0.1 is used for gamma.

VARIABLES Subcommand

VARIABLES specifies the series names and is the only required subcommand. The actual keyword VARIABLES can be omitted.

- For seasonal models, the series must contain at least four full seasons of data.

MODEL Subcommand

MODEL specifies the type of model to be used.

- The only specification on MODEL is a model keyword.
- Only one model keyword can be specified. If more than one is specified, only the first is used.

The following models are available. Table 1 summarizes the models by trend and seasonal component.

No trend models:

NN   *No trend and no seasonality.* This is the default model. Keyword SINGLE is an alias for NN.

NA   *No trend and an additive seasonal component.*

NM   *No trend and a multiplicative seasonal component.*

Linear trend models:

LN   *Linear trend component and no seasonality.* Keyword HOLT is an alias for LN.

LA   *Linear trend component and an additive seasonal component.*

LM   *Linear trend component and a multiplicative seasonal component.* Keyword WINTERS is an alias for LM.

Exponential trend models:

EN   *Exponential trend component and no seasonality.*

EA   *Exponential trend component and an additive seasonal component.*

EM   *Exponential trend component and a multiplicative seasonal component.*

Damped trend models:

DN   *Damped trend component and no seasonality.*

DA   *Damped trend component and an additive seasonal component.*

DM   *Damped trend component and a multiplicative seasonal component.*

Table 1   Models for different types of Trends and seasons

		Seasonal component		
		None	**Additive**	**Multiplicative**
Trend component	**None**	NN	NA	NM
	Linear	LN	LA	LM
	Exponential	EN	EA	EM
	Damped	DN	DA	DM

Example

```
EXSMOOTH VAR1.
```

- This example uses the default model NN for series *VAR1*.

Example

```
EXSMOOTH VAR2
  /MODEL=LN.
```

- This example uses model LN (linear trend with no seasonality) for series *VAR2*.

PERIOD Subcommand

PERIOD indicates the periodicity of the seasonal component for seasonal models.

- The specification on PERIOD indicates how many observations are in one period or season and can be any positive integer.
- PERIOD is ignored if it is specified with a nonseasonal model.
- If PERIOD is not specified, the periodicity established on TSET PERIOD is in effect. If TSET PERIOD is not specified, the periodicity established on the DATE command is used. If periodicity was not established anywhere and a seasonal model is specified, EX-SMOOTH will terminate.

Example

```
EXSMOOTH VAR1
  /MODEL=LA
  /PERIOD=12.
```

- This example specifies a periodicity of 12 for the seasonal *VAR1* series.

SEASFACT Subcommand

SEASFACT specifies initial seasonal factor estimates for seasonal models.

- The specification on SEASFACT is either a value list enclosed in parentheses or a variable name.
- If a value list is specified, the number of values in the list must equal the periodicity. For example, if the periodicity is 12, then 12 initial values must be specified.
- For multiplicative models, the sum of the values in the list should equal the periodicity. For additive models, the sum of the values should equal 0.
- A variable specification on SEASFACT indicates the name of a variable in the working data file containing the seasonal factor estimates (see SEASON).
- If the model is seasonal and SEASFACT is not specified, EXSMOOTH calculates the initial seasonal factors.
- The seasonal factor estimates of a SEASFACT subcommand are not used when the model is respecified using the APPLY subcommand (see the APPLY subcommand on p. 281).

Example

```
EXSMOOTH VAR2
  /MODEL=LA
  /PERIOD=8
  /SEASFACT=(-25.30 -3 -14.70 17 4 3 13 6).
```

- This command uses the list of values specified on the SEASFACT subcommand as the initial seasonal factor estimates.
- Eight values are specified, since the periodicity is 8.
- The eight values sum to 0, since this is an additive seasonal model.

Example

```
EXSMOOTH VAR3
  /MODEL=LA
  /SEASFACT=SAF#1.
```

- This command uses the initial seasonal factors contained in variable *SAF#1*, which was saved in the working data file by a previous SEASON command.

Smoothing Parameter Subcommands

ALPHA, GAMMA, DELTA, and PHI specify the values that are used for the smoothing parameters.

- The specification on each subcommand is either a value within the valid range, or the keyword GRID followed by optional range values.
- If GAMMA, DELTA, or PHI are not specified but are required for the model, the default values are used.
- ALPHA is applied to all models. If it is not specified, the default value is used.

ALPHA   *General smoothing parameter.* This parameter is applied to all models. Alpha can be any value between and including 0 and 1. (For EM models, alpha must be greater than 0 and less than or equal to 1.) The default value is 0.1.

GAMMA   *Trend smoothing parameter.* Gamma is used only with models that have a trend component, excluding damped seasonal (DA, DM) models. It is ignored if it is specified with a damped seasonal or no-trend model. Gamma can be any value between and including 0 and 1. The default value is 0.1.

DELTA   *Seasonal smoothing parameter.* Delta is used only with models that have a seasonal component. It is ignored if it is specified with any of the nonseasonal models. Delta can be any value between and including 0 and 1. The default value is 0.1.

PHI   *Trend modification parameter.* Phi is used only with models that have a damped trend component. It is ignored if it is specified with models that do not have a damped trend. Phi can be any value greater than 0 and less than 1. The default value is 0.1.

Table 2 summarizes the parameters that are used with each EXSMOOTH model. An *X* indicates that the parameter is used for the model.

Table 2   Parameters that can be specified with EXSMOOTH models

		Smoothing parameter			
		ALPHA	DELTA	GAMMA	PHI
Model	NN	x			
	NA	x	x		
	NM	x	x		
	LN	x		x	
	LA	x	x	x	
	LM	x	x	x	
	EN	x		x	
	EA	x	x	x	
	EM	x	x	x	
	DN	x		x	x
	DA	x	x		x
	DM	x	x		x

Keyword GRID

Keyword GRID specifies a range of values to use for the associated smoothing parameter. When GRID is specified, new variables are saved only for the optimal set of parameters on the grid.

- The first value on GRID specifies the start value, the second value is the end value, and the last value is the increment.
- The start, end, and increment values on GRID are separated by commas or spaces and enclosed in parentheses.
- If you specify any grid values, you must specify all three.
- If no values are specified on GRID, the default values are used.
- Grid start and end values for alpha, gamma, and delta can range from 0 to 1. The defaults are 0 for the start value and 1 for the end value.
- Grid start and end values for phi can range from 0 to 1, exclusive. The defaults are 0.1 for the start value and 0.9 for the end value.
- Grid increment values must be within the range specified by start and end values. The default is 0.1 for alpha, and 0.2 for gamma, delta, and phi.

Example

```
EXSMOOTH VAR1
  /MODEL=LA
  /PERIOD=12
  /GAMMA=0.20
  /DELTA=0.20.
```

- This example uses a model with a linear trend and additive seasonality.

- The parameters and values are alpha = 0.10, gamma = 0.20, and delta = 0.20. Alpha is not specified but is always used by default.
- This command generates one *FIT* variable and one *ERR* variable to contain the forecasts and residuals generated by this one set of parameters.

Example

```
EXSMOOTH VAR2
  /MODEL=EA
  /ALPHA=GRID
  /DELTA=GRID(0.2,0.6,0.2).
```

- This example specifies a model with an exponential trend component and an additive seasonal component.
- The default start, end, and increment values (0, 1, and 0.1) are used for the grid search of alpha. Thus, the values used for alpha are 0, 0.1, 0.2, 0.3, . . . , 0.9, and 1.
- The grid specification for delta indicates a start value of 0.2, an end value of 0.6, and an increment of 0.2. Thus, the values used for delta are 0.2, 0.4, and 0.6.
- Since this is an exponential trend model, the parameter gamma will be supplied by EXS-MOOTH with the default value of 0.1, even though it is not specified on the command.
- Two variables (*FIT* and *ERR*) will be generated for the parameters resulting in the best-fitting model.

INITIAL Subcommand

INITIAL specifies the initial start and trend values used in the models.

- The specification on INITIAL is the start and trend values enclosed in parentheses. You must specify both values.
- The values specified on INITIAL are saved as part of the model and can be reapplied with the APPLY subcommand (see the APPLY subcommand on p. 281).
- If INITIAL is not specified, the initial start and trend values are calculated by EXSMOOTH. These calculated initial values are *not* saved as part of the model.
- To turn off the values specified on INITIAL when the model is used on an APPLY subcommand, specify INITIAL=CALCULATE. New initial values will then be calculated by EXS-MOOTH (see the APPLY subcommand on p. 281).

Example

```
EXSMOOTH VAR2
  /MODEL=LA
  /PERIOD=4
  /SEASFACT=(23 -14.4 7 -15.6)
  /ALPHA=0.20
  /GAMMA=0.20
  /DELTA=0.30
  /INITIAL=(112,17).
```

- In this example, an initial start value of 112 and trend value of 17 is specified for series *VAR2*.

APPLY Subcommand

APPLY allows you to use a previously defined EXSMOOTH model without having to repeat the specifications. For general rules on APPLY, see the APPLY subcommand on p. 256.

- The only specification on APPLY is the name of a previous model in quotes. If a model name is not specified, the model specified on the previous EXSMOOTH command is used.

- To change one or more model specifications, specify the subcommands of only those portions you want to change after the APPLY subcommand.

- If no series are specified on the command, the series that were originally specified with the model being reapplied are used.

- To change the series used with the model, enter new series names before or after the APPLY subcommand. If a series name is specified before APPLY, the slash before the subcommand is required.

- Initial values from the previous model's INITIAL subcommand are applied unless you specify INITIAL = CALCULATE or a new set of initial values. Initial values from the original model are not applied if they were calculated by EXSMOOTH.

- Seasonal factor estimates from the original model's SEASFACT subcommand are not applied. To use seasonal factor estimates, you must respecify SEASFACT.

Example

```
EXSMOOTH VAR1
  /MODEL=NA
  /PERIOD=12
  /ALPHA=0.2
  /DELTA=0.2.
EXSMOOTH APPLY
  /DELTA=0.3.
EXSMOOTH VAR2
  /APPLY.
```

- The first command uses a model with no trend but additive seasonality for series *VAR1*. The length of the season (PERIOD) is 12. A general smoothing parameter (ALPHA) and a seasonal smoothing parameter (DELTA) are used, both with values set equal to 0.2.

- The second command applies the same model to the same series but changes the delta value to 0.3. Everything else stays the same.

- The last command applies the model and parameter values used in the second EXSMOOTH command to series *VAR2*.

Example

```
EXSMOOTH VAR3
  /MOD=NA
  /ALPHA=0.20
  /DELTA=0.4
  /INITIAL=(114,20).
EXSMOOTH VAR4
  /APPLY
  /INITIAL=CALCULATE.
```

- The first command uses a model with no trend and additive seasonality model with alpha set to 0.2 and delta set to 0.4. Initial start and trend values of 114 and 20 are specified.
- The second command applies the previous model and parameter values to a new variable, *VAR4*, but without the initial starting values. The initial starting values will be calculated by EXSMOOTH.

References

Abraham, B., and J. Ledolter. 1983. *Statistical methods of forecasting.* New York: John Wiley & Sons.

Gardner, E. S. 1985. Exponential smoothing: The state of the art. *Journal of Forecasting* 4: 1–28.

Ledolter, J., and B. Abraham. 1984. Some comments on the initialization of exponential smoothing. *Journal of Forecasting* 3: 79–84.

Makridakis, S., S. C. Wheelwright, and V. E. McGee. 1983. *Forecasting: Methods and applications.* New York: John Wiley & Sons.

MODEL NAME

```
MODEL NAME [model name] ['model label']
```

Example:
```
MODEL NAME PLOTA1 'PLOT OF THE OBSERVED SERIES'.
```

Overview

MODEL NAME specifies a model name and label for the next procedure in the session.

Basic Specification

The specification on MODEL NAME is either a name, a label, or both.

- The default model name is *MOD_n*, where *n* increments by 1 each time an unnamed model is created. This default is in effect if it is not changed on the MODEL NAME command, or if the command is not specified. There is no default label.

Syntax Rules

- If both a name and label are specified, the name must be specified first.
- Only one model name and label can be specified on the command.
- The model name must be unique. It can contain up to 8 characters and must begin with a letter (A–Z).
- The model label can contain up to 60 characters and must be specified in apostrophes.

Operations

- MODEL NAME is executed at the next model-generating procedure.
- If the MODEL NAME command is used more than once before a procedure, the last one is in effect.
- If a duplicate model name is specified, the default *MOD_n* name will be used instead.
- *MOD_n* reinitializes at the start of every session and when the READ MODEL command is specified (see READ MODEL). If any models in the working data file are already named *MOD_n*, those numbers are skipped when new *MOD_n* names are assigned.

Examples

```
MODEL NAME ARIMA1 'First ARIMA model'.
ARIMA VARX
  /MODEL=(0,1,1).
ARIMA VARY
  /MODEL=(1,1,1).
ARIMA VARZ
   /APPLY 'ARIMA1'.
```

- In this example, the model name *ARIMA1* and the label *First ARIMA model* are assigned to the first ARIMA command.
- The second ARIMA command has no MODEL NAME command before it, so it is assigned the name *MOD_1*.
- The third ARIMA command applies the model named *ARIMA1* to the series *VARZ*. This model is named *MOD_2.*

READ MODEL

```
READ MODEL FILE='filename'

  [/KEEP={ALL**      }]
         {model names}
         {procedures  }

  [/DROP={model names}]
         {procedures  }

  [/TYPE={MODEL** }]
         {COMMAND }

  [/TSET={CURRENT** }]
         {RESTORE   }
```

**Default if the subcommand is omitted.

Example:

```
READ MODEL FILE='ACFMOD.DAT'
  /DROP=MOD_1.
```

Overview

READ MODEL reads a model file that has been previously saved on the SAVE MODEL command (see SAVE MODEL). A model file contains the models generated by Trends procedures for use with the APPLY subcommand.

Options

You can restore a subset of models from the model file using the DROP and KEEP subcommands. You can control whether models are specified by model name or by the name of the procedure that generated them using the TYPE subcommand. With the TSET subcommand you can restore the TSET settings that were in effect when the model file was created.

Basic Specification

The basic specification is the FILE subcommand specifying the name of a previously saved model file.

- By default, all models contained in the specified file are restored, replacing all models that are currently active. The restored models have their original *MOD_n* default names or names assigned by the MODEL NAME command.

Subcommand Order

- Subcommands can be specified in any order.

Syntax Rules

- If a subcommand is specified more than once, only the last one is executed.

Operations

- READ MODEL is executed immediately.
- Models that are currently active are erased when READ MODEL is executed. To save these models for later use, specify the SAVE MODEL command before READ MODEL.
- Model files are designed to be read by Trends only and should not be edited.
- DATE specifications are not saved in model files. Therefore, the DATE specifications from the current session are applied to the restored models.
- The following procedures can generate models: AREG, ARIMA, EXSMOOTH, SEASON, SPECTRA, and X11ARIMA in SPSS Trends; ACF, CASEPLOT, CCF, CURVEFIT, NPPLOT, PACF, and TSPLOT in the SPSS Base System; and WLS and 2SLS in SPSS Professional Statistics.

Limitations

- Maximum 1 filename can be specified.

Example

```
READ MODEL FILE='ACFMOD.DAT'
  /DROP=MOD_1.
```

- In this example, all models except *MOD_1* in the model file *ACFMOD.DAT* are restored.

FILE Subcommand

FILE names the model file to be read and is the only required subcommand.
- The only specification on FILE is the name of the model file.
- The filename must be enclosed in apostrophes.
- Only one filename can be specified.
- Only files saved with the SAVE MODEL command can be read.
- You can specify files residing in other directories by supplying a fully qualified filename.

KEEP and DROP Subcommands

DROP and KEEP allow you to restore a subset of models. By default, all models in the model file are restored.
- KEEP specifies the models to be restored.

- DROP specifies the models to be excluded.
- Models can be specified using either individual model names or the names of the procedures that created them. To use procedure names, you must specify COMMAND on the TYPE subcommand.
- Model names are either the default *MOD_n* names or the names assigned with MODEL NAME.
- If a procedure name is specified on KEEP, all models created by that procedure are restored; on DROP, all models created by the procedure are dropped.
- Model names and procedure names cannot be mixed on a single READ MODEL command.
- If more than one KEEP or DROP subcommand is specified, only the last one is executed.
- You can specify keyword ALL on KEEP to restore all models in the model file. This is the default.
- The stored model file is not affected by the KEEP or DROP specification on READ MODEL.

Example

```
READ MODEL FILE='ACFCCF.DAT'
  /KEEP=ACF1 ACF2.
```

- In this example, only models *ACF1* and *ACF2* are restored from model file *ACFCCF.DAT*.

TYPE Subcommand

TYPE indicates whether models are specified by model name or procedure name on DROP and KEEP.

- One keyword, MODEL or COMMAND, can be specified after TYPE.
- MODEL is the default and indicates that models are specified as model names.
- COMMAND indicates that models are specified by procedure name.
- TYPE has no effect if KEEP or DROP is not specified.
- The TYPE specification applies only to the current READ MODEL command.

Example

```
READ MODEL FILE='ARIMA1.DAT'
  /KEEP=ARIMA
  /TYPE=COMMAND.
```

- In this example, all models created by ARIMA are restored from model file *ARIMA1.DAT*.

TSET Subcommand

TSET allows you to restore the TSET settings that were in effect when the model was created.

- The specification on TSET is either CURRENT or RESTORE.
- CURRENT (the default) indicates you want to continue to use the current TSET settings.

- RESTORE indicates you want to restore the TSET settings that were in effect when the model file was saved. The current TSET settings are replaced with the model file settings when the file is restored.

SAVE MODEL

```
SAVE MODEL OUTFILE='filename'

[/KEEP={ALL**     }]
       {model names}
       {procedures }

[/DROP={model names}]
       {procedures }

[/TYPE={MODEL** }]
       {COMMAND}
```

**Default if the subcommand is omitted.

Example:

```
SAVE MODEL OUTFILE='ACFMOD.DAT'
  /DROP=MOD_1.
```

Overview

SAVE MODEL saves the models created by Trends procedures into a model file. The saved model file can be read later on in the session or in another session with the READ MODEL command.

Options

You can save a subset of models into the file using the DROP and KEEP subcommands. You can control whether models are specified by model name or by the name of the procedure that generated them using the TYPE subcommand.

Basic Specification

The basic specification is the OUTFILE subcommand followed by a filename.

- By default, SAVE MODEL saves all currently active models in the specified file. Each model saved in the file includes information such as the procedure that created it, the model name, the variable names specified, subcommands and specifications used, and parameter estimates. The names of the models are either the default *MOD_n* names or the names assigned on the MODEL NAME command. In addition to the model specifications, the TSET settings currently in effect are saved.

Subcommand Order

- Subcommands can be specified in any order.

Syntax Rules

- If a subcommand is specified more than once, only the last one is executed.

Operations

- SAVE MODEL is executed immediately.
- Model files are designed to be read and written by Trends only and should not be edited.
- The active models are not affected by the SAVE MODEL command.
- DATE specifications are not saved in the model file.
- Models are not saved in SPSS data files.
- The following procedures can generate models: AREG, ARIMA, EXSMOOTH, SEASON, SPECTRA, and X11ARIMA in SPSS Trends; ACF, CASEPLOT, CCF, CURVEFIT, NPPLOT, PACF, and TSPLOT in the SPSS Base System; and WLS and 2SLS in SPSS Professional Statistics.

Limitations

- Maximum 1 filename can be specified.

Example

```
SAVE MODEL OUTFILE='ACFMOD.DAT'
  /DROP=MOD_1.
```

- In this example, all models except *MOD_1* that are currently active are saved in the file *ACFMOD.DAT*.

OUTFILE Subcommand

OUTFILE names the file where models will be stored and is the only required subcommand.
- The only specification on OUTFILE is the name of the model file.
- The filename must be enclosed in apostrophes.
- Only one filename can be specified.
- You can store models in other directories by specifying a fully qualified filename.

KEEP and DROP Subcommands

DROP and KEEP allow you to save a subset of models. By default, all currently active models are saved.
- KEEP specifies models to be saved in the model file.
- DROP specifies models that are not saved in the model file.

- Models can be specified using either individual model names or the names of the procedures that created them. To use procedure names, you must specify COMMAND on the TYPE subcommand.
- Model names are either the default *MOD_n* names or the names assigned with MODEL NAME.
- If you specify a procedure name on KEEP, all models created by that procedure are saved; on DROP, any models created by that procedure are not included in the model file.
- Model names and procedure names cannot be mixed on a single SAVE MODEL command.
- If more than one KEEP or DROP subcommand is specified, only the last one is executed.
- You can specify keyword ALL on KEEP to save all models that are currently active. This is the default.

Example

```
SAVE MODEL OUTFILE='ACFCCF.DAT'
  /KEEP=ACF1 ACF2
```

- In this example, only models *ACF1* and *ACF2* are saved in model file *ACFCCF.DAT*.

TYPE Subcommand

TYPE indicates whether models are specified by model name or procedure name on DROP and KEEP.

- One keyword, MODEL or COMMAND, can be specified after TYPE.
- MODEL is the default and indicates that models are specified as model names.
- COMMAND indicates that the models are specified by procedure name.
- TYPE has no effect if KEEP or DROP is not specified.
- The TYPE specification applies only to the current SAVE MODEL command.

Example

```
SAVE MODEL OUTFILE='ARIMA1.DAT'
  /KEEP=ARIMA
  /TYPE=COMMAND.
```

- This command saves all models that were created by the ARIMA procedure into the model file *ARIMA1.DAT*.

SEASON

```
SEASON [VARIABLES=] series names

[/MODEL={MULTIPLICATIVE**}]
       {ADDITIVE        }

[/MA={EQUAL   }]
     {CENTERED}

[/PERIOD=n]

[/APPLY [='model name']]
```

**Default if the subcommand is omitted.

Example:

```
SEASON VARX
  /MODEL=ADDITIVE
  /MA=EQUAL.
```

Overview

SEASON estimates multiplicative or additive seasonal factors for time series using any spec-ified periodicity. SEASON is an implementation of the Census Method I, otherwise known as the ratio-to-moving-average method (see Makridakis et al., 1983, and McLaughlin, 1984).

Options

Model Specification. You can specify either a multiplicative or additive model on the MODEL subcommand. You can specify the periodicity of the series on the PERIOD subcommand.

Computation Method. Two methods of computing moving averages are available on the MA subcommand for handling series with even periodicities.

Statistical Output. Specify TSET PRINT=BRIEF to display only the initial seasonal factor esti-mates. TSET PRINT=DETAILED produces the same output as the default.

New Variables. To evaluate the displayed averages, ratios, factors, adjusted series, trend-cycle, and error components without creating new variables, specify TSET NEWVAR=NONE prior to SEASON. This can result in faster processing time. To add new variables without erasing the values of previous Trends-generated variables, specify TSET NEWVAR=ALL. This saves all new variables generated during the current session in the working data file and may require extra processing time.

Basic Specification

The basic specification is one or more series names.

• By default, SEASON uses a multiplicative model to compute and display moving averag-es, ratios, seasonal factors, the seasonally adjusted series, the smoothed trend-cycle components, and the irregular (error) component for each series (variable) specified. The default periodicity is the periodicity established on TSET or DATE.

- Unless the default on TSET NEWVAR is changed prior to the procedure, SEASON creates four new variables for each series specified: *SAF#n* to contain the seasonal adjustment factors, *SAS#n* to contain the seasonally adjusted series, *STC#n* to contain the smoothed trend-cycle components, and *ERR#n* to contain the irregular (error) component. These variables are automatically named, labeled, and added to the working data file. (For variable naming and labeling conventions, see "New Variables" on p. 253.)

Subcommand Order

- Subcommands can be specified in any order.

Syntax Rules

- VARIABLES can be specified only once.
- Other subcommands can be specified more than once, but only the last specification of each one is executed.

Operations

- The endpoints of the moving averages and ratios are displayed as system-missing in the output.
- Missing values are not allowed anywhere in the series. (You can use the RMV command to replace missing values, and USE to ignore missing observations at the beginning or end of a series. See RMV and USE in the *SPSS Base System Syntax Reference Guide* for more information.)

Limitations

- Maximum 1 VARIABLES subcommand. There is no limit on the number of series named on the list.

Example

```
SEASON VARX
  /MODEL=ADDITIVE
  /MA=EQUAL.
```

- In this example, an additive model is specified for the decomposition of *VARX*.
- The moving average will be computed using the EQUAL method.

VARIABLES Subcommand

VARIABLES specifies the series names and is the only required subcommand. The actual keyword VARIABLES can be omitted.

- Each series specified must contain at least four full seasons of data.

MODEL Subcommand

MODEL specifies whether the seasonal decomposition model is multiplicative or additive.

- The specification on MODEL is keyword MULTIPLICATIVE or ADDITIVE.
- If more than one keyword is specified, only the first is used.
- MULTIPLICATIVE is the default if the MODEL subcommand is not specified or if MODEL is specified without any keywords.

Example

```
SEASON VARX
  /MODEL=ADDITIVE.
```

- This example uses an additive model for the seasonal decomposition of *VARX*.

MA Subcommand

MA specifies how to treat an even-periodicity series when computing moving averages.

- MA should be specified only when the periodicity is even. When periodicity is odd, the EQUAL method is always used.
- For even-periodicity series, keyword EQUAL or CENTERED can be specified. CENTERED is the default.
- EQUAL calculates moving averages with a span (number of terms) equal to the periodicity and all points weighted equally.
- CENTERED calculates moving averages with a span (number of terms) equal to the periodicity plus 1 and endpoints weighted by 0.5.
- The periodicity is specified on the PERIOD subcommand (see the PERIOD subcommand on p. 295).

Example

```
SEASON VARY
  /MA=CENTERED
  /PERIOD=12.
```

- In this example, moving averages are computed with spans of 13 terms and endpoints weighted by 0.5.

PERIOD Subcommand

PERIOD indicates the size of the period.

- The specification on PERIOD indicates how many observations are in one period or season and can be any positive integer.
- If PERIOD is not specified, the periodicity established on TSET PERIOD is in effect. If TSET PERIOD is not specified, the periodicity established on the DATE command is used. If periodicity was not established anywhere, the SEASON command will not be executed.

Example

```
SEASON SALES
  /PERIOD=12.
```

- In this example, a periodicity of 12 is specified for *SALES*.

APPLY Subcommand

APPLY allows you to use a previously defined SEASON model without having to repeat the specifications. For general rules on APPLY, see the APPLY subcommand on p. 256.

- The only specification on APPLY is the name of a previous model in quotes. If a model name is not specified, the model specified on the previous SEASON command is used.
- To change one or more model specifications, specify the subcommands of only those portions you want to change after the APPLY subcommand.
- If no series are specified on the command, the series that were originally specified with the model being reapplied are used.
- To change the series used with the model, enter new series names before or after the APPLY subcommand. If a series name is specified before APPLY, the slash before the subcommand is required.

Example

```
SEASON X1
  /MODEL=ADDITIVE.
SEASON Z1
  /APPLY.
```

- The first command specifies an additive model for the seasonal decomposition of *X1*.
- The second command applies the same type of model to series *Z1*.

Example

```
SEASON X1 Y1 Z1
  /MODEL=MULTIPLICATIVE.
SEASON APPLY
  /MODEL=ADDITIVE.
```

- The first command specifies a multiplicative model for the seasonal decomposition of *X1*, *Y1*, and *Z1*.

- The second command applies an additive model to the same three variables.

References

Makridakis, S., S. C. Wheelwright, and V. E. McGee. 1983. *Forecasting: Methods and applications.* New York: John Wiley & Sons.

McLaughlin, R. L. 1984. *Forecasting techniques for decision making.* Rockville, Md.: Control Data Management Institute.

SPECTRA

```
SPECTRA [VARIABLES=] series names

[/{CENTER NO**}]
  {CENTER   }

[/{CROSS NO**}]
  {CROSS   }

[/WINDOW={HAMMING** [({5    })]      }]
         {           {span}           }
         {BARTLETT [(span)]           }
         {PARZEN [(span)]             }
         {TUKEY [(span)]              }
         {UNIT or DANIELL [(span)]    }
         {NONE                        }
         {w_-p, ..., w_0, ..., w_p   }

[/PLOT= [P] [S] [CS] [QS] [PH] [A]
        [G] [K] [ALL] [NONE]
        [BY {FREQ  }]]
           {PERIOD}

[/SAVE = [FREQ (name)] [PER (name)] [SIN (name)]
         [COS (name)]  [P (name)]   [S (name)]
         [RC (name)]   [IC (name)]  [CS (name)]
         [QS (name)]   [PH (name)]  [A (name)]
         [G (name)]    [K (name)]]

[/APPLY [='model name']]
```

**Default if the subcommand is omitted.

Example:

```
SPECTRA HSTARTS
  /CENTER
  /PLOT P S BY FREQ.
```

Overview

SPECTRA plots the periodogram and spectral density function estimates for one or more series. You can also request bivariate spectral analysis. Moving averages, termed *windows,* can be used for smoothing the periodogram values to produce spectral densities.

Options

Output. In addition to the periodogram, you can produce a plot of the estimated spectral density with the PLOT subcommand. You can suppress the display of the plot by frequency or the plot by period using keyword BY on PLOT. To display intermediate values and the plot legend, specify TSET PRINT=DETAILED before SPECTRA. To reduce the range of values displayed in the plots, you can center the data using the CENTER subcommand.

Cross-Spectral Analysis. You can specify cross-spectral (bivariate) analysis with the CROSS subcommand and select which bivariate plots are produced using PLOT.

New Variables. Variables computed by SPECTRA can be saved in the working data file for use in subsequent analyses with the SAVE subcommand.

Spectral Windows. You can specify a spectral window and its span for calculation of the spectral density estimates.

Basic Specification

The basic specification is one or more series names.

- By default, SPECTRA plots the periodogram for each series specified. The periodogram is shown first by frequency and then by period. No new variables are saved by default.

Figure 1 and Figure 2 show the default plots produced by the basic specification.

Figure 1   SPECTRA=PRICE (by frequency)

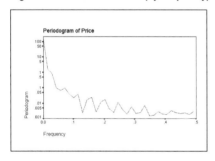

Figure 2   SPECTRA=PRICE (by period)

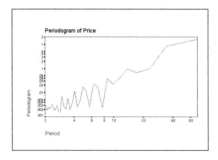

Subcommand Order

- Subcommands can be specified in any order.

Syntax Rules

- VARIABLES can be specified only once.
- Other subcommands can be specified more than once, but only the last specification of each one is executed.

Operations

- SPECTRA cannot process series with missing observations. (You can use the RMV command to replace missing values, and USE to ignore missing observations at the beginning or end of a series. See RMV and USE in the *SPSS Base System Syntax Reference Guide* for more information.)
- If the number of observations in the series is odd, the first case is ignored.
- If the SAVE subcommand is specified, new variables are created for each series specified. For bivariate analyses, new variables are created for each series pair.
- SPECTRA requires memory both to compute variables and to build plots. Requesting fewer plots may enable you to analyze larger series.

Limitations

- Maximum 1 VARIABLES subcommand. There is no limit on the number of series named on the list.

Example

```
SPECTRA HSTARTS
 /CENTER
 /PLOT P S BY FREQ.
```

- This example produces a plot of the periodogram and spectral density estimate for series *HSTARTS*.
- CENTER adjusts the series to have a mean of 0.
- PLOT specifies that the periodogram (P) and the spectral density estimate (S) should be plotted against frequency (BY FREQ).

VARIABLES Subcommand

VARIABLES specifies the series names and is the only required subcommand. The actual keyword VARIABLES can be omitted.

- VARIABLES must be specified before the other subcommands.
- Each series specified is analyzed separately unless the CROSS subcommand is specified.
- The series must contain at least six cases.

Example

```
SPECTRA VARX VARY.
```

- This command produces the default display for two series, *VARX* and *VARY*.

CENTER Subcommand

CENTER adjusts the series to have a mean of 0. This reduces the range of values displayed in the plots.

- If CENTER is not specified, the ordinate of the first periodogram value is $2n$ times the square of the mean of the series, where n is the number of cases.
- You can specify CENTER NO to suppress centering when applying a previous model with APPLY.

Example

```
SPECTRA VARX VARY
   /CENTER.
```

- This example produces the default display for *VARX* and *VARY*. The plots are based on the series after their means have been adjusted to 0.

WINDOW Subcommand

WINDOW specifies a spectral window to use when the periodogram is smoothed to obtain the spectral density estimate. If WINDOW is not specified, the Tukey-Hamming window with a span of 5 is used.

- The specification on WINDOW is a window name and a span in parentheses, or a sequence of user-specified weights.
- The window name can be any one of the keywords listed below.
- Only one window keyword is accepted. If more than one is specified, the first is used.
- The span is the number of periodogram values in the moving average and can be any integer. If an even number is specified, it is decreased by 1.
- Smoothing near the end of series is accomplished via reflection. For example, if the span is 5, the second periodogram value is smoothed by averaging the first, third, and fourth values and twice the second value.

The following data windows can be specified. Each formula defines the upper half of the window. The lower half is symmetric with the upper half. In all formulas, p is the integer part of the number of spans divided by 2, D_p is the Dirichlet kernel of order p, and F_p is the Fejer kernel of order p (Priestley, 1981).

HAMMING   *Tukey-Hamming window.* The weights are

$$W_k = 0.54 D_p (2\pi f_k) + 0.23 D_p (2\pi f_k + \frac{\pi}{p}) + 0.23 D_p (2\pi f_k + \frac{\pi}{p})$$

where $k=0, \dots p$. This is the default.

TUKEY	*Tukey-Hanning window.* The weights are

$$W_k = 0.5D_p\,(2\pi f_k) + 0.25D_p\,(2\pi f_k + \frac{\pi}{p}) + 0.25D_p\,(2\pi f_k - \frac{\pi}{p})$$

where $k=0, \dots p$.

PARZEN	*Parzen window.* The weights are

$$W_k = \frac{1}{p}\,(2 + \cos\,(2\pi f_k))\,(F_{p/2}\,(2\pi f_k))^2$$

where $k=0, \dots p$.

BARTLETT	*Bartlett window.* The weights are $W_k = F_p\,(2\pi f_k)$ where $k=0, \dots p$.
UNIT	*Equal-weight window.* The weights are $w_k = 1$ where $k=0, \dots p$. DANIELL is an alias for UNIT.
NONE	*No smoothing.* If NONE is specified, the spectral density estimate is the same as the periodogram.
w_-p,...w_0,...,w_p	*User-specified weights.* W_0 is applied to the periodogram value being smoothed, and the weights on either side are applied to preceding and following values. If the number of weights is even, it is assumed that w_p is not supplied. The weight after the middle one is applied to the periodogram value being smoothed. W_0 must be positive.

Example

```
SPECTRA VAR01
  /WINDOW=TUKEY(3)
  /PLOT=P S.
```

- In this example, the Tukey window weights with a span of three are used.
- The PLOT subcommand plots both the periodogram and the spectral density estimate, both by frequency and period.

PLOT Subcommand

PLOT specifies which plots are displayed.

- If PLOT is not specified, only the periodogram is plotted for each series specified. Each periodogram is shown both by frequency and by period.
- You can specify more than one plot keyword.
- Keywords can be specified in any order.
- Plot keywords K, CS, QS, PH, A, and G apply only to bivariate analyses. If subcommand CROSS is not specified, these keywords are ignored.
- The period (horizontal) axis on a plot BY PERIOD is scaled in natural logarithms from 0.69 to $\ln(n)$, where n is the number of cases.
- The frequency (horizontal) axis on a plot BY FREQ is scaled from 0 to 0.5, expressing the frequency as a fraction of the length of the series.
- The periodogram and estimated spectrum (vertical axis) are scaled in natural logs.

The following plot keywords are available:

P   *Periodogram.* This is the default.

S   *Spectral density estimate.*

K   *Squared coherency.* Applies only to bivariate analyses.

CS   *Cospectral density estimate.* Applies only to bivariate analyses.

QS   *Quadrature spectrum estimate.* Applies only to bivariate analyses.

PH   *Phase spectrum.* Applies only to bivariate analyses.

A   *Cross amplitude.* Applies only to bivariate analyses.

G   *Gain.* Applies only to bivariate analyses.

ALL   *All plots.* For bivariate analyses, this includes all plots listed above. For univariate analyses, this includes the periodogram and the spectral density estimate.

BY Keyword

By default, SPECTRA displays both frequency and period plots. You can use BY to produce only frequency plots or only period plots.

- BY FREQ indicates that all plots are plotted by frequency only. Plots by period are not produced.
- BY PERIOD indicates that all plots are plotted by period only. Plots by frequency are not produced.

Example

```
SPECTRA SER01
  /PLOT=P S BY FREQ.
```

- This command plots both the periodogram and the spectral density estimate for *SER01*. The plots are shown by frequency only.

CROSS Subcommand

CROSS is used to specify bivariate spectral analysis.

- When CROSS is specified, the first series named on the VARIABLES subcommand is the independent variable. All remaining variables are dependent.
- Each series after the first is analyzed with the first series independently of other series named.
- Univariate analysis of each series specified is still performed.
- You can specify CROSS NO to turn off bivariate analysis when applying a previous model with APPLY.

Example

```
SPECTRA VARX VARY VARZ
  /CROSS.
```

- In this example, bivariate spectral analyses of series *VARX* with *VARY* and *VARX* with *VARZ* are requested in addition to the usual univariate analyses of *VARX*, *VARY*, and *VARZ*.

SAVE Subcommand

SAVE saves computed SPECTRA variables in the working data file for later use. SPECTRA displays a list of the new variables and their labels, showing the type and source of those variables.

- You can specify any or all of the output keywords listed below.
- A name to be used for generating variable names must follow each output keyword. The name must be enclosed in parentheses.
- For each output keyword, one variable is created for each series named on SPECTRA and for each bivariate pair.
- Keywords RC, IC, CS, QS, PH, A, G, and K apply only to bivariate analyses. If CROSS is not specified, these keywords are ignored.
- SAVE specifications are not used when models are reapplied using APPLY. They must be specified each time variables are to be saved.
- The output variables correspond to the Fourier frequencies. They do not correspond to the original series.
- Since each output variable has only ($n/2 + 1$) cases (where n is the number of cases), the values for the second half of the series are set to system-missing.
- Variable names are generated by adding _n to the specified name, where n ranges from 1 to the number of series specified.
- For bivariate variables, the suffix is _n_n, where the n's indicate the two variables used in the analysis.
- The frequency (FREQ) and period (PER) variable names are constant across all series and do not have a numeric suffix.
- If the generated variable name is longer than eight characters, or if the specified name already exists, the variable is not saved.

The following output keywords are available:

FREQ   *Fourier frequencies.*

PER   *Fourier periods.*

SIN   *Value of a sine function at the Fourier frequencies.*

COS   *Value of a cosine function at the Fourier frequencies.*

P   *Periodogram values.*

S   *Spectral density estimate values.*

RC   *Real part values of the cross-periodogram.* Applies only to bivariate analyses.

IC   *Imaginary part values of the cross-periodogram.* Applies only to bivariate analyses.

CS   *Cospectral density estimate values.* Applies only to bivariate analyses.

QS   *Quadrature spectrum estimate values.* Applies only to bivariate analyses.

PH   *Phase spectrum estimate values.* Applies only to bivariate analyses.

A   *Cross-amplitude values.* Applies only to bivariate analyses.

G   *Gain values.* Applies only to bivariate analyses.

K   *Squared coherency values.* Applies only to bivariate analyses.

Example

```
SPECTRA VARIABLES=STRIKES RUNS
   /SAVE= FREQ (FREQ) P (PGRAM) S (SPEC).
```

- This example creates five variables: *FREQ, PGRAM_1, PGRAM_2, SPEC_1,* and *SPEC_2.*

APPLY Subcommand

APPLY allows you to use a previously defined SPECTRA model without having to repeat the specifications. For general rules on APPLY, see the APPLY subcommand on p. 256.

- The only specification on APPLY is the name of a previous model in quotes. If a model name is not specified, the model specified on the previous SPECTRA command is used.

- To change one or more model specifications, specify the subcommands of only those portions you want to change after the APPLY subcommand.

- If no series are specified on the command, the series that were originally specified with the model being reapplied are used.

- To change the series used with the model, enter new series names before or after the APPLY subcommand. If a variable name is specified before APPLY, the slash before the subcommand is required.

- The SAVE specifications from the previous model are *not* reused by APPLY. They must be specified each time variables are to be saved.

Examples

```
SPECTRA VAR01
   /WINDOW=DANIELL (3)
   /CENTER
   /PLOT P S BY FREQ.
SPECTRA APPLY
   /PLOT P S.
```

- The first command plots both the periodogram and the spectral density estimate for *VAR01.* The plots are shown by frequency only.

- Since the PLOT subcommand is respecified, the second command produces plots by both frequency and period. All other specifications remain the same as in the first command.

References

Bloomfield, P. 1976. *Fourier analysis of time series.* New York: John Wiley & Sons.

Fuller, W. A. 1976. *Introduction to statistical time series.* New York: John Wiley & Sons.

Gottman, J. M. 1981. *Time-series analysis: A comprehensive introduction for social scientists.* Cambridge: Cambridge University Press.

Priestley, M. B. 1981. *Spectral Analysis and Time Series.* Volumes 1 & 2. London: Academic Press.

TDISPLAY

```
TDISPLAY  [ {ALL            } ]
            {model names     }
            {command names   }

[/TYPE={MODEL**}]
       {COMMAND}
```

**Default if the subcommand is omitted.

Example:

```
TDISPLAY MOD_2 MOD_3
  /TYPE=MODEL.
```

Overview

TDISPLAY displays information about currently active Trends models. These models are automatically generated by many Trends procedures for use with the APPLY subcommand (see the APPLY subcommand on p. 256).

Options

If models are specified on TDISPLAY, information about just those models is displayed. You can control whether models are specified by model name or by the name of the procedure that generated them using the TYPE subcommand.

Basic Specification

The basic specification is simply the command keyword TDISPLAY.

- By default, TDISPLAY produces a list of all currently active models. The list includes the model names, the commands that created each model, model labels if specified, and creation dates and times.

Syntax Rules

- To display information on a subset of active models, specify those models after TDISPLAY.
- Models can be specified using either individual model names or the names of the procedures that created them. To use procedure names, you must specify the TYPE subcommand with keyword COMMAND.
- Model names are either the default *MOD_n* names or the names assigned with MODEL NAME.
- If procedure names are specified, all models created by those procedures are displayed.
- Model names and procedure names cannot be mixed on the same TDISPLAY command.

- You can specify keyword ALL after TDISPLAY to display all models that are currently active. This is the default.

Operations

- Only models currently active are displayed.
- The following procedures can generate models: AREG, ARIMA, EXSMOOTH, SEASON, SPECTRA, and X11ARIMA in SPSS Trends; ACF, CASEPLOT, CCF, CURVEFIT, NPPLOT, PACF, and TSPLOT in the SPSS Base System; and WLS and 2SLS in SPSS Professional Statistics.

Example

```
TDISPLAY.
```

- The command keyword by itself displays information about all currently active models.

TYPE Subcommand

TYPE indicates whether models are specified by model name or procedure name.

- One keyword, MODEL or COMMAND, can be specified after TYPE.
- MODEL is the default and indicates that models are specified as model names.
- COMMAND specifies that models are specified by procedure name.
- TYPE has no effect if model names or command names are not listed after TDISPLAY.
- If more than one TYPE subcommand is specified, only the last one is used.
- The TYPE specification applies only to the current TDISPLAY command.

Example

```
TDISPLAY ACF ARIMA
  /TYPE=COMMAND.
```

- This command displays all currently active models that were created by procedures ACF and ARIMA.

X11ARIMA

```
X11ARIMA [VARIABLES=] series names [/APPLY [='model name']]

[/TITLE={'title'  }]  [/MODEL={MULTIPLICATIVE**}]
        {'X11ARIMA'}           {ADDITIVE        }
                               {LOGARITHMIC     }

[/PERIOD={MONTHLY or 12 }]  [/{NOSUMMARY          }]
         {QUARTERLY or 4}     {SUMMARY [=varlist]}

[/{NOARIMA                                            }]
  {ARIMA=[EXTREMES ({ACCEPT**})]][{BACKCAST  }]}
  {                {REPLACE }    {NOBACKCAST}}

[/{NOUSERMODEL                                         }]
  {USERMODEL=(p,d,q) [(sp,sd,sq)]  [MXITER ({30   })]  }
  {                                        {value}     }

    [{NOINITIAL        }]    [{NOCONSTANT}]
     {INITIAL (values)}      {MACONSTANT}
                             {ARCONSTANT}

    [{NOTRANSFORM            }]
     {LN [({0    })]}
     {     {value}}
     {POWER (value [,{0    }]}
     {               {value}}

    [{NOORDERS                                                      }]
     {[ARORDER (values)][MAORDER (values)][SARORDER (values)] SMAORDER (values)]}

[/FORMAT=[TABLES ({0**  })]  [D10 ({2**  })]]
                 {value}           {value}

[/PRINT=[{STANDARD**}][   [{NOEXTRA**}]]
         {BRIEF     }      {EXTRA    }
         {ANALYSIS  }
         {SHORT     }
         {LONG      }
         {FULL      }

[/PLOTS={STANDARD**}]  [/{NOYEARTOTAL**}]  [/{EXTREMETC**}]]
        {NONE      }     {YEARTOTAL    }     {NOEXTREMETC}
        {ALL       }

[/LOWSIGMA={1.5**}]  [/HISIGMA={2.5**}]
          {value}             {value}

[/MONTHLEN={SEASONAL**}]  [/{NOPRVARS**     }]
           {TRADEDAY  }     {PRVARS=varlist}

[/{NODAYWGTS**                          }]
  {DAYWGTS=[MON (value) . . . SUN (value)]}

[/{NOTRADAYREG**                              }]
  {TRADAYREG=[{NOADJUST}]  [TDSIGMA ({2.5  }]]}
  {          {ADJUST  }             {value}   }
  {          {SIGNIF  }                        }

    [{NOCOMPUTE    }]  [{NOBEGIN    }]
     {COMPUTE (year)}   {BEGIN (year)}
```

```
[/MACURVES= [SEASFACT ({HYBRID**})]    [TR20DCYC ({4††})]
                      {3X3    }                  {8   }
                      {3X5    }                  {12††}
                      {3X9    }                  {24  }
                      {STABLE }
                      {SELECT }

            [HENDERSON ({SELECT**})]
                       {9      }
                       {13     }
                       {23     }
                       {5      }
                       {7      }

   [{NOPERMONTH**                                            }]
    {PREMONTH [(JAN {3X3   })...(DEC {3X3   })]               }
                   {3X5   }         {3X5   }
                   {3X9   }         {3X9   }
                   {STABLE}         {STABLE}
    {NOPERQUARTER**                                          }
    {PERQUARTER} [(FIRST {3X3   })...(FOURTH {3X3   })]]
                        {3X5   }           {3X5   }
                        {3X9   }           {3X9   }
                        {STABLE}           {STABLE}


    [DEFAULTS]]
```

**Default if the subcommand or keyword is not specified.
†† Default is 12 for monthly data and 4 for quarterly data.

Example:

```
X11ARIMA PRICES
  /PERIOD=4
  /ARIMA
  /USERMODEL=(0,1,1)(0,1,1).
```

Overview

X11ARIMA estimates multiplicative or additive seasonal factors for monthly or quarterly series. ARIMA forecasts and backcasts can be added to the series before seasonal decomposition. The procedure is based on the Statistics Canada version of the U.S. Bureau of Labor Statistics Census-II X-11 program.

Options

Seasonal Adjustment. You can select one of three seasonal adjustment models (multiplicative, additive, or log additive) on the MODEL subcommand. You can use the SUMMARY subcommand to specify that you want summary statistics on already adjusted series and that no seasonal adjustment is to be done. On the PERIOD subcommand you can specify the periodicity of the series.

ARIMA Adjustment. You can add ARIMA forecasts and, optionally, backcasts, to the series before seasonal adjustment using the ARIMA subcommand. You can specify the ARIMA model on the USERMODEL subcommand or let the program select the best one from three default models.

Other Adjustments. A wide variety of other optional adjustments can be made, such as a yearly total adjustment (YEARTOTAL), replacement of extreme values (NOEXREMETC), length of month allowances (MONTHLEN), prior adjustment based on specified variables (PRVARS), prior daily weights adjustment (DAYWGTS), trading-day regression (TRADAYREG), and application of many different types of moving averages (MACURVES). You can specify the upper and lower sigma limits for generating extreme values using HISIGMA and LOWSIGMA.

Output. Depending on the subcommands and specifications you use, you can display from 3 to 76 tables. The PRINT subcommand provides control over the general number and type of tables. You can specify the number of decimal places displayed using FORMAT. In addition to the standard plots, you can request the irregular (error) series chart, seasonal factors plot, and the Kolmogorov-Smirnov cumulative periodogram using the PLOTS subcommand. You can also suppress all plots. You can specify a title for the X11ARIMA output using the TITLE subcommand.

Basic Specification

The basic specification is one or more series names.

- By default, X11ARIMA estimates a multiplicative seasonal model without doing any prior ARIMA adjustment. The default periodicity is the periodicity established on the DATE command (the DATE command must be specified before X11ARIMA; see "Operations" on p. 311). Extreme values are included in estimating the trend-cycle curve. The trend-cycle moving average is based on 12 if the series are monthly and 4 if the series are quarterly. A Henderson moving average appropriate for the series is selected by the program. In estimating the seasonal factors, the length-of-month allowance is included. A 3×3 moving average is used for the first estimate and a 3×5 moving average is used for the final estimate.

- Default output consists of 19 to 40 tables, depending on the subcommands and specifications chosen. Values are displayed as integers in most tables except D10 (final seasonal factors), where values are displayed with two decimal places by default. Original series, seasonal, and trend-cycle plots are produced.

- For each series specified, four new variables are automatically created, labeled, and added to the working data file: the seasonal adjustment factors, the seasonally adjusted series, the smoothed trend-cycle components, and the irregular (error) component. (For variable naming and labeling conventions, see "New Variables" on p. 253.)

Subcommand Order

- If the SUMMARY subcommand is used, the VARIABLES subcommand must be specified before it. Otherwise, subcommands can be specified in any order.

Syntax Rules

- VARIABLES can be specified only once.
- Other subcommands can be specified more than once, but only the last specification of each one is executed.

Operations

- The starting year and month (or quarter) must be specified on the DATE command before the X11ARIMA procedure is used. The year specification must be in the range 1900 to 1999 and *cannot* be abbreviated to the last two digits. (See DATE in the *SPSS Base System Syntax Reference Guide*.)
- The PREDICT command has no effect on X11ARIMA. X11ARIMA provides one-year forecasts/backcasts where relevant. (See PREDICT in the *SPSS Base System Syntax Reference Guide*.)
- Missing data are not allowed anywhere in the series. (You can use the RMV command to replace missing values, and USE to ignore missing observations at the beginning or end of a series. See RMV and USE in the *SPSS Base System Syntax Reference Guide* for more information.)

Limitations

- Maximum 1 VARIABLES subcommand. There is no limit on the number of series named on the list.
- Each series must contain at least three full years of data. Five full years of data are required for ARIMA extrapolation and some MACURVES specifications.

Example

```
X11ARIMA PRICES
  /PERIOD=4
  /ARIMA
  /USERMODEL=(0,1,1)(0,1,1).
```

- This command seasonally adjusts the series *PRICES* using a multiplicative seasonal model after forecasts and backcasts generated from the specified ARIMA model have been added.

VARIABLES Subcommand

VARIABLES specifies the series names and is the only required subcommand. The actual keyword VARIABLES is optional.

TITLE Subcommand

Use TITLE to specify a title for the first page of the X11ARIMA output.

- The title can be up to 77 characters in length and must be specified in single quotes.
- The default title is *X11ARIMA*.
- The TITLE subcommand on X11ARIMA is unrelated to the TITLE command in the SPSS Base system, which prints a heading at the top of every page of output for the entire session.

Example

```
X11ARIMA PRHSTART
  /TITLE='New Private Housing Starts'.
```

- The TITLE subcommand assigns the title *New Private Housing Starts*, which will appear on the first page of the X11ARIMA output.

MODEL Subcommand

MODEL specifies whether the seasonal adjustment is multiplicative, additive, or logarithmic (log additive).

- The specification on MODEL is one of three keywords: MULTIPLICATIVE, ADDITIVE, or LOGARITHMIC.
- MULTIPLICATIVE is the default if the MODEL subcommand is not specified.
- The series must contain only positive values for MULTIPLICATIVE or LOGARITHMIC models.

Example

```
X11ARIMA PRHSTART
  /TITLE='New Private Housing Starts'
  /MODEL=ADDITIVE.
```

- The MODEL subcommand requests an additive model of seasonal adjustment.

PERIOD Subcommand

PERIOD indicates the size of the period.

- The specification on PERIOD indicates how many data points are in one period or season. You can specify one of two keywords, MONTHLY or QUARTERLY, or one of two values, 12 or 4. The value 12 is an alias for MONTHLY and the value 4 is an alias for QUARTERLY.
- If the PERIOD subcommand is not specified, the periodicity established on the DATE command is used. (See DATE in the *SPSS Base System Syntax Reference Guide*.)

Example

```
X11ARIMA PRHSTART
  /MODEL=MULTIPLICATIVE
  /PERIOD=MONTHLY.
```

- The PERIOD subcommand specifies that the data in the series have a monthly periodicity.

SUMMARY and NOSUMMARY Subcommands

SUMMARY indicates that the series are already seasonally adjusted and should be summarized without seasonal adjustment. NOSUMMARY indicates that the series should be seasonally adjusted. NOSUMMARY is the default.

- Following SUMMARY, a series or series list can be specified to indicate which series should not be seasonally adjusted.
- The series named on SUMMARY must first be specified on the VARIABLES subcommand.
- If no series are specified, the SUMMARY subcommand applies to all series specified on VARIABLES. None of the series will be seasonally adjusted.
- There are no additional specifications on NOSUMMARY.
- NOSUMMARY is generally used with an APPLY subcommand to turn off a previous SUMMARY specification.

Example

```
X11ARIMA ADJSTART
  /SUMMARY.
```

- The SUMMARY subcommand indicates that the series *ADJSTART* has already been seasonally adjusted. Only summary measures of the series will be produced.

ARIMA and NOARIMA Subcommands

ARIMA indicates that an ARIMA model should be used to generate forecasts. NOARIMA is the default and indicates that no ARIMA adjustment is done to the series before seasonal decomposition.

- There are no additional specifications for NOARIMA.
- NOARIMA is generally used with an APPLY subcommand to turn off a previous ARIMA specification.
- If ARIMA is specified, the series must contain at least 5 and not more than 29 years of observations.

The following optional keywords can be specified on subcommand ARIMA. BACKCAST and NOBACKCAST are alternatives.

EXTREMES *Treatment of extreme values (outliers).* The specification on EXTREMES is either ACCEPT or REPLACE, enclosed in parentheses. With ACCEPT, extreme values are used in the ARIMA extrapolation. ACCEPT is the default. With REPLACE, extreme values in the original series are replaced with fitted values generated by the ARIMA model. The same ARIMA model is then retested with the modified series to obtain the extrapolated values. No replacements are made, however, for any extreme values in the first $2(p + sp + d + sd(\text{period}))$ observations of the series.

BACKCAST *Backcast the series.* ARIMA-extrapolated values are added to the beginning of the series as well as the end of the series. BACKCAST is the default.

NOBACKCAST *No backcasting.* Values will not be added to the beginning of the series.

Example

```
X11ARIMA PRHSTART
  /ARIMA.
```

- This command specifies that ARIMA modeling should be done.
- Forecasts and backcasts from the ARIMA model are added to the original series before the seasonal adjustment process begins. Extreme values are used in the ARIMA extrapolation.

USERMODEL Subcommand

USERMODEL specifies an ARIMA model used in ARIMA adjustment.

- The ARIMA subcommand must be specified for USERMODEL to be executed. If you specify USERMODEL without ARIMA in effect, the procedure terminates with an error message.
- The ARIMA parameters (p,d,q) (sp,sd,sq) must be specified on USERMODEL.
- (p,d,q) specifies the nonseasonal ARIMA parameters. These values must be integers ranging from 0 to 4, inclusive. The (p,d,q) specification is required. If p, d, and q are not to be included in the model, specify them as (0,0,0).
- (sp,sd,sq) specifies the seasonal ARIMA parameters. These values must be integers ranging from 0 to 4, inclusive. The (sp,sd,sq) specification is optional. If sp, sd, and sq are omitted, they are set to (0,0,0) by default.
- If the model does not have a deterministic constant, the sum of p, q, sp, and sq must be less than or equal to 10. If the model has a deterministic constant, the sum of p, q, sp, and sq must be less than or equal to 9.

Transformation Keywords

Use one of the following keywords on USERMODEL to transform the series before modeling:

LN   *Natural (base* e) *logarithmic transformation.* After LN, you can optionally specify a constant value to be added to the series before the transformation. The default constant is 0.

POWER   *Power transformation.* After POWER, specify the power to which the series is raised. After the power value, you can optionally specify a constant value to be added to the series before the transformation. The default constant is 0. There is no default power value.

NOTRANSFORM *No transformation.* NOTRANSFORM is the default and is generally used on an APPLY subcommand to turn off a previous LN or POWER specification.

Termination Criteria Keyword

Use the following keyword on USERMODEL to indicate the maximum number of iterations:

MXITER   *Maximum number of iterations.* The value specified on MXITER must be an integer between 1 and 50, inclusive. The default number of iterations is 30.

Constant Parameter Keywords

Use one of the following keywords on USERMODEL to include deterministic constants in the model:

MACONSTANT   *Use a constant deterministic moving-average parameter.*

ARCONSTANT   *Use a constant deterministic autoregressive parameter.*

NOCONSTANT   *No deterministic constant.* NOCONSTANT is the default and is generally used with an APPLY subcommand to turn off a previous MACONSTANT or ARCONSTANT specification.

Initial Value Keywords

Use keyword INITIAL on USERMODEL to specify initial values for the parameters in the model:

INITIAL   *Use the specified initial values for the model parameters.* The list of values is enclosed in parentheses following keyword INITIAL. You must specify one initial value for every parameter in the model.

NOINITIAL   *Do not use initial values.* NOINITIAL is the default and is generally used with the APPLY subcommand to turn off a previous INITIAL specification.

Parameter-Order Keywords

Use one or more of the parameter-order keywords to specify the orders of the ARIMA model parameters or turn off all previously specified orders with NOORDERS, which is the default.

ARORDER   *Order values of the regular autoregressive parameters.*

MAORDER   *Order values of the regular moving-average parameters.*

SARORDER   *Order values of the seasonal autoregressive parameters.*

SMAORDER   *Order values of the seasonal moving-average parameters.*

NOORDERS   *No orders.* NOORDERS is the default and is generally used with an APPLY subcommand to turn off previously specified orders.

- Orders are specified by listing the order values, one for each parameter, enclosed in parentheses following the keyword.
- If the model contains a deterministic constant, the order of the constant is automatically zero.
- The order of every parameter in the model (except the constant) must be specified after the order keyword.
- The order values must be integers. A single value n indicates that only lag n should be fit. A list of values denotes specific lags.
- The maximum number of orders that can be specified across all lists is 10.

- For seasonal parameters, the values denote *seasonal* lags. Thus, a seasonal parameter of 1 indicates lag 12 for monthly data, and a seasonal parameter of 2 indicates lag 24.

Example

```
X11ARIMA PRHSTART
  /ARIMA
  /USERMODEL=(0,1,1)(0,1,1) LN.
```

- An ARIMA (0,1,1)(0,1,1) model is specified. The series is transformed using the natural logarithm before modeling.

NOUSERMODEL Subcommand

NOUSERMODEL indicates that a user-specified model is not supplied and that one of three default ARIMA models is used. The three default models are automatically fit to the series and X11ARIMA selects the one that fits best. NOUSERMODEL is the default.

- For series that are seasonally adjusted multiplicatively or logarithmically, the three models are:

  (0,1,1) (0,1,1) LN
  (0,2,2) (0,1,1) LN
  (2,1,2) (0,1,1)

  For series that are seasonally adjusted additively, the default models are:

  (0,1,1) (0,1,1)
  (0,2,2) (0,1,1)
  (2,1,2) (0,1,1)

- NOUSERMODEL is generally used with an APPLY subcommand to turn off a previous USERMODEL specification.

- If the series is not fit adequately by one of the default models, no ARIMA modeling will be done. The criteria used to judge the models is displayed in case you want to specify one of the models anyway.

- The ARIMA subcommand must be specified for NOUSERMODEL to be executed. If you specify NOUSERMODEL without ARIMA in effect, the procedure terminates with an error message.

FORMAT Subcommand

FORMAT controls the number of decimal places displayed in output tables. The specification on FORMAT is either or both of the following keywords:

TABLES (n)   *The number of decimal places displayed in most tables except Table D10.* The integer specified after TABLES indicates the number of digits to the right of the decimal point. The integer can range from 0 to 5. The default is 0.

D10 (n) *The number of decimal places displayed in Table D10 (Final Seasonal Factors).* The integer specified after D10 indicates the number of digits to the right of the decimal point. The integer can range from 1 to 5. The default is 2.

Example

```
X11ARIMA PRHSTART
  /FORMAT=TABLES (2) D10 (4).
```

- This command specifies that the values in all tables except D10 will display two decimal places.
- In Table D10, the values are displayed with four decimal places.

PRINT Subcommand

PRINT provides control over the general number and type of tables displayed. The exact tables displayed depend on other subcommand specifications. Table 1 lists all of the available tables.

You can specify any one of the following keywords on PRINT:

BRIEF *Print 3 to 13 tables.* Depending on other subcommand specifications, these tables can include tables from group A, B1, C16A, C16B, C16C, D10, D10A, D11, D11A, D16, D16A, and group F.

ANALYSIS *Print 7 to 29 tables.* The tables displayed are mainly from groups A, D, E, and F.

SHORT *Print 7 to 26 tables.* The tables displayed are mainly from groups A, D, and F.

LONG *Print 28 to 60 tables.* The tables that are omitted are a few of the intermediate ratio, seasonal factor, and seasonally adjusted series tables from the B, C, and D groups.

FULL *Print 45 to 76 tables.* All possible tables given other subcommand specifications are displayed.

STANDARD *Print 19 to 40 tables.* This is the default.

In addition to the keywords above, one of the following two keywords can also be specified:

EXTRA *Additional information in Tables A5 and A6.* The forecasted values for the last 36 months and the absolute percent differences between forecasted values for the last 36 months are added to Table A5. The backcasted values for the last 36 months and the absolute percent differences between backcasted values for the last 36 months are added to Table A6.

NOEXTRA *No additional information in Tables A5 and A6.* NOEXTRA is generally used with an APPLY subcommand to turn off a previous EXTRA specification.

Example

```
X11ARIMA PRHSTART
  /PRINT=BRIEF EXTRA.
```

- The PRINT subcommand limits output to BRIEF
- Keyword EXTRA specifies extra output for Tables A5 and A6.

Table 1   Tables produced by X11ARIMA

Table	Contents
A1	Original series
A2	Prior monthly adjustment factors
A3	Adjusted original series, modified by prior monthly adjustment factors
A4A	Prior trading-day adjustment daily weights
A4B	Prior trading-day adjustment factors without length of month adjustment
A4C	Prior trading-day adjustment factors, one year ahead
A5	ARIMA extrapolation model (forecast)
A6	ARIMA extrapolation model (backcast)
B1	Prior adjusted original series
B2	Trend cycle: centered 12-term moving average
B3	Modified SI ratios
B4	Replacement ratios
B5	Seasonal factors
B6	Seasonally adjusted series
B7	Trend cycle: Henderson curve
B8	Modified SI ratios
B9	Replacement ratios
B10	Seasonal factors
B11	Seasonally adjusted series
B13	Irregular series
B14	Extreme irregular values excluded from trading-day regression
B15	Preliminary trading-day regression
B16	Trading-day adjustment factors derived from regression coefficients
B17	Preliminary weights for irregular component
B18	Trading-day factors derived from the combined daily weights
B19	Adjusted original series, modified for trading-day variation
B20	Extreme values
C1	Adjusted original series modified by preliminary weights
C2	Trend cycle: centered 12-term moving average
C4	Modified SI ratios
C5	Seasonal factors

Table 1   Tables produced by X11ARIMA (Continued)

Table	Contents
C6	Seasonally adjusted series
C7	Trend cycle: Henderson curve
C9	Modified SI ratios
C10	Seasonal factors
C11	Seasonally adjusted series
C13	Irregular series
C14	Extreme irregular values excluded from trading-day regression
C15	Final trading-day regression
C16A	Regression coefficients used to derive trading-day adjustment factors
C16B	Regression trading-day adjustment factors
C16C	Regression trading-day adjustment factors, one year ahead
C17	Final weights for irregular component
C18A	Combined daily weights
C18B	Combined trading-day adjustment factors without length-of-month adjustment
C18C	Combined trading-day adjustment factors, one year ahead
C19	Adjusted original series, modified for trading-day variation
C20	Extreme values
D1	Adjusted original series modified by final weights
D2	Trend cycle: centered 12-term moving average
D4	Modified SI ratios
D5	Seasonal factors
D6	Seasonally adjusted series
D7	Trend cycle: Henderson curve
D8	Final modified SI ratios
D9	Final replacement ratios
D9A	Yearly change in error, seasonal components, and moving seasonality ratio
D10	Final seasonal factors
D10A	Seasonal factors, one year ahead
D11	Final seasonally adjusted series
D11A	Final seasonally adjusted series with revised yearly totals
D12	Final trend cycle—Henderson curve
D13	Final irregular series
D16	Combined seasonal and trading-day factors
D16A	Combined seasonal and trading-day factors, one year ahead
E1	Original series modified for extremes with 0 final weights
E2	Final seasonally adjusted series modified for extremes with 0 weight
E3	Modified irregular series

Table 1   Tables produced by X11ARIMA (Continued)

Table	Contents
E4	Ratios of annual totals, original and adjusted series
E5	Month-to-month changes in the original series
E6	Month-to-month changes in the final seasonally adjusted series (D11)
E6A	Month-to-month changes in the final seasonally adjusted series (D11A)
F1	MCD moving average
F2A	Average percent change without regard to sign over the indicated span
F2B	Contributions of the percent change in the components of the original series
F2C	Average percent change with regard to sign and standard deviation
F2D	Average duration of run
F2E	I/C ratio for months span
F2F	Contribution of the components to the stationary portion of variance
F2G	Autocorrelation of the irregulars for spans 1 to 14
F2H	Final I/C ratio and the final I/S ratio
F2I	Statistical tests of trading-day regressions and seasonality
F3	Monitoring and quality assessment statistics

PLOTS Subcommand

PLOTS controls which plots are displayed. You can specify any one of the following key-words on PLOTS:

STANDARD   *Standard plots.* These include a plot of the original series, the original series with ARIMA-extrapolated values, and the original series modified for extremes with 0 final weights; a plot of the final seasonally adjusted series and the final trend-cycle; and a plot of the final seasonal factors, final unmodified seasonal-irregular ratios, final ratios modified for extremes, and extrapolated seasonal factors for each month or quarter. STANDARD is the default.

ALL   *All available plots.* These include all the standard plots plus a plot of the final seasonal factors, final unmodified seasonal-irregular ratios, final ratios modified for extremes, and extrapolated seasonal factors for the series; a plot of the final irregular series and the final modified irregular series; and a list of the values and plot of the cumulative periodogram bounded by 95% confidence limits from the Kolmogorov-Smirnov significance tests of the final irregulars.

NONE   *No plots.*

Example

```
X11ARIMA PRHSTART
  /PLOT=ALL.
```

- The PLOTS subcommand of this X11ARIMA procedure produces standard plots plus three additional plots.

YEARTOTAL and NOYEARTOTAL Subcommands

YEARTOTAL indicates that the seasonally adjusted series in Table D11 should be adjusted to make the yearly totals the same as those of the original series. NOYEARTOTAL indicates that the series should not be adjusted and is the default.

- There are no additional specifications on YEARTOTAL or NOYEARTOTAL.
- If YEARTOTAL is specified, the seasonally adjusted series with the revised yearly totals is presented in Table D11A.
- NOYEARTOTAL is generally used with an APPLY subcommand to turn off a previous YEARTOTAL specification.

Example

```
X11ARIMA PRHSTART
   /YEARTOTAL.
```

- The seasonally adjusted series will be adjusted so that its yearly totals are the same as those of the original series.

EXTREMETC and NOEXTREMETC Subcommands

EXTREMETC and NOEXTREMETC specify whether extreme values should be modified before computing the trend-cycle estimates in Table B7.

- NOEXTREMETC indicates that extreme values should be modified before computing the trend-cycle estimates. This is useful when unusual events such as strikes or catastrophes cause major irregularities in the series. Modifying the extreme values reduces the effect of these events on the trend-cycle estimates.
- EXTREMETC is the default and indicates that extreme values should be included in the trend-cycle estimates without any modification.
- EXTREMETC is generally used with an APPLY subcommand to turn off a previous NOEXTREMETC specification.
- There are no additional specifications on EXTREMETC or NOEXTREMETC.

Example

```
X11ARIMA PRHSTART
   /NOEXTREMETC.
```

- In this X11ARIMA analysis, extreme scores will be modified before seasonal adjustment.

MONTHLEN Subcommand

MONTHLEN controls whether the differences in the number of days in each month are accounted for in the seasonal factors or in the trading-day factors.

- MONTHLEN is ignored unless it is used with monthly series and MODEL=MULTIPLICATIVE is in effect.

The specification on MONTHLEN is one of the following two keywords:

SEASONAL   *Include length-of-month variation in the seasonal factors.* SEASONAL is the default.

TRADEDAY   *Include length-of-month variation in the trading-day factors.*

Example

```
X11ARIMA PRHSTART
  /MONTHLEN=TRADEDAY.
```

- Here the length-of-month differences are accounted for in the trading-day factors rather than in the seasonal factors.

HISIGMA and LOWSIGMA Subcommands

HISIGMA and LOWSIGMA set the upper and lower sigma limits for graduating extreme values in estimating seasonal and trend-cycle components.

- The specification on LOWSIGMA is a value ranging from 0.1 to 9.9. The default is 1.5.
- The specification on HISIGMA is a value ranging from 0.1 to 9.9. The default is 2.5.
- The value of HISIGMA must be larger than the value of LOWSIGMA.

Example

```
X11ARIMA PRHSTART
  /NOEXTREMETC
  /LOWSIGMA 2.5
  /HISIGMA 3.5.
```

- The LOWSIGMA and HISIGMA subcommands set the sigma limits for graduating extreme values to 2.5 and 3.5.

PRVARS and NOPRVARS Subcommands

PRVARS specifies the variables to be used in adjusting the series before the seasonal adjustment process. NOPRVARS is the default and indicates that there is no PRVARS adjustment.

- The specification on PRVARS is one or more variable names.
- The variables specified on PRVARS adjust the series specified on the VARIABLES subcommand on a one-to-one basis: the first variable named on PRVARS adjusts the first series named on VARIABLES, the second variable adjusts the second series, and so forth.
- You do not have to specify a PRVARS variable for every series named on VARIABLES.
- The maximum number of variables specified on PRVARS is the number of series named on the VARIABLES subcommand.
- When MODEL=MULTIPLICATIVE or LOGARITHMIC, the PRVARS variables are divided into the original series before seasonal adjustment.

- When MODEL=ADDITIVE, the PRVARS variables are subtracted from the original series before seasonal adjustment.
- There are no additional specifications on NOPRVARS.
- NOPRVARS is generally used with an APPLY subcommand to turn off a previous PRVARS specification.

Example

```
X11ARIMA PRHSTART
 /PRVARS=ADJINDEX.
```

- In this example, the variable *ADJINDEX* is used to make a prior adjustment to the *PRHSTART* series.

DAYWGTS and NODAYWGTS Subcommands

DAYWGTS allows you to specify prior daily weights to adjust for trading-day variation before seasonal adjustment. NODAYWGTS is the default and indicates that prior daily weights should not be applied.

- DAYWGTS can only be used with monthly series and with MODEL=MULTIPLICATIVE or LOGARITHMIC.
- The specification on DAYWGTS is one or more day keywords (MON, TUES, WED, THUR, FRI, SAT, and SUN) with their weights.
- Each weight is specified in parentheses following the day keyword to which it applies.
- The weights must be in the range 0 to 9.999.
- Days that are not specified are assigned a weight of 0. The weights of specified days are adjusted, if necessary, to total 7.0. The weights may also be adjusted by trading-day regression calculations.
- There are no additional specifications on NODAYWGTS. NODAYWGTS is equivalent to setting all day weights to 0.
- NODAYWGTS is generally used with an APPLY subcommand to turn off a previous DAYWGTS specification.

Example

```
X11ARIMA PRHSTART
 /DAYWGTS=MON(1.4) TUES(1.4) WED(1.4) THUR(1.4) FRI(1.4).
```

- The DAYWGTS subcommand in this example assigns equal weights to Monday through Friday. Saturday and Sunday are assigned weights of 0 by default.

TRADAYREG and NOTRADAYREG Subcommands

TRADAYREG computes and displays trading-day regression estimates. NOTRADAYREG indicates trading-day regression estimates should not be computed. NOTRADAYREG is the default.

- There are no additional specifications on NOTRADAYREG.

- NOTRADAYREG is generally used with an APPLY command to turn off a previous TRA-DAYREG specification.

The following keywords on TRADAYREG control whether and how the regression estimates are used to adjust the series. You can specify only one of these keywords:

NOADJUST   *Do not adjust the series by the factors computed.* This is the default specification for TRADAYREG.

ADJUST   *Adjust the series by the regression estimates.* If prior daily weights have been supplied on a DAYWGTS subcommand, they are corrected on the basis of these estimates.

SIGNIF   *Adjust the series by the regression estimates or prior factors corrected by the regression estimates to obtain preliminary estimates for the error series in B tables.* In C tables, SIGNIF uses the regression estimates only if they explain significant variation on the basis of the F test.

The following additional keywords can be specified on TRADAYREG: COMPUTE or NOCOMPUTE, BEGIN or NOBEGIN, and TDSIGMA:

COMPUTE   *Starting date for computing the trading-day regression.* The specification after COMPUTE is a year in the range 1900 to 1999 in parentheses. The estimates are derived using only the part of the series from January of the year specified to the end of the series (or the end of the USE period).

NOCOMPUTE   *Use the entire series in the regression.* NOCOMPUTE is the default and is generally used with an APPLY subcommand to override a previous COMPUTE specification.

BEGIN   *Starting date for applying the trading-day regression.* BEGIN can be specified only if TRADAYREG=ADJUST or SIGNIF. The specification on BEGIN is a year in the range 1900 to 1999 in parentheses. BEGIN applies the estimates only to the part of the series from January of the year specified to the end of the series (or the end of the USE period). If prior daily weights are supplied on the DAYWGTS subcommand, BEGIN adjusts the part of the series before the specified date by the prior weights only. The part of the series after the specified date is adjusted by the prior weights corrected by the regression estimates.

NOBEGIN   *Apply trading-day corrections to the entire series.* NOBEGIN is the default and is generally used with an APPLY subcommand to override a previous BEGIN specification.

TDSIGMA   *Sigma limit for excluding extreme values from the trading-day regression.* The specification on TDSIGMA is a value in the range 0.1 to 9.9 in parentheses. The default value is 2.5.

Example

```
X11ARIMA PRHSTART
  /TRADAYREG=ADJUST.
```

- The TRADAYREG subcommand indicates that a trading-day regression is to be calculated.

- The ADJUST keyword after TRADAYREG indicates the series is to be adjusted by the computed regression coefficients.

MACURVES Subcommand

MACURVES specifies the types of seasonal and trend-cycle moving averages. The following keywords are available for MACURVES:

SEASFACT *Moving average for the seasonal factor curves.* Specify one of the following types in parentheses after SEASFACT: HYBRID, which uses a 3×3 average for the first estimate and a 3×5 average for the final estimate; 3X3, which uses a 3×3 average for all iterations; 3X5, which uses a 3×5 average for all iterations; 3X9, which uses a 3×9 average for all iterations; STABLE, which is an average of all values; or SELECT, which chooses a different moving average for each month based on the I/S ratio. The default is HYBRID.

TRENDCYC *Trend-cycle moving average.* The specification after TRENDCYC is 12 or 24 in parentheses for monthly series, and 4 or 8 in parentheses for quarterly series. The defaults are 12 for monthly and 4 for quarterly.

HENDERSON *Moving average for variable trend-cycles.* The specification after HENDERSON is a moving-average value or keyword SELECT in parentheses. For monthly series, 9 specifies a 9-term Henderson moving average, 13 specifies a 13-term moving average, and 23 specifies a 23-term moving average. For quarterly series, 5 specifies a 5-term Henderson moving average and 7 specifies a 7-term moving average. SELECT requests that Trends select an appropriate moving average based on the randomness in the series. SELECT is the default.

PERMONTH *Seasonal moving-average method per month for monthly series.* The specification on PERMONTH is followed by one or more month keywords (JAN, FEB, MAR, APR, MAY, JUN, JUL, AUG, SEP, OCT, NOV, DEC) and their averages in parentheses. The averages that can be specified are 3X3, 3X5, 3X9, and STABLE.

PERQUARTER *The seasonal moving-average method per quarter for quarterly series.* The specification on PERQUARTER is one or more quarter keywords (FIRST, SECOND, THIRD, FOURTH) and their averages in parentheses. The averages that can be specified are 3X3, 3X5, 3X9, and STABLE.

DEFAULT *Reset all MACURVES specifications to their defaults.* DEFAULT is in effect if MACURVES is not specified.

- Any month or quarter that is not included on a PERMONTH or PERQUARTER specification will be averaged according to the method specified by the SEASFACT entry of the MACURVES subcommand. 3×3, 3×5, and 3×9 specify those moving averages. STABLE specifies that the program should average all of the values.
- Monthly and quarterly specifications cannot be mixed.
- NOPERMONTH and NOPERQUARTER can be used to turn off PERMONTH or PERQUARTER specifications from a previous model.

Example

```
X11ARIMA PRHSTART
  /MACURVES=SEASFACT (SELECT).
```

- In this example, a different seasonal moving average is chosen for each month based on the Irregular/Seasonal ratio.

APPLY Subcommand

APPLY allows you to use a previously defined X11ARIMA model without having to repeat the specifications. For general rules on APPLY, see the APPLY subcommand on p. 256.

- The only specification on APPLY is the name of a previous model in quotes. If a model name is not specified, the model specified on the previous X11ARIMA command is used.
- To change one or more of the specifications of the model, specify the subcommands of only those portions you want to change after the subcommand APPLY.
- If no series are specified, the series that were originally specified with the model being reapplied are used.
- To change the series used with the model, enter new series names before or after the APPLY subcommand. If a series name is specified before APPLY, the slash before the subcommand is required.

Example

```
X11ARIMA TOTALHS
  /ARIMA
  /USERMODEL=(0,1,1)(0,1,1)
  /TRADAYREG=SIGNIF.
X11ARIMA APPLY
  /NOTRADAYREG.
```

- In this example, the same X11ARIMA procedure is done a second time without making any trading-day regression adjustments.

References

Dagum, E. B. 1983. *The X-11-ARIMA seasonal adjustment method.* Ottawa, Ont.: Statistics Canada.

Makridakis, S., S. C. Wheelwright, and V. E. McGee. 1983. *Forecasting: Methods and applications.* New York: John Wiley & Sons.

McLaughlin, Robert L. 1984. *Forecasting techniques for decision making.* Rockville, Md.: Control Data Management Institute.

Shiskin, J., A. H. Young, and J. C. Musgrave. 1967. *The X-11 variant of census method II seasonal adjustment.* Technical Paper No. 15, Bureau of the Census, U.S. Department of Commerce.

Appendix A
Durbin-Watson Significance Tables

The Durbin-Watson test statistic tests the null hypothesis that the residuals from an ordinary least-squares regression are not autocorrelated against the alternative that the residuals follow an AR1 process. The Durbin-Watson statistic ranges in value from 0 to 4. A value near 2 indicates nonautocorrelation; a value toward 0 indicates positive autocorrelation; a value toward 4 indicates negative autocorrelation.

Because of the dependence of any computed Durbin-Watson value on the associated data matrix, exact critical values of the Durbin-Watson statistic are not tabulated for all possible cases. Instead, Durbin and Watson established upper and lower bounds for the critical values. Typically, tabulated bounds are used to test the hypothesis of zero autocorrelation against the alternative of *positive* first-order autocorrelation, since positive autocorrelation is seen much more frequently in practice than negative autocorrelation. To use the table, you must cross-reference the sample size against the number of regressors, excluding the constant from the count of the number of regressors.

The conventional Durbin-Watson tables are not applicable when you do not have a constant term in the regression. Instead, you must refer to an appropriate set of Durbin-Watson tables. The conventional Durbin-Watson tables are also not applicable when a lagged dependent variable appears among the regressors. Durbin has proposed alternative test procedures for this case.

Statisticians have compiled Durbin-Watson tables from some special cases, including:

- Regressions with a full set of quarterly seasonal dummies.

- Regressions with an intercept and a linear trend variable (CURVEFIT MODEL=LINEAR).

- Regressions with a full set of quarterly seasonal dummies and a linear trend variable.

In addition to obtaining the Durbin-Watson statistic for residuals from REGRESSION, you should also plot the ACF and PACF of the residuals series. The plots might suggest either that the residuals are random, or that they follow some ARMA process. If the residuals resemble an AR1 process, you can estimate an appropriate regression using the AREG procedure. If the residuals follow any ARMA process, you can estimate an appropriate regression using the ARIMA procedure.

In this appendix, we have reproduced two sets of tables. Savin and White (1977) present tables for sample sizes ranging from 6 to 200 and for 1 to 20 regressors for models in which an intercept is included. Farebrother (1980) presents tables for sample sizes ranging from 2 to 200 and for 0 to 21 regressors for models in which an intercept is not included.

Let's consider an example of how to use the tables. In Chapter 9, we look at the classic Durbin and Watson data set concerning consumption of spirits. The sample size is 69, there are 2 regressors, and there is an intercept term in the model. The Durbin-Watson test statistic value is 0.24878. We wish to test the null hypothesis of zero autocorrelation in the residuals against the alternative that the residuals are positively autocorrelated at the 1% level of significance. If you examine the Savin and White tables (Table A.2 and Table A.3), you will not find a row for sample size 69, so go to the next *lowest* sample size with a tabulated row, namely $N=65$. Since there are two regressors, find the column labeled $k=2$. Cross-referencing the indicated row and column, you will find that the printed bounds are dL = 1.377 and dU = 1.500. If the observed value of the test statistic is less than the tabulated lower bound, then you should reject the null hypothesis of nonautocorrelated errors in favor of the hypothesis of positive first-order autocorrelation. Since 0.24878 is less than 1.377, we reject the null hypothesis. If the test statistic value were greater than dU, we would not reject the null hypothesis.

A third outcome is also possible. If the test statistic value lies between dL and dU, the test is inconclusive. In this context, you might err on the side of conservatism and not reject the null hypothesis.

For models with an intercept, if the observed test statistic value is greater than 2, then you wish to test the null hypothesis against the alternative hypothesis of negative first-order autocorrelation. To do this, compute the quantity 4-d and compare this value with the tabulated values of dL and dU as if you were testing for positive autocorrelation.

When the regression does not contain an intercept term, refer to Farebrother's tabulated values of the "minimal bound," denoted dM (Table A.4 and Table A.5), instead of Savin and White's lower bound dL. In this instance, the upper bound is the conventional bound dU found in the Savin and White tables. To test for negative first-order autocorrelation, use Table A.6 and Table A.7.

To continue with our example, had we run a regression with no intercept term, we would cross-reference N equals 65 and k equals 2 in Farebrother's table. The tabulated 1% minimal bound is 1.348.

We have reprinted the tables exactly as they originally appeared. There have been subsequent corrections to them, however, as published in Farebrother, *Econometrica* 48(6): 1554 and *Econometrica* 49(1): 277. The corrections are as follows:

Table A.1   Corrections for Table A.2—Table A.7

	k'	n	Bound	Incorrect	Correct
Table A.2	6	75	dU	1.646	1.649
	8	75	dU	1.716	1.714
	9	75	dU	1.746	1.748
	10	40	dL	0.789	0.749
	10	75	dU	1.785	1.783
	18	80	dU	2.057	2.059
Table A.3	10	40	dL	0.945	0.952

	k	n	Bound	Incorrect	Correct
Table A.4	0	7		0.389	0.398
Table A.5	8	15		9.185	0.185
	19	90		1.617	1.167
Table A.6	8	70		2.089	2.098
	10	200		1.116	2.116
	14	34		1.295	1.296
Table A.7	1	39		2.645	2.615
	3	15		2.432	2.423
	8	14		0.984	0.948

Table A.2 Models with an intercept (from Savin and White)

DURBIN–WATSON STATISTIC: 1 PER CENT SIGNIFICANCE POINTS OF dL AND dU[a]

	k'=1		k'=2		k'=3		k'=4		k'=5		k'=6		k'=7		k'=8		k'=9		k'=10	
n	dL	dU	dL	dU	dL	dU	dL	dU	dL	dU	dL	dU	dL	dU	dL	dU	dL	dU	dL	dU
6	0.390	1.142	-----	-----	-----	-----	-----	-----	-----	-----	-----	-----	-----	-----	-----	-----	-----	-----	-----	-----
7	0.435	1.036	0.294	1.676	-----	-----	-----	-----	-----	-----	-----	-----	-----	-----	-----	-----	-----	-----	-----	-----
8	0.497	1.003	0.345	1.489	0.229	2.102	-----	-----	-----	-----	-----	-----	-----	-----	-----	-----	-----	-----	-----	-----
9	0.554	0.998	0.408	1.389	0.279	1.875	0.183	2.433	-----	-----	-----	-----	-----	-----	-----	-----	-----	-----	-----	-----
10	0.604	1.001	0.466	1.333	0.340	1.733	0.230	2.193	0.150	2.690	-----	-----	-----	-----	-----	-----	-----	-----	-----	-----
11	0.653	1.010	0.519	1.297	0.396	1.640	0.286	2.030	0.193	2.453	0.124	2.892	-----	-----	-----	-----	-----	-----	-----	-----
12	0.697	1.023	0.569	1.274	0.449	1.575	0.339	1.913	0.244	2.280	0.164	2.665	0.105	3.053	-----	-----	-----	-----	-----	-----
13	0.738	1.038	0.616	1.261	0.499	1.526	0.391	1.826	0.294	2.150	0.211	2.490	0.140	2.838	0.090	3.182	-----	-----	-----	-----
14	0.776	1.054	0.660	1.254	0.547	1.490	0.441	1.757	0.343	2.049	0.257	2.354	0.183	2.667	0.122	2.981	0.078	3.287	-----	-----
15	0.811	1.070	0.700	1.252	0.591	1.464	0.488	1.704	0.391	1.967	0.303	2.244	0.226	2.530	0.161	2.817	0.107	3.101	0.068	3.374
16	0.844	1.086	0.737	1.252	0.633	1.446	0.532	1.663	0.437	1.900	0.349	2.153	0.269	2.416	0.200	2.681	0.142	2.944	0.094	3.201
17	0.874	1.102	0.772	1.255	0.672	1.432	0.574	1.630	0.480	1.847	0.393	2.078	0.313	2.319	0.241	2.566	0.179	2.811	0.127	3.053
18	0.902	1.118	0.805	1.259	0.708	1.422	0.613	1.604	0.522	1.803	0.435	2.015	0.355	2.238	0.282	2.467	0.216	2.697	0.160	2.925
19	0.928	1.132	0.835	1.265	0.742	1.415	0.650	1.584	0.561	1.767	0.476	1.963	0.396	2.169	0.322	2.381	0.255	2.597	0.196	2.813
20	0.952	1.147	0.863	1.271	0.773	1.411	0.685	1.567	0.598	1.737	0.515	1.918	0.436	2.110	0.362	2.308	0.294	2.510	0.232	2.714
21	0.975	1.161	0.890	1.277	0.803	1.408	0.718	1.554	0.633	1.712	0.552	1.881	0.474	2.059	0.400	2.244	0.331	2.434	0.268	2.625
22	0.997	1.174	0.914	1.284	0.831	1.407	0.748	1.543	0.667	1.691	0.587	1.849	0.510	2.015	0.437	2.188	0.368	2.367	0.304	2.548
23	1.018	1.187	0.938	1.291	0.858	1.407	0.777	1.534	0.698	1.673	0.620	1.821	0.545	1.977	0.473	2.140	0.404	2.308	0.340	2.479
24	1.037	1.199	0.960	1.298	0.882	1.407	0.805	1.528	0.728	1.658	0.652	1.797	0.578	1.944	0.507	2.097	0.439	2.255	0.375	2.417
25	1.055	1.211	0.981	1.305	0.906	1.409	0.831	1.523	0.756	1.645	0.682	1.776	0.610	1.915	0.540	2.059	0.473	2.209	0.409	2.362
26	1.072	1.222	1.001	1.312	0.928	1.411	0.855	1.518	0.783	1.635	0.711	1.759	0.640	1.889	0.572	2.026	0.505	2.168	0.441	2.313
27	1.089	1.233	1.019	1.319	0.949	1.413	0.878	1.515	0.808	1.626	0.738	1.743	0.669	1.867	0.602	1.997	0.536	2.131	0.473	2.269
28	1.104	1.244	1.037	1.325	0.969	1.415	0.900	1.513	0.832	1.618	0.764	1.729	0.696	1.847	0.630	1.970	0.566	2.098	0.504	2.229
29	1.119	1.254	1.054	1.332	0.988	1.418	0.921	1.512	0.855	1.611	0.788	1.718	0.723	1.830	0.658	1.947	0.595	2.068	0.533	2.193
30	1.133	1.263	1.070	1.339	1.006	1.421	0.941	1.511	0.877	1.606	0.812	1.707	0.748	1.814	0.684	1.925	0.622	2.041	0.562	2.160
31	1.147	1.273	1.085	1.345	1.023	1.425	0.960	1.510	0.897	1.601	0.834	1.698	0.772	1.800	0.710	1.906	0.649	2.017	0.589	2.131
32	1.160	1.282	1.100	1.352	1.040	1.428	0.979	1.510	0.917	1.597	0.856	1.690	0.794	1.788	0.734	1.889	0.674	1.995	0.615	2.104
33	1.172	1.291	1.114	1.358	1.055	1.432	0.996	1.510	0.936	1.594	0.876	1.683	0.816	1.776	0.757	1.874	0.698	1.975	0.641	2.080
34	1.184	1.299	1.128	1.364	1.070	1.435	1.012	1.511	0.954	1.591	0.896	1.677	0.837	1.766	0.779	1.860	0.722	1.957	0.665	2.057
35	1.195	1.307	1.140	1.370	1.085	1.439	1.028	1.512	0.971	1.589	0.914	1.671	0.857	1.757	0.800	1.847	0.744	1.940	0.689	2.037
36	1.206	1.315	1.153	1.376	1.098	1.442	1.043	1.513	0.988	1.588	0.932	1.666	0.877	1.749	0.821	1.836	0.766	1.925	0.711	2.018
37	1.217	1.323	1.165	1.382	1.112	1.446	1.058	1.514	1.004	1.586	0.950	1.662	0.895	1.742	0.841	1.825	0.787	1.911	0.733	2.001
38	1.227	1.330	1.176	1.388	1.124	1.449	1.072	1.515	1.019	1.585	0.966	1.658	0.913	1.735	0.960	1.816	0.807	1.899	0.754	1.985
39	1.237	1.337	1.187	1.393	1.137	1.453	1.085	1.517	1.034	1.584	0.982	1.655	0.930	1.729	0.878	1.807	0.826	1.887	0.774	1.970
40	1.246	1.344	1.198	1.398	1.148	1.457	1.098	1.518	1.048	1.584	0.997	1.652	0.946	1.724	0.895	1.799	0.844	1.876	0.789	1.956
45	1.288	1.376	1.245	1.423	1.201	1.474	1.156	1.528	1.111	1.584	1.065	1.643	1.019	1.704	0.974	1.768	0.927	1.834	0.881	1.902
50	1.324	1.403	1.285	1.446	1.245	1.491	1.205	1.538	1.164	1.587	1.123	1.639	1.081	1.692	1.039	1.748	0.997	1.805	0.955	1.864
55	1.356	1.427	1.320	1.466	1.284	1.506	1.247	1.548	1.209	1.592	1.172	1.638	1.134	1.685	1.095	1.734	1.057	1.785	1.018	1.837
60	1.383	1.449	1.350	1.484	1.317	1.520	1.283	1.558	1.249	1.598	1.214	1.639	1.179	1.682	1.144	1.726	1.108	1.771	1.072	1.817
65	1.407	1.468	1.377	1.500	1.346	1.534	1.315	1.568	1.283	1.604	1.251	1.642	1.218	1.680	1.186	1.720	1.153	1.761	1.120	1.802
70	1.429	1.485	1.400	1.515	1.372	1.546	1.343	1.578	1.313	1.611	1.283	1.645	1.253	1.680	1.223	1.716	1.192	1.754	1.162	1.792
75	1.448	1.501	1.422	1.529	1.395	1.557	1.368	1.587	1.340	1.617	1.313	1.646	1.284	1.682	1.256	1.716	1.227	1.746	1.199	1.785
80	1.466	1.515	1.441	1.541	1.416	1.568	1.390	1.595	1.364	1.624	1.338	1.653	1.312	1.683	1.285	1.714	1.259	1.745	1.232	1.777
85	1.482	1.528	1.458	1.553	1.435	1.578	1.411	1.603	1.386	1.630	1.362	1.657	1.337	1.685	1.312	1.714	1.287	1.743	1.262	1.773
90	1.496	1.540	1.474	1.563	1.452	1.587	1.429	1.611	1.406	1.636	1.383	1.661	1.360	1.687	1.336	1.714	1.312	1.741	1.288	1.769
95	1.510	1.552	1.489	1.573	1.468	1.596	1.446	1.618	1.425	1.642	1.403	1.666	1.381	1.690	1.358	1.715	1.336	1.741	1.313	1.767
100	1.522	1.562	1.503	1.583	1.482	1.604	1.462	1.625	1.441	1.647	1.421	1.670	1.400	1.693	1.378	1.717	1.357	1.741	1.335	1.765
150	1.611	1.637	1.598	1.651	1.584	1.665	1.571	1.679	1.557	1.693	1.543	1.708	1.530	1.722	1.515	1.737	1.501	1.752	1.486	1.767
200	1.664	1.684	1.653	1.693	1.643	1.704	1.633	1.715	1.623	1.725	1.613	1.735	1.603	1.746	1.592	1.757	1.582	1.768	1.571	1.779

	k'=11		k'=12		k'=13		k'=14		k'=15		k'=16		k'=17		k'=18		k'=19		k'=20	
n	dL	dU	dL	dU	dL	dU	dL	dU	dL	dU	dL	dU	dL	dU	dL	dU	dL	dU	dL	dU
16	0.060	3.446	-----	-----	-----	-----	-----	-----	-----	-----	-----	-----	-----	-----	-----	-----	-----	-----	-----	-----
17	0.084	3.286	0.053	3.506	-----	-----	-----	-----	-----	-----	-----	-----	-----	-----	-----	-----	-----	-----	-----	-----
18	0.113	3.146	0.075	3.358	0.047	3.557	-----	-----	-----	-----	-----	-----	-----	-----	-----	-----	-----	-----	-----	-----
19	0.145	3.023	0.102	3.227	0.067	3.420	0.043	3.601	-----	-----	-----	-----	-----	-----	-----	-----	-----	-----	-----	-----
20	0.178	2.914	0.131	3.109	0.092	3.297	0.061	3.474	0.038	3.639	-----	-----	-----	-----	-----	-----	-----	-----	-----	-----
21	0.212	2.817	0.162	3.004	0.119	3.185	0.084	3.358	0.055	3.521	0.035	3.671	-----	-----	-----	-----	-----	-----	-----	-----
22	0.246	2.729	0.194	2.909	0.148	3.084	0.109	3.252	0.077	3.412	0.050	3.562	0.032	3.700	-----	-----	-----	-----	-----	-----
23	0.281	2.651	0.227	2.822	0.178	2.991	0.136	3.155	0.100	3.311	0.070	3.459	0.046	3.597	0.029	3.725	-----	-----	-----	-----
24	0.315	2.580	0.260	2.744	0.209	2.906	0.165	3.065	0.125	3.218	0.092	3.363	0.065	3.501	0.043	3.629	0.027	3.747	-----	-----
25	0.348	2.517	0.292	2.674	0.240	2.829	0.194	2.982	0.152	3.131	0.116	3.274	0.085	3.410	0.060	3.538	0.039	3.657	0.025	3.766
26	0.381	2.460	0.324	2.610	0.272	2.758	0.224	2.906	0.180	3.050	0.141	3.191	0.107	3.325	0.079	3.452	0.055	3.572	0.036	3.682
27	0.413	2.409	0.356	2.552	0.303	2.694	0.253	2.836	0.208	2.976	0.167	3.113	0.131	3.245	0.100	3.371	0.073	3.490	0.051	3.602
28	0.444	2.363	0.387	2.499	0.333	2.635	0.283	2.772	0.237	2.907	0.194	3.040	0.156	3.169	0.122	3.294	0.093	3.412	0.068	3.524
29	0.474	2.321	0.417	2.451	0.363	2.582	0.313	2.713	0.266	2.843	0.222	2.972	0.182	3.098	0.146	3.220	0.114	3.338	0.087	3.450
30	0.503	2.283	0.447	2.407	0.393	2.533	0.342	2.659	0.294	2.785	0.249	2.909	0.208	3.032	0.171	3.152	0.137	3.267	0.107	3.379
31	0.531	2.248	0.475	2.367	0.422	2.487	0.371	2.609	0.322	2.730	0.277	2.851	0.234	2.970	0.193	3.087	0.160	3.201	0.128	3.311
32	0.558	2.216	0.503	2.330	0.450	2.446	0.399	2.563	0.350	2.680	0.304	2.797	0.261	2.912	0.221	3.026	0.184	3.137	0.151	3.246
33	0.585	2.187	0.530	2.296	0.477	2.408	0.426	2.520	0.377	2.633	0.331	2.746	0.287	2.858	0.246	2.969	0.209	3.078	0.174	3.184
34	0.610	2.160	0.556	2.266	0.503	2.373	0.452	2.481	0.404	2.590	0.357	2.699	0.313	2.808	0.272	2.915	0.233	3.022	0.197	3.126
35	0.634	2.136	0.581	2.237	0.529	2.340	0.478	2.444	0.430	2.550	0.383	2.655	0.339	2.761	0.297	2.865	0.257	2.969	0.221	3.071
36	0.658	2.113	0.605	2.210	0.554	2.310	0.504	2.410	0.455	2.512	0.409	2.614	0.364	2.717	0.322	2.818	0.282	2.919	0.244	3.019
37	0.680	2.092	0.628	2.186	0.578	2.282	0.528	2.379	0.480	2.477	0.434	2.576	0.389	2.675	0.347	2.774	0.306	2.872	0.268	2.969
38	0.702	2.073	0.651	2.164	0.601	2.256	0.552	2.350	0.504	2.445	0.458	2.540	0.414	2.637	0.371	2.733	0.330	2.828	0.291	2.923
39	0.723	2.055	0.673	2.143	0.623	2.232	0.575	2.323	0.528	2.414	0.482	2.507	0.438	2.600	0.395	2.694	0.354	2.787	0.315	2.879
40	0.744	2.039	0.694	2.123	0.645	2.210	0.597	2.297	0.551	2.386	0.505	2.476	0.461	2.566	0.418	2.657	0.377	2.748	0.338	2.838
45	0.835	1.972	0.790	2.044	0.744	2.118	0.700	2.193	0.655	2.269	0.612	2.346	0.570	2.424	0.528	2.503	0.488	2.582	0.448	2.661
50	0.913	1.925	0.871	1.987	0.829	2.051	0.787	2.116	0.746	2.182	0.705	2.250	0.665	2.318	0.625	2.387	0.586	2.456	0.548	2.526
55	0.979	1.891	0.940	1.945	0.902	2.002	0.863	2.059	0.825	2.117	0.786	2.176	0.748	2.237	0.711	2.298	0.674	2.359	0.637	2.421
60	1.037	1.865	1.001	1.914	0.965	1.964	0.929	2.015	0.893	2.067	0.857	2.120	0.822	2.173	0.786	2.227	0.751	2.283	0.716	2.338
65	1.087	1.845	1.053	1.889	1.020	1.934	0.986	1.980	0.953	2.027	0.919	2.075	0.886	2.123	0.852	2.172	0.819	2.221	0.786	2.272
70	1.131	1.831	1.099	1.870	1.068	1.911	1.037	1.953	1.005	1.995	0.974	2.038	0.943	2.082	0.911	2.127	0.880	2.172	0.849	2.217
75	1.170	1.819	1.141	1.856	1.111	1.893	1.082	1.931	1.052	1.970	1.023	2.009	0.993	2.049	0.964	2.090	0.934	2.131	0.905	2.172
80	1.205	1.810	1.177	1.844	1.150	1.878	1.122	1.913	1.094	1.949	1.066	1.984	1.039	2.022	1.011	2.057	0.983	2.097	0.955	2.135
85	1.236	1.803	1.210	1.834	1.184	1.866	1.158	1.898	1.132	1.931	1.106	1.965	1.080	1.999	1.053	2.033	1.027	2.068	1.000	2.104
90	1.264	1.798	1.240	1.827	1.215	1.856	1.191	1.886	1.166	1.917	1.141	1.948	1.116	1.979	1.091	2.012	1.066	2.044	1.041	2.077
95	1.290	1.793	1.267	1.821	1.244	1.848	1.221	1.876	1.197	1.905	1.174	1.934	1.150	1.963	1.126	1.993	1.102	2.023	1.079	2.054
100	1.314	1.790	1.292	1.816	1.270	1.841	1.248	1.868	1.225	1.895	1.203	1.922	1.181	1.949	1.158	1.977	1.136	2.006	1.113	2.034
150	1.473	1.783	1.458	1.799	1.444	1.814	1.429	1.830	1.414	1.847	1.400	1.863	1.385	1.880	1.370	1.897	1.355	1.913	1.340	1.931
200	1.561	1.791	1.550	1.801	1.539	1.813	1.528	1.824	1.518	1.836	1.507	1.847	1.495	1.860	1.484	1.871	1.474	1.883	1.462	1.896

[a] k' is the number of regressors excluding the intercept

Reprinted, with permission, from *Econometrica* 45(8): 1992-1995.

Table A.3   Models with an intercept (from Savin and White)

DURBIN–WATSON STATISTIC: 5 PER CENT SIGNIFICANCE POINTS OF dL AND dU[a]

n	k'=1 dL	dU	k'=2 dL	dU	k'=3 dL	dU	k'=4 dL	dU	k'=5 dL	dU	k'=6 dL	dU	k'=7 dL	dU	k'=8 dL	dU	k'=9 dL	dU	k'=10 dL	dU
6	0.610	1.400	-----	-----	-----	-----	-----	-----	-----	-----	-----	-----	-----	-----	-----	-----	-----	-----	-----	-----
7	0.700	1.356	0.467	1.896	-----	-----	-----	-----	-----	-----	-----	-----	-----	-----	-----	-----	-----	-----	-----	-----
8	0.763	1.332	0.559	1.777	0.368	2.287	-----	-----	-----	-----	-----	-----	-----	-----	-----	-----	-----	-----	-----	-----
9	0.824	1.320	0.629	1.699	0.455	2.128	0.296	2.588	-----	-----	-----	-----	-----	-----	-----	-----	-----	-----	-----	-----
10	0.879	1.320	0.697	1.641	0.525	2.016	0.376	2.414	0.243	2.822	-----	-----	-----	-----	-----	-----	-----	-----	-----	-----
11	0.927	1.324	0.758	1.604	0.595	1.928	0.444	2.283	0.316	2.645	0.203	3.005	-----	-----	-----	-----	-----	-----	-----	-----
12	0.971	1.331	0.812	1.579	0.658	1.864	0.512	2.177	0.379	2.506	0.268	2.832	0.171	3.149	-----	-----	-----	-----	-----	-----
13	1.010	1.340	0.861	1.562	0.715	1.816	0.574	2.094	0.445	2.390	0.328	2.692	0.230	2.985	0.147	3.266	-----	-----	-----	-----
14	1.045	1.350	0.905	1.551	0.767	1.779	0.632	2.030	0.505	2.296	0.389	2.572	0.286	2.848	0.200	3.111	0.127	3.360	-----	-----
15	1.077	1.361	0.946	1.543	0.814	1.750	0.685	1.977	0.562	2.220	0.447	2.472	0.343	2.727	0.251	2.979	0.175	3.216	0.111	3.438
16	1.106	1.371	0.982	1.539	0.857	1.728	0.734	1.935	0.615	2.157	0.502	2.388	0.398	2.624	0.304	2.860	0.222	3.090	0.155	3.304
17	1.133	1.381	1.015	1.536	0.897	1.710	0.779	1.900	0.664	2.104	0.554	2.318	0.451	2.537	0.356	2.757	0.272	2.975	0.198	3.184
18	1.158	1.391	1.046	1.535	0.933	1.696	0.820	1.872	0.710	2.060	0.603	2.257	0.502	2.461	0.407	2.667	0.321	2.873	0.244	3.073
19	1.180	1.401	1.074	1.536	0.967	1.685	0.859	1.848	0.752	2.023	0.649	2.206	0.549	2.396	0.456	2.589	0.369	2.783	0.290	2.974
20	1.201	1.411	1.100	1.537	0.998	1.676	0.894	1.828	0.792	1.991	0.692	2.162	0.595	2.339	0.502	2.521	0.416	2.704	0.336	2.885
21	1.221	1.420	1.125	1.538	1.026	1.669	0.927	1.812	0.829	1.964	0.732	2.124	0.637	2.290	0.547	2.460	0.461	2.633	0.380	2.806
22	1.239	1.429	1.147	1.541	1.053	1.664	0.958	1.797	0.863	1.940	0.769	2.090	0.677	2.246	0.588	2.407	0.504	2.571	0.424	2.734
23	1.257	1.437	1.168	1.543	1.078	1.660	0.986	1.785	0.895	1.920	0.804	2.061	0.715	2.208	0.628	2.360	0.545	2.514	0.465	2.670
24	1.273	1.446	1.188	1.546	1.101	1.656	1.013	1.775	0.925	1.902	0.837	2.035	0.751	2.174	0.666	2.318	0.584	2.464	0.506	2.613
25	1.288	1.454	1.206	1.550	1.123	1.654	1.038	1.767	0.953	1.886	0.868	2.012	0.784	2.144	0.702	2.280	0.621	2.419	0.544	2.560
26	1.302	1.461	1.224	1.553	1.143	1.652	1.062	1.759	0.979	1.873	0.897	1.992	0.816	2.117	0.735	2.246	0.657	2.379	0.581	2.513
27	1.316	1.469	1.240	1.556	1.162	1.651	1.084	1.753	1.004	1.861	0.925	1.974	0.845	2.093	0.767	2.216	0.691	2.342	0.616	2.470
28	1.328	1.476	1.255	1.560	1.181	1.650	1.104	1.747	1.028	1.850	0.951	1.958	0.874	2.071	0.798	2.188	0.723	2.309	0.650	2.431
29	1.341	1.483	1.270	1.563	1.198	1.650	1.124	1.743	1.050	1.841	0.975	1.944	0.900	2.052	0.826	2.164	0.753	2.278	0.682	2.396
30	1.352	1.489	1.284	1.567	1.214	1.650	1.143	1.739	1.071	1.833	0.998	1.931	0.926	2.034	0.854	2.141	0.782	2.251	0.712	2.363
31	1.363	1.496	1.297	1.570	1.229	1.650	1.160	1.735	1.090	1.825	1.020	1.920	0.950	2.018	0.879	2.120	0.810	2.226	0.741	2.333
32	1.373	1.502	1.309	1.574	1.244	1.650	1.177	1.732	1.109	1.819	1.041	1.909	0.972	2.004	0.904	2.102	0.836	2.203	0.769	2.306
33	1.383	1.508	1.321	1.577	1.258	1.651	1.193	1.730	1.127	1.813	1.061	1.900	0.994	1.991	0.927	2.085	0.861	2.181	0.795	2.281
34	1.393	1.514	1.333	1.580	1.271	1.652	1.208	1.728	1.144	1.808	1.080	1.891	1.015	1.979	0.950	2.069	0.885	2.162	0.821	2.257
35	1.402	1.519	1.343	1.584	1.283	1.653	1.222	1.726	1.160	1.803	1.097	1.884	1.034	1.967	0.971	2.054	0.908	2.144	0.845	2.236
36	1.411	1.525	1.354	1.587	1.295	1.654	1.236	1.724	1.175	1.799	1.114	1.877	1.053	1.957	0.991	2.041	0.930	2.127	0.868	2.216
37	1.419	1.530	1.364	1.590	1.307	1.655	1.249	1.723	1.190	1.795	1.131	1.870	1.071	1.948	1.011	2.029	0.951	2.112	0.891	2.198
38	1.427	1.535	1.373	1.594	1.318	1.656	1.261	1.722	1.204	1.792	1.146	1.864	1.088	1.939	1.029	2.017	0.970	2.098	0.912	2.180
39	1.435	1.540	1.382	1.597	1.328	1.658	1.273	1.722	1.218	1.789	1.161	1.859	1.104	1.932	1.047	2.007	0.990	2.085	0.932	2.164
40	1.442	1.544	1.391	1.600	1.338	1.659	1.285	1.721	1.230	1.786	1.175	1.854	1.120	1.924	1.064	1.997	1.008	2.072	0.945	2.149
45	1.475	1.566	1.430	1.615	1.383	1.666	1.336	1.720	1.287	1.776	1.238	1.835	1.189	1.895	1.139	1.958	1.089	2.022	1.038	2.088
50	1.503	1.585	1.462	1.628	1.421	1.674	1.378	1.721	1.335	1.771	1.291	1.822	1.246	1.875	1.201	1.930	1.156	1.986	1.110	2.044
55	1.528	1.601	1.490	1.641	1.452	1.681	1.414	1.724	1.374	1.768	1.334	1.814	1.294	1.861	1.253	1.909	1.212	1.959	1.170	2.010
60	1.549	1.616	1.514	1.652	1.480	1.689	1.444	1.727	1.408	1.767	1.372	1.808	1.335	1.850	1.298	1.894	1.260	1.939	1.222	1.984
65	1.567	1.629	1.536	1.662	1.503	1.696	1.471	1.731	1.438	1.767	1.404	1.805	1.370	1.843	1.336	1.882	1.301	1.923	1.266	1.964
70	1.583	1.641	1.554	1.672	1.525	1.703	1.494	1.735	1.464	1.768	1.433	1.802	1.401	1.837	1.369	1.873	1.337	1.910	1.305	1.948
75	1.598	1.652	1.571	1.680	1.543	1.709	1.515	1.739	1.487	1.770	1.458	1.801	1.428	1.834	1.399	1.867	1.369	1.901	1.339	1.935
80	1.611	1.662	1.586	1.688	1.560	1.715	1.534	1.743	1.507	1.772	1.480	1.801	1.453	1.831	1.425	1.861	1.397	1.893	1.369	1.925
85	1.624	1.671	1.600	1.696	1.575	1.721	1.550	1.747	1.525	1.774	1.500	1.801	1.474	1.829	1.448	1.857	1.422	1.886	1.396	1.916
90	1.635	1.679	1.612	1.703	1.589	1.726	1.566	1.751	1.542	1.776	1.518	1.801	1.494	1.827	1.469	1.854	1.445	1.881	1.420	1.909
95	1.645	1.687	1.623	1.709	1.602	1.732	1.579	1.755	1.557	1.778	1.535	1.802	1.512	1.827	1.489	1.852	1.465	1.877	1.442	1.903
100	1.654	1.694	1.634	1.715	1.613	1.736	1.592	1.758	1.571	1.780	1.550	1.803	1.528	1.826	1.506	1.850	1.484	1.874	1.462	1.898
150	1.720	1.746	1.706	1.760	1.693	1.774	1.679	1.788	1.665	1.802	1.651	1.817	1.637	1.832	1.622	1.847	1.608	1.862	1.594	1.877
200	1.758	1.778	1.748	1.789	1.738	1.799	1.728	1.810	1.718	1.820	1.707	1.831	1.697	1.841	1.686	1.852	1.675	1.863	1.665	1.874

n	k'=11 dL	dU	k'=12 dL	dU	k'=13 dL	dU	k'=14 dL	dU	k'=15 dL	dU	k'=16 dL	dU	k'=17 dL	dU	k'=18 dL	dU	k'=19 dL	dU	k'=20 dL	dU
16	0.098	3.503	-----	-----	-----	-----	-----	-----	-----	-----	-----	-----	-----	-----	-----	-----	-----	-----	-----	-----
17	0.138	3.378	0.087	3.557	-----	-----	-----	-----	-----	-----	-----	-----	-----	-----	-----	-----	-----	-----	-----	-----
18	0.177	3.265	0.123	3.441	0.078	3.603	-----	-----	-----	-----	-----	-----	-----	-----	-----	-----	-----	-----	-----	-----
19	0.220	3.159	0.160	3.335	0.111	3.496	0.070	3.642	-----	-----	-----	-----	-----	-----	-----	-----	-----	-----	-----	-----
20	0.263	3.063	0.200	3.234	0.145	3.395	0.100	3.542	0.063	3.676	-----	-----	-----	-----	-----	-----	-----	-----	-----	-----
21	0.307	2.976	0.240	3.141	0.182	3.300	0.132	3.448	0.091	3.583	0.058	3.705	-----	-----	-----	-----	-----	-----	-----	-----
22	0.349	2.897	0.281	3.057	0.220	3.211	0.166	3.358	0.120	3.495	0.083	3.619	0.052	3.731	-----	-----	-----	-----	-----	-----
23	0.391	2.826	0.322	2.979	0.259	3.128	0.202	3.272	0.153	3.409	0.110	3.535	0.076	3.650	0.048	3.753	-----	-----	-----	-----
24	0.431	2.761	0.362	2.908	0.297	3.053	0.239	3.193	0.186	3.327	0.141	3.454	0.101	3.572	0.070	3.678	0.044	3.773	-----	-----
25	0.470	2.702	0.400	2.844	0.335	2.983	0.275	3.119	0.221	3.251	0.172	3.376	0.130	3.494	0.094	3.604	0.065	3.702	0.041	3.790
26	0.508	2.649	0.438	2.784	0.373	2.919	0.312	3.051	0.256	3.179	0.205	3.303	0.160	3.420	0.120	3.531	0.087	3.632	0.060	3.724
27	0.544	2.600	0.475	2.730	0.409	2.859	0.348	2.987	0.291	3.112	0.238	3.233	0.191	3.349	0.149	3.460	0.112	3.563	0.081	3.658
28	0.578	2.555	0.510	2.680	0.445	2.805	0.383	2.928	0.325	3.050	0.271	3.168	0.222	3.283	0.178	3.392	0.138	3.495	0.104	3.592
29	0.612	2.515	0.544	2.634	0.479	2.755	0.418	2.874	0.359	2.992	0.305	3.107	0.254	3.219	0.208	3.327	0.166	3.431	0.129	3.528
30	0.643	2.477	0.577	2.592	0.512	2.708	0.451	2.823	0.392	2.937	0.337	3.050	0.286	3.160	0.238	3.266	0.195	3.368	0.156	3.465
31	0.674	2.443	0.608	2.553	0.545	2.665	0.484	2.776	0.425	2.887	0.370	2.996	0.317	3.103	0.269	3.208	0.224	3.309	0.183	3.406
32	0.703	2.411	0.638	2.517	0.576	2.625	0.515	2.733	0.457	2.840	0.401	2.946	0.349	3.050	0.299	3.153	0.253	3.252	0.211	3.348
33	0.731	2.382	0.668	2.484	0.606	2.588	0.546	2.692	0.488	2.796	0.432	2.899	0.379	3.000	0.329	3.100	0.283	3.198	0.239	3.293
34	0.758	2.355	0.695	2.454	0.634	2.554	0.575	2.654	0.518	2.754	0.462	2.854	0.409	2.954	0.359	3.051	0.312	3.147	0.267	3.240
35	0.783	2.330	0.722	2.425	0.662	2.521	0.604	2.619	0.547	2.716	0.492	2.813	0.439	2.910	0.388	3.005	0.340	3.099	0.295	3.190
36	0.808	2.306	0.748	2.398	0.689	2.492	0.631	2.586	0.575	2.680	0.520	2.774	0.467	2.868	0.417	2.961	0.369	3.053	0.323	3.142
37	0.831	2.285	0.772	2.374	0.714	2.464	0.657	2.555	0.602	2.646	0.548	2.738	0.495	2.829	0.445	2.920	0.397	3.009	0.351	3.097
38	0.854	2.265	0.796	2.351	0.739	2.438	0.683	2.526	0.628	2.614	0.575	2.703	0.522	2.792	0.472	2.880	0.424	2.968	0.378	3.054
39	0.875	2.246	0.819	2.329	0.763	2.413	0.707	2.499	0.653	2.585	0.600	2.671	0.549	2.757	0.499	2.843	0.451	2.929	0.404	3.013
40	0.896	2.228	0.840	2.309	0.785	2.391	0.731	2.473	0.678	2.557	0.626	2.641	0.575	2.724	0.525	2.808	0.477	2.892	0.430	2.974
45	0.988	2.156	0.938	2.225	0.887	2.296	0.838	2.367	0.788	2.439	0.740	2.512	0.692	2.586	0.644	2.659	0.598	2.733	0.553	2.807
50	1.064	2.103	1.019	2.163	0.973	2.225	0.927	2.287	0.882	2.350	0.836	2.414	0.792	2.479	0.747	2.544	0.703	2.610	0.660	2.675
55	1.129	2.062	1.087	2.116	1.045	2.170	1.003	2.225	0.961	2.281	0.919	2.338	0.877	2.396	0.836	2.454	0.795	2.512	0.754	2.571
60	1.184	2.031	1.145	2.079	1.106	2.127	1.068	2.177	1.029	2.227	0.990	2.278	0.951	2.330	0.913	2.382	0.874	2.434	0.836	2.487
65	1.231	2.006	1.195	2.049	1.160	2.093	1.124	2.138	1.088	2.183	1.052	2.229	1.016	2.276	0.980	2.323	0.944	2.371	0.908	2.419
70	1.272	1.986	1.239	2.026	1.206	2.066	1.172	2.106	1.139	2.148	1.105	2.189	1.072	2.232	1.038	2.275	1.005	2.318	0.971	2.362
75	1.308	1.970	1.277	2.006	1.247	2.043	1.215	2.080	1.184	2.118	1.153	2.156	1.121	2.195	1.090	2.235	1.058	2.275	1.027	2.315
80	1.340	1.957	1.311	1.991	1.283	2.024	1.253	2.059	1.224	2.093	1.195	2.129	1.165	2.165	1.136	2.201	1.106	2.238	1.076	2.275
85	1.369	1.946	1.342	1.977	1.315	2.009	1.287	2.040	1.260	2.073	1.232	2.105	1.205	2.139	1.177	2.172	1.149	2.206	1.121	2.241
90	1.395	1.937	1.369	1.966	1.344	1.995	1.318	2.025	1.292	2.055	1.266	2.085	1.240	2.116	1.213	2.148	1.187	2.179	1.160	2.211
95	1.418	1.929	1.394	1.956	1.370	1.984	1.345	2.012	1.321	2.040	1.296	2.068	1.271	2.097	1.247	2.126	1.222	2.156	1.197	2.186
100	1.439	1.923	1.416	1.948	1.393	1.974	1.371	2.000	1.347	2.026	1.324	2.053	1.301	2.080	1.277	2.108	1.253	2.135	1.229	2.164
150	1.579	1.892	1.564	1.908	1.550	1.924	1.535	1.940	1.519	1.956	1.504	1.972	1.489	1.989	1.474	2.006	1.458	2.023	1.443	2.040
200	1.654	1.885	1.643	1.896	1.632	1.908	1.621	1.919	1.610	1.931	1.599	1.943	1.588	1.955	1.576	1.967	1.565	1.979	1.554	1.991

[a] k' is the number of regressors excluding the intercept.

Table A.4 Models with no intercept (from Farebrother): positive serial correlation

DURBIN-WATSON ONE PER CENT MINIMAL BOUND

N	K=0	K=1	K=2	K=3	K=4	K=5	K=6	K=7	K=8	K=9	K=10	K=11	K=12	K=13	K=14	K=15	K=16	K=17	K=18	K=19	K=20	K=21
2	0.001																					
3	0.034	0.000																				
4	0.127	0.022	0.000																			
5	0.233	0.089	0.014	0.000																		
6	0.322	0.175	0.065	0.010	0.000																	
7	0.389	0.253	0.135	0.049	0.008	0.000																
8	0.469	0.324	0.202	0.106	0.038	0.006	0.000															
9	0.534	0.394	0.268	0.164	0.086	0.031	0.005	0.000														
10	0.591	0.457	0.333	0.223	0.136	0.070	0.025	0.004	0.000													
11	0.643	0.515	0.394	0.284	0.189	0.114	0.059	0.021	0.003	0.000												
12	0.691	0.568	0.451	0.341	0.244	0.161	0.097	0.050	0.018	0.003	0.000											
13	0.733	0.617	0.503	0.396	0.298	0.212	0.139	0.083	0.043	0.015	0.002	0.000										
14	0.773	0.662	0.552	0.448	0.350	0.262	0.185	0.121	0.072	0.037	0.013	0.002	0.000									
15	0.809	0.703	0.598	0.496	0.400	0.311	0.232	0.163	0.107	0.063	0.032	0.011	0.002	0.000								
16	0.842	0.741	0.640	0.541	0.447	0.358	0.278	0.206	0.145	0.094	0.056	0.028	0.010	0.002	0.000							
17	0.873	0.776	0.679	0.583	0.491	0.404	0.323	0.249	0.184	0.129	0.084	0.050	0.025	0.009	0.001	0.000						
18	0.901	0.808	0.715	0.623	0.533	0.447	0.366	0.292	0.225	0.166	0.116	0.075	0.044	0.023	0.008	0.001	0.000					
19	0.928	0.839	0.749	0.660	0.572	0.488	0.408	0.333	0.265	0.204	0.150	0.105	0.068	0.040	0.020	0.007	0.001	0.000				
20	0.952	0.867	0.780	0.694	0.609	0.527	0.448	0.374	0.304	0.241	0.185	0.136	0.095	0.062	0.036	0.018	0.006	0.001	0.000			
21	0.976	0.893	0.810	0.727	0.644	0.564	0.486	0.413	0.343	0.279	0.221	0.169	0.124	0.087	0.056	0.033	0.017	0.006	0.001	0.000		
22	0.997	0.918	0.838	0.757	0.677	0.599	0.523	0.450	0.381	0.316	0.257	0.203	0.155	0.114	0.079	0.051	0.030	0.015	0.005	0.001	0.000	
23	1.018	0.942	0.864	0.786	0.709	0.632	0.558	0.486	0.417	0.352	0.292	0.237	0.187	0.143	0.104	0.073	0.047	0.027	0.014	0.005	0.001	0.000
24	1.037	0.964	0.889	0.813	0.738	0.664	0.591	0.520	0.452	0.387	0.327	0.270	0.219	0.172	0.131	0.096	0.067	0.043	0.025	0.013	0.004	0.001
25	1.056	0.984	0.912	0.839	0.766	0.693	0.622	0.553	0.486	0.421	0.361	0.304	0.251	0.203	0.160	0.122	0.089	0.062	0.040	0.023	0.012	0.004
26	1.073	1.004	0.934	0.863	0.792	0.722	0.652	0.584	0.518	0.454	0.394	0.336	0.283	0.233	0.189	0.148	0.113	0.083	0.057	0.037	0.022	0.011
27	1.089	1.023	0.955	0.886	0.817	0.749	0.681	0.614	0.549	0.486	0.426	0.368	0.314	0.264	0.218	0.176	0.138	0.105	0.077	0.053	0.034	0.020
28	1.105	1.040	0.974	0.908	0.841	0.774	0.708	0.643	0.579	0.517	0.457	0.400	0.345	0.294	0.247	0.204	0.164	0.129	0.098	0.071	0.050	0.032
29	1.120	1.057	0.993	0.929	0.864	0.798	0.734	0.670	0.607	0.546	0.487	0.430	0.376	0.324	0.276	0.232	0.191	0.154	0.120	0.091	0.067	0.046
30	1.134	1.073	1.011	0.948	0.885	0.822	0.759	0.696	0.635	0.574	0.516	0.460	0.405	0.354	0.305	0.260	0.217	0.179	0.144	0.113	0.086	0.062
31	1.147	1.088	1.028	0.967	0.905	0.844	0.782	0.721	0.661	0.602	0.544	0.488	0.434	0.383	0.334	0.288	0.244	0.205	0.168	0.135	0.106	0.080
32	1.160	1.103	1.044	0.985	0.925	0.865	0.805	0.745	0.686	0.628	0.571	0.516	0.462	0.411	0.362	0.315	0.271	0.230	0.193	0.158	0.127	0.100
33	1.173	1.117	1.060	1.002	0.944	0.885	0.826	0.768	0.710	0.653	0.597	0.542	0.489	0.438	0.389	0.342	0.298	0.256	0.218	0.182	0.149	0.120
34	1.185	1.130	1.075	1.018	0.961	0.904	0.847	0.790	0.733	0.677	0.622	0.568	0.516	0.465	0.416	0.369	0.324	0.282	0.243	0.206	0.172	0.141
35	1.196	1.143	1.089	1.034	0.978	0.923	0.867	0.811	0.755	0.700	0.646	0.593	0.541	0.491	0.442	0.395	0.350	0.308	0.268	0.230	0.195	0.163
36	1.207	1.155	1.102	1.049	0.995	0.940	0.886	0.831	0.777	0.723	0.669	0.617	0.566	0.516	0.467	0.421	0.376	0.333	0.292	0.254	0.218	0.185
37	1.217	1.167	1.116	1.063	1.010	0.957	0.904	0.850	0.797	0.744	0.692	0.640	0.590	0.540	0.492	0.446	0.401	0.358	0.317	0.278	0.241	0.207
38	1.228	1.178	1.128	1.077	1.026	0.974	0.921	0.869	0.817	0.765	0.713	0.663	0.613	0.564	0.516	0.470	0.425	0.382	0.341	0.302	0.265	0.230
39	1.237	1.189	1.140	1.090	1.040	0.989	0.938	0.887	0.836	0.785	0.734	0.684	0.635	0.587	0.540	0.494	0.449	0.406	0.365	0.325	0.288	0.252
40	1.247	1.200	1.152	1.103	1.054	1.004	0.954	0.904	0.854	0.804	0.754	0.705	0.657	0.609	0.562	0.517	0.473	0.430	0.388	0.349	0.311	0.275
45	1.289	1.247	1.204	1.160	1.116	1.071	1.026	0.981	0.936	0.890	0.845	0.800	0.755	0.710	0.666	0.623	0.581	0.539	0.499	0.459	0.421	0.384
50	1.325	1.287	1.248	1.208	1.168	1.128	1.087	1.046	1.004	0.963	0.921	0.880	0.838	0.797	0.756	0.715	0.675	0.636	0.597	0.559	0.521	0.485
55	1.356	1.321	1.286	1.250	1.213	1.176	1.139	1.101	1.063	1.025	0.987	0.948	0.910	0.872	0.833	0.796	0.758	0.721	0.684	0.647	0.611	0.576
60	1.383	1.351	1.319	1.285	1.252	1.218	1.183	1.149	1.114	1.078	1.043	1.008	0.972	0.936	0.901	0.865	0.830	0.795	0.760	0.725	0.691	0.657
65	1.408	1.378	1.348	1.317	1.286	1.254	1.222	1.190	1.158	1.125	1.092	1.059	1.026	0.993	0.960	0.927	0.894	0.861	0.828	0.795	0.762	0.730
70	1.429	1.401	1.373	1.345	1.316	1.286	1.257	1.227	1.197	1.166	1.136	1.105	1.074	1.043	1.012	0.981	0.950	0.919	0.888	0.857	0.826	0.795
75	1.448	1.423	1.396	1.369	1.342	1.315	1.287	1.260	1.231	1.203	1.174	1.146	1.117	1.088	1.058	1.029	1.000	0.971	0.941	0.912	0.883	0.854
80	1.466	1.442	1.417	1.392	1.367	1.341	1.315	1.289	1.262	1.236	1.209	1.182	1.155	1.127	1.100	1.072	1.045	1.017	0.989	0.962	0.934	0.907
85	1.482	1.459	1.436	1.412	1.388	1.364	1.340	1.315	1.290	1.265	1.240	1.214	1.189	1.163	1.137	1.111	1.085	1.059	1.033	1.006	0.980	0.954
90	1.497	1.475	1.453	1.431	1.408	1.385	1.362	1.339	1.315	1.292	1.268	1.244	1.220	1.195	1.171	1.146	1.121	1.097	1.072	1.047	1.022	0.997
95	1.510	1.490	1.469	1.448	1.426	1.405	1.383	1.361	1.338	1.316	1.293	1.271	1.248	1.225	1.201	1.178	1.155	1.131	1.108	1.084	1.060	1.037
100	1.523	1.503	1.483	1.463	1.443	1.422	1.402	1.381	1.359	1.338	1.317	1.295	1.273	1.251	1.229	1.207	1.185	1.162	1.140	1.118	1.095	1.072
150	1.611	1.598	1.585	1.571	1.558	1.544	1.530	1.516	1.502	1.488	1.474	1.460	1.445	1.431	1.416	1.402	1.387	1.372	1.357	1.342	1.327	1.312
200	1.664	1.654	1.644	1.634	1.624	1.613	1.603	1.593	1.582	1.572	1.561	1.551	1.540	1.529	1.519	1.508	1.497	1.486	1.475	1.464	1.453	1.442

Reprinted, with permission, from *Econometrica* 48(6): 1556-1563.

Table A.5   Models with no intercept (from Farebrother): positive serial correlation

DURBIN-WATSON FIVE PER CENT MINIMAL BOUND

N	K=0	K=1	K=2	K=3	K=4	K=5	K=6	K=7	K=8	K=9	K=10	K=11	K=12	K=13	K=14	K=15	K=16	K=17	K=18	K=19	K=20	K=21
2	0.012																					
3	0.168	0.006																				
4	0.355	0.105	0.004																			
5	0.478	0.248	0.070	0.002																		
6	0.584	0.358	0.180	0.050	0.002																	
7	0.677	0.462	0.275	0.136	0.037	0.001																
8	0.754	0.556	0.371	0.217	0.106	0.029	0.001															
9	0.820	0.635	0.460	0.303	0.175	0.085	0.023	0.001														
10	0.877	0.706	0.539	0.385	0.251	0.143	0.069	0.019	0.001													
11	0.927	0.768	0.610	0.460	0.326	0.211	0.120	0.058	0.016	0.001												
12	0.972	0.823	0.674	0.530	0.397	0.279	0.180	0.101	0.049	0.013	0.001											
13	1.012	0.872	0.731	0.593	0.464	0.345	0.241	0.154	0.087	0.042	0.011	0.001										
14	1.047	0.916	0.783	0.651	0.525	0.408	0.302	0.210	0.134	0.075	0.036	0.010	0.001									
15	1.079	0.955	0.829	0.704	0.583	0.467	0.361	0.266	0.185	0.118	0.066	0.031	0.008	0.001								
16	1.109	0.992	0.872	0.752	0.635	0.523	0.418	0.322	0.237	0.164	0.104	0.058	0.028	0.007	0.000							
17	1.136	1.024	0.911	0.797	0.684	0.575	0.472	0.376	0.288	0.211	0.146	0.093	0.052	0.025	0.007	0.000						
18	1.160	1.055	0.946	0.837	0.729	0.624	0.523	0.427	0.339	0.260	0.190	0.131	0.083	0.046	0.022	0.006	0.000					
19	1.183	1.082	0.979	0.875	0.771	0.669	0.570	0.476	0.388	0.307	0.235	0.171	0.118	0.075	0.041	0.020	0.005	0.000				
20	1.204	1.108	1.010	0.910	0.810	0.711	0.615	0.523	0.436	0.354	0.280	0.213	0.156	0.107	0.067	0.037	0.018	0.005	0.000			
21	1.224	1.132	1.038	0.942	0.846	0.751	0.657	0.567	0.481	0.400	0.324	0.256	0.195	0.142	0.097	0.061	0.034	0.016	0.004	0.000		
22	1.242	1.154	1.064	0.972	0.879	0.787	0.697	0.609	0.524	0.443	0.368	0.298	0.235	0.178	0.130	0.089	0.056	0.031	0.015	0.004	0.000	
23	1.259	1.175	1.088	1.000	0.911	0.822	0.734	0.648	0.565	0.485	0.410	0.339	0.274	0.216	0.164	0.119	0.081	0.051	0.028	0.014	0.004	0.000
24	1.275	1.194	1.111	1.026	0.940	0.854	0.769	0.685	0.604	0.525	0.450	0.380	0.314	0.254	0.199	0.151	0.110	0.075	0.047	0.026	0.012	0.003
25	1.290	1.212	1.132	1.050	0.967	0.884	0.802	0.720	0.641	0.563	0.489	0.419	0.353	0.291	0.235	0.184	0.140	0.101	0.069	0.044	0.024	0.011
26	1.304	1.229	1.152	1.073	0.993	0.913	0.833	0.753	0.676	0.600	0.527	0.457	0.390	0.328	0.271	0.218	0.171	0.130	0.094	0.064	0.040	0.022
27	1.318	1.245	1.171	1.094	1.017	0.940	0.862	0.785	0.709	0.635	0.563	0.493	0.427	0.365	0.306	0.252	0.203	0.159	0.120	0.087	0.060	0.037
28	1.330	1.260	1.188	1.115	1.040	0.965	0.889	0.815	0.741	0.668	0.597	0.529	0.463	0.400	0.341	0.286	0.236	0.190	0.148	0.112	0.081	0.055
29	1.342	1.275	1.205	1.134	1.062	0.989	0.916	0.843	0.770	0.699	0.630	0.562	0.497	0.435	0.376	0.320	0.268	0.221	0.177	0.139	0.105	0.076
30	1.354	1.288	1.221	1.152	1.082	1.011	0.940	0.869	0.799	0.729	0.661	0.595	0.530	0.468	0.409	0.353	0.301	0.252	0.207	0.166	0.130	0.098
31	1.365	1.301	1.236	1.169	1.101	1.033	0.964	0.895	0.826	0.758	0.691	0.626	0.562	0.501	0.442	0.386	0.333	0.283	0.237	0.195	0.156	0.122
32	1.375	1.313	1.250	1.185	1.120	1.053	0.986	0.919	0.852	0.785	0.720	0.656	0.593	0.532	0.474	0.418	0.364	0.314	0.267	0.223	0.183	0.147
33	1.385	1.325	1.264	1.201	1.137	1.072	1.007	0.942	0.876	0.811	0.747	0.684	0.623	0.563	0.504	0.449	0.395	0.344	0.297	0.252	0.211	0.173
34	1.394	1.336	1.277	1.216	1.153	1.091	1.027	0.963	0.900	0.836	0.774	0.712	0.651	0.592	0.534	0.479	0.425	0.374	0.326	0.280	0.238	0.199
35	1.403	1.347	1.289	1.230	1.169	1.108	1.046	0.984	0.922	0.860	0.799	0.738	0.678	0.620	0.563	0.508	0.455	0.404	0.355	0.309	0.266	0.225
36	1.412	1.357	1.301	1.243	1.184	1.125	1.064	1.004	0.943	0.883	0.823	0.763	0.705	0.647	0.591	0.536	0.483	0.432	0.384	0.337	0.293	0.252
37	1.420	1.367	1.312	1.256	1.199	1.141	1.082	1.023	0.964	0.905	0.846	0.787	0.730	0.673	0.618	0.564	0.511	0.460	0.412	0.365	0.321	0.279
38	1.428	1.376	1.323	1.268	1.212	1.156	1.099	1.041	0.983	0.925	0.868	0.811	0.754	0.698	0.644	0.590	0.538	0.488	0.439	0.392	0.347	0.305
39	1.436	1.385	1.333	1.280	1.225	1.170	1.114	1.058	1.002	0.945	0.889	0.833	0.778	0.723	0.669	0.616	0.564	0.514	0.466	0.419	0.374	0.331
40	1.443	1.394	1.343	1.291	1.238	1.184	1.130	1.075	1.020	0.965	0.909	0.854	0.800	0.746	0.693	0.641	0.590	0.540	0.492	0.445	0.400	0.357
45	1.476	1.432	1.387	1.341	1.294	1.246	1.197	1.148	1.099	1.049	1.000	0.950	0.900	0.851	0.802	0.753	0.706	0.658	0.612	0.567	0.523	0.480
50	1.504	1.464	1.424	1.382	1.340	1.297	1.253	1.209	1.164	1.120	1.075	1.029	0.984	0.939	0.894	0.849	0.804	0.760	0.717	0.674	0.631	0.590
55	1.528	1.492	1.455	1.417	1.379	1.340	1.300	1.260	1.219	1.179	1.138	1.096	1.055	1.013	0.972	0.930	0.889	0.848	0.807	0.766	0.726	0.687
60	1.549	1.516	1.482	1.447	1.412	1.376	1.340	1.303	1.266	1.229	1.191	1.153	1.115	1.077	1.038	1.000	0.962	0.923	0.885	0.847	0.810	0.772
65	1.568	1.537	1.505	1.474	1.441	1.408	1.375	1.341	1.307	1.272	1.238	1.202	1.167	1.132	1.096	1.061	1.025	0.989	0.953	0.918	0.882	0.847
70	1.584	1.555	1.526	1.497	1.467	1.436	1.405	1.374	1.342	1.310	1.278	1.245	1.213	1.180	1.147	1.113	1.080	1.047	1.013	0.980	0.947	0.914
75	1.599	1.572	1.545	1.517	1.489	1.461	1.432	1.403	1.373	1.344	1.313	1.283	1.253	1.222	1.191	1.160	1.129	1.098	1.066	1.035	1.004	0.972
80	1.612	1.587	1.561	1.536	1.509	1.483	1.456	1.429	1.401	1.373	1.345	1.317	1.288	1.259	1.230	1.201	1.172	1.143	1.113	1.084	1.054	1.025
85	1.624	1.600	1.576	1.552	1.527	1.502	1.477	1.452	1.426	1.400	1.373	1.347	1.320	1.293	1.266	1.238	1.211	1.183	1.155	1.128	1.100	1.072
90	1.635	1.613	1.590	1.567	1.544	1.520	1.497	1.472	1.448	1.423	1.399	1.373	1.348	1.323	1.297	1.271	1.245	1.219	1.193	1.167	1.141	1.114
95	1.645	1.624	1.603	1.581	1.559	1.537	1.514	1.491	1.468	1.445	1.422	1.398	1.374	1.350	1.326	1.301	1.277	1.252	1.227	1.202	1.177	1.152
100	1.654	1.634	1.614	1.593	1.573	1.551	1.530	1.508	1.487	1.465	1.442	1.420	1.397	1.374	1.352	1.328	1.305	1.282	1.258	1.235	1.211	1.187
150	1.720	1.706	1.693	1.679	1.666	1.652	1.638	1.624	1.609	1.595	1.580	1.566	1.551	1.536	1.521	1.506	1.491	1.476	1.461	1.445	1.430	1.414
200	1.759	1.748	1.738	1.728	1.718	1.708	1.697	1.687	1.676	1.666	1.655	1.644	1.633	1.622	1.611	1.600	1.589	1.578	1.567	1.556	1.544	1.533

Reprinted, with permission, from *Econometrica* 48(6): 1556-1563.

Table A.6   Models with no intercept (from Farebrother): negative serial correlation

DURBIN-WATSON NINETY FIVE PER CENT MINIMAL BOUND

N	K=0	K=1	K=2	K=3	K=4	K=5	K=6	K=7	K=8	K=9	K=10	K=11	K=12	K=13	K=14	K=15	K=16	K=17	K=18	K=19	K=20	K=21
2	1.988																					
3	2.761	0.994																				
4	2.871	1.836	0.582																			
5	2.857	2.178	1.267	0.380																		
6	2.844	2.320	1.655	0.917	0.266																	
7	2.828	2.398	1.871	1.283	0.690	0.197																
8	2.805	2.453	2.008	1.521	1.017	0.537	0.151															
9	2.783	2.483	2.110	1.687	1.251	0.823	0.429	0.120														
10	2.762	2.501	2.181	1.816	1.427	1.044	0.678	0.350	0.097													
11	2.742	2.511	2.231	1.913	1.569	1.218	0.881	0.567	0.291	0.080												
12	2.723	2.516	2.268	1.987	1.682	1.364	1.049	0.752	0.481	0.245	0.068											
13	2.705	2.518	2.296	2.044	1.771	1.484	1.193	0.911	0.649	0.413	0.210	0.058										
14	2.688	2.517	2.316	2.090	1.843	1.582	1.316	1.051	0.797	0.565	0.358	0.181	0.050									
15	2.672	2.515	2.332	2.126	1.902	1.664	1.419	1.172	0.931	0.703	0.497	0.314	0.158	0.043								
16	2.657	2.512	2.344	2.155	1.950	1.732	1.506	1.276	1.049	0.829	0.624	0.439	0.277	0.139	0.038							
17	2.644	2.508	2.353	2.179	1.990	1.789	1.580	1.367	1.153	0.944	0.743	0.557	0.391	0.246	0.124	0.034						
18	2.631	2.504	2.359	2.199	2.024	1.838	1.644	1.445	1.244	1.045	0.852	0.669	0.501	0.351	0.220	0.110	0.030					
19	2.618	2.499	2.364	2.215	2.053	1.880	1.699	1.513	1.324	1.136	0.951	0.773	0.605	0.452	0.316	0.198	0.099	0.027				
20	2.607	2.494	2.368	2.228	2.077	1.916	1.747	1.573	1.395	1.216	1.040	0.868	0.704	0.550	0.410	0.286	0.179	0.090	0.025			
21	2.596	2.489	2.370	2.239	2.098	1.947	1.789	1.625	1.457	1.289	1.120	0.955	0.796	0.644	0.502	0.373	0.260	0.162	0.081	0.022		
22	2.585	2.484	2.372	2.249	2.116	1.974	1.825	1.671	1.513	1.353	1.193	1.034	0.880	0.731	0.591	0.460	0.341	0.238	0.148	0.074	0.020	
23	2.575	2.479	2.373	2.257	2.131	1.998	1.858	1.712	1.563	1.411	1.258	1.107	0.957	0.813	0.674	0.544	0.422	0.313	0.218	0.136	0.068	0.019
24	2.566	2.474	2.373	2.263	2.145	2.019	1.886	1.749	1.607	1.463	1.318	1.172	1.029	0.888	0.753	0.623	0.502	0.389	0.289	0.201	0.125	0.062
25	2.557	2.470	2.373	2.269	2.156	2.037	1.912	1.782	1.647	1.510	1.371	1.232	1.094	0.958	0.826	0.699	0.578	0.465	0.360	0.267	0.185	0.115
26	1.073	1.004	0.934	0.863	0.792	0.722	0.652	0.584	0.518	0.454	0.394	0.336	0.283	0.233	0.189	0.148	0.113	0.083	0.057	0.037	0.022	0.011
27	1.089	1.023	0.955	0.886	0.817	0.749	0.681	0.614	0.549	0.486	0.426	0.368	0.314	0.264	0.218	0.176	0.138	0.105	0.077	0.053	0.034	0.020
28	1.105	1.040	0.974	0.908	0.841	0.774	0.708	0.643	0.579	0.517	0.457	0.400	0.345	0.294	0.247	0.204	0.164	0.129	0.098	0.071	0.050	0.032
29	1.120	1.057	0.993	0.929	0.864	0.798	0.734	0.670	0.607	0.546	0.487	0.430	0.376	0.324	0.276	0.232	0.191	0.154	0.120	0.091	0.067	0.046
30	1.134	1.073	1.011	0.948	0.885	0.822	0.759	0.696	0.635	0.574	0.516	0.460	0.405	0.354	0.305	0.260	0.217	0.179	0.144	0.113	0.086	0.062
31	1.147	1.088	1.028	0.967	0.905	0.844	0.782	0.721	0.661	0.602	0.544	0.488	0.434	0.383	0.334	0.288	0.244	0.205	0.168	0.135	0.106	0.080
32	1.160	1.103	1.044	0.985	0.925	0.865	0.805	0.745	0.686	0.628	0.571	0.516	0.462	0.411	0.362	0.315	0.271	0.230	0.193	0.158	0.127	0.100
33	1.173	1.117	1.060	1.002	0.944	0.885	0.826	0.768	0.710	0.653	0.597	0.542	0.489	0.438	0.389	0.342	0.298	0.256	0.218	0.182	0.149	0.120
34	1.185	1.130	1.075	1.018	0.961	0.904	0.847	0.790	0.733	0.677	0.622	0.568	0.516	0.465	0.416	0.369	0.324	0.282	0.243	0.206	0.172	0.141
35	1.196	1.143	1.089	1.034	0.978	0.923	0.867	0.811	0.755	0.700	0.646	0.593	0.541	0.491	0.442	0.395	0.350	0.308	0.268	0.230	0.195	0.163
36	1.207	1.155	1.102	1.049	0.995	0.940	0.886	0.831	0.777	0.723	0.669	0.617	0.566	0.516	0.467	0.421	0.376	0.333	0.292	0.254	0.218	0.185
37	1.217	1.167	1.116	1.063	1.010	0.957	0.904	0.850	0.797	0.744	0.692	0.640	0.590	0.540	0.492	0.446	0.401	0.358	0.317	0.278	0.241	0.207
38	1.228	1.178	1.128	1.077	1.026	0.974	0.921	0.869	0.817	0.765	0.713	0.663	0.613	0.564	0.516	0.470	0.425	0.382	0.341	0.302	0.265	0.230
39	1.237	1.189	1.140	1.090	1.040	0.989	0.938	0.887	0.836	0.785	0.734	0.684	0.635	0.587	0.540	0.494	0.449	0.406	0.365	0.325	0.288	0.252
40	1.247	1.200	1.152	1.103	1.054	1.004	0.954	0.904	0.854	0.804	0.754	0.705	0.657	0.609	0.562	0.517	0.473	0.430	0.388	0.349	0.311	0.275
45	1.289	1.247	1.204	1.160	1.116	1.071	1.026	0.981	0.936	0.890	0.845	0.800	0.755	0.710	0.666	0.623	0.581	0.539	0.499	0.459	0.421	0.384
50	1.325	1.287	1.248	1.208	1.168	1.128	1.087	1.046	1.004	0.963	0.921	0.880	0.838	0.797	0.756	0.715	0.675	0.636	0.597	0.559	0.521	0.485
55	1.356	1.321	1.286	1.250	1.213	1.176	1.139	1.101	1.063	1.025	0.987	0.948	0.910	0.872	0.833	0.796	0.758	0.721	0.684	0.647	0.611	0.576
60	1.383	1.351	1.319	1.285	1.252	1.218	1.183	1.149	1.114	1.078	1.043	1.008	0.972	0.936	0.901	0.865	0.830	0.795	0.760	0.725	0.691	0.657
65	1.408	1.378	1.348	1.317	1.286	1.254	1.222	1.190	1.158	1.125	1.092	1.059	1.026	0.993	0.960	0.927	0.894	0.861	0.828	0.795	0.762	0.730
70	1.429	1.401	1.373	1.345	1.316	1.286	1.257	1.227	1.197	1.166	1.136	1.105	1.074	1.043	1.012	0.981	0.950	0.919	0.888	0.857	0.826	0.795
75	1.448	1.423	1.396	1.369	1.342	1.315	1.287	1.260	1.231	1.203	1.174	1.146	1.117	1.088	1.058	1.029	1.000	0.971	0.941	0.912	0.883	0.854
80	1.466	1.442	1.417	1.392	1.367	1.341	1.315	1.289	1.262	1.236	1.209	1.182	1.155	1.127	1.100	1.072	1.045	1.017	0.989	0.962	0.934	0.907
85	1.482	1.459	1.436	1.412	1.388	1.364	1.340	1.315	1.290	1.265	1.240	1.214	1.189	1.163	1.137	1.111	1.085	1.059	1.033	1.006	0.980	0.954
90	1.497	1.475	1.453	1.431	1.408	1.385	1.362	1.339	1.315	1.292	1.268	1.244	1.220	1.195	1.171	1.146	1.121	1.097	1.072	1.047	1.022	0.997
95	1.510	1.490	1.469	1.448	1.426	1.405	1.383	1.361	1.338	1.316	1.293	1.271	1.248	1.225	1.201	1.178	1.155	1.131	1.108	1.084	1.060	1.037
100	1.523	1.503	1.483	1.463	1.443	1.422	1.402	1.381	1.359	1.338	1.317	1.295	1.273	1.251	1.229	1.207	1.185	1.162	1.140	1.118	1.095	1.072
150	1.611	1.598	1.585	1.571	1.558	1.544	1.530	1.516	1.502	1.488	1.474	1.460	1.445	1.431	1.416	1.402	1.387	1.372	1.357	1.342	1.327	1.312
200	1.664	1.654	1.644	1.634	1.624	1.613	1.603	1.593	1.582	1.572	1.561	1.551	1.540	1.529	1.519	1.508	1.497	1.486	1.475	1.464	1.453	1.442

Table A.7 Models with no intercept (from Farebrother): negative serial correlation

DURBIN-WATSON NINETY NINE PER CENT MINIMAL BOUND

N	K=0	K=1	K=2	K=3	K=4	K=5	K=6	K=7	K=8	K=9	K=10	K=11	K=12	K=13	K=14	K=15	K=16	K=17	K=18	K=19	K=20	K=21
2	1.999																					
3	2.951	0.999																				
4	3.221	1.967	0.586																			
5	3.261	2.462	1.359	0.382																		
6	3.235	2.682	1.878	0.983	0.268																	
7	3.198	2.776	2.177	1.459	0.740	0.198																
8	3.166	2.817	2.347	1.776	1.158	0.576	0.153															
9	3.133	2.837	2.448	1.983	1.465	0.937	0.460	0.121														
10	3.101	2.847	2.514	2.121	1.684	1.224	0.773	0.375	0.098													
11	3.071	2.847	2.560	2.220	1.842	1.441	1.035	0.647	0.312	0.081												
12	3.043	2.843	2.592	2.294	1.961	1.607	1.244	0.885	0.549	0.263	0.069											
13	3.017	2.836	2.612	2.349	2.054	1.737	1.410	1.082	0.764	0.471	0.225	0.059										
14	2.992	2.828	2.626	2.391	2.127	1.842	1.544	1.244	0.984	0.666	0.409	0.195	0.051									
15	2.969	2.818	2.635	2.432	2.185	1.928	1.656	1.379	1.104	0.837	0.585	0.358	0.170	0.044								
16	2.948	2.808	2.640	2.447	2.231	1.997	1.749	1.494	1.237	0.985	0.743	0.517	0.316	0.150	0.039							
17	2.927	2.797	2.643	2.466	2.269	2.055	1.827	1.591	1.351	1.114	0.883	0.664	0.461	0.281	0.133	0.035						
18	2.908	2.787	2.644	2.480	2.299	2.102	1.893	1.675	1.451	1.227	1.007	0.796	0.597	0.413	0.251	0.119	0.031					
19	2.890	2.776	2.643	2.492	2.324	2.142	1.948	1.746	1.538	1.327	1.118	0.915	0.721	0.539	0.372	0.226	0.107	0.028				
20	2.874	2.766	2.641	2.500	2.344	2.176	1.996	1.807	1.613	1.415	1.217	1.022	0.834	0.656	0.489	0.337	0.204	0.096	0.025			
21	2.858	2.756	2.638	2.506	2.361	2.204	2.036	1.861	1.678	1.492	1.305	1.119	0.937	0.763	0.598	0.446	0.307	0.185	0.087	0.023		
22	2.842	2.746	2.635	2.511	2.375	2.228	2.071	1.907	1.736	1.561	1.384	1.207	1.032	0.862	0.700	0.548	0.408	0.280	0.169	0.080	0.021	
23	2.828	2.736	2.631	2.515	2.387	2.249	2.102	1.947	1.786	1.621	1.454	1.285	1.118	0.954	0.796	0.645	0.504	0.374	0.257	0.155	0.073	0.019
24	2.814	2.727	2.627	2.517	2.396	2.267	2.128	1.983	1.831	1.675	1.516	1.356	1.196	1.038	0.884	0.736	0.596	0.465	0.345	0.237	0.143	0.067
25	2.801	2.717	2.623	2.518	2.404	2.282	2.151	2.014	1.871	1.723	1.572	1.420	1.267	1.115	0.966	0.821	0.683	0.552	0.430	0.319	0.218	0.132
26	2.789	2.709	2.618	2.519	2.411	2.295	2.171	2.042	1.906	1.766	1.623	1.478	1.331	1.186	1.042	0.901	0.765	0.635	0.512	0.399	0.295	0.202
27	2.777	2.700	2.614	2.519	2.416	2.306	2.189	2.066	1.938	1.805	1.669	1.530	1.390	1.250	1.111	0.975	0.842	0.714	0.592	0.477	0.371	0.274
28	2.766	2.692	2.609	2.519	2.421	2.316	2.205	2.088	1.966	1.839	1.710	1.577	1.444	1.309	1.176	1.043	0.914	0.788	0.667	0.553	0.445	0.346
29	2.755	2.684	2.604	2.518	2.425	2.325	2.219	2.107	1.991	1.871	1.747	1.621	1.493	1.364	1.235	1.107	0.981	0.858	0.739	0.625	0.517	0.416
30	2.745	2.676	2.600	2.517	2.428	2.332	2.231	2.125	2.014	1.899	1.781	1.660	1.537	1.414	1.290	1.166	1.044	0.924	0.807	0.695	0.587	0.485
31	2.735	2.668	2.595	2.515	2.430	2.339	2.242	2.140	2.035	1.925	1.812	1.696	1.579	1.460	1.340	1.221	1.102	0.986	0.872	0.761	0.654	0.552
32	2.725	2.661	2.590	2.514	2.432	2.344	2.252	2.155	2.053	1.948	1.840	1.729	1.616	1.502	1.387	1.272	1.157	1.043	0.932	0.823	0.718	0.617
33	2.716	2.654	2.586	2.512	2.433	2.349	2.260	2.167	2.070	1.970	1.866	1.759	1.651	1.541	1.430	1.319	1.208	1.097	0.989	0.882	0.779	0.678
34	2.707	2.647	2.581	2.510	2.434	2.353	2.268	2.179	2.086	1.989	1.889	1.787	1.683	1.577	1.470	1.363	1.255	1.148	1.042	0.938	0.836	0.737
35	2.699	2.640	2.576	2.508	2.435	2.357	2.275	2.189	2.100	2.007	1.911	1.813	1.713	1.611	1.507	1.404	1.299	1.196	1.093	0.991	0.891	0.794
36	2.690	2.634	2.572	2.506	2.435	2.360	2.281	2.199	2.113	2.023	1.931	1.837	1.740	1.642	1.542	1.442	1.341	1.240	1.140	1.041	0.943	0.847
37	2.683	2.627	2.567	2.503	2.435	2.363	2.287	2.207	2.124	2.038	1.950	1.859	1.765	1.670	1.574	1.477	1.379	1.282	1.184	1.088	0.992	0.898
38	2.675	2.621	2.563	2.501	2.435	2.365	2.292	2.215	2.135	2.052	1.967	1.879	1.789	1.697	1.604	1.510	1.416	1.321	1.226	1.132	1.039	0.947
39	2.667	2.615	2.559	2.499	2.435	2.367	2.296	2.222	2.145	2.065	1.982	1.898	1.811	1.722	1.632	1.541	1.450	1.358	1.266	1.174	1.083	0.993
40	2.660	2.609	2.555	2.496	2.434	2.369	2.300	2.229	2.154	2.077	1.997	1.915	1.831	1.746	1.659	1.570	1.482	1.392	1.303	1.213	1.124	1.036
45	2.628	2.583	2.535	2.484	2.430	2.374	2.315	2.253	2.190	2.124	2.056	1.986	1.914	1.841	1.767	1.691	1.614	1.537	1.459	1.381	1.302	1.224
50	2.600	2.559	2.516	2.471	2.424	2.374	2.323	2.269	2.214	2.157	2.098	2.037	1.975	1.911	1.847	1.781	1.714	1.646	1.578	1.509	1.439	1.370
55	2.575	2.538	2.500	2.459	2.417	2.373	2.327	2.280	2.231	2.180	2.128	2.075	2.020	1.964	1.907	1.849	1.790	1.730	1.669	1.608	1.546	1.484
60	2.553	2.519	2.484	2.448	2.409	2.370	2.329	2.286	2.242	2.197	2.151	2.103	2.054	2.004	1.954	1.902	1.849	1.796	1.742	1.687	1.631	1.576
65	2.534	2.503	2.470	2.437	2.402	2.366	2.329	2.290	2.250	2.210	2.168	2.125	2.081	2.036	1.990	1.944	1.896	1.848	1.799	1.750	1.700	1.650
70	2.516	2.487	2.458	2.427	2.395	2.361	2.327	2.292	2.256	2.219	2.181	2.142	2.102	2.061	2.020	1.977	1.934	1.891	1.846	1.802	1.756	1.710
75	2.500	2.473	2.446	2.417	2.387	2.357	2.325	2.293	2.260	2.226	2.191	2.155	2.118	2.081	2.043	2.005	1.965	1.926	1.885	1.844	1.802	1.760
80	2.486	2.461	2.436	2.408	2.380	2.352	2.323	2.293	2.262	2.231	2.198	2.165	2.132	2.098	2.063	2.027	1.991	1.954	1.917	1.879	1.841	1.803
85	2.473	2.449	2.425	2.399	2.374	2.347	2.320	2.292	2.263	2.234	2.204	2.174	2.143	2.111	2.079	2.046	2.012	1.979	1.944	1.909	1.874	1.838
90	2.460	2.438	2.415	2.391	2.367	2.342	2.317	2.291	2.264	2.237	2.209	2.181	2.152	2.122	2.092	2.061	2.030	1.999	1.967	1.935	1.902	1.869
95	2.449	2.428	2.406	2.384	2.361	2.338	2.314	2.289	2.264	2.239	2.212	2.186	2.159	2.131	2.103	2.075	2.046	2.016	1.986	1.956	1.926	1.895
100	2.438	2.418	2.398	2.377	2.355	2.333	2.310	2.287	2.264	2.240	2.215	2.190	2.165	2.139	2.113	2.086	2.059	2.031	2.003	1.975	1.946	1.917
150	2.363	2.349	2.336	2.322	2.308	2.294	2.279	2.265	2.250	2.235	2.220	2.204	2.188	2.173	2.156	2.140	2.124	2.107	2.090	2.073	2.056	2.039
200	2.317	2.307	2.296	2.286	2.276	2.265	2.255	2.244	2.233	2.222	2.211	2.200	2.189	2.177	2.166	2.154	2.142	2.131	2.119	2.106	2.094	2.082

Appendix B
Guide to ACF/PACF Plots

The plots shown here are those of pure or theoretical ARIMA processes. Here are some general guidelines for identifying the process:

- Nonstationary series have an ACF that remains significant for half a dozen or more lags, rather than quickly declining to zero. You must difference such a series until it is stationary before you can identify the process.

- Autoregressive processes have an exponentially declining ACF and spikes in the first one or more lags of the PACF. The number of spikes indicates the order of the autoregression.

- Moving average processes have spikes in the first one or more lags of the ACF and an exponentially declining PACF. The number of spikes indicates the order of the moving average.

- Mixed (ARMA) processes typically show exponential declines in both the ACF and the PACF.

At the identification stage you do not need to worry about the sign of the ACF or PACF, nor about the speed with which an exponentially declining ACF or PACF approaches zero. These depend upon the sign and actual value of the AR and MA coefficients. In some instances an exponentially declining ACF alternates between positive and negative values.

ACF and PACF plots from real data are never as clean as the plots shown here. You must learn to pick out what is essential in any given plot. Always check the ACF and PACF of the residuals, in case your identification is wrong. Bear in mind that:

- Seasonal processes show these patterns at the seasonal lags (the multiples of the seasonal period).

- You are entitled to treat nonsignificant values as zero. That is, you can ignore values that lie within the confidence intervals on the plots. You do not have to ignore them, however, particularly if they continue the pattern of the statistically significant values.

- An occasional autocorrelation will be statistically significant by chance alone. You can ignore a statistically significant autocorrelation if it is isolated, preferably at a high lag, and if it does not occur at a seasonal lag.

Consult any text on ARIMA analysis for a more complete discussion of ACF and PACF plots.

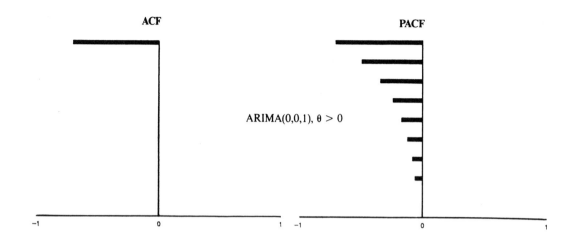

ARIMA(0,0,1), $\theta > 0$

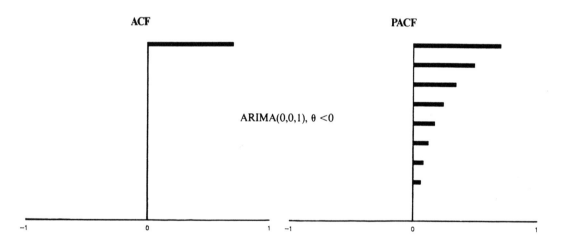

ARIMA(0,0,1), $\theta < 0$

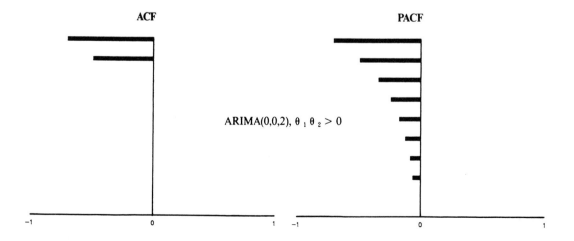

ARIMA(0,0,2), $\theta_1 \theta_2 > 0$

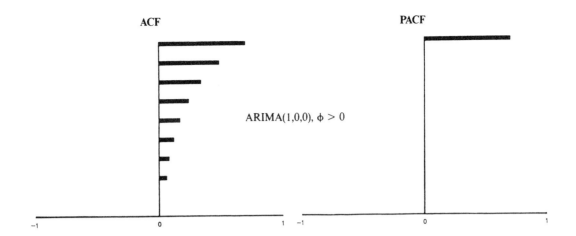

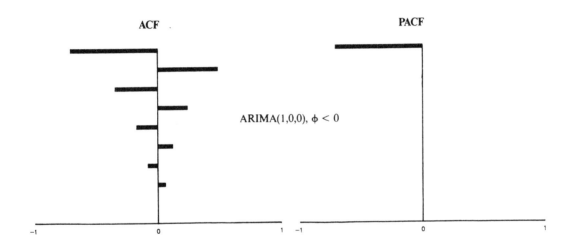

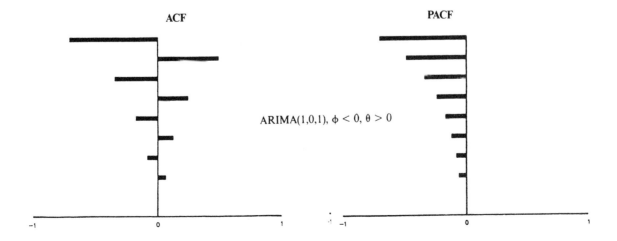

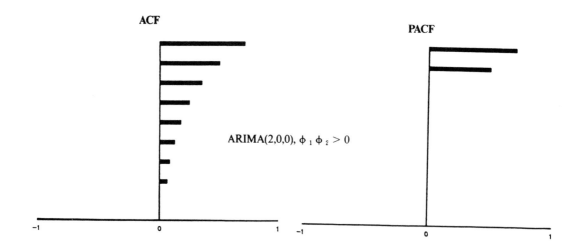

ARIMA(2,0,0), $\phi_1 \phi_2 > 0$

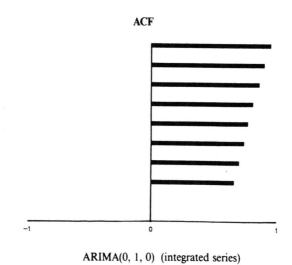

ARIMA(0, 1, 0) (integrated series)

Bibliography

Box, G. E. P., and G. C. Tiao. 1975. Intervention analysis with applications to economic and environmental problems. *Journal of the American Statistical Association* 70(3): 70–79.

Box, G. E. P., and G. M. Jenkins. 1976. *Time series analysis: Forecasting and control*, rev. ed. San Francisco: Holden-Day.

Draper, N. R., and H. Smith. 1981. *Applied regression analysis*, 2nd ed. New York: John Wiley & Sons.

Durbin, J. 1969. Tests for serial correlation in regression analysis based on the periodogram of least-squares residuals. *Biometrika* (March 1969).

Durbin, J., and G. S. Watson. 1951. Testing for serial correlation in least-squares regression II. *Biometrika* 38: 159–178.

Gardner, E. S. 1985. Exponential smoothing: The state of the art. *Journal of Forecasting* 4: 1–28.

Kelejian, H. H., and W. E. Oates. 1976. *Introduction to econometrics: Principles and applications.* New York: Harper & Row.

Makridakis, S., S. C. Wheelwright, and V. E. McGee. 1983. *Forecasting: Methods and applications*, 2nd ed. New York: John Wiley & Sons.

McCleary, R., and R. A. Hay. 1980. *Applied time series analysis for the social sciences.* Beverly Hills, Calif.: Sage Publications.

Montgomery, D. C., and E. A. Peck. 1982. *Introduction to linear regression analysis.* New York: John Wiley & Sons.

Thompson, H. E., and G. C. Tiao. 1971. Analysis of telephone data: A case study of forecasting seasonal time series. *The Bell Journal of Economics and Management Science* 2(2): 515–541.

Tiao, G. C., et al. 1986. A statistical trend analysis of ozonesonde data. *Journal of Geophysical Research*, no. 11 (November 1986).

Wichern, D. W., and R. H. Jones. 1977. Assessing the impact of market disturbances using intervention analysis. *Management Science*

Subject Index

additive model
    for seasonal decomposition 159–161
    in Seasonal Decomposition procedure 187, 294
    in X11 ARIMA procedure 240, 312

Akaike Information Criterion 68

Akaike information criterion 106

ARIMA modeling 59–72, 83–90, 95–109, 138–151,
    264–272
    autoregression 60
    components of 59–61
    diagnosis 63, 101–102, 108, 149, 202–203
    differencing 60–61, 150–151
    estimation 63, 98–101, 106, 145–146, 198–202
    identification 61–62, 96–98, 105–106, 139,
        196–201
    identification of seasonal models 194
    in X11 ARIMA procedure 230–232, 313–316
    interpretation of constant 98
    moving averages 61
    notation 59, 140–141, 193–194
    predictor variables (regressors) 145–151
    seasonal 192–205
    steps 61–63
    with outliers 95–109

ARIMA procedure 66–68, 73–77, 83–85, 98–101,
    106, 145–148, 264–272
    and missing values 12, 20–21, 103, 108–109, 252
    confidence interval 271
    confidence intervals 75
    display alternatives 77
    efficiency 20–21
    error series and log transformations 17
    forecasting 75–76, 88–89, 201–205
    including constant 74, 268
    initial parameter values 77, 269–270
    iterations 76, 270–271
    model parameters 74, 267–268, 268–269
    saving new variables 74–75
    single or nonsequential parameters 268–269
    specifying periodicity 267–268
    termination criteria 76–77, 270–271
    transforming values 74, 267–268
    using a previously defined model 271–272

autocorrelated errors
    in regression 55, 111–132

autocorrelation 27, 45, 112, 124
    in ARIMA diagnosis 63, 68–70, 202–203
    in ARIMA model identification 62, 83, 96–98,
        105–106, 139, 196–198

autocorrelation function 62

Autocorrelations procedure 64–65, 87–88, 96–97,
    101, 123, 195–196
    efficiency 21
    seasonal differencing 196–197

autoregression
    compared to differencing 61
    compared to exponential smoothing 60
    compared to moving averages 61
    in ARIMA 60

Autoregression procedure 55, 125–132, 132–136,
    258–263
    and missing values 12, 21, 252
    Cochrane-Orcutt method 133, 261
    confidence intervals 134
    display alternatives 136
    efficiency 21
    forecasting 128–132, 134–135
    including constant 133, 261
    iterations 136
    maximum iterations 261–262
    maximum-likelihood estimation 133, 261
    Prais-Winsten method 133, 261
    rho value 261
    saving new variables 133–134
    termination criteria 136
    using a previously defined model 262–263

backcasting
    in X11 ARIMA procedure 313

backshift operator 140–141
    seasonal 193

Bartlett window
    in spectral analysis 220–221
    in Spectral Plots procedure 224, 301

Syntax Index